Mold Town and Country

an historical account

T. W. Pritchard

Mold Town and Country an historical account
was first published in Wales in 2012
on behalf of the author
by
BRIDGE BOOKS
61 Park Avenue
WREXHAM
LL12 7AW

A CIP entry for this book is available from the British Library

ISBN 978-1-84494-085-1

Printed and bound by
Gutenberg Press Ltd
Malta

Contents

Acknowledgements

A great debt of gratitude is owed to so many people for their assistance, encouragement, kindness and expertise in enabling me to complete this book. A mere list of names fails to do justice to those concerned. I long resisted the suggestions of Alister Williams of Bridge Books and Ken Lloyd Gruffydd that I write a book on the history of Mold and from the time that I finally succumbed to their hints they gave me invaluable encouragement and assistance. The editorship of Alister Williams has been patient, thorough and sympathetic and made a considerable improvement to the finished book. Ken Lloyd Gruffydd has illuminated and ornamented the text throughout with a series of maps and diagrams. These superb aids demonstrate and strengthen his dictum that we can only understand history when it is placed in its geographical setting. By his own explorations into the early history of Ystrad Alun he has made an outstanding contribution to this story.

I am indebted to Kevin Matthias for his interpretation of the fifteenth-century account roll of Thomas Stanley. This document provides what little evidence we have for the manor and lordship of medieval Mold. He also made available to me his transcript and notes of the eighteenth-century diary of Thomas Griffith of Rhual. Councillor Christopher Bithell readily provided answers to my questions on twentieth-century Mold and much of this information is incorporated in the final pages. David Rowe, with his characteristic knowledge and enthusiasm, made available images from the Mold Civic Society archive. Paul Temple was of great assistance with his photographic and computer skills. Lawrence Rawsthorne, Simon Gott, Debbie Seymour and members of the Answers Centre Mold and the staff of Flintshire Library, Museums and Leisure Services were unfailing in responding to my requests for material as was the Flintshire Planning Librarian, Peter Brownhill. John R. Williams, churchwarden at St Mary's, was very helpful in his explanation of the architectural development of this beautiful parish church as was the architectural historian, Dr Clare Haynes.

I was prevented from countless errors by the proof reading of David and Carol Shone and Len and Shirley Walls. Claire Harrington, principal archivist at the Flintshire Office Record Office Hawarden, and her staff were patient and generous in meeting the demands I made on them for access to the Mold and district records. Gladstone's Library, Hawarden, through the kindness of the warden, Peter Francis, and the librarian, Patsy Williams, was an ideal place for background reading. There are many other people who have provided generous support and encouragement and I thank them most sincerely.

Acknowledgement of images and permission to use them is by courtesy of the following copyright holders (images in the colour section are prefixed 'C'):

Mr A. Chrimes: 83 (bottom).
Clwyd Fine Arts Trust via Bodelwyddan Castle: C.9.
Frome Society for Local Studies via Mr Michael McGarbie: 150.
Mr Richard Furse and Dame Clara Furse: 153, 154, C.5.
Mr Ken Lloyd Gruffydd: 12, 18, 23, 25, 26 (bottom), 28, 29, 30, 38, 39, 41, 44, 46, 49, 51, 52, 53, 59, 61, 62, 77, 82, 83 (bottom), 88, 117, 137, 139, 145, 175, 207, 208, 217, 234, 244.
Flintshire Historical Society: 15 (top).
Flintshire Museum Service: 156 (both).
Flintshire Record Office: 20, 80, 84, 85, 86 (top), 93, 96, 97, 111, 113, 141, 147, 149, 160, 161, 164, 168, 169, 170, 172,

180, 181 (both), 182, 188, 194, 199, 205, 209, 210, 211 (both), 213, 221, 225, 230 (both), 235, 236 (top), 237 (both), 238 (both), 240 (top), 243, 245, 247, 251, C.7, C.12.
Mold Civic Society Archive: 26 (top), 81, 102, 105, 167, 174, 176, 177 (top), 189, 212, 218, 219 (both), 220, 236 (bottom), 239, 230 (bottom), 241, 242, 246, 250, 254.
Mold Library and Museum: 179, 228, C.1.
Mold Town Council: illustration of Mold motte and bailey castle used on the dust jacket.
National Library of Wales/Llyfrgell Genedlaethol Cymru: 134, 144, 158, c.4, C.5, C.6, C.8, C.13, C.14.
Rhydymwyn Valley History Society via Mr Colin Barber: 248.
Wikipedia: 69 (both).
Mr J.R. Williams: 70, 71 (both), 72, 76, C.2.
W. Alister Williams Collection: 67, 72, 79, 80, 92, 114, 124, 125, 127, 130, 162, 249, 253, 254, 255, C.3.

I would also like to thank the vicar and churchwardens of St Mary the Virigin, Mold for their support and for granting access to the church.
Every effort has been made to ensure that wherever possible permission has been obtained to reproduce the images in this book.

Introduction

The aim of this book is to provide a comprehensive historical account of the town of Mold from the beginning of the Ice Age (20,000 BC) to the end of the twentieth century. The narrative is divided into major time periods which are illuminated by illustrations of relevant artefacts and extracts from documentary evidence. In this way the book stands as a useful record of the town of Mold.

Locating Mold

The geographical location of Mold like most places in the world today has never been easier to find than in the twenty-first century CE (Christian Era); we press a button and the computer marks its position in a matter of seconds. The screen shows not only its place on a map; it gives directions to get there and, as a bonus, proceeds to show a film of the area. Such pictorial accuracy leaves very little to the imagination and it is not until one arrives at a destination that further enquiry begins. Then the quest starts for the identity of the inhabitants, their culture, language, religion and everything we wish to know about their past. This is the information the local historian is challenged to provide. This book attempts to answer these questions about the neighbourhood of Mold and its peoples over the centuries.

Mold is not an isolated community. Like all towns it is part of a region, the county of Flintshire, and a nation, Wales. As such, it shares certain characteristics with the area of which it is a part. In addition, Mold has much in common with other small towns in Britain, but equally there are things which make it different. This study attempts to identify these similarities and differences and discover in what way the town is unique. This may only be revealed by a close examination of many factors, among which are geographical setting, historical experience, economic development and the way of life of successive waves of invaders and settlers who have come to Mold through the ages. Throughout the centuries, incoming foreign influences and the native reception of these ideas and customs, by either acceptance or rejection, have created their own particular pattern of events and left behind distinctive marks.

Landscape[1]

We begin with a discussion of what is common to all historical accounts from prehistory through to the present day, the relationship between humans and their environment, the struggle of man to come to terms with his existence on this earth. The local landscape is the back-cloth against which this struggle has taken place and it is made up of both natural features which have been shaped in geological time and those features that were created by human activity. For example, war can have a destructive effect on the landscape, irrigation can turn a desert into a garden and every human activity has the potential to upset the balance of nature and bring either poverty or prosperity as a result.

The word landscape, with its variety of meanings, is a useful term to begin with. It is a word not only used by artists like the great Mold landscape painter, Richard Wilson (1713–82), but also by geologists, archaeologists and historians.

We cannot understand the history of Mold without being aware of a geological explanation of how hills, valleys, moors, rocks, mineral deposits, rivers, lakes and other features were formed. Archaeologists continue the story of the earth with their account of human settlers, their evidence coming from the land itself, from the remains left behind by the first human inhabitants. Archaeologists and historians have used the concept of landscape as a background against which to record the gradual evolution and advance of human activity and the changes in societies and civilisations.[2]

Imprints on the landscape

The advance of human activity has progressed from hunting with hand-made weapons of stone to modern technology. This has taken thousands of years and many generations to accomplish. People have lived in the Mold area for at least two thousand years and each generation has left something useful for the next. This is what we sometimes describe as heritage which is the story of a particular place, its individual biography.

Is there any way in which we can explain, describe and recreate what has happened in Mold over the last two thousand years? How do we provide the answer to the simple questions: who lived here in Mold? Where did they come from? How did they make a living? What have they left behind? In order to answer these questions we will have to build up our knowledge piece by piece from wherever we can find clues. Let us imagine each piece as an imprint upon the landscape. Historians are using examples of natural and man-made imprints which they find in the local landscape as material as well as documentary evidence to assist them in their explanation of the past. They have learnt from geologists and archaeologists the relevance and importance of landscape. W.G. Hoskins emphasised in a pioneering study the importance of interpreting the landscape, describing landscape as 'the richest historical record we possess' and spoke of the relationship between geologist and historian.

> He (the geologist) explains to us the bones of the landscape, the fundamental structure that gives form and colour to the scene and produces a certain kind of topography and natural vegetation. But the flesh that covers the bones, and the details of the features, are the concern of the historian, whose task is to show how man has clothed the geological skeleton during the comparatively recent past – mostly within the last fifteen centuries, though in some regions much longer than this.[3]

Frank Emery, a historian writing about Wales, followed the ideas of Hoskins and it is from his work that I have taken the idea of using the word 'imprint' to describe a succession of created landscapes, each with its own identifiable features, to explain the history of Mold. Emery describes 'landscape as the imprint of past communities as they went about their business of using the land and its resources. Nor should this preclude their tangibles, whether social, artistic, or technological.'[4]

A summary of the formation of the landscape of Mold

Set out below is a chronological list or summary of successive changes or imprints on the landscape of Mold, a separate discussion of each will form the chapters in this story of Mold.

The geological formation of the landscape of Mold took place over a long period from the ice ages of the Pleistocene period, from 2.5 mil to 10,000 years ago, the major features being the Alun river valley, and higher land. In this period the highlands and lowlands of Britain were formed, a division of geological formations broadly arranged NW–SE. The northern and western parts are composed of harder and older rock with uplands, high moors and mountains. Lowland Britain is the belt of land south of a line from the Humber to the Bristol Channel and part of the area of Mold is in a transitional area between the two. Human habitation was sparse in north-east Wales at this time and consisted of hunter-gatherers. The first farmers appeared between 4,500 and 2,500 BC.

In the Early Bronze Age (2400–1400 BC) and Later Bronze Age (1400–600 BC) mining and smelting expanded leading to the production of bronze tools, weapons and ornaments. Evidence of human settlement in the Mold area in this period is limited to a few finds by archaeologists, most of which were on higher land and in settlements either along the Alun valley or in the neighbouring hillforts. The main examples of landscape features yielding artefacts are funerary barrows, some of which have been found along the Alun valley: the Mold Cape, discovered in 1833 at Bryn yr Ellyllon (dated *c.*1900–1600 BC); a necklace of jet beads at Llong, discovered in 1955; and a group of Bronze Age axes from higher land on Hafod Mountain, discovered in 1989.

The outstanding landscape imprint from the Romano-British period *(c.*1100 BC–100 AD) was the construction of hillforts that took place from the late Bronze Age. There were other small settlements in north-east Wales throughout the Iron Age *c.*500 BC which practised mixed, settled farming in which the growth of cereals and herding of cattle were the basis of the economy. There was no Roman settlement in the area of Mold town as such and, although a few artefacts have been found, they predate the Romans and discovered in districts beyond the town boundaries. The Decangli, a British tribe, controlled the land between the river Dee westwards to the river Conwy and Mold was positioned between them and another tribe, the Ordovices, to the south west. There is virtually nothing we can say about this period until the fifth century AD.

The next major imprint on the landscape was over a thousand years in its making, occurring during the period between the Iron Age and the Norman Conquest. During this first millennium AD the lowland areas of Mold were transformed by the ploughs, spades and axes of successive Welsh, Saxon and Norman settlers as they worked the land, cultivating fields and clearing woodland. This resulted in recognisable differences in field patterns and settlements between Welsh natives and Anglo-Norman colonisers. Another difference was the contrast between the cultivated landscape of the lowland Alun valley and the waste and commons on higher land used primarily for grazing beasts. This was to continue until the Mold enclosure award of 1800 left another lasting imprint, that of newly enclosed allotments and roads.

Other major imprints on the landscape were made by the landmarks of conquest and domination: Celtic hill-forts in the last century BC; Mercian dykes in the eighth and ninth centuries; Norman motte and bailey castles in the eleventh century; tower houses in the fifteenth century and country houses in the seventeenth and eighteenth centuries.

Religious beliefs have always had a major impact on the landscape from pagan times onwards. Prehistoric standing stones and Christian church steeples have been silhouetted on the horizon to beckon the worshipper through the ages. The imprint of sacred wells and groves on both the landscape and the imagination has however faded in Mold as elsewhere.

Over the centuries the physical landscape of Mold has been blasted, scarred, scoured and stripped of its woodland by the extraction of mineral resources, the development of industrial sites, the impact of technology and economic forces from primitive times until the industrial revolution.

A major and continuing imprint on the landscape is population growth and the built environment.

Finally there are non-material influences on landscape such as language, belief, culture, customs and law which have determined the region's social, religious and political organisation.

Sorting out the imprints

If you have ever attempted to restore an old and long-occupied house you may have found yourself with the task of stripping off layers of wallpaper. Imagine how much more difficult it would be if you had to preserve each layer when it was removed so as to record the pattern, interpret the design and date the material. Archaeologists and historians often attempt the same task with the landscape. They look for the kind of pattern, design and material we have described above in our survey of imprints on the landscape of Mold through the ages. The surface layer, either stripped off a wall or excavated from the ground, is often described as a palimpsest. The surface which has been inscribed bears evidence of more than one inscription. One historian has described the landscape as 'a dense and complex system of signs and symbols that can be decoded and deciphered, a porous surface upon which each generation inscribes its own values and preoccupations without ever being able to erase those of the preceding one.'[5] Maps are often described in this way and we will make good use of them in interpreting the pattern of events in the story of Mold.

Two other ingredients are essential to illuminate, illustrate and enrich this story which will be added throughout each section of the narrative. The first of these are artefacts, objects selected to provide a human dimension to the landscape: the sort of object found by an archaeologist or hand made or manufactured in the locality through the ages in connection with all human activities, such as a medieval gargoyle, a boundary marker, an early bank note. The final common dimension is the documentary evidence relating to the landscape which ranges from early historical records of events, to church and estate records.

Notes

1. Landscape is a Dutch word that has changed its meaning in modern usage. Originally it meant the depiction of a scene painted on canvas seen through the artist's eyes or those of a spectator. Now the word landscape has come to mean a physical tract of land with its distinguishing features and characteristics.
2. The first evidence for habitation by Neanderthal people in Wales is at Pontnewydd Cave *c.*220,000 BC, an Old Stone Age site in Denbighshire (OS 116 SJ015711). Most of the recorded finds in north-east Wales date from Neolithic and Bronze Ages *c.*4500 BC to 600 BC.
3. W.G. Hoskins, *The Making of the English Landscape*, London, 1955, p.14.
4. F. Emery, 'The Landscape' in *Settlement and Society in Wales*, edited by D. Huw Owen, Cardiff, 1989, p.57.
5. A. Walsham, *The Reformation of the Landscape*, Oxford, 2011, p.6.

Prologue

The purpose of this Prologue is to bring the story of Mold and district into being. In the absence of any other account of the subject known to me, I have attempted to construct such an entrance. I believe that the discovery and recording of some archaeological remains here does suggest that, although there is no recorded prehistoric settlement as such, there was in all probability some form of habitation in the area. Having stated so firmly in the Introduction the importance of landscape and artefacts, I feel it is imperative to begin with a discussion of these themes and the appearance of settlers in north Wales.

The Welsh place name for the extensive area of Mold, its town and countryside is Ystrad Alun, the vale of the river Alun, flowing west to east through the region. But the valley of the Alun is only one of two main features of the landscape of this area for the district of Mold is in the northern borderland of Wales and England, an area which straddles that zone of contact between highland and lowland Britain. The northern borderland is situated between north-east Wales, on the edge of the Welsh highland zone, and the adjacent Cheshire–Shropshire plain, the beginning of the lowland zone. The outlying southern townships to the south of Mold, on the upland plateau of Nercwys and Rhydtalog, mark the beginning of the highland zone.

Geological action has determined the height of land and sea, the formation of rock strata and soil deposits, the creation of rivers and valleys, features that are responsible for local scenery. Another factor that has determined the variety of landscape is climate. Geological time and climate change are the joint agents that have produced and continue to create an astonishing variety of landscapes. Clear examples of the influence of geology on the area are the sources of rich mineral deposits which have played an important role in the prosperity and industrial life of the Mold area over hundreds of years and had a considerable effect on the landscape through the extraction of stone, clay, coal, and lead.

Climate change, brought about by the extreme cold of a number of ice ages interspersed with warmer periods, has been responsible for the most important features in the landscape of north Wales. Glacial action, by reason of its nature and the extent of its occurrence and reoccurrence over a long period of time, has left an indelible mark as the movement or drift of glaciers and their retreat, by the process of erosion and deposition of large amounts of varied glacial drift material, transformed old surfaces and created new ones in valleys, lowlands and uplands. In this way, the climatic events which shaped the Alun valley began when the glaciation of Wales occurred sometime within the last million years. The glacial features of the Alun valley and elsewhere in north Wales are a result of the final retreat of the ice around 10,000 BC. By 8300 BC, Wales was free of glaciers and the temperature continued to rise until 3000 BC when northern Europe was some 2.5°C warmer than it is today.

What was the effect in the Alun valley of glaciation and melting ice? The area of glaciation was extensive throughout north Wales where two vast glaciers met, one coming from Scotland and the Lake District and the other, a slowly moving mountain of ice travelling eastward into Ystrad Alun, from Snowdonia. Somewhere about Tyddyn, near Mold, is the boundary where the northern Lake District and Scottish glacier met the ice from Snowdonia and retreated. The northern glacier divided into two wings, one of which crossed into Anglesey and Llŷn and into Cardigan Bay, the other branching south-east to the Cheshire Plain and into north Shropshire. The drift from the west met the drift from the north. The glacial deposit of the valley of the

Alun and the Halkyn range travelled from the west, whilst that along the coast came from the north. It was in this geological period that the red sandstone of the vale of Clwyd travelled up the valley of the Wheeler, and several hillocks and rounded outlines of sandhills called 'eskers' or '*bryniau*' were formed, one of the most notable being Bailey Hill, Mold.

The map shows the pre-Pleistocene course of the river Alun (before 1 million years BC), the changes made during the glacial period and the retreat stages of the ice sheets.[1] Before the Ice Age the upper Alun, which rises near Llandegla, flowed northward between the Clwydian Range and the main limestone escarpment to Pont Cilcain and was the head waters of the pre-glacial river Wheeler. At Pont Cilcain, it was glacially diverted through the escarpment to Rhydymwyn where it entered the valley of a south-easterly flowing stream, which in consequence became the present lower river Alun. From this valley the pre-glacial lower river Alun maintained a south-easterly direction, through the wider valley in which Mold now stands, joined on the right bank by two major streams from the slopes of the mountain, the Terrig and Cegidog. During the retreat stages of the ice sheet, the great volume of melt water formed temporary glacial lakes.[2] The Mold lake was held up by the Irish Sea ice against the hills west of Mold between the two great buttresses of Halkyn Mountain to the north and Hope Mountain, with its northerly extension, Leeswood Hill, to the south. At the head of this lake the intake was by way of the Bellan Gorge, two miles above Mold. The town of Mold has been built on the low elevations in the middle of the valley.[3] 'It seems unquestionable that the sand and gravel

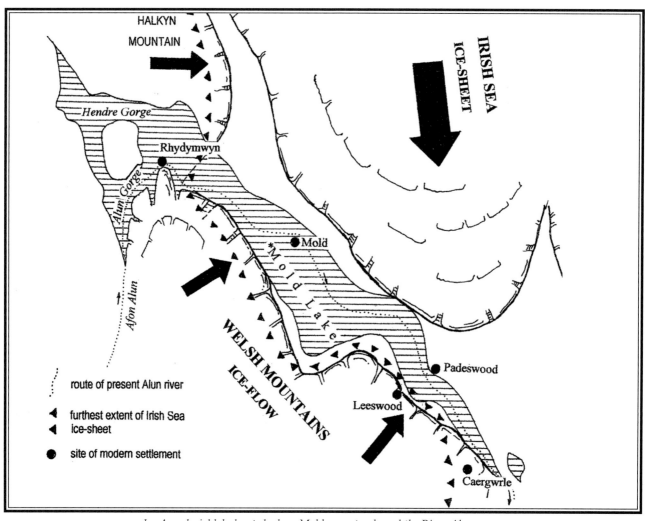

Ice Age glacial lake located where Mold now stands and the River Alun runs.

mounds on which the town [Mold] is built are the dissected remnants of a large delta falling from over 400 feet to 340 feet, which was built out into the Mold Lake at the Pontblyddyn stage above the Bellan Gorge.'[4]

There is no certainty when the uplands, lowlands or valley of the Alun in the Mold district were first settled. The only things of which we are certain are that throughout prehistoric times the area we now know as Wales was very thinly populated, that the first inhabitants of what we now call Flintshire were cave dwellers in the carboniferous limestone rocks, and that they survived by hunting animals, wandering over a large area in their pursuit. On the higher ground, there is evidence of settlement in the Early Bronze Age around 2,400 BC, when pottery and metal objects appear. By 600 BC, Iron Age hillforts and small, circular defended farms were built in increasing numbers and iron tools first appear. The period before the Roman occupation in the first century AD saw the consolidation of tribal groups in Wales and the establishment of a way of life which persisted until the early middle ages and beyond. By this time animals had become domesticated and a pastoral economy was practised, with seasonal transhumance from the valley bottoms to land above 1,000 feet.

Three artefacts which, amongst others, have been discovered in Mold district, are illustrative of the culture of the Mold area before recorded history.

The Mold Cape

Two of the artefacts chosen to represent objects from prehistory were both found in separate funerary barrows in the proximity of the town of Mold and near the river Alun. Both artefacts have been dated to the Early Bronze Age (*c.*2150–1550 BC).

In 2010, the town of Mold received a rare historical accolade in the form of a unique tribute paid by Neil MacGregor, Director of the British Museum, in a celebrated BBC Radio 4 series, *A History of the World in 100 Objects*, designed as an 'an original approach to the history of humanity, using objects which previous civilizations have left behind them.' Wales received its only mention through the object selected from Mold in a section *The Beginnings of Science and Literature, 2000–700 BC*. MacGregor described the Mold Cape as 'a breathtaking object … a short golden poncho,' worn by a young person of considerable power in local society in the Bronze Age. It is an example, he said, of the sophisticated Bronze Age society with its trade connections stretching from the copper mine at the Great Orme in Llandudno throughout north-west Europe. Viewing the beautifully fashioned cape filled him with 'a strange mix of sensations' which he described as 'exhilaration that such a supreme work of art has survived, and frustration that the surrounding material, which would have told us so much about this great and mysterious civilization that flourished in north Wales 4,000 years ago, was recklessly discarded.' MacGregor lamented that the workmen of Mold were only anxious to get their hands on the precious gold and failed to preserve the skeleton of the wearer and other grave goods, for as he concluded, 'it's that context of material that turns treasure into history.' Most of the pieces of the gold object were purchased by the British Museum in 1836, three years after it was found. Other pieces were obtained later and attempts were made in the 1950s to restore the cape. A new restoration in 2002 filled in all the missing parts for the first time since its discovery.

The site where the Mold Cape was discovered[3] was a round burial mound in the Alun valley, north of Chester Road, between a quarter and a half-mile east to the south east of Mold parish church. The burial cairn was known as Bryn yr Ellyllon, or the Hill of Goblins (or perhaps idols). Prior to the discovery, the tumulus had the reputation of being haunted by a formidable golden sceptre, the sighting of which was capable of sobering the local drunks!

The cape was discovered on 11 October 1833 by the workmen of John Langford, the Overseer of Highways, who were in the process of filling in a gravel pit from which they had extracted material. On shovelling stones from the cairn above they broke into it and disturbed its contents which consisted of a skeleton and grave goods. Unfortunately, the nature and value of the find were not immediately appreciated as the vicar of Mold reported:

I regret to say that the Corslet suffered considerable mutilation. Mr Langford upon its discovery, having no idea of its value, threw it into a hedge, and told the workmen to bring it with them when they returned home to dinner. In the meantime several persons broke small pieces off it, and after I saw it, one piece of gold, apparently a shoulder strap, which was entire from front to the back of the arm was taken away: two small pieces of which I believe to have been from its similarity to what I had seen, the other shoulder strap with several small pieces of copper upon which gold was fixed, are still in Mr Langford's possession; several rings and breast pins have been made out of pieces carried away.[6]

No report on the skeleton was possible because of its dispersal, but it was suggested that it may have been that of a woman. The grave goods also included two or three hundred amber beads, strips of bronze and a second gold object. A short distance away was a pottery vessel containing cremated human bones and charcoal. None of these goods has survived.

The cape suffered great damage on excavation and the dispersal of pieces on discovery made it difficult to appreciate its original purpose for the major portion was itself broken into three. Over a long period, a variety of functions were suggested for it. For many years it was thought to be a peytrel or breast ornament for a pony, but, on restoration of the object, this interpretation was abandoned in favour of '[a] … seamless cape … made from over half a kilo of gold, originally stitched to a lining of cloth or leather and decorated with embossed patterns like strings of beads'. It was, as noted above, found with a large number of amber beads. The constriction of movement the wearer would have experienced has led to the belief that the cape would have restricted upper body movement suggesting that it had a rather formal and ceremonial purpose. Archaeologist Frances Lynch of Bangor University has suggested that the person (a man) who wore the Mold Cape had no weapons, suggesting that it may have been some priestly vestment.[7] Another suggestion made by the British Museum is that the cape was worn by a female, 'The Mantle of a woman of distinction from the Early Bronze Age 1900–1600 BC … The Mold woman, thus cloaked in gold with an arrangement of amber beads and bearing a bronze knife, would have stood out amongst her drabber costumed people'. The conclusion of other archaeologists[8] of the Clwyd Powys Archaeological Trust was that 'analysis of the composition of the bronze and gold shows it to be typical of the period 1950–1550 BC, and that it was made towards the end of the Early Bronze Age in about 1800 BC.'

It is not surprising that the discovery, rescue and restoration of the Gold Cape serves to illuminate the beginning of the history of Mold. The contents of this Early Bronze Age barrow reveal the probable prosperity of the community settled on the present site of the town of Mold in the Alun river valley. The ceremonial and ritual use of the Cape indicate a highly organised society which contained not only priests and warriors, but also skilled metal workers who had contacts with traders from Ireland and the western sea-routes. As archaeologist Dr H.N. Savory suggested, the Mold Cape '… may well be the product of a local school of craftsmanship ultimately of central European origin, but locally established in those lands round the northern part of the Irish Sea … '[9]

The bead necklace from the Bronze Age Barrow at Llong
Less than two miles away from the 'Golden Barrow' at Bryn yr Ellyllon is another Bronze Age monument in a field which is significantly named Dol yr Orsedd, the meadow of the burial monument. This lies close to the small hamlet of Llong and is one of a series of Early Bronze Age barrows in the bottom of the Alun valley in a distribution pattern which is in contrast to those usually sited on the tops of hills and ridge-tops. The cairn's low-lying situation on a river terrace suggests a settlement of farmers around 2000 BC, contemporary with the folk who owned the Gold Cape.

The site was investigated in the 1950s under the direction of Peter Hayes and a report, edited by Frances Lynch in the 1980s, contained details of the excavation of the Llong barrow and its contents.[10] The structure of the excavated cairn suggested that it '… may have been a two-period monument, an initial small cairn covering a central inhumation, later enlarged asymmetrically for the insertion of unaccompanied (i.e. no grave goods) cremation burials. These were dated in the second half of the Early Bronze Age.' The barrow had been built over a small natural hillock of coarse sand. In the primary burial a crouched body had been placed in a shallow grave dug into the summit. What is of especial interest is the artefact discovered amongst the stones of the cairn above the body, a group of tiny jet beads, 954 of them disc beads, as if they had come from a single necklace. This, states the author of the report, is the first

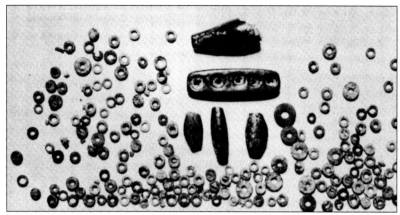
Jet bead necklace discovered at Llong during the 1950s.

disc-bead necklace to have been found in Wales, and likely to have originated in Yorkshire. Another unusual aspect of the necklace is that it was not on the body when the girl was placed in the grave and must be regarded as a separate and later deposit. Frances Lynch made it quite clear that the artefact was not directly associated with the body.

The discovery of the jet bead necklace from the second half of the Early Bronze Age suggests a group of farmers settled along the fertile terraces of the valley of the river Alun. The rarity of the jet necklace indicates that there were trading links or migratory routes across the uplands into Yorkshire (where the only British deposits of the mineraloid lignite, or jet, are found). It also implies a level of prosperity in the area.

The Gwernymynydd hoard of Bronze Age axes
A hoard of six axes and a bronze mould, dating from about 1000 BC, was found on Hafod Mountain in 1989 by means of a metal detector.[11] The find consisted of four palstaves, two socketed axes and a rare object of a bronze two piece mould, all dating from *c.*1000 BC. Archaeologist K. Brassil suggested that it is possible that they may have been deposited for ritual purposes, perhaps to placate the gods of the Bronze Age world.

These three separate and distinctive prehistoric artefacts are an intriguing glimpse into settlement in the Alun Valley and the vicinity of Mold 3–4,000 years ago and the only knowledge we possess of its first settlers.

Right: The bronze, two-piece axe mould found on Hafod Mountain in 1989.

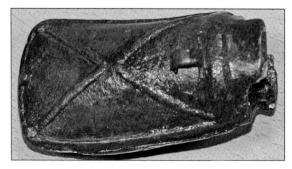

Left: One of the socketed axe heads found on Hafod Mountain in 1989.

Notes

1. See 'Glacial changes in the Alyn River System and their significance,' in the 'Glaciology of the North Welsh Border.' D.S. Peake, *Journal of the Geological Society of London*, vol. 11, pp.335–66.

2. ibid. Lakes named Wheeler, Upper Alun, Rhydymwyn, Cymau, Caergwrle and Wrexham.

3. During road widening at the parish church in 1958, horizontally-bedded clean red sands were revealed, with thin bands of small, rounded pebbles deposited when the Mold lake had widened to a broad sheet of water.

4. Peake, op cit, p.347.

5. This is based on information from a leaflet prepared by the British Museum and the National Museums and Galleries of Wales for an exhibition held at Wrexham County Borough Museum in 2005, a leaflet prepared by the Clwyd-Powys Archaeological Trust and Canon Ellis Davies, *The Prehistoric and Roman Remains of Flintshire*, Cardiff, 1949, pp.256–63.

6. ibid. Ellis Davies, p.257.

7. 'Report on the Excavation of a Bronze Age Barrow at Llong near Mold', edited by Francis Lynch, *Flintshire Historical Society Journal*, vol 31, 1983–1984, p.23.

8. Clwyd Powys Archaeological Trust.

9. *Prehistoric and Early Wales*, edited by I. Ll Foster & Glyn Daniels, London, 1965, p.91.

10. See fn 7 above.

11. Discovered by Stanley Morris of Buckley who, with the landowner, R. J. Peyton, donated them to Clwyd County Council who placed them in the museum in Mold Library. I am grateful to the Flintshire Museum Officer, Debbie Seymour, for this information and photographs.

1: The formation of Ystrad Alun

The time span of this chapter covers over a thousand years, the period from the later centuries of the first millenium BC, before the Roman occupation of Britain in the first century AD, to the Norman invasion at the end of the eleventh century. After the Romans withdrew from Britain in the fifth century AD, the old British tribes eventually emerged as six separate new kingdoms within an independent nation sharing a common language, laws, customs and Christian religion. By the time of the Norman invasion, each of the indigenous royal dynasties was firmly established and, until the end of Welsh independence in 1284, their ruling families regularly intermarried, quarrelled amongst themselves and fought the English foe.

Against this background Ystrad Alun came into being as a commote or territorial division of the kingdom of Powys and was subdivided into townships that retain their integrity to the present day. Throughout this period, and more so after the Norman conquest, the fortunes of Ystrad Alun had a troubled connection with Powys until the Welsh were conquered in 1282. This northern commote of Powys was often in the hands of Mercian kings or in an uneasy alliance with the princes of Gwynedd. During these formative years, the main weakness of Ystrad Alun was its vulnerability to attack from its enemies. Its geographical position close to the English border left it in continual danger of invasion from the east. Chester had been the gateway to Wales from prehistoric times and the new Roman system of roads provided excellent routes for peaceful settlers and armed invaders. After the Northumbrians won a famous victory over the Welsh at the battle of Chester in c.616 AD there was a steady colonization of Ystrad Alun by Saxon settlers. In order to mark out the boundary of their settlements, they engineered two great earthworks, Wat's Dyke and Offa's Dyke, sometime at the end of the eighth and beginning of the ninth centuries AD.

Historians have always acknowledged that it is difficult to construct an accurate chronological narrative for a history of Wales in the period between the end of the Roman occupation of Britain and the Norman invasion. For this reason, the period is often dubbed the 'Dark Ages.' Most local historians prefer not to mention the period and remain virtually silent about this most critical part of Welsh history. The same applies to Mold and Ystrad Alun because of the difficulty of finding straightforward sources from which to construct its history. All accounts of Ystrad Alun belong to the same framework as that of the origin and foundation of the kingdom of Powys. In turn, this framework is derived from events relating to Britain after the departure of the Romans in the fifth century AD.

There are no documents, apart from accounts of the origin of the Welsh kingdom of Powys of which Ystrad Alun was an integral unit. Here an attempt is made to describe the history of Ystrad Alun by the only available option; some kind of chronological framework has been constructed making use of a combination of early literary sources and surviving artefacts. All events and personalities associated with the story of Ystrad Alun given in this chapter are derived from written material in existence before the Norman invasion.[1]

These ancient writers provide the only framework we possess for the history of Britain and the early history of Ystrad Alun. From the piecing together of their accounts, we follow the departure of the Romans, the beginnings of Christianity, the arrival of the Saxons, and the foundation of the kingdom and royal dynasty of Powys. Remarkable surviving artefacts of the eighth and ninth centuries provide outstanding memorials to the activities of the Welsh and Mercian Saxons in Ystrad Alun. One of these artefacts is Eliseg's Pillar, erected in memory of a king of Powys in c.854, on a site which now overlooks Valle Crucis Abbey, near

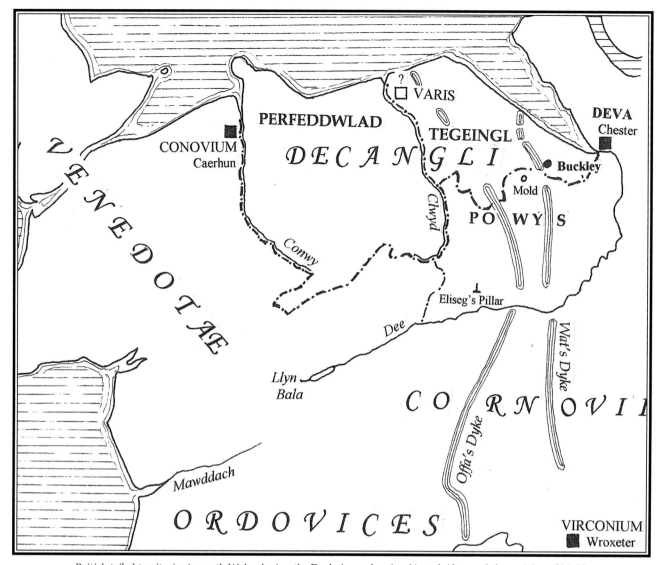

British tribal territories in north Wales during the Dark Ages, showing Ystrad Alun and the position of Mold.

Llangollen. Its importance to Ystrad Alun in these formative years is that it links together all the main figures in the story of the foundation of the kingdom of Powys and the growth of Christianity. The Mercian artefacts in Ystrad Alun date from the late eighth and early ninth centuries and take the form of linear earthworks which define the north-eastern boundary between Wales and the Saxon kingdom. These major landscape features are evidence of the penetration of Anglo-Saxon culture into the land of the tribal Welsh.

The people of Ystrad Alun were relatively undisturbed during the three hundred years of Roman rule. The nearest points of contact were on the road along which the legions marched into north Wales, in the direction of Bala, between Treuddyn, Llanfynydd and Llandegla. At Ffrith, near Llanfynydd, on the fringes of the clan lands of the Deceangli, tiles were discovered marked 'LEG XX,' indicating the twentieth legion. This site, occupied by the Romans from the first to the fourth century AD, may have marked a settlement connected with the mining of lead at Minera near Wrexham. To the north-west of Mold were lead mines at Halkyn and the military settlement and smelting centre at Pentre, Flint. Here, ore was smelted and then taken along Roman roadways by trains of pack-horses to be sold to the traders at the market at Heronbridge on the Dee where, on the border of Deceangli territory, the route from east Wales joined Watling Street which linked Deva (Chester) to Londunium (London). A lead ingot (pig) in the Grosvenor Museum, Chester is stamped

'*IMP. VESP. V. T. IMP III COS/DECEANGLI*', made when the Emperor Vespasian was consul for the fifth time and the Emperor Titus was consul for the third time, i.e. in AD 74.

From *c.*500 BC onwards until after the departure of the Romans in 410 AD, north Wales was divided between three major tribes. Further to the west of Ystrad Alun, at the river Conwy, were the Ordovices who inhabited what is now southern Gwynedd. To the east, across the Dee, were the Cornovii, of modern Shropshire, with territory extending into Staffordshire, Cheshire and the eastern parts of Powys. In between the Ordovices and Cornovii were the Deceangli, the tribe of the people of Ystrad Alun. Heronbridge, later part of the Saxon hundred of Atiscross, was in the territory of the Deceangli.

In the century after the departure of the Romans, these former Iron Age tribes emerged as newly-established Welsh kingdoms. Out of the Ordovician territory came the kingdom of Gwynedd, with the traditions of Cunedda and his eight sons as founders. The geographical origins of the kingdom of Powys are more problematic as it probably emerged from parts of the tribal territories of the Deceangli and the Cornovii. Powys was to suffer throughout its history, particularly on its

The 'Allelulia' Monument at Rhual (from Camden's Britannia*).*

boundaries, from inroads from the new Welsh kingdom of Gwynedd and from Mercia to the east. The destiny of Ystrad Alun was determined by its situation as the most northerly commote of Powys, exposed as it was on the edge of the kingdom in a disputed border territory.

The 'Alleluia' Monument at Rhual, Mold, is a local artefact which represents the beginnings of Christianity in Ystrad Alun, whose boundaries became the original ecclesiastical parish of Mold by the twelfth century. The illustration of the obelisk is accompanied by an account of the event recorded by the Northumbrian chronicler, the Venerable Bede (*c.*673–735), which is quoted below. It is taken from his report of the visit of St Germanus to Britain in 429 AD. The obelisk was erected in 1736 by Nehemiah Griffith, a prominent Baptist Dissenter of Rhual, to commemorate the victory of St Germanus and the Britons over the Picts and Saxons. Bede gathered his information from the *Life of St Germanus*, written by Constantius of Lyons *c.*480 AD. Bede emphasised the religious nature of the mission of Germanus, bishop of Auxerre, and his fellow bishop, Lupus of Troyes. Germanus had the advantage of his experience as a former Roman military commander.

> In the season of Lent Germanus baptised the British army and after Easter led them into battle. He chose as the place of conflict a valley among the hills and prepared an ambush.
>
> Suddenly Germanus, raising the standard, called upon them all to join him in a mighty shout. While the enemy advanced confidently, expecting to take the Britons unawares, the bishops three times shouted, 'Alleluia!' The whole army joined in this shout, until the surrounding hills echoed with the sound. The enemy column panicked, thinking that the very rocks and sky were falling on them, and they were so terrified that they could not run fast enough … the Christian forces rejoiced in the triumph of heaven. So the bishops overcame the enemy without bloodshed, winning a victory by faith and not by force.[2]

The Welsh sited the battle at Maes Garmon in Mold. Most commentators, however, do not identify the battlefield. One writer, Leslie Alcock, is of the opinion that the story belongs 'not to sober history but to Welsh folk-tale' and another, Sheppard Frere, leaves the question open, describing the battle as being 'fought in a mountainous district which was probably in North Wales.'

The location of a meeting Between St Augustine of Canterbury and the British bishops in 603 AD is another event in Bede's *History* which legend linked with Ystrad Alun, but such a connection is difficult to prove. It has been suggested that this event took place at Bistre, a township in Ystrad Alun. This is based on the belief that the place-name is derived from a combination of *biscop*, bishop, with tree or cross. The place where a bishop set up his Christian cross for preaching, or as a boundary marker for his territory, or even in this instance, Augustine's Oak, the spot of the ill-fated encounter.[3]

A second meeting followed at Chester and included learned men from the monastery of Bangor-is-y-coed in the kingdom of Powys. Both parties failed to agree on the date on which to keep Easter and on a common rite of Baptism, and the British bishops declined to join Augustine in the conversion of the Saxons. On hearing of their refusal, Augustine prophesied that the bishops would suffer divine judgement at the hands of their enemies. According to Bede, Augustine's prophecy of divine retribution was visited on the kingdom of Powys and the monks of Bangor at the Battle of Chester *c.*616.

The evidence for Christianity in Ystrad Alun during this period is obscure. There is no doubt however of missionary activities throughout Wales in this 'Age of the Saints'. Founders of churches in Powys included Deiniol, Beuno, Tysilio, Garmon and other 'saints' and monastic communities, such as the monastery at Bangor on the north-easterly border of the newly established kingdom of Powys, witnessed to the faith.

Bede also provides us with details of one of the landmark events in the delineation of what was to become Wales, the Battle of Chester c.616 AD.

The powerful King Ethelfrid [Aethelfrith, king of Northumbria] raised a great army at the City of Legions [Chester] and made a great slaughter of the faithless Britons. Before battle was joined, he noticed that their priests were assembled apart in a safer place to pray for their soldiers, and he enquired who they were and what they had come to do. Most of these priests came from the monastery of Bangor, where there are said to have been so many monks that although it was divided into seven sections, each under its own head none of these sections contained less than three hundred monks, all of whom supported themselves by manual work. Most of these monks, who had kept a three-day fast, had gathered to pray at the battle, guarded by a certain Brocmail [Brochfael], who was there to protect them from the swords of the barbarians while they were intent on prayer. As soon as King Ethelfrid was informed of their purpose, he said if they are crying to their God against us, they are fighting against us even if they do not bear arms. He therefore directed his first attack against them, and then destroyed the rest of the accursed army, not without heavy loss to his own forces. It is said that of the monks who had come to pray about twelve hundred perished in this battle and only fifty escaped by flight. Brocmail and his men took to their heels at the first assault, leaving those whom they should have protected unarmed and exposed to the sword-strokes of the enemy. Thus, long after his death, was fulfilled Bishop Augustine's prophecy that the faithless Britons, who had rejected the offer of eternal salvation, would incur the punishment of temporal destruction.[4]

Bede probably obtained this account from a monastic source and presented it in a manner favourable to the Roman Church's mission and antagonistic to British Christianity. The battle was one of the key events in post-Roman Britain, marking the split between the Britons in the north from those in Wales. It was the prelude to the struggle for supremacy between Northumbria and the kingdoms of western Britain. In the period 616–54 AD, five

Nineteenth-century print depicting the massacre of the monks at the Battle of Chester.

major battles can be identified. After the Battle of Chester, the kingdom of Powys collapsed, overshadowed by the supremacy of its neighbour, Gwynedd. In the seventh century, the Mercian frontier extended as far as Pulford on the boundary of Powys, and in the eighth century, the Mercians made inroads into Ystrad Alun. During the ninth century part of Powys was conquered by the Mercians and the remainder absorbed into the kingdom of Gwynedd.

Bede's account of the battle brings the ruling dynasty of Powys onto the stage of conflict which was to affect its northern borders for over six hundred years. We turn from Bede to Nennius to discover the origins of the dynasty of Powys.

Ystrad Alun was at the northerly extremity of the kingdom of Powys, part of the *cantref* of Rhiw, and, with its next door neighbour Iâl, remained a part of Powys until the loss of Welsh independence in 1284. Although from time to time it was overrun by foreign invaders, the major influence came from the Welsh kingdom of Powys. Ystrad Alun received distinctively Welsh foundations. As part of the territory of a Welsh tribe, the Decangli, for a thousand years its agricultural economy and political organisation were shaped by its native laws and customs which were the same as those codified for the rest of Wales by Hywel Dda at the end of the tenth century. Its position on the northern border of Powys made it vulnerable to invasion and settlement from Gwynedd to the west and Saxon-Mercia to the east.

These formative centuries in the history of Ystrad Alun are recorded on Eliseg's Pillar, an extant monument that was originally a high-cross which, when erected in 855 AD, was nearly twenty feet in height. The cross was thrown down and broken in two during the English Civil War in the 1640s and re-erected in its present state in 1779. Of supreme importance is the extensive genealogical inscription on the pillar which covers a number of generations in a period of five hundred years. It is an historical link extending from the final years of Roman occupation in the fifth century to the recovery of the kingdoms of Powys and Gwynedd under Rhodri Mawr in opposition to the English. The original inscription was written to record 'the ancestry and ancient glories of the kings of Powys' to 855 AD and the expulsion of the Anglo Saxons.[5]

Eliseg's Pillar by Moses Griffith, from Thomas Pennant's Tour in Wales.

The inscription provided a unique insight into the origins of the kings of Powys and owed its composition to Welsh traditions relating to the early history of the region compiled by Nennius in the ninth century entitled *Historia Brittonum*, 'The history of the Britons',[6] which is a compilation from a variety of sources, learned, oral and legendary. Amongst these sources is a life of Germanus, whose identity was conflated by Nennius with that of a later Welsh saint named Garmon. The deeds of this 'later' St Germanus are described in a series of fantastic tales, many of which are set in the two northerly parts of the kingdom of Powys, the commotes of Iâl and Ystrad Alun. From this mixture of the improbable with the miraculous there emerged tales of the origins of the kings of Powys.

The earliest genealogies of the kings of Powys cover a period from the early fifth century until the death of Cyngen on pilgrimage to Rome in 854 AD. Amongst the names which occur in the inscription are Welsh literary figures, heroes and villains. Vortigen, who lived in the first part of the fifth century, whose patron and father-in-law was the Roman Emperor Magnus Maximus (d.383 AD), and his grandson Cadell (*fl.* 450–80 AD), to whom Nennius attributes the origin of the dynasty of Powys.

The royal house of Powys remained Christian after the departure of the Romans in the fifth century and was sympathetic to missionary activity of the Celtic saints. Many of the churches in northern Powys were dedicated to St Tysilio, a member of the royal houses and a son of Brochfael Ysgithrog (*fl.* 550). Brochfael was a son of Cyngen and grandson of Cadell Ddyrnllug, who had legendary associations with the hillfort at Moel Fenlli. In the heartland of northern Powys, bordering on Mold, Cadell had made the original grant of land the *clas* settlement which became the church at Llanarmon-yn-Iâl, dedicated to St Garmon of Man. The cult of Garmon flourished where he laboured in Powys and Gwynedd. The missionary route of the saint is marked by a trail of nine churches dedicated to him, sacred sites which have a close connection with the topographical setting in the Nennius narrative of the *Life of St Germanus*. The dependence of the house of Powys on the activities of Garmon is clearly brought out by Nennius who used the genealogies, not as a historical record, but to express the political claims of the kingdom of Gwynedd. It has been suggested that he used the name of Cadell for the dynastic head because the king of Powys at the time was Cadell ap Brochfael (d. 808 AD). The following extract from Nennius described 'the first of the miracles' of Garmon as occurring near the tribal headquarters on Moel Fenlli.

> There was a wicked king called Benlli, a great tyrant. The holy man wanted to visit him, and to hasten to preach to the wicked king. But when the man of God came to the city gate with his companions, the porter came to greet them, and they sent him to the king; and the king answered roughly with an oath, saying, 'Even if they are here and stay here till the end of the year, they shall never enter within my city.' While they were waiting for the gate-keeper to bring them the tyrant's message, the day turned to evening, and night drew near, and they knew not where to go. Then one of the king's servants came from within the city, and bowed before the man of God, and told him all the tyrant's words; and invited them to go out with them to his own house. They went out with him, and he welcomed them. But he had no animal of any kind, except a cow with a calf and he killed the calf, and cooked it and placed it before them …

The next day Garmon was again refused admission and warned his host and nine sons not to stay in the fortress with the words, 'Be watchful, and if anything happens in the fortress, do not look, but continue praying and calling upon your God without pause.' After a short interval, night fire fell from heaven and burnt the fortress and all the men who were with the tyrant and they have never been seen to this day and the fortress was never rebuilt. The following morning, the man who had been their host, with all his sons and the whole country with him, was baptised a Christian. His name was Cadell and he was blessed by Germanus who said, 'From your seed a king shall not fail for ever (for he is Cadell Ddyrnyllug), and you alone shall be king from this day.' According to St Germanus' words, he was made a king from a servant, and all his sons were made kings and from their seed the whole country of Powys was ruled.[7]

From time to time the kingdom of Powys was absorbed by that of Gwynedd. The result of this union was that the commote of Ystrad Alun became part of a stronger unit that was better able to resist the advances of its English enemies in the east. Ancient Gwynedd consisted of only that part of north-west Wales which lay beyond the river Conwy. But, when the kingdom of Gwynedd was strong and its neighbours weak, it expanded eastwards to absorb territory known as the Middle Country or *Y Berfeddwlad,* lying between Gwynedd proper and Powys.

In the twelfth century, the kingdom of Powys was divided into two parts with the river Rhaeadr as the boundary; to the south lay Powys Wenwywyn, to the north Powys Fadog. The northern kingdom consisted of the commotes of Ystrad Alun, Hope, Maelor Saesneg, Nanheudwy, Cynllaith, Penllyn, Dinmael, Edeirnion, Mochnant and Iâl.

During the period *c.*600–850 much of later Powys was in English hands, for Offa's and Wat's Dykes cut through Tegeingl and Ystrad Alun, Hope and the two Maelors. The heart of northern Powys (or Powys Fadog) therefore was the commote of Iâl. In it were the western part of the valley of the Alun and that part of the Dee valley near Llangollen. In 814, Elise, king of Powys, slew his brother Gruffudd which led to violence, fratricide, disputed succession and the conquest of Powys by Mercia in 822. The English were not

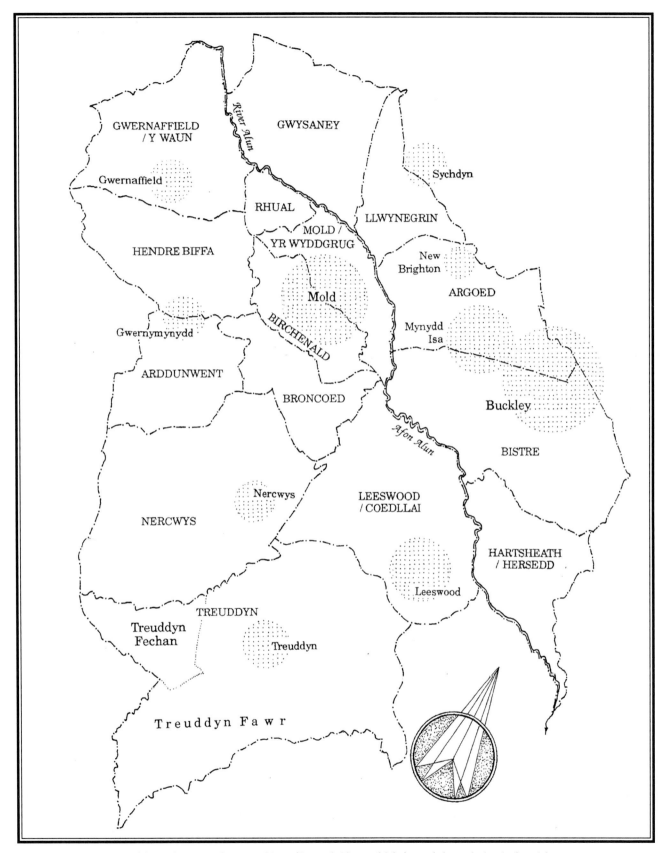

Mold in relation to the townships of Ystrad Alun, which formed the ecclesiastical parish.

driven back east until more than half a century later when the sons of Rhodri Mawr won the battle of Conwy and incorporated Powys into the kingdom of Gwynedd.

The administrative unit of Ystrad Alun was a commote of Powys in the *cantref* of Rhiw. It was of manageable size and, from its formation to the present day, has been used as an essential core area of local government and as such has had various names. Originally known as Ystrad Alun, under the Normans and during the later Middle Ages, it became the manor and lordship of Moldsdale, as well as forming the ancient ecclesiastical parish of Mold from the twelfth or thirteenth century.

Powys was ruled by a king whose court was at the centre of the *gwlad* (kingdom) which he ruled through the officers of his *llys*, or royal household. The most important officials were the *distain* (steward), the judge, the court priest, and the court bard and others. In each commote the king had a lesser court-house which served as the centre for local government, where the local officers, the *rhaglaw*, held a court and the *maer* collected the dues of the *taeogion* (bondmen), while the *rhingyll* was answerable for those of the freemen. At two seasons of the year, the king and his entire court went on progress around the commotes of his *cantref* to review the work of his local officials and hear appeals. On such occasions the freemen of the commote made a contribution of food and drink, known as the *gwestfa*, or feast, while the *taeogion* repaired the court-house and provided fuel and a certain proportion of food. In each commote was the royal village, or *maerdref*, where the local bondmen of the king carried out their services on the king's 'home farm'. Other villages in the commote were also inhabited by bondmen who performed special services and paid certain dues in money or in kind. The bond villages were the only villages to be found in Wales before the coming of the Normans.[8]

The townships, *trefi* to the Welsh, and *vill* to the Mercians, were the smallest divisions of the commote and later of civil and ecclesiastical parishes. Due to their size and convenience, they were used for taxation purposes throughout the centuries, including the collection of tithes and much later, for electoral divisions. Their origins go back to the Dark Ages. Some of the names of the fifteen townships in Ystrad Alun appear in the Domesday survey of 1086 and the first dates of others are listed below with a brief explanation of a derivation of names.[9] All of them play a basic and unique part in the history of the town and district of Mold and recur throughout.

Arddunwent: Welsh. There is no clear explanation of the name. Arddun a personal name with *gwent* field.

Argoed: Welsh.'edge or border of a forest,' or 'circle or enclosure of trees.' The Swerdwood was the name of an extensive forest of which Argoed was a part.

Birchenald: Welsh or English. The Welsh word *brecanor, brycan* 'blanket, canopy' (of trees). To this was added the English 'hill' which became cymricised.

Bistre: name appears in the Domesday Survey. Old English *biscop*, either personal name, or 'bishop' and 'trow' [tree]. The tree may refer to a boundary. Eventually contracted and cymricised.

Broncoed: Old English *brun*, brown, dark, and 'cot' 'cottage, shelter'. But it could be Welsh – possibly *bryn* hill with *coed* wood.

Gwernaffield/Y Waun: Welsh *gwern*, 'alder tree, alder grove, damp meadow, wet ground'. English 'field'. It may have been land which was a relatively early example of enclosure for arable purposes, possibly encouraged by the Rhual or Gwysaney estates.

Gwysaney/Quisan: The Welsh etymology of Gwysaney suggests that it is named after a brook which burrowed through the land in the manner of a sow or pig. *Gwys* with a personal name Aneu. A brook flowing through from Sychdyn is called Afon Ddu or Black Brook.

Hartsheath/Hersedd: Old English Harts' heath. The English pronunciation in *c*.1500 was consistent with the Welsh or cymricised form. In 1699, Edward Lluhyd used the form Herseth.

Hendre Biffa: Welsh. Hendre Bifau means winter dwelling located in the valley. *Hendre* being a permanent residence as opposed to the *hafod* which was a summer residence, with Piffa being a personal name whose identity is unknown.

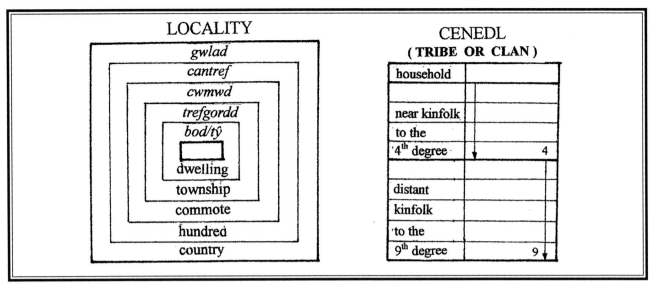

Social relationships in Wales in pre-Norman times.

Leeswood/Coed-llai: Old English Legge 'at the clearing' from OE 'leah' meaning 'a settlement at the clearing' or a 'settlement at or near to pasture or a meadow,' especially near a river.

Llwynegryn: Welsh *llwyn* (bush, hedge, small wood, copse or grove) with personal name Egryn.

Mold/Yr Wyddrug: The place name Mold refers to the same prominent topographic feature as the place name 'Yr Wyddgrug,' namely the Bailey Hill upon which was built the Norman castle. The antecedent of Mold was the Norman-French *mont haut*, meaning high hill. By 1595 it was known as 'Mohaut … otherwise Molde.' Moldesdale 1314 and 1506.

Nercwys: Welsh 'at the dark furrow, '*yn,- erch. – cwys.*' Possibly refers to the narrow course of the stream Afon Terrig or one of its tributaries as a burrowing *gwys* 'sow, pig.'

Rhual: Welsh *Yr* the and *Hual* fetter. *Hual* may have referred to a dam or weir on the River Alun or a sheepfold or pound.

Treuddyn: Welsh, *tref* and *dyn* meaning homestead.

The map of the boundaries of the townships of Ystrad Alun shows that their origins go back further than we have knowledge of. The same may be said about the native Welsh clans and tribes who settled on the land and first established the *trefi* (townships) of Ystrad Alun and Powys.

The *tref* (township) was inhabited by a subdivision of a *cenedl* (clan) and organised as an economic unit. In the free *tref* it was divided into four holdings, each with a homestead site (*tyddyn*) of four *erwau* (small acres) and arable land of sixty *erwau*, lying in four arable or meadow *rhandir* (sharelands) which were divided between free men. The laws provided evidence of the way the practice of mixed farming was organised, generally on an open-field basis and with a degree of communal control. Ploughing was an essential joint activity and demonstrated the way in which the resources of the *tref* were shared and utilised, especially on the *cytir* (joint land). The plough team was ideally made up of twelve men – a ploughman and driver, a person who contributed a plough, another who gave the irons, and the remaining eight brought an ox each. In Bistre it was recorded that each of the six men of King Gruffudd appear to have owned a plough team in the years before 1063. The law went so far as to determine the complementary resources of a hamlet as nine houses, one plough, one kiln, one churn, one cat, one bull and one herdsman.

One of the fascinating features of the ancient Welsh landscape is that many of the field names relating to Welsh agricultural customs and organization survive. A great list of these was made in the nineteenth century in the tithe apportionment surveys, that for the parish of Mold and its ancient townships being made in 1839. Through a study of the field names we may trace the story of agriculture in Ystrad Alun for over a thousand years. There are the names of *tyddynod* (homesteads) and many of field names incorporate one of the various Welsh words for field: *maes, erw, llain, dryll, cyfar, talar, cytir*. Other names are associated with former wooded areas such as *llwyn, celli, coed* or meadow, *cae, dôl, gweirglodd*. There are names which relate to outbuildings that were not originally used for human occupation which later developed into independent farmsteads. These were situated on or near the old summer pastures (*hafodau*) where they functioned as dairies, cowsheds, barns *llaethdy, beudy, lluesty, ysgubor*[10] and names relating to transhumance – summer dwelling *hafod*, – winter *hendre*. By way of contrast, in the neighbouring parish and lordship of Hawarden the names have an Anglo-Saxon/Mercian dominance which is explained by their almost continuous non-Welsh settlement since the eighth century. Townships have the names of Aston, Broughton, Shotton and Rake and field names are Shawfield, Springwell, Home Field, Big Town Field, the Great Hay Rake, Crooked Lounds, etc.

Still recognisable today are many of the homesteads, remarkable as being ancient dwelling sites which were continuously inhabited by Welsh freeholders from before the building of the Mercian dykes in the eighth and ninth centuries. Over the years, these habitations were part of the tour by kings (and later princes) of Powys and Gwynedd on their progress in the commote of Ystrad Alun. In later centuries, some of them fought with the Black Prince in France in the Hundred Years War, fulfilling their military obligations of tenure for the privilege of holding their homesteads. The difference in prosperity amongst the *uchelwyr* was notable later on in the sixteenth and seventeenth centuries. Increasing wealth, education and greater opportunity to follow a career in the professions of the law, church or military, for the Crown or at Court, gave them places of importance and influence. Many of the more prosperous rose in the ranks of the gentry and built new mansion houses and others improved their modest *plasau*. Amongst the most notable of the former were the houses at Gwysaney, Leeswood, Nerquis, Pentrehobyn, Rhual and Tower.

However, most of the homesteads remained as farm-houses of modest arrangement. Tyddyn is one of these with a string of others situated and scattered above the flood plain. They all enjoy the benefit of excellent

meadow, pasture and arable land with orchards. Their solid, stone buildings, cosily sheltered against the side of the valley. Examples of these are Tyddyn, Trebeirdd, Broncoed, Garreg Lwyd, Hendre Biffa and Rhos Ithel.

The 1653 survey of the manor of Mold lists the size of dwelling houses in the town of Mold and homesteads scattered in the country townships[11] and details of the simple cottages of peasants. The survey was a summary of the property on the manorial roll of the earl of Derby, an inventory made of the size of homestead, number of buildings, the extent of arable, pasture, meadow and woodland. In some cases even the number of trees are recorded.

From records such as these and those from elsewhere in rural Wales, it is possible to draw an elementary ground plan to demonstrate the simple variety of houses in the countryside of Ystrad Alun. There were three main sections. The first section, which was the

Nant Ori Cottage, Nercwys.

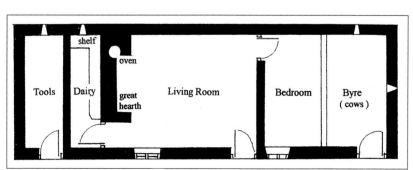

Ground plan of a typical Welsh farmhouse.

central and largest, was called the *cegin*, the living room or literally the kitchen, where the fireplace was, its rear towards the back kitchen. On one side of the central section was the *cegin gefn*, the back kitchen. The third section was divided into two: the parlour in the front at the upper end, and a dairy or pantry at the lower end. The ceilings were normally no higher than six or seven feet. Upstairs, access to which was via a narrow, wooden staircase, the headroom was restricted by the slope of the roof. The cottage home of the smallholder was even more basic in its arrangement and limited to a house and chamber.

The property descriptions in the 1653 survey show a typical diversity of native Welsh rural dwellings such as 'a thatched house of six bays of building,' 'a thatched house containing three rooms', 'one cottage of two rooms, and one cow house' 'one small thatched house, of two rooms, and one close of arable and pasture', 'a thatched house of three rooms, one barn of three bays or sections, a cow house,' 'a thatched house containing four rooms, a barn, a cow house.'

We have seen that basic to the formation of Ystrad Alun was the influence of laws and customs. As in all societies, the primary things that concerned them were expressed in terms of rights, duties and obligations. Gradually, communal activities were governed by custom which became refined into a code of law, the basic rules for the organization of the society. The laws gave all members of the respective groups a status and a role, each being assigned a specific place within the hierarchy. Nations codified their own laws to make clear the position of all members of society from the slave and the foreigner, to the king. All aspects of life were governed by regulations for communal activities such as agriculture, law, crime, punishment and arbitration on occasions of dispute or injury. Gradually in Britain, Christianity became a common and shared religion for transmitting the values of the gospels. This is not to say that there was uniformity in the law and custom of the Welsh, Saxons and Normans. Language differences were often a barrier, but in time a shared Christian inheritance, transmitted through the administration of justice, scholarship and the Church, became a bridge of understanding and eventually, by the sixteenth century, a basis of national unity.

By the tenth century, throughout the various kingdoms of Wales, society was regulated by codes of law. In 945, Hywel Dda 'King of All Wales' assembled thirteen learned men at Tŷ Gwyn on the banks of the Taf in Dyfed. They were 'to determine and expound to him and his kingdom the laws and customs in their perfection and as near as may be to truth and justice.' Hywel commanded that 'they be written in three parts: firstly the law of his daily court; secondly the law of the land; and thirdly the custom of each of them.' Hywel's action codified Welsh law and made it universal throughout each of the kingdoms. It was recognized as such by Edward I in 1284 and remained in force in Wales until the Act of Union in 1536.

Mutual responsibility, rights and obligations within the *cenedl* (clan or people) were determined by kinship. Knowledge of descent and genealogy was vital in determining land holding and the responsibility for the payment of compensation for injury and in many other circumstances.

Hywel Dda's laws divided Welsh society into five classes at the head of which was the *brenin* (king). Next in order of status and privilege was the *boneddig/uchelwyr* (the free-born) who dwelt in homesteads scattered throughout free townships. It was from this class that the gentry emerged at the end of the Middle Ages when their more fortunate representatives acquired estates and built comfortable *plasau*. This group was to make a significant contribution to Mold society, particularly from the sixteenth century onwards. Below them were the *aillt* or *taeog* (villein) class, the bondmen, who dwelt in the bond townships. It was this class who performed special services for the king in his *maerdref* and paid certain dues of money. Almost at the bottom of the class list were the *alltudion* or foreigners who were outside the tribal system but, if they chose to settle in a district, received full legal protection. At the very bottom of Welsh tribal society were the *caethion* (slaves). They were the property of their owners and belonged to no *cenedl* (clan) and were expected to perform heavy and menial work in the fields and the *tref*.

The Battle of Chester *c*.616, already noted above, was an event which made Powys vulnerable to the Saxon kingdoms of Northumbria and Mercia as well as the Welsh kingdom of Gwynedd. The gateway was now open for Saxon expansion westwards to settle on good farmland. The success of Mercian aggrandisement in

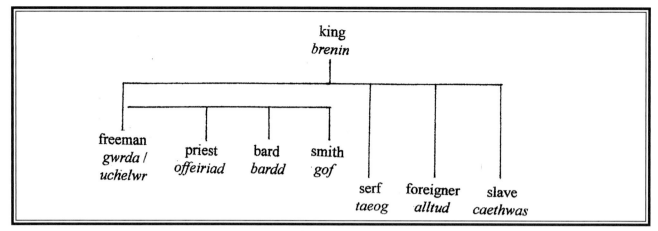

Structure of medieval Welsh society.

north-east Wales in the eighth and ninth centuries led to the division of Ystrad Alun between the native Welsh and the colonisers from the east, a struggle for dominance which lasted for over four centuries. The Welsh kingdoms of Gwynedd and Powys were often united against the Mercian invaders with their respective fortunes ebbing and flowing in the tide of war.

The seventh century was a prelude to Mercian success. The Battle of Chester had cut off the Britons in the west (Wales) from those in the north (Cumbria). For the next forty years, the northern Welsh kingdoms allied themselves with the Mercians against Northumbria so that by the early eighth century, Mercia emerged supreme among Anglo-Saxon kingdoms and began to colonise westwards from Chester during the reigns of Aethelbald (716–57) and his successor Offa (757–96). This was a time of consolidation and expansion of Saxon settlements into north-east Wales. There was pressure from Mercian settlers east of Chester for new land to the west across the Dee which gave rise to a time of major change in the landscape history of north-east Wales and Ystrad Alun. The English immigrants brought with them their own customs and system of farming. They altered the once universal Celtic pattern and replaced it in part with their own field systems. From now on there was an inter-relationship of two systems, English and Welsh, and sometimes a mixture of both. It was a time of forest clearances which are recognised in place-names such as Aberllannerch (*llannerch* Welsh for 'glade, clearing'), Buckley ('clearing in a beech wood' or perhaps a personal name Bocca), Leeswood (a settlement at the clearing adjacent to a river) and Argoed ('edge or border of a forest').[12]

The infant Mercian settlements were vulnerable to attack from the native Welsh, their ancient occupiers. Protection was given to the colonisers by the construction of two massive, parallel earthworks comprising a ditch and a bank known as a dyke. Both were probably engineered as military and political frontiers by Mercian kings along the northern marches to defend their newly-acquired lands from the Welsh. In times of war, they were meant to act as a frontier and in peace-time as a trading contact point.

Offa's Dyke is the longer of the two dykes and stretches 157 miles along the Welsh-English border from near Prestatyn in the north to the Wye, near Monmouth, in the south. It nearest point in Ystrad Alun is at Treuddyn. The date and order of construction of the dykes have always been debatable. Although the date attributed by Asser (d. 909), a Welshman, was 783 AD. 'There was in Mercia in fairly recent times a certain vigorous king called Offa who terrified all the neighbouring kings and provinces around him, and who had a great dyke built between Wales and Mercia from sea to sea.' Wat's Dyke, at forty miles, is considerably shorter. It runs parallel to Offa's Dyke following a more easterly alignment across mostly low-lying agricultural land. The dyke begins at Basingwerk and follows the north and east side of the Alun Valley, running parallel to the Dee estuary before turning towards Wrexham then crossing the Dee at Ruabon and terminating to the south of Oswestry. Excavations of Wat's Dyke at Sychdyn show it to be a well-engineered earthwork, better built and sited than Offa's. Here the bank probably originally stood some 2m high, with a ditch 2m deep and 6m wide, probably topped with a palisade.

The tradition and date of Offa's Dyke are not generally questioned but it is more difficult to date Wat's Dyke. This is important because of the dyke's prominent position in Ystrad Alun east of, and parallel to, the river Alun and as an important boundary line between native Welsh and Mercian settlers. It is reputed that the latter derived their name Mercians from *Mierce*, meaning 'boundary folk.' The date suggested for the construction of the dyke varies between the fifth and the tenth centuries.[13] Offa's Dyke has been described as 'much the most striking man-made boundary in the whole of western Europe.'[14] Those living in north-east Wales have the privilege of seeing magnificent views of both dykes. The dykes contribute to the landscape a sense of mystery and awe similar to the finest of Iron Age hillforts. Their mystery lies in the magnitude of their conception and the awesome task confronting those responsible for their execution. The only comparisons we may make perhaps are the construction of Roman roads and Hadrian's Wall, the

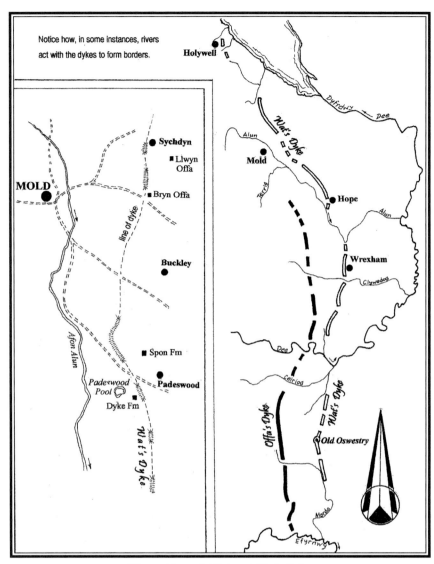

The positions of Offa's and Wat's Dykes

engineering and labour involved in making waterways and canals, or perhaps the work of the Enclosure Commissioners in *c*.1800.

In the creation of the dykes, communal activity was prompted by security. The colonisers sought to protect settlements and crops against hostile native tribesmen. The line of the boundary was chosen to coincide with, and make use of, the strongest features of the landscape: to defend territory, warn of approaching enemies, provide a look out and impede surprise attack. An experienced surveyor with a vision to choose and mark the line of bank and ditch was essential and so was knowledge of the terrain. Success depended on good leadership. Local decisions were made with the witan (king's council) which stipulated the drafting of able-bodied gangs to clear woodland, dig ditches and raise-up embankments and mark out the length to be undertaken by each group. Sir Cyril Fox, who surveyed Offa's Dyke in the 1920s, appreciated the difficulties encountered by the builders and was sympathetic to their failure to complete the task. 'To the Mercians,' he wrote, 'it was a remote, difficult and dangerous countryside, and that in the case of both dykes the constructional and perhaps also military effort involved was too great to be sustained to the end … it shows how essential the control of the south shore of the Dee estuary must have been presumably for securing the safety of Chester.'[15]

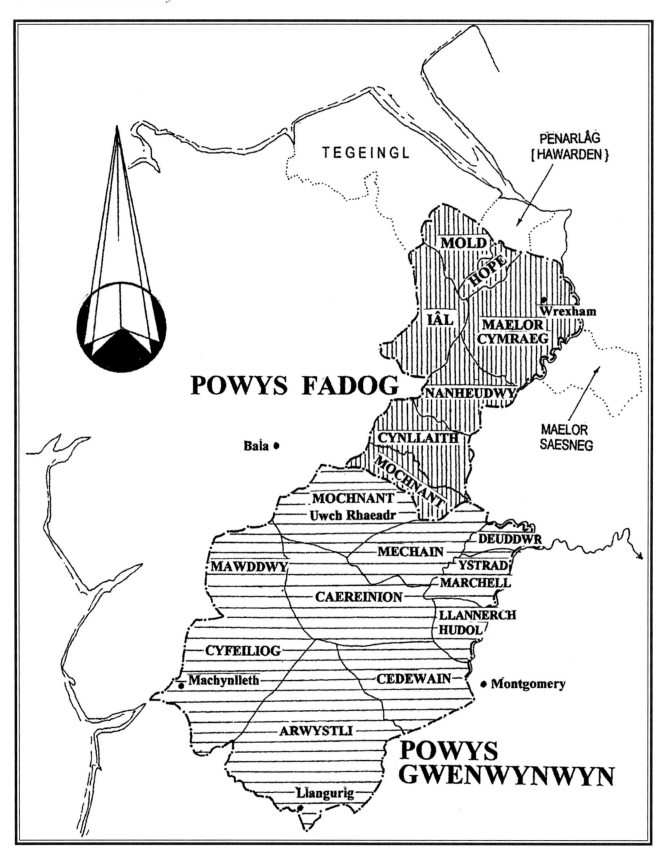

The principalities of Powys Fadog and Powys Gwenwynwyn.

Mercian expansion continued in the ninth century, although it began to meet opposition from the rise of a strong kingdom of Gwynedd under Rhodri Mawr (*fl.* 844–78) who, on the death of Cyngen in 855, absorbed Powys. Further hostility came from the leadership of Wessex under Alfred and the Norse threat to Britain. How great the peril was to Mercia is seen in the report that the Norsemen occupied 'a deserted city in Wirral called Chester' in 893. The Norsemen had occupied the city by 907 but were halted when a Mercian recovery took place. Its boundary on the west, in north-east Wales, may have been extended as far as the river Clwyd and to Derby in the south. By 921, the Mercians felt secure enough, under King Edward the Elder, to establish a new town, intended to be modelled on Chester, which they called *Cledemutha* 'Clwydmouth', at Rhuddlan near the north Wales coast.

This resurgence of Mercia was to have an effect upon Ystrad Alun until the time of the Norman invasion 150 years later. In 1086, the Domesday survey revealed that most of the land between the Clwyd and the Dee was a border province. In the 920s, after opposition from Gwynedd and the Norsemen, they rearranged the boundaries of their kingdom. Cheshire was constituted as the northernmost shire and the line of Wat's Dyke in Ystrad Alun was chosen as the western boundary. The new Cheshire was divided into units called hundreds. These subdivisions had military, judicial and administrative functions which were to endure for centuries. The names of the hundreds were taken from their original meeting place which were usually remote from settlements, often at a river crossing or by a major highway, and the site was often marked by a stone, tree or other landmark. Ystrad Alun was in the hundred of Atiscross, named after *Croes Ati*.[16]

Wales achieved some kind of unity in the years before the Norman invasion of 1066. The four kingdoms had emerged from the Dark Ages temporarily united for the first time in their history. This was achieved under the rule of Gruffudd ap Llywelyn (*fl.* 1039–63) king of Gwynedd and Powys and, after 1055, king of all Wales. Gruffudd was judged to be 'the head and shield and defender of the Britons' by the *Brut y Tywysogion* (The Chronicle of the Princes) and by a modern historian as 'the most effective king Wales had ever possessed.' He had the reputation of being a brutal leader in an age noted for violence and cruelty. The *Brut* records twenty-eight murders and four blindings in the years 950 to 1150. It is not surprising that Gruffudd was counted amongst them, slain 'through the treachery of his own men.' On the eve of her greatest challenge from the Norman French, Wales had lost her greatest leader. On the death of Gruffudd, separate kingdoms became the norm with a new dynasty, the second house of Powys, emerging.

Notes

1. The earliest historical description which had some connection with Wales was written by a British monk named Gildas (*c.*495–570) in his writing *De Excido Britanniae* (On the destruction of Britain). It is not a history but a diatribe, written in the style of an Old Testament prophet in which Gildas denounced the contemporary kings of Britain, including Vortigern (*Gwytheryn*), for inviting Saxon tribes to Britain. Gildas interprets the success of the mercenaries as the vengeance of God upon the Britons for their sins. From the time of Gildas, Vortigern became the scapegoat for the disasters which struck the Britons at the hand of the Saxons. He is mentioned by the Venerable Bede (*c.*673–735), the most reliable writer of them all, in his *Historia Ecclesiastica* (The History of the English Church and People). This is an invaluable account of Christianity in Anglo-Saxon England, in spite of his biased account of the Welsh Church. A later Welsh account of this period by Nennius (*c.*830), entitled *Historia Brittonum* (A History of the Britons), was made up of a jumble of sources, some of them relating to Powys. It was composed on behalf of the royal dynasty of Gwynedd as an act of deliberate propaganda to discredit the house of Powys.
2. *A History of the English Church and People*, the Venerable Bede (d. 735), translated by Leo Shirley Price, London, 1955, p.63.
3. Other suggestions for the siting of Augustine's Oak are Down Ampney, Aust on the Severn, Cressage in Shropshire, Abberley in Worcestershire.
4. Bede, op cit, pp.103–4.
5. 'Concenn son of Cattell son of Brochmail, Brohcmail son of Eliseg, Eliseg son of Guoillauc. Concenn therefore being great-grandson of Eliseg erected this stone to his great-grandfather Eliseg. It is Eliseg who annexed the inheritance of Powys … throughout nine [years] from the power of the English, which he made into a sword-land by fire. Whosoever shall read this hand-inscribed stone, let him give a blessing on the soul of Eliseg. It is Concenn who … with his hand … to his own kingdom of Powys … and which … the mountain … the monarchy Maximus … of Britain … Concenn, Pascent … Maun, Annan, Britu, moreover [was] the son of *Guorthigirn* [Vortigern], whom Germanus blessed and whom Sevira bore to him, the daughter of Maximus the king, who slew the king of the Romans. Conmarch painted this writing at the command of his king, Concenn. The blessing of the Lord upon Concenn and all members of his family and upon all the land of Powys until the day of judgement. Amen.' The inscription no longer survives but was transcribed by Edward Lhuyd in the late seventeenth

century. It is quoted in *The Welsh Kings, Warriors, Warlords and Princes*, Kari Maund, Stroud, 2006, p.41.

6. J. Morris, *Arthurian Period Sources*, vol. 8, *British History and the Welsh Annals*, London, 1980, which includes Nennius.

7. Ibid, pp.26–8.

8. *An Historical Atlas of Wales,* William Rees, London, 1966, pp.24–5.

9. This relies on 'Names of the Townships of Ystrad Alun', by Hywel Wynn Owen in *Ystrad Alun, 2*, 2001.

10. See 'Place-names Analysis in the Geographical Study of the Rural Landscape of Wales,' by Colin Thomas, *Studia Celtica,* 1973–4, p.314.

11. FRO D/KK/263.

12. Ken Lloyd Gruffydd, 'The Manor of Ewloe and the Place-Name Buckley,' *Buckley*, 5, pp.25–30.

13. The earliest date was postulated by Hannaford as being a fifth-century earthwork cast up as a political frontier between the post-Roman British kingdom of the Cornovii and the Welsh Decangli tribes. Other dates for the dyke are of the eighth century in the reign of Aethelbald (716–47) before Offa, or early in the ninth century in the time of Coenwulf (*fl.* 796–821) who was killed at Basingwerk, or his successor Coelwulf (*fl.* 821–23). The latest date is the middle of the tenth century by Moore 'as marking off the reorganised land around Chester from territories controlled by the Welsh.'

14. *The Age of Conquest in Wales 1063–1415,* R. R. Davies, Oxford, 1987, p.3.

15. Wat's Dyke: A Field Survey, [Sir] Cyril Fox, *Archaeologia Cambrensis, lxxxix,* 1934, p.229.

16. Croes Ati stood somewhere in the village of Pentre, about a mile from the town of Flint. Thomas Pennant records seeing the spot in *Tours in Wales, vol I*, p.68.Morris,

2: The Norman town

The town of Mold was probably planned at the end of the eleventh century, a time of the most momentous events in a thousand years of the history of Ystrad Alun. The year 1066 was a troubled one in England. Between Christmas 1065 and Christmas 1066, the English nation had had three kings: Edward the Confessor, who died on 5 January, was immediately succeeded by Earl Harold Godwinson who was slain in October at the Battle of Hastings and his adversary, the Duke William of Normandy was crowned king on Christmas Day. For the Welsh, disaster had struck three years earlier when in August 1063, Gruffudd ap Llywelyn, king of Gwynedd and Powys, lord of the manors of Rhuddlan, Hawarden and Bistre, suffered defeat by Earl Harold and betrayal and death from his own men. As a result, territory in north-east Wales was returned to the earl of Mercia. Over the next few years, young Earl Edwin and his Mercian and Welsh followers faced one danger after another. They survived the enmity of Earl Harold, missed the Battle of Hastings, swore submission to King William and then rebelled against him in company with Bleddyn ap Cynfyn of Powys.

Few Saxon leaders survived the regime change and amongst them perished Edwin and his brother Morcar. Their allies, the Welshmen of Ystrad Alun, mourned Bleddyn the founder of a new dynasty of Powys, who was killed in the southern Welsh kingdom of Deuheubarth in 1071. He was for a brief season the short-lived hope of the men of Powys and was mourned as 'the gentlest and most merciful of kings, who wrought good to all and did harm to no-one, terrible in war, beloved and meek in peace and a defence for all.'

Rumours of the violence and brutality of the new Norman king, William, were soon proved to be a reality. The nearer the Normans came to Wales, the more men feared him. Understandably, for his attitude to war has been summed up as 'Destroy your enemies and waste their country; let everything be set alight by flame and burning, leave nothing for them … on which they could have dinner … this is how war should be begun.'[1] William came to Chester in the late winter of 1069–70 to subdue the Chester-men and Earl Edwin's Welsh allies, and to break up the great Saxon earldom of Mercia. His pursuit of his enemies became a byword for devastation and cruelty. He 'harried the north' with the 'population reduced to great wretchedness' as he brought his unhappy army which 'feared the wilderness of the region, the severity of the winter, the scarcity of food, and the terrible ferocity of the enemy,' from Yorkshire, across the Pennines, to continue their destruction in Cheshire, north-east Wales, Shropshire and Staffordshire. At Chester, King William conscripted the soldiers who had once formed part of the fighting forces of Gruffudd ap Llywelyn and Earl Edwin to build a new castle. Gherbord the Flemish was installed as earl of Chester but was soon replaced by Hugh d'Avranches (d. 1101).

William decided that the kingdoms of Wales were to be conquered not by him but by his barons, and controlled from the border towns of Chester, Shrewsbury and Hereford. Hugh was the strong man chosen for Chester, to act in conjunction with his barons one of whom would eventually hold the lordships and manors of Mold and Hawarden. The Normans moved their new regional capital to Chester, adopting the same site at Deva as the Romans had a thousand years before.

Earl Hugh was richly rewarded with forty manors in Cheshire and counted Bistre amongst them, controlling Ystrad Alun. More significantly, it was probably through his initiative that the town of Mold was planted and gradually developed into an urban centre and as a focus for military presence, government, and trade. Earl Hugh stood out amongst his contemporaries for his power, energy and flamboyance in enforcing

The Norman knights in action at Hastings, 1066. An extract from the Bayeux Tapestry.

the Conqueror's rule in north Wales. The description of him given by Orderic Vitalis emphasises his exuberance and vitality:

> He loved the world and worldly pomp and thought that they were the highest blessing that human beings could attain. He was always the first in battle, lavish in his giving, took great pleasure in games and luxuries, in actors, horses, dogs and other vanities of this kind. He was surrounded by a huge household, in which there were crowds of boys, both nobles and commoners, making a great noise, as well as honourable clerks and Knights with whom he shared his labours and his wealth.[2]

Hugh d'Avranches knew what William expected of him and his barons in Cheshire and north Wales. The Norman agenda was to impose a cultural change on Anglo-Saxon England, by replacing it with Norman-French values and institutions, a transformation made under the leadership of King William and his followers – an aristocracy of two hundred families, close-knit in a feudal hierarchy, whose patronage extended down the social scale. They were rewarded by the gift of estates taken from Anglo-Saxon aristocrats in the most wide-spread land transfer in English history. In Wales, Anglo-Norman invaders enforced their rule wherever they could but allowed the continuation of the Welsh legal and administrative systems, and collected traditional taxes. The Welsh Church was by the eleventh century integrated into the Province of Canterbury. The assimilation of cultures took place gradually and throughout the Middle Ages the two communities with their own officials lived in separate areas called a Welshry and Englishry.

In the implementation of this agenda the man-made landscape of Ystrad Alun was changed dramatically with stone buildings as the most impressive new additions. The first of these changes began to occur during the last decade of the eleventh century, but many did not appear until much later. The only Mercian *burh* in north-east Wales was at Rhuddlan. At Mold they had to start from scratch: to conquer, colonise and create an urban settlement. Development therefore took place according to priority, necessity, opportunity and success. Priority and necessity in Wales were always dictated by fortifications, building castles for attack, defence, domination and colonisation. The castle came first; around it grew the town; trade and a market followed. The origin, dedication, dating and background of religious buildings depended on the transformation of the native Welsh Church by the Normans.

Earl Hugh rewarded one of his barons, Hugh Fitz Norman, with lands in Ystrad Alun. As the Norman clerks preferred to use either Latin or French place-names, the new town eventually became known as Mold or Moldsdale as a preferred alternative usage for Anglo-Normans and later the English. There is no accepted derivation for the place-name, but the following alternatives are favoured. One is from the Welsh *Yr Wyddgrug* (meaning *gŵydd* 'cairn' and *crug* 'hillock') on which the Normans built a castle, and may be a reference to a cairn of stones or tumulus. The Latin name is *monte alto, mons altus* 'high hill', with its equivalent the French *mont haut*. Another suggestion is that the town was named after the French baron whose family became hereditary lords of Mold, diversely written as de Mohaut, de Montalt or de Monthaut. Moldsdale was the name given to the manor which was coterminous with the lordship and ancient ecclesiastical parish, retaining the ancient boundaries of the commote of Ystrad Alun.

King William was as curious as we are about the domains he had acquired. In 1085 at his Christmas council held in Gloucester, it was reported that

> [He] had important deliberations and exhaustive discussions with his council about this land, how it was peopled, and with what sort of men. Then he sent his men all over England into every shire to ascertain how many hundreds of 'hides' of land … how much land and live stock the king himself owned in the country, and what annual dues were lawfully his from each shire.
> So very thoroughly did he have the enquiry carried out that there was not … even one ox, nor one cow, nor one pig which escaped notice in his survey.[3]

Within a year his commissioners' task of visiting every shire throughout the kingdom was finished. Their survey and enquiry, together with the written returns, were lodged with the king on large rolls of parchment and later re-entered into the Domesday Book.[4]

The clerks visited the manor of Bistre, a jurisdiction probably equivalent to the extent of Ystrad Alun. The manor was in the hundred of Atiscross in Cheshire. The entry in Domesday Book is the first major information we have of life in Ystrad Alun and its significance may be compared in modern parlance as having access to the tax returns of Gruffudd ap Llywelyn, Earl Edwin and Earl Hugh, together with details in the land registry of information relating to their property. The Domesday survey refers not only to the principal landowners but also to their tenants. When the commissioners made their report on Ystrad Alun they did so on the lines of a prospectus for a business company which had recently changed hands. The first owner was of Welsh nationality, the second Anglo-Saxon, and the incumbent landowner, the most powerful of them all, a Norman-French adventurer and, in every way, the largest shareholder.

The survey was an exercise in the evaluation of assets. King William wanted to know what was in his kingdom and how much it was worth. The purpose of the survey was to record property and not settlements. The king's clerks were ordered to record only those who owned specific property in Norman land terms and units of administration such as hundreds, manors and lordships. The only persons named are those individuals who legally held these properties. The other inhabitants involved in the working of the land and fisheries rather than given their personal names, were simply numbered according to status. They were the 'agricultural labourers'[5] who were bound to the soil of their townships no matter the ethnicity of their masters.[5] The Domesday commissioners went about their arduous task throughout the year of 1086. What an insight they have left of the English countryside. But it was not at all idyllic as they were surveying land that was the spoils of war, taken from the vanquished and given to the victor. Much of the land they visited in the north of the kingdom had been 'utterly laid waste' by the new king himself and the clerks said so.

The clerks who made the survey were chiefly concerned with arable land, making note of the numbers of plough teams that were in use and how many were ideally necessary to generate the best use of the land. The clerks appeared to be reticent about pasture and meadowland. The farming in Ystrad Alun at this time was a mixture of all three.

There are other limitations in the survey. The accuracy of the figures for woodland is questioned as are numbers of livestock which at this time played an important part in the economy. The only buildings mentioned are churches and mills and entries for these are minimal and some religious buildings which we know were then in existence are not recorded. In some places there are notices of priests but no churches are recorded.

Domesday Book gives an abstract of the land secured by King William by right of conquest. In 1066 in England there was a completely new start in the practice of landholding. All secular land came into the hands of the king and he gave it out again to men he made his tenants, bestowed as a reward for assistance in the conquest of his new kingdom. They shared in the victory and were now bound even closer to the king by fealty and service. Secondly, it was the method by which the king was to maintain a following which would serve him in the field or garrison his castles. This arrangement was called feudalism, the political and economic system by which land was held on condition of homage and service to a superior lord. Service deserved a reward and the fee commonly took the form of land. Land was held from a lord of which there was more than one class. The land *holder* was a tenant of the land *owner* and there were various forms of land tenure. The nobility held their estates in return for military service to the Crown e.g. Earl Hugh of Chester was a tenant-in-chief to the king. Other tenants-in-chief included barons, who were followed in the feudal hierarchy by the knights who were the fighting men who had accompanied William to England and whom he rewarded by grants of land, a knight's fee which they held in return for a knight's service.

Earl Hugh had eight barons to whom he granted land and who assisted him in war and administration. One of them, mentioned in Domesday Book, was Hugh Fitz Norman, baron of Mold and Hawarden. Baron Fitz Norman held the hereditary office of seneschal (or steward) of Chester and from him descended the lords of Mold who figure so prominently in this story until they died out in 1329. Odin, resident in Bistre, is mentioned in Domesday and was a tenant-in-chief of Earl Hugh, on the same social level as Hugh Fitz Norman. Other landholders named in the survey with holdings from Earl Hugh are Ralph at Rhos Ithel (who may have been the brother of Baron Fitz Norman) and his son William at Gwysaney. The only other named tenant of Earl Hugh is Warmund the Hunter who may have been a survivor of the Mercian regime, retained because of his usefulness as a hunter and knowledge of the forest which was described as: 'In this manor the woodland is 1 league in length and ½ league in width; there is a hawk's eyrie. The Earl has this woodland, which he has put in to a forest.'

No other persons than those given above are named in the entry for Bistre manor and its berewicks. Other unnamed individuals are grouped together in general categories which were deemed useful to describe the number of the workforce and the chief means of production, usually given as the number of plough teams. An exception is one unnamed priest from Gwysaney. Every township has a number of small holders, described as *bordars* (unfree tenants holding land by agricultural service), the number of ploughs employed and the number of ploughs deemed necessary for the correct tillage of the land.

The survey clerks noted every detail capable of providing evidence of the potential of the manor. They recorded what had happened in the time of Gruffudd ap Llywelyn (*c*.1056–1063) and that when the Welsh king came on circuit to his *maerdref* (here called the manor of Bistre) there were seven plough teams and it was the duty of each team to make provision of 200 loaves, a barrel of beer and a vessel of butter for the king and his household. The English ploughland was the area capable of being tilled by one plough team (which usually meant eight oxen) in a year and able to support one family. It varied in area between 60 and 180 acres depending on the size of the acre. The Domesday acre was not the statute acre, but the amount of land a yoke of oxen could plough in a day.

The Domesday survey enables us to deduce for the first time the names of settlements in what became the parish, manor and lordship of Mold. Some of the recognisable names on the map were those of existing townships whilst others were homesteads such as Hendre Biffa, Broncoed, Rhos Ithel, Gwysaney, which had belonged to previous Welsh or Mercian settlers and were now being taken over by Norman colonists. Other places named in the survey are unidentified and have been lost, although it may be possible to deduce their probable location. The location of familiar places is shown on the map together with those whose position has been speculatively deduced: Legge (Leeswood), Munentone, Horsepol (Padeswood Pool), Mulintone (it has been suggested is between Rhyd y Golau and Rhyd Alun water mill), Sudfell, Wiselei (may have been the precursor of Llong), Weltune (well town, possibly in Rhual), Ffynnon Tysilio (or Maes y Ffynnon near Bailey Hill). It has been suggested that the demesne land (the land which the lord farmed himself) and the lord's hall of Fitz Norman was located below the Wylfa Hill and was farmed for him by two smallholders, or *bordars*, one living at Hill farm and the other at Garreg Llwyd. There was a large field on Wylfa Hill called 'the Lord's Meadow.' Even from this slender evidence it is possible to see that the earl of Chester used his gift from the king of the manor of Bistre to reward his own followers with rich agricultural land in the Alun valley. The survey shows the first stage in the Norman colonisation of Ystrad Alun as the taking of the land by the king and its redistribution by him amongst his followers as a reward for military service.

THE DESCRIPTION OF YSTRAD ALUN IN ATISCROSS HUNDRED IN THE DOMESDAY SURVEY OF CHESHIRE

Before 1066 BISTRE was a manor of Earl Edwin. It never paid tax, nor was it hidated. It was then waste, and was likewise waste when Earl Hugh acquired it.

Now Hugh fitz Norman holds half of this manor from the Earl, and all of LEGGE and SUDFELL. Land for 1 plough, which is there in lordship, with 2 smallholders. Meadow, 1 acre. Value 10s.

Odin holds the other half of the manor from the earl and half of MULINTONE and all of WISELE. Land for 1 plough, which is there with 2 slaves and 1 smallholder. Value 10s.

Berewicks of the manor of Bistre.

Hugh fitz Norman holds from the earl HENDREBIFA, WELTUNE, MUNETONE, the two HORSEPOOLS and half of MULINTONE. Land for 2 ploughs. These 2 ploughs are there with 3 villagers and 2 smallholders. Value 18s.

Warmund Hunter holds BRONCOED from the Earl. Land for 1 plough. 1 villager with ½ plough and 2 oxen. Value 10s.

Ralph holds RHOS ITHEL from the Earl. Land for 1 plough. It is there with 4 smallholders. Value 8s.

William holds GWYSANEY from the Earl. Land for 1 plough. The plough is there with 2 villagers and a priest. Woodland 1 league long and ½ wide. Value 10s.

All this land belongs to BISTRE. It was waste. It never paid tax nor was it hidated.

In this HUNDRED of ATI's CROSS King Gruffydd had 1 manor at BISTRE. He had 1 plough in demesne/lordship; his men ploughs. When the King came there himself every plough paid him 200 loaves, a barrel of beer and a vessel of butter.

Having secured the crown and kingdom of England, the Normans ensured that they retained them. We have seen the methods which they employed at work in Ystrad Alun. Through the introduction of the feudal system they enforced a strict, inflexible and disciplined approach to the holding of land. New Norman occupiers received their estates in return for military service. In reality the town and countryside of England was policed and ruled by Norman knights as a military cavalry élite. The Welsh kingdoms, however, were still to be conquered and Ystrad Alun was part of the long borderland west of Offa's Dyke penetrated by the Normans where they were determined to create a permanent presence. Fortifications in the form of motte and bailey castles were raised in a very short time to create a defensive position and establish control over the surrounding countryside.

It is against this background that we may provide some kind of explanation for the uncertainty about the

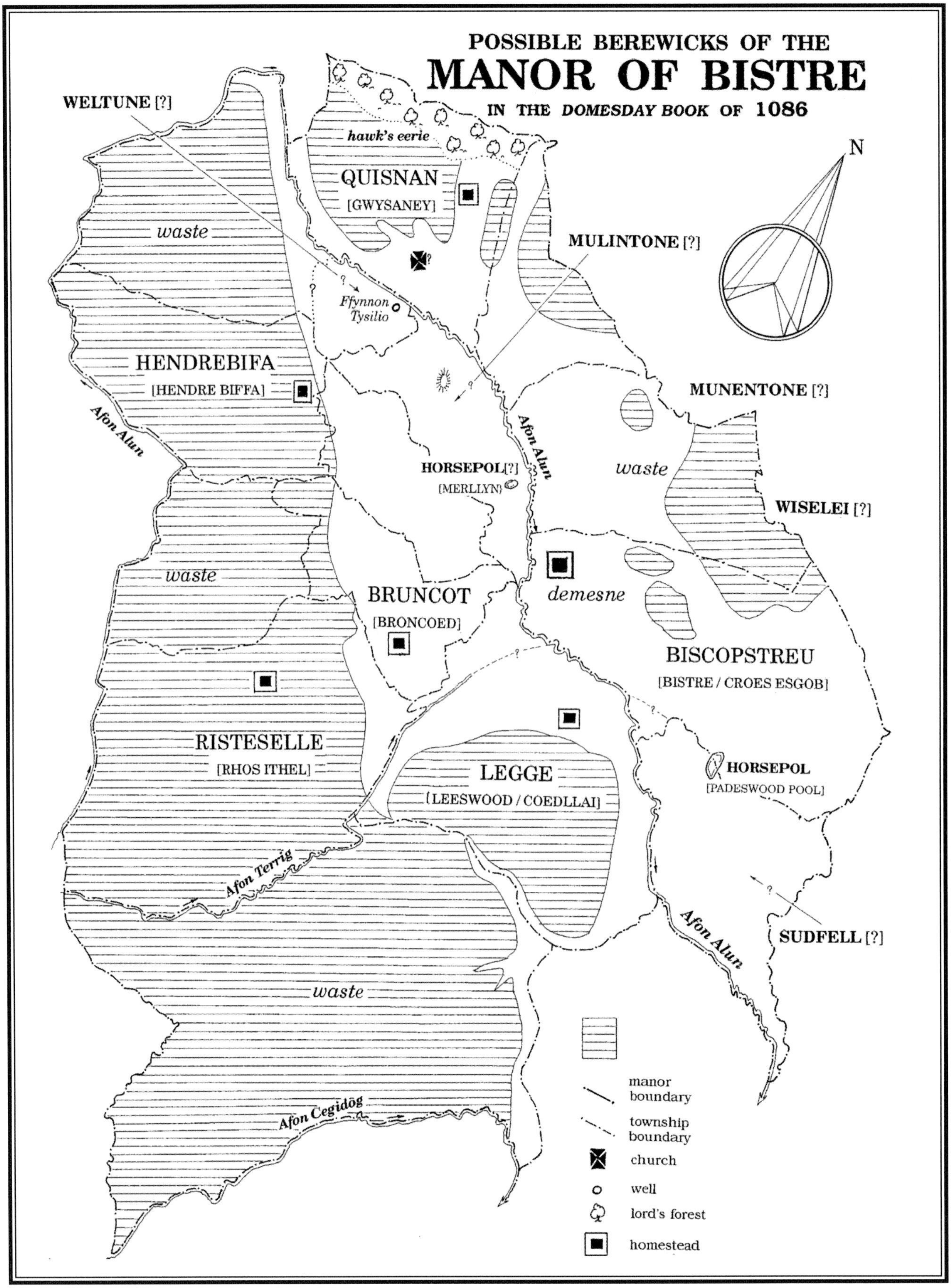

POSSIBLE BEREWICKS OF THE
MANOR OF BISTRE
IN THE *DOMESDAY BOOK* OF 1086

N

WELTUNE [?]

hawk's eerie

QUISNAN
[GWYSANEY]

waste

MULINTONE [?]

Ffynnon Tysilio

HENDREBIFA
[HENDRE BIFFA]

MUNENTONE [?]

waste

HORSEPOL [?]
[MERLLYN]

WISELEI [?]

Afon Alun

waste

demesne

BRUNCOT
[BRONCOED]

BISCOPSTREU
[BISTRE / CROES ESGOB]

RISTESELLE
[RHOS ITHEL]

LEGGE
[LEESWOOD / COEDLLAI]

HORSEPOL
[PADESWOOD POOL]

Afon Terrig

Afon Alun

SUDFELL [?]

waste

Afon Cegidog

manor boundary

township boundary

church

well

lord's forest

homestead

TENANT IN CHIEF : HUGH, earl of CHESTER				
LAND / BEREWICKS	LAND HOLDERS	NUMBER PLOUGHS	OCCUPANTS	VALUE
1 *Biscopestreu* [Bistre]	Odin			10s.0d. includes Odin's other lands
demesne	Hugh fitz Norman	1	2 smallholders	10s.0d
2 *Legge* [Leeswood]				
3 *Sudfell*				
4 *Horsepol*				18s.0d.
5 *Horsepol*				
6 *Hendrebifau*				
7 *Weltune*		2	2 smallholders 3 villagers	
8 *Munentone*				
9 *Mulintone*				
10 *Wiselei*	Odin			see Bistre
11 *Bruncot* [Broncoed]	Waermund the Hunter	1½ 2 oxen	1 villager	10s.0d.
12 *Risteselle* [Rhos Ithel]	Ralph	1	4 smallholders	8s.0d.
13 *Quisnan* [Gwysaney]	William	1 woodland	1 priest 2 villagers	10s.0d.

Land tenure in the manor of Bistre, 1086.

The Normans building a motte and bailey castle, 1066.
Detail from the Bayeux Tapestry.

nature of possible sites of motte and bailey castles in Ystrad Alun.[6] If we assume that all the sites are of Norman origin, then in all probability they date at the earliest from the time of Hugh Fitz Norman, (*c*.1070 until his death in 1128) and others mentioned in the Domesday Survey. Hugh Fitz Norman, one of the eight barons appointed by Hugh d'Avranches, was a very powerful man and one of the leaders of the earl's expeditionary force into north Wales.

A motte and bailey castle site at Tyddyn may be that of Fitz Norman's original fortification in the Alun valley, established on his entry into the manor of Bistre. It is feasible that its former occupants would have chosen Tyddyn for its strategic position as a vantage point in the valley. The Welsh call the vicinity *Yr Wylfa* (lookout, watching-place).[7] Fitz Norman strengthened the position of what was possibly a former earthwork by raising a motte and bailey.

There is much more uncertainty about the validity of other probable sites which are arranged in line down the Alun valley but they may have been used as look-out posts located at the Mount, a large-based motte with a hint of a bailey, Bryn Castell (near to Padeswood) and Maes William (on a site which guarded the narrow defile created by the Afon Terrig).

There is no mention in the Domesday survey of the existence of a castle in the immediate area of Mold in 1086 and one may have been established during the following two decades. It is impossible to know the actual reaction of the locally resident English and Welsh when this occurred, but one can surmise that it would have caused considerable distress. These castles became signs of oppression and a cause of resentment because of the behaviour of their occupiers who terrorised the locality by plundering, pillaging, extorting, abducting and imprisoning the local population. Did the native Welsh suffer feelings of fear and trepidation as they entered the settlement in the newly-planted town of Mold or as they walked up Bailey Hill on the way to till their fields? Many of them would probably have been conscripted into the workforce during the construction of the new castle[8] which was on a far greater scale than those at Tyddyn or elsewhere in Ystrad Alun.

The building of the castle and the planting of the town was the major man-made landscape change, sited as they were at the highest point overlooking the church with the river Alun below. There was much movement of earth as a large motte was raised up on which to construct the ultimate bastion of defence, a round keep.[9] The earth had been excavated out of a natural hillock from which two large baileys, separated by a ditch, were laid out.[10] These baileys provided an area for the billeting of the garrison with additional quarters prepared for the the earl of Chester's baronial retinue. There were huts to service horses, store equipment and prepare food. The steward and other officers had their specialised chambers, the most important of them in the keep itself, where they would be joined by visiting dignitaries. Local officials had their own quarters in the upper bailey. The lower bailey had space where cattle could be sheltered from

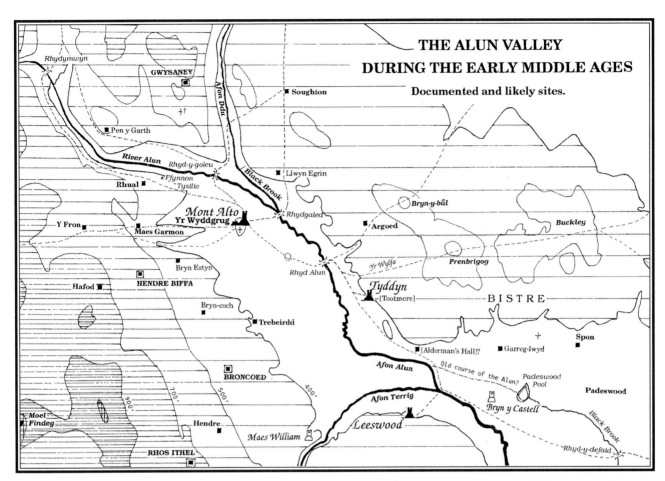

slaughter or in order to provide food during a siege. In one of the enclosures was a well known as Ffynnon y Beili. The height of the motte and the keep were designed to provide an additional defence against assault and the motte was surrounded by a defensive ditch. Fire could be a hazard if siege engines were employed and was as much to be feared as starvation or disease.[11]

Earl Hugh placed great trust in the ability of Hugh Fitz Norman and raised him to the position of hereditary seneschal (steward) of Chester which gave him responsibility for controlling his master's affairs during his frequent absences. For over 250 years, from the 1070s until the early fourteenth century, the fortunes of the earls of Chester and barons of Mold and Hawarden were inextricably linked and is depicted in the sixteenth century engraving 'Hugh Lupus, Earl of Chester, sitting in his Parliament with the Barons and Abbots of that County Palatine.'

The office of hereditary seneschal and the barony passed eventually through inheritance to Robert de Mohaut I (1135–62) who also held the lordships of both Hawarden and Mold which acted as buffer zones between Chester and the Welsh. For 200 years, the Mohauts exercised political and religious patronage and served both the earl of Chester and the English Crown and in the process became extremely rich. In Mold, as can be seen in the synopsis of events detailed below, their power fluctuated with that of the rulers of Gwynedd to whom, on more than one occasion, they were forced to yield both the castle and their lordship. On these occasions, for short periods during the twelfth century or longer during the thirteenth, they were compelled to reside at their castle in Hawarden, or elsewhere when that fortress also fell to the Welsh. Without any evidence to the contrary we must assume that the castle at Mold was equal to that of Hawarden and the one built by Llywelyn ap Iorwerth at Ewloe *c.*1210.

Details of the succession of the hereditary barons of Mold and Hawarden and the periods when they were expelled from Mold are given below.

Hugh Fitz Norman, d. *c.*1128
William Fitz Hugh, d. *c.*1141
Radulph 'Ralph' Fitz Norman, d. *c.*1124, hereditary seneschal of Chester
Robert de Mohaut I, 1135–62
Ralph de Mohaut, *c.*1162–99
Robert de Mohaut I, 1210–32
Roger de Mohaut II, 1232–60
Robert de Mohaut III, 1260–75
Roger de Mohaut III, 1282–96
Robert de Mohaut IV, 1296–1329, died without issue and the barony passed to the Crown

During the period 1066 to 1282, the main theme in the history of north-east Wales was a struggle between Welsh princes and Norman kings in which the invaders had a distinct superiority in military technology and fiscal resources. The Welsh economy was weaker, its military organisation less advanced and the will and ability to unite against a common foe fickle and unreliable. The Welsh ability to repel Norman invasion in north Wales was dependent upon a strong leader of Gwynedd, who could unite support from other Welsh kingdoms and create an alliance and for this to happen, a combination of diplomatic and military success was necessary.

On the other hand a feudal state needed internal stability and the loyalty of its barons in fulfilling their military obligations to the king in order to pursue a successful policy of political aggrandisement. During this period, the Norman English state was weakened by the anarchy of King Stephen's reign, the absence of King Richard, the distrust of King John (culminating in Magna Carta in 1215) and the weakness of the long reign of King Henry III.

The recognised complexity of this conflict, in which Mold castle was frequently involved, is seen in the following quotation and chronology of events:

The political and military history of Wales in the twelfth and thirteenth centuries is a story of perennial violent competition between a large number of Welsh and Anglo-Norman powers, in which fortunes rose and fell with dramatic suddenness, alliances were made and betrayed, and conflict was as often between Welsh and Welsh or Norman and Norman as it was between Norman and Welsh.[12]

Hugh Lupus, earl of Chester and his 'parliament' of eight barons and abbots. De Mohout is seated on the right, second from bottom. Illustration taken from George Ormerod's History of Cheshire.

1099–1110	Powys dominant over Gwynedd and prominent in north and central Wales.
1135–54	Anglo-Norman collapse under King Stephen. The Welsh recovery, the first major and sustained relief to Anglo-Norman expansion, particularly in north-east Wales – considerable Welsh re-colonisation of Ystrad Alun and restoration of their settlements and customs.
1140s–1150s	Powys witnessed an era of expansion. Madog ap Maredudd (1132–60) who 'held Powys from end to end, from Pulford near Chester to Arwystli in mid Wales.'
1146	Robert de Mohaut I in possession of the castle when it was captured by Owain Gwynedd who built a castle in Iâl at Tomen-y-Rhodwydd.
1150	Madog of Powys allied with Earl Ranulf of Chester is defeated by Owain Gwynedd at the Battle of Coleshill.
1156	Castle recaptured by Robert I.
1157–8	King Henry II led first expedition into Wales since 1121. Owain Gwynedd compelled to surrender Tegeingl.
	Madog of Powys recovered the commote of Iâl and destroyed Owain's castle there.
1160	Death of Madog of Powys whose kingdom was divided between five heirs. Eventually Powys Fadog was formed in north and Powys Gwenwynwyn in the southern portion.
1166	Owain Gwynedd (d. 1170) re-occupied the Alun valley.
1177	Dafydd ab Owain Gwynedd returned lands east of the Conwy to Henry II. Radulph de Mohaut II re-established himself.
1199	6 January: Llywelyn ab Iorwerth recaptured the castle and held it until his death in 1240. Ralph de Mohaut was slain at Mold. According to the poet Cynddelw Brydydd Mawr (c.1155–1200) the river Alun ran red with blood and the castle was badly damaged if not destroyed. Llywelyn's court bard, Llywarch ap Llywelyn (c.1150–1220), proudly informs us that it was a complete victory, involving a great fire, with the local inhabitants fleeing in panic.
1211	Llywelyn allied to Earl Ranulf III of Chester in a war against King John. Llywelyn forced to take refuge in Snowdonia. Roger de Mohaut I in occupation of Mold.
1215	Magna Carta.
1218	Treaty of Worcester. Llywelyn reoccupies Mold.
1241	Dafydd ap Owain agreed to return the lordship to Henry III who in turn returned it to Roger Mohaut II.
1244	Henry III instructed John le Strange of Chester to pay £40 to rebuild and strengthen the castle which he termed 'a royal stronghold.'
1245	Dafydd recaptured the castle on 28 March and held it until his death in 1246. Account in the *Annales Cestriensis*, also in Matthew Paris:

> But Dafydd, undertaking it himself, with his followers besieging Munthaut (Mold) with a siege camp, violently seized the same within a short space of time, and slaughtering those whom he found, or carrying them off with him, gained his victory as he had vowed. However, the lord of that castle, namely Roger de Munthaut, who was not found in the castle strove against him more cautiously in that district. Thereafter, there accordingly arose a very bloody war. Nor did they spare one party or another, on this side or that, because of their sex, age, or condition, they gathered all the people together to eliminate them.[13]

> £16 was spent on relieving Mold Castle from Prince Dafydd, son of Llywelyn, who besieged it early in 1245. The Welsh princes, Gruffudd of Bromfield and Gruffudd (son of Gwenwynwyn), lord of Upper Powys, were in the King's service, having done homage, but Tudor son of Ednyfed and others had been taken to the Tower of London.[14]

1246–56	Roger de Mohaut II held the castle until he lost it in 1256.
1256	Llywelyn ap Gruffudd destroyed the castle.
1265	Agreement between Llywelyn and Robert de Mohaut III not honoured.
1267	Treaty of Montgomery. Llywelyn agreed to release Robert de Mohaut III of Mold and to restore

Mold Castle on Bailey Hill

An artist's impression of how the motte and bailey castle might have appeared at the time of its construction.

Keep

Motte

Pallisade

Inner Gate

Inner Bailey

Bridge

Ditch

Outer Bailey

Outer Gate

Animal Compound

Modern Access

Compound Gate

to him the lordships of Mold and Hawarden, on condition that he would not rebuild his castles for thirty years.

1277	Treaty of Conwy. King Edward I regained Moldsdale and Roger de Mohaut III (during his minority Roger de Clifford had ruled the lordships on his behalf) restored by English king.
1282	Dafydd ap Gruffydd attacked Hawarden Castle on Palm Sunday 1282. Llywelyn ap Gruffydd regained Mold castle. After death of Llywelyn, Roger de Mohaut III and his successors retained the lordships of Mold and Hawarden until the main line died out in 1329. It is doubtful if the castle was rebuilt after 1282. There are later references to the 'castle and town' of Mold in the Charter and Patent Rolls of the 1330s, and in an *Inquisition Post Mortem* of 1415 and again in 1421.

As already noted there was no mention of a town in Ystrad Alun in 1086. The Domesday survey showed that it was a group of agricultural townships with its centre probably focused in the Welsh prince's *maerdref* in Bistre where the Royal household received hospitality on its routine progress. Normally we would expect another township in the commote to have contained a church and its burial place, the *llan* or sacred enclosure. But the survey gave no evidence of this and no alternative site has been suggested for an ecclesiastical centre in Ystrad Alun other than the present church of St Mary in Mold.

The Normans had selected Bailey Hill as an ideal site upon which to build a castle and establish a settlement but it is more than likely that an agricultural community, with a church sited opposite, had been present there for centuries before the arrival of the Normans. If we reject this hypothesis of a previous settlement then we are left with an alternative conclusion that the town of Mold was planned by the Normans on an entirely new site. Whatever its previous history, the site was developed by the Normans as a community of foreign settlers, planted by them to strengthen their military presence and provide economic growth and financial benefit.

If we assume that the building of the castle was the first act of a planned urban development of the town of Mold, then the earliest likely date we have for this occurring is in the 1090s. At that period any major decision regarding Norman expansion in north-east Wales would have been made by Hugh d'Avranches, earl of Chester, in consultation with his barons. His chief supporter, his cousin Robert of Rhuddlan, was killed in 1088, but there were others fighting for the earl as Oderic Vitalis reported, 'This man with the help of many cruel barons, shed much Welsh blood.' Amongst his advisers was Hugh Fitz Norman who held half the manor of Bistre and land in the outlying berewicks. It is natural that he would encourage the strengthening of Ystrad Alun against Welsh resistance and revival. In 1093, the earl was endowing his religious foundation of St Werburgh's Abbey with tithes from north-east Wales[15] and, more importantly, conducting a reinvigorated campaign of expansion into Wales in the course of extending his frontiers.

The development of new towns was a speciality of the Normans and between 1066 and the 1220s more than 125 planned towns were founded in England. In Wales, a smaller nation not yet conquered, very few new towns developed and then only in areas occupied by the invaders and each dominated by a castle. The Normans built a castle at Hawarden in 1072 but there is no evidence that they attempted to turn the Saxon settlement into a town.

The town was planned as the centre of a Norman settlement and was the centre of a lordship where there was a castle, church, and market place to service a military community and exploit the economic resources of the lordship. Conquest was not only undertaken by force of arms, but also by trade following the banner. Deliberate colonisation was introduced in order to implement a policy of eventual assimilation.

Modest as the size of the town was, we can see that it was characterised by a regular compact plan, with a grid pattern that could still be seen on the first OS map survey of *c*.1870. The 'grids' are made up of burgage plots which were occupied by the burgesses at the beginning of the twelfth century.

The burgesses were 'foreigners' who were settled into the town on an area of land, a burgage plot, which was of a standard size. Their admission to their plot was entered in the records of the lord's court on a court

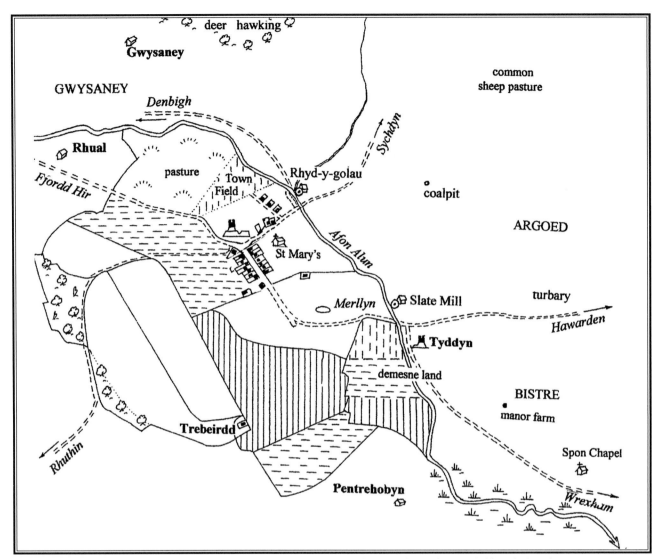

Manor town of Mold, c.1250, showing the castle, church and town. The market was held in the broad street.
Notice the burgage plots on either side of the broad main street.

roll and in return, they paid a small rent and performed certain services for their lord such as guarding the town and repairing the town ditch. They were not required to plead at the ordinary local courts or shire or hundred but only at their own *portemannemon* – the court of the men of the town. Their burgage rents were small monetary payments which continued in perpetuity, no matter who succeeded in the tenure.

The burgage plots were located around the market place and on main streets. Space fronting the high street into the market place was an ideal sales position. Here the burgage plots are long and narrow with outbuildings stretching to the rear of the house and shop. The people holding these plots were able to carry on trades and crafts independently of agriculture, though they often cultivated parts of their plots and kept livestock in outhouses, for which they might have rights on the common pastures.

In times of peace, the town and market place flourished and the number of craftsmen and tradesmen increased and the opportunities to enjoy these privileges attracted a wide variety of trades and crafts to the town e.g. butchers, bakers, brewers, vintners, cloth-makers, tailors, dyers, weavers, fullers, blacksmiths, tanners, masons and carpenters. The main attraction for the burgesses was the hope that they would be able to prosper in peace and enjoy their freedom.

There is no evidence of a charter being granted to the new town of Mold, but this does not preclude it being a medieval borough for it is not uncommon for documentary material relating to the granting of a charter to be lost. In England, of the 609 towns which probably were boroughs, there is surviving charter material for only around twenty-two. Positive evidence for the probable borough status of Mold is the arrangement of burgage plots which conform to that of a planned town. Other evidence is the existence of the office of mayor, other officials, its own manorial courts, the right to hold a weekly market and a number of annual fairs. At the time the town was planted the Norman lords were familiar with the form of customary borough charters and it would have been unusual for them not to have followed the practice.

The establishment of the town of Mold in the twelfth century preceded the creation of a number of Royal Boroughs in the shire county of Flint in 1284. These were towns planted at the places where King Edward I built his great ring of castles to subdue the Welsh, amongst which in Flintshire were the boroughs of Flint (1284), Rhuddlan (1284), Caerwys (1290) and Caergwrle and Hope (1351). By this time Mold had been in existence for over 150 years and there would have been no reason for it to have received the king's attention and be given a charter as it (and Hawarden) was outside the new shire arrangement in north Wales and remained so until the Acts of Union of 1536–41.

The Norman planners of Mold, in setting out the two main streets, arranged the frontage of the burgage plots in line with a broad market place. The new town was designed to attract a Norman-French merchant class and the burgesses were to be recruited from foreign merchants, tradesmen and craftsmen and, if commercially successful, would evolve into an urban middle-class with their guilds.

There does not appear to be an early charter in existence which granted the right to hold a market in Mold. Such charter rights were first granted in the late twelfth century, nearly 100 years after the probable establishment of Mold market which has remained the centre of economic activity for the neighbourhood for 900 years.

The first weekly market in Mold as well as annual fairs would have been established under the de Mahouts because they would have acted as an incentive to attract merchants and traders to the town and generated an income from tolls. The market was the place of exchange where craftsmen and manufacturers obtained raw materials from the countryside such as wool, hides, timber and metal and merchants and traders sold finished goods. It was the centre of the local rural economy. To the market and fairs flocked cattle dealers, farmers, small holders and housewives, bringing with them livestock, cereals and dairy products. The burgesses were the ideal residents and middlemen to encourage market trade and for this role received special privileges such as exemption from tolls and a voice in market regulation.

At the beginning of the eighteenth century, the right of the lord of the manor of Mold to charge tolls was challenged and Anthony Langley Swymmer, legal successor to the Norman baron, had this right confirmed in the Court of Chancery on the 14 December 1732.

Manor of Mold, 20 September 1732, LICENCE to Anthony Langley Swymmer Lord of the Manor of Mold to hold a Market.[16]

By an inquisition held at Mold, co Flint, on 20 September 1732 before Robert Price, esq, sheriff of the county, it was ascertained on the oath of worthy and law-abiding men of the said county that it would not do any harm or prejudice to the Crown or to the merchants and traders in the neighbourhood if we were to grant to Anthony Langley Swymmer, esq, Lord of the manor of Mold, and his heirs, licence to hold a market within the boundaries of the said town on Wednesday in each week and four fairs annually, viz on 22 July (unless it happens to fall on a Sunday and then on the Monday next following) for two days, on 11 November, being the feast of St Martin (unless it happens to fall on a Sunday and then on the Monday next following) and on the Wednesday immediately preceding Ascension Day, for ever, for buying and selling all kinds of fowl, meat, fish, grains, roots and herbs and other provisions and all other kinds of merchandise usually bought or sold at markets and fairs, together with a court of 'pie powder'[17] at the time of the said fairs. And the said inquisition is filed in the Court of Chancery as a permanent, full and open record.

Know therefore that we have granted and by these presents do grant on behalf of ourselves and our heirs and successors to the said Anthony Langley Swymmer and his heirs licence to hold a market in the town of Mold on

Wednesday each week and four fairs (as above) together with the court of 'pie powder,' tolls and profits (as above). To have, hold, and enjoy the said markets and fairs etc to his and his heirs use for ever without any charge or other payment to us, our heirs and successors or and it is our meaning and clear intention that they should continue without let or hindrance from our successors or any of our sheriffs, escheators, bailiffs, officials or ministers or their successors. Signed and sealed at Westminster 14 December 1732.

The origins of Welsh Christianity, dating to the time of Roman occupation, is well attested by the remains of carved stones and allusions to individuals and places in the histories of Bede and Nennius and lives of Welsh saints, particularly those associated with the kingdom of Powys, such as Tysilio and Garmon. From Bede's History (735 AD) of the English Church and the Saxon conversion we learn of the strength of Christianity in north-east Wales and the author's contempt for the Welsh Church for its rejection of the authority of the Roman Church and its emissary Augustine of Canterbury *c*.600. When the Normans arrived in Wales *c*.1070 they viewed the Welsh Church as 'archaic and backward looking, isolated (probably more so than in earlier centuries) from England and Europe, and idiosyncratic in many of its customs. Two centuries later it was an integral part of a papally dominated Western Christendom. Its peculiarities had not been entirely eliminated, but they were now little more than the curious fossils of former days.'[18]

The energetic Normans, whose campaign to conquer England had received the Pontiff's blessing, set about reforming the Welsh Church in an attempt to bring it into line with continental practices. They achieved their objective by imposing conformity and regulation upon it at every level: episcopal, diocesan and parochial. Customs that were considered archaic, undesirable or unnecessary were purged, or allowed to fall out of use. In this way a transformation took place between *c*.1070 and 1284 which eradicated former customs and institutions. Being on the border of the English diocese of Lichfield, and with the Welsh diocese of St Asaph in suspense, Ystrad Alun was one of the areas to experience the reformers' zeal.

In Wales, the clergy, who were vowed to celibacy, were ill-disciplined and living in concubinage and sons succeeded fathers in the priesthood. Churches and church lands were in the ownership of families and shared between laymen and clerics in portions. This arrangement was an abomination to the Normans who were accustomed to churches organised into parishes that were grouped together into rural deaneries and then into larger groups of archdeaconries, all under the control and authority of bishops in dioceses. What they found in Wales were churches that were localised. Each district had its own mother church or *clas* church which claimed ecclesiastical authority over areas such as a *cantref* or commote. The bishop, who had been chosen by the prince, would generally have oversight over the kingdom or smaller districts. Another difference between the Normans and the Welsh was the organisation of monasticism. Welsh monasticism was again locally based whilst the Norman equivalent was part of the great European orders of Benedictines, Augustinians, Cistercians, etc. Welsh monasteries were supported by the Welsh princes who endowed them with land and food-rents.

The Normans gradually gained control over the Welsh Church by appointing Welsh diocesan bishops who swore allegiance to the king and became his tenants-in-chief and then imposed the ways of the Province of Canterbury on the Welsh dioceses. This transformation took about two hundred years to achieve and was completed by the end of the thirteenth century and enables us, for the first time, to have an accurate description of religious organisation in the commote of Ystrad Alun.

In all probability the pre-Norman situation was that the mother church for the commote of Ystrad Alun may have had as its *clas* a church dedicated to St Tysilio, with the possibility of other churches at Bistre and Nercwys dedicated to other Welsh saints. In the commote of Iâl there was a church dedicated to St Garmon (associated with St Germanus) and in Hawarden a church dedicated to St Deiniol.[19] In all probability, the site of the *clas* church for Ystrad Alun was on the site of the present-day church in Mold. This assumption is based on the curvilinear shape of the churchyard and the absence of an alternative site for a burial ground. This identification is, however, by no means certain due the vagueness of the exact location of Bistre in the commote of Ystrad Alun. Another difficulty which cannot be explained is the mention in Domesday of a priest dwelling within Gwysaney township, an individual whom no-one has ever suggested was a Norman. Other factors which are difficult to explain are the existence of holy wells with Welsh dedications which could be either pre-Norman or post-Norman, of interest more for their names than their known association with a particular *clas*.[20]

After the arrival of the Normans in north-east Wales, there is evidence of their involvement in the Welsh Church in Ystrad Alun. The first is the gift by Hugh d'Avranches of the tithes of his demesne manors of Hawarden, Coleshill and Bistre for the endowment of the abbey in Chester. But there is no indication of the origin and ownership of church tithes in Ystrad Alun. In 1125, north-east Wales was described as being 'without a bishop because of the desolation of the country and rudeness of the inhabitants' but, by 1143, the Normans are known to have re-created the territorial diocese of St Asaph and appointed Gilbert as its first bishop. They had the choice of either establishing a new diocese, annexing north-east Wales to the bishopric of Chester-Lichfield or re-establishing the old Welsh diocese of St Asaph which was coincident with the kingdom of Powys. The latter option was chosen and Ystrad Alun was joined with Iâl into a newly-created

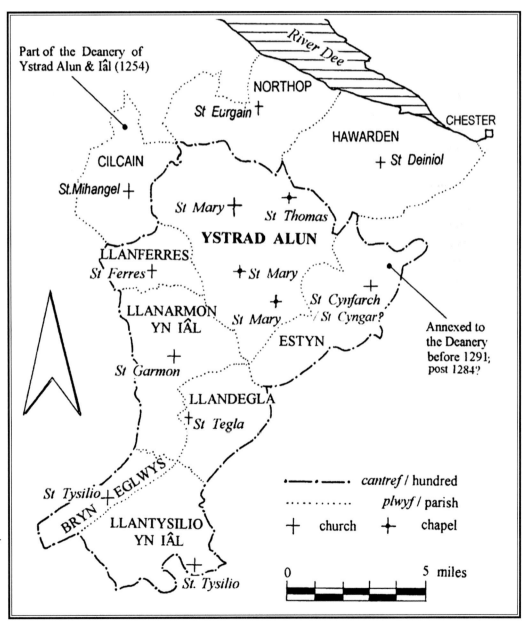

The arrangement of parishes in the thirteenth century with the large parish of Mold (Ystrad Alun).

rural deanery.[21] It is conjectured that this reform took place sometime in the middle of the twelfth century, between 1146 and 1157, during a brief interval when these two commotes were united politically under Owain, prince of Gwynedd. This slender information is the first evidence of the introduction locally of church organisation which conformed with the western Roman Church. However, we have to wait a hundred years for the Valuation of Norwich in 1254, which is the first extant list of parishes in the diocese of Asaph.

> The valuation of the churches of the Deanery of de Monte Alto [Mold] made by Kenwric, Dean there; Iefad, chaplain of Lantesiliau [Llantysilio-yn-Iâl] and John Rufus, rector of the same church, jurors.

> The church of Mohald [Mold] 9 marks 12s
> The church of Kilkeyn [Cilcain] 3 marks 4s
> The church of Lanwertys [Llanferres] 2 marks 2s 8d
> The church of Germanus [Llanarmon-yn-Ial] 3 marks 4s
> The church of de Sancto Tessiliao [Llantysilio-yn-Ial] 3 marks 4s
> Total £13 6s 8d – Tenth [tithe] 26s 8d[21]

In another valuation, made in 1291, in the time of Pope Nicholas IV, when the name of the deanery had been changed from de Monte Alto [Mold] to Yall [Iâl] and Stratalwen [Strath Alun or Ystrad Alun], the parishes were listed as:

> Llanferres
> Llanarmon
> Llandegla
> Llantysillio
> Bryn Eglwys
> *De Monte alto cum capella sua de Nerchgwys*

A list of the religious buildings which came under the patronage of the Norman Barons of Mold is detailed below, together with brief details of any record of this association seen in the respective buildings and surviving artefacts. Some speculation is made concerning the foundation of the Norman church at Mold which was repaired after the Edwardian Conquest of 1284, although the tower survived until *c*.1768. The main body of the church was completely replaced *c*.1490–1590.

St Mary's Church

St Mary's, the pre-eminent church in Ystrad Alun, dedicated to the Nativity of the Blessed Virgin Mary (feast day 8 September), was built on the site of the present-day church by the Normans sometime in the twelfth century, probably to replace an earlier Welsh church dedicated to a native local saint. The patrons of the church were the barons of Mold, members of the de Mohaut family, chief of whom were, in the twelfth century, Hugh Fitz Norman (d. *c*.1128), William Fitz Hugh (d. *c*.1141), Robert de Mohaut (1135–62) and Ralph de Mohaut (1162–99).

The Norman barons of Mold were powerful, rich and religious. In an age of church building they were patrons of religious buildings throughout their barony and beyond. Their piety and devotion were sometimes mixed with greed and rapacity and one of the barons was known as the 'black steward.' Nevertheless, their wealth and position made them knowledgeable and familiar with masons and craftsmen engaged on the continuing large scale construction of churches.

We know nothing of the structure of the Welsh church which the Normans found in Mold but we may assume that in all probability it was made of wood. As soon as they had planned a new town at Mold it would be their ambition to also build a fine, new, stone church. We may also assume that the person responsible for the building of a new church was one of the twelfth-century barons of Mold. If it was built

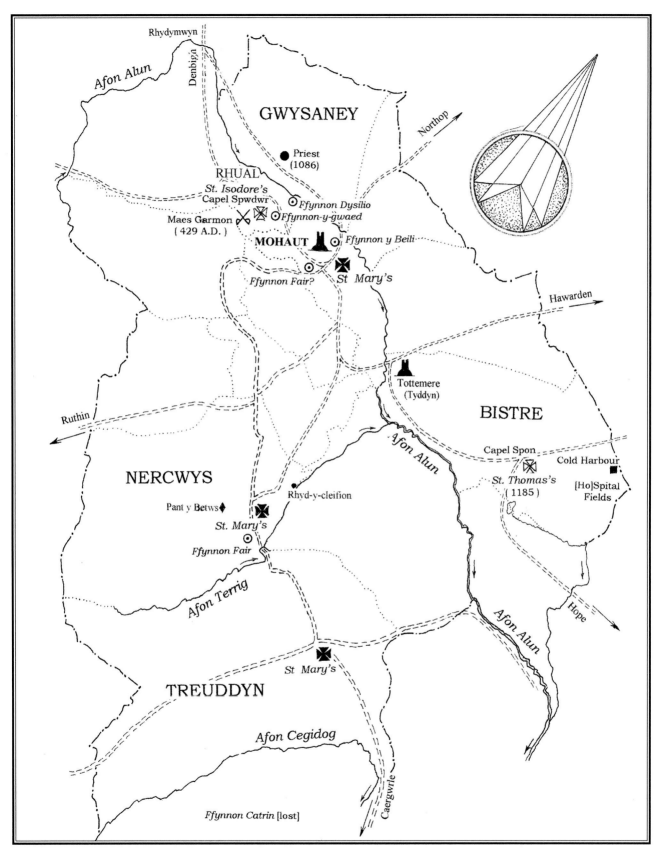

Rhydymwyn

Afon Alun

Denbigh

GWYSANEY

Northop

● Priest
(1086)

RHUAL

St. Isodore's
Capel Spwdwr

⊙ *Ffynnon Dysilio*

Maes Garmon
(429 A.D.)

⊙ *Ffynnon-y-gwaed*

MOHAUT

⊙ *Ffynnon y Beili*

⊙

Ffynnon Fair?

St Mary's

Hawarden

Tottemere
(Tyddyn)

BISTRE

Ruthin

Capel Spon

Cold Harbour

NERCWYS

St. Thomas's
(1185)

[Ho]Spital
Fields

Afon Alun

Rhyd-y-cleifion

Pant y Betws ◆

St. Mary's

⊙
Ffynnon Fair

Afon Terrig

Hope

St Mary's

TREUDDYN

Afon Cegidog

Caergwrle

Ffynnon Catrin [lost]

Christian sites in medieval Ystrad Alun.

during the first part of the twelfth century then it would have taken place during the reign of Henry I, when Richard, earl of Chester, was a minor and ward of the king. The baron of Mold would be aware of the friendly relationship that existed between Gruffudd ap Cynan, king of Gwynedd, and the English monarch. Moreover, he would know that the Welsh prince was using masons recruited from Chester to enrich the churches in his chief places in Gwynedd in the Romanesque style. Penmon Priory in Anglesey still remains as a testimony of what was achieved under Norman influence in north Wales; church building of the highest workmanship, equal to that of any in Europe. A modest assessment of the achievement of the baron might suggest that his new church building was smaller than the church which succeeded it. If we assume that it was built on the existing site, it would have had the traditional ground plan of nave, chancel and tower, possibly with doorways on the south, north and west. If it was bigger than the modest chapel built at Nercwys, it may have had a porch and side aisles. One clue to the size of the Mold church may be found in the sum of money awarded for compensation for damage to Welsh churches during Edward I's wars of conquest. After numerous churches were plundered and devastated by English soldiers and their mercenaries, over a hundred claims were submitted to the King's Commission. By November 1284, more than £1,730 was distributed in compensation payments, ranging from a few shillings to £250 allowed to the bishop of Bangor. Other awards normally only amounted to a few pounds and rarely exceeded £10, but the vicar of Mold received £26.

The masons responsible for undertaking work on Mold church were recruited by the patron. Medieval masons travelled from place to place to undertake whatever commissions they received from the king or his barons. When they came to Mold they lived in temporary lodges, single-storied timber sheds that were thatched with straw. The gangs of workmen were made up of a variety of craftsmen which included a master-mason, a digger, free and rough masons, carvers, setters and wallers, paviors (to lay the floors) and tilers (who were the brick layers). Another group of specialists was employed at a quarry; diggers and hewers of stone, quarry men who gave the stone a rough shape leaving it to be finished by the free masons. Choosing the stone was important and there were several considerations which included accessibility of an outcrop for quarrying, the colour and quality of the stone and the low cost of transport.

Other craftsmen who made up the team of builders were carpenters (to make the scaffolding, templates, construct the roofs and furnish the church), plumbers (who put the lead on the roof) and smiths (who sharpened the tools and provided nails).

We have a brief glimpse of the quality and skill of medieval craftsmen employed at Mold in the surviving grotesque carvings from the barons' church. In order to identify and date them, photographs of the stones which have been incorporated in a wall in the vicinity of the church were sent to an expert who dated them between the twelfth century and the late fifteenth century. The late twelfth century group of carvings included

Corbels (roof supports) from the late twelfth-century church in the form of grotesque carvings.

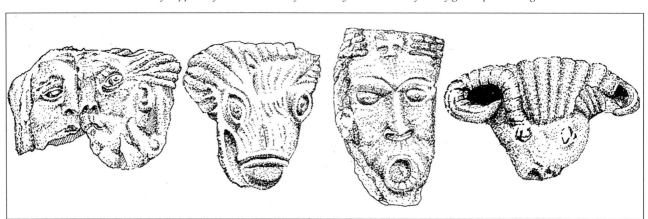

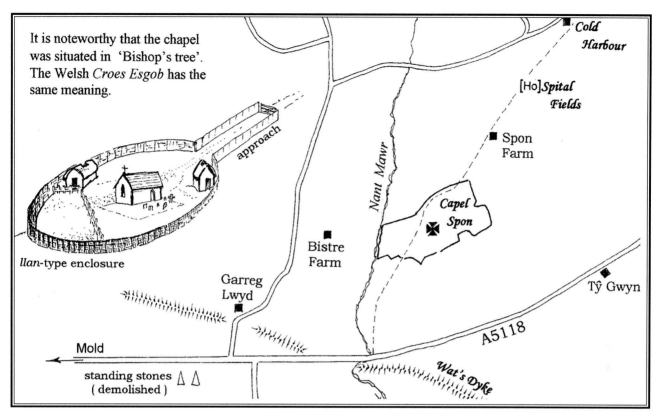

It is noteworthy that the chapel was situated in 'Bishop's tree'. The Welsh *Croes Esgob* has the same meaning.

approach

llan-type enclosure

Nant Mawr

Cold Harbour

[Ho]*Spital Fields*

■ Spon Farm

Capel Spon

■ Bistre Farm

◆ Tŷ Gwyn

Garreg Lwyd

A5118

Mold

standing stones (demolished) △ △

Wat's Dyke

The site of Capel Spon with an inset showing the layout of the llan.

corbels which were described as being possibly 'provincial school working ... say in the first half of the thirteenth century, but still employing some of the features of Romanesque carving.[22]

Possibly the building of Mold Church coincided with the foundation of Capel Spon sometime between 1157 and 1199.

Capel Spon

Ralph de Mohaut (1162–99) invited the abbot of the Augustinian abbey at Haughmond, Shrewsbury, to establish a daughter house in his lordship of Mold. The Augustinian, or Black, canons arrived at Spon, near Wat's Dyke in the township of Bistre, to build their priory in about the year 1185. It was dedicated to St Thomas Becket (*c.* 1120–70), archbishop of Canterbury, who was murdered in his cathedral. Baron Ralph was probably acquainted with him and may have witnessed the act of penitence of King Henry II.

The new priory consisted of a modest chapel and domestic quarters, with a burial place in the enclosure. The Augustinians occupied the site until 1260 when they were recalled to the mother house in Shropshire, during the time of the hostile Roger de Mohaut II (d. 1260) who sought to dispossess the monks of St Werburgh's in Chester of some of their property. The annals of Chester recorded that as a result of his misdeeds, Roger died in poverty 'the common people being ignorant of his place of burial'. The Augustinians were recruited almost exclusively from a non-Welsh population and were noted for their association with hospitals, which probably accounts for the nearby place-name 'Spital fields'. It has been suggested that *c.*1300 Robert de Mohaut IV (1296–1329) granted William of Hawarden some leper's land, which might be the spital fields.

The charters which were granted to Spon by Ralph de Mohaut gave the Augustinians lands, rights and privileges in Bistre and the adjacent townships.[23] They are also extremely important in that they provide information about the settlement in the Bistre area a hundred years after Domesday, showing that the area was being cleared of forest to provide arable land and pasture for existing inhabitants and new settlers.

The map below shows the location of priory lands attached to Spon and their variety, rights, privileges and usage. It was situated in a compact area which can be identified from the place-names cited in the charter. The canons received the whole of Spon and Padeswood in order to bring waste and forest land under cultivation. They were given permission to clear, enclose and convert the forests of Bistre and Swerdewod, adjacent to the priory, into arable land. They also had the right to feed 100 pigs in the forests. In addition, the charter gave the monks freedom from all secular dues and other taxes. The new priory did not receive an endowment from tithes or any further gifts from the de Mohaut barons. Relations between the canons and their patron later became strained because of the temperament and behaviour of the founder's grandson and the former eventually returned to their mother house at Haughmond in Shropshire.

The later history of Capel Spon is uncertain. The owner and occupier of the building did not appear in the list of those compensated in 1284 and by 1392–7, it had been annexed to 'the free chapel in the castle of Ewloe', coming under the jurisdiction of the rector of Hawarden. Edward Lhuyd in 1697–9 counted it as one of the three chapelries of Mold (together with Nercwys and Treuddyn) and reported a great decay, 'whereof a small part of ye wall only is now to be seen.' In 1854, it was reported that the foundations of the de Mohaut's priory were being ploughed.

Nercwys Chapel
Nercwys Chapel is medieval in origin, built in the shape of a simple parallelogram, separated into a nave and chancel by a rood screen. The building is distinguished by having, in the tower arch at the west-end, the only surviving examples of Norman ecclesiastical architecture in Flintshire. It now serves as a baptistery, on the window sill of which may be seen the remains of a headstone of a Norman window and a holy water stoup. Incorporated in the stone credence table in the sanctuary is a flat stone, ornamented with a ball-flower decoration. The dating of carved stones to the middle of the thirteenth century supports the claim to a church being in existence at that time.

St Mary's, Nercwys was founded by the de Mohaut barons at the end of the twelfth century as a chapel of ease in the township of the same name and is first mentioned in the taxation of 1291. Its dedication to the Blessed Virgin Mary follows that of the parent church at Mold. For centuries it has served as the place of worship for the inhabitants of this outlying township who farmed the homesteads. Amongst stone fragments unearthed when the church was restored in 1847 are eight carved stones made of the fine-grained sandstone of north Flintshire, the earliest of which dates from *c.*1250–80 and the most recent from the end of the fourteenth century; the latter bears an inscription in Lombardic capitals 'HIC: IACET [Here lies]: ATHVN / YT F: DD [Athunyd daughter of Dafydd]'. Nearby are a holy well, Ffynnon Fair, Rhyd-y-Cleifion (lepers' ford) and Pant-y-Betws (the oratory's hollow) where perhaps a small religious house stood.

Treuddyn Chapel
Similar to Nercwys, Treuddyn was founded as a chapel of ease to Mold but the original building was replaced in 1874. Notable in the context of the church's founders, the de Mohaut barons, it has pieces of fourteenth-century stained glass. One piece, dated *c.*1305, shows a monastic saint and is the earliest such stained-glass work in north Wales. Another, dated *c.*1330, shows the arms of the last baron de Mohaut who died in 1329.

Capel Spwdwr
Capel Spwdwr was the name given to a small chapel said to have been dedicated to St Isidore of Seville (*fl. c.*560–636) which was used 'for the singing of masses for the souls of the dead'. Although now lost, the chapel is thought to have been located near Maes Garmon. Because of its dedication to St Isidore, Capel Spwdwr may have been founded by local Norman knights, perhaps including a de Mohaut baron, on their return from a crusade to the Holy Land.

*

Between 1086 and the loss of Welsh independence in 1284 a period of transformation took place when agricultural land was created from forest, waste and river valley and the fifteen townships of Ystrad Alun, with their homesteads and settlements, emerged from the Dark Ages. The solidity of these small territorial units, the *trefi*, forms the basis of a new society with lordship, manor and parish planted, as it were, alongside the native Welsh and Mercian colonial settlements. Although sometimes they subjugated, the older patterns were never extinguished and adapted, inter-mingled and retained their unique identity.

The Normans imprinted their own organisation and authority on both the urban and rural landscapes. Two important nineteenth-century surveys are essential tools in understanding the period of transformation outlined above, both of which are particularly useful in the interpretation of the rural landscape. The first, the tithe survey and apportionment, provides us with many field names which go back through the centuries, giving invaluable information on land use be it Welsh, Saxon, Norman or later, which suggests the way in which the parish was colonised, the farming practices employed, road construction and land enclosure. The second source is the series of large-scale Ordnance Survey maps (1869–70) which are useful in interpreting the urban landscape and locating burgage plots and town fields. These show how close the urban landscape was to the original rural settlement around the town of Mold. In other words

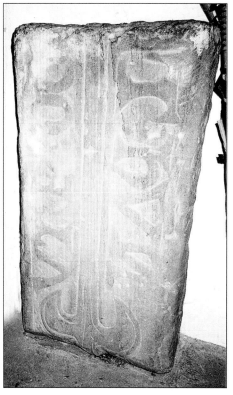

Nercwys Chapel carved stone c.1300 with inscription to Athunyd.

when we compare the township of Mold in the tithe apportionment with the OS map, it becomes obvious from the field names that many of the first townsfolk carried on farming after they had settled in the town. The open fields and meadows surrounded the town and continued to be farmed and grazed for centuries, until built on after 1850. Here are some examples.

Exquisitely carved late medieval furnishings from Nercwys Chapel.

Open fields were subdivided into strips or *erwau*, the singular form of which *erw*, later became generally used to describe a field, whether open or enclosed. The name of the field e.g *cyfer pedwar* and *cyfer saith* indicated the size of the field by the number of days it took to plough it (in these cases four and seven). Other field names are: *Maes* (field); *Maes Glas* (green field); *Maes Garmon* (refers to the 'Alleluia' battlefield 429 AD); *Maes y dre* (the town field); *Maes y ffynnon* (well field); *Maes y Dderwen* (oak field, used for communal grazing); *Maes yr Arglwydd* (lord's field, relating to Gwysaney).

The River Alun provided good meadow land. *Weirglodd* (the Welsh name for the common hayfield meadow) gives us *weirglodd Bromfield* (just north of Broncoed); *weirglodd y felin* (meadow of the mill at Pen y bont); *dôl* (water meadow); *Dôl y bont* (water meadow by the bridge).

At the close of the twelfth century Mold was under siege. Llywelyn ab Iorwerth (Llywelyn the Great, 1173–1240), prince of Gwynedd, triumphed and Ralph de Mohaut, lord of Mold, was killed defending his own castle in 1199. In 1275, Llywelyn ap Gruffydd, prince of Gwynedd, was in dispute with the English king, Edward I, over his demand for fealty. This led to the king summoning Llywelyn to meet him at Gresford. The prince went as far as Treuddyn but, probably afraid of being surrounded by his enemies, refused to cross the boundary into English territory. Whilst at Treuddyn he wrote to Pope Gregory X, listing his grievances against the king of England, saying that Edward was holding lands of some Welsh lords on Llywelyn's border.

> Lands of which we have been in peaceful possession for a long time after … the peace treaty [and the king] calls us to pay him homage, and to profess our loyalty to him at a place which is less safe for us … amongst fugitives and felons who are our deadly enemies. However he refuses absolutely to do this … so that he may obtain justification for departing entirely from the treaty.

On Palm Sunday 1282, Dafydd ap Gruffudd, brother of Llywelyn ap Gruffudd, raided Hawarden Castle sparking off a full-scale war of independence. Before Christmas the following year, both the princes of the House of Gwynedd had been killed and the other Welsh royal dynasties effectively ceased to exist. King Edward I had achieved what William the Conqueror had set out to do, to conquer the Welsh, and he proclaimed the finality of his victory in the settlement of 1284 known as the Statute of Rhuddlan.

> Divine providence has entirely transferred under our proper dominion the land of Wales with its inhabitants, heretofore subject to us in feudal right, and has annexed and united the same into the Crown of the realm [of England].

The lordships of Mold and Hawarden then reverted to the de Mohaut family and Ystrad Alun was no longer a commote of the former kingdom of Powys but, becoming known as Molesdale, was administered as the Anglo-Norman lordship, manor, and parish of Mold.

Llywelyn ap Gruffydd's letter to Pope Gregory X. The last line reads: 'Datum apud Trofthyn idus Septembris Anno Dom. MCCLXX quinto' (Dated at Treuddyn 11th September AD 1275).

Notes

1. R. Bartlett, *England under the Normans and Angevin Kings, 1075–1225,* Oxford, 2000, p.255.
2. Ibid, p.235.
3. *The Anglo-Saxon Chronicle,* translated and edited by G. N. Garmonsway, London, 1953, p.216.
4. By 1179 it was being referred to as Domesday Book because of the thoroughness of the survey and it was compared to 'the book by which the dead were to be judged. (Revelations, xx, 12).
5. Known as villeins, cottars and bordars.
6. Ken Lloyd Gruffydd, 'The Manor and Marcher Lordship of Mold during the Early Middle Ages, 1039–1247, *Ystrad Alun,* 2003, p.11f.
7. Ibid, p.11.
8. No one knows when the castle was built. David Powel gave the year 1093, Sir John Lloyd 1110, and Cathcart King 1146. I prefer *c.*1093, the years of penetration into north-east Wales, when Hugh d'Avranches was exercising his patronage on behalf of the abbey of St Werburgh.
9. The original keep was a timber construction, later replaced by stone.
10. R. J. Sylvester, Mold Castle and its Environs, *Clwyd Powys Archaeological Trust Report No 882* who estimated 2.2ha and 19–20m in diameter at the top.
11. ibid.
12. Bartlett, op cit, p.73.
13. Account in *Annales Cestriensis* and the Chronicle of Matthew Paris.
14. Cheshire in the Pipe Rolls, notes on Account xviii *Record Society of Lancashire and Cheshire,* vol 92, 1938, p.83.
15. Holywell and Bistre.
16. Licence to hold a market, FRO NT/1435.
17. 'Court of Piepoudre,' the court by which the owner of the right to hold a market or fair settled disputes, regulated measures and maintained order. The name comes from French words for 'dusty feet,' which the English in their ignorance translate as 'pie powder.' There was a need for some discipline because market places were frequented by middlemen, or chapmen, who made a living travelling from fair to fair throughout the realm.
18. R. R. Davies, *The Age of Conquest, Wales 1063–1415,* Oxford, 1987, p.179.
19. See Ken Lloyd Gruffydd, 'Early Christianity in Ystrad Alun,' *Ystrad Alun,* 2004.
20. See Ken Lloyd Gruffydd, 'The Holy Wells of Ystrad Alun,' *Ystrad Alun,* 2006.
21. D. Pratt, 'St Asaph Diocese, 1254', *Denbighshire Historical Society Transactions, 42,* 1993, p.113.
22. G. Lloyd, 'Medieval carved stones at Mold', *Flintshire Historical Society Publications, 18,* 1960, p.164–8.
23. See J. R. Cole and D. Pratt, 'Capel Spon, Buckley, Clwyd', *Archaeology in Wales, 33,* 1983, pp.25–30.

3: The lordship and manor of Mold, 1284–1536

The two hundred years between the Act of Settlement 1284 and the victory of Henry VII at Bosworth in 1485 were a time of slow change. From this point onwards in royal documents Ystrad Alun was known as Moldsdale. The conquest of Edward I had brought to an end the great native Welsh kingdoms and their dynasties and the lordships of Hawarden and Moldsdale, created by the earl of Chester around the end of the eleventh century, were now secure and able to flourish unhindered by Welsh political opposition. In Wales and the Marches, both lordship and manor prospered.

The conquered and dispossessed Welsh gradually found a way back into positions of responsibility and ownership of land. What we see happening in Moldsdale was a similar pattern to that in other lordships along the March. At first, in the fourteenth century, it was a process of enforced toleration. At the beginning of the fifteenth century, in the crisis precipitated by the revolt of Owain Glyndŵr (c.1359–c.1415), there was a renewed attempt by the Welsh to assert themselves and re-establish an independent state, although Mold appears to have been hardly affected by the rebellion. The only mention in the records was a comment that beer purchased in Chester c.1400 should not be sold to the 'Glendower' rebels. Following on from this major crisis in Wales, the English state had its own ongoing struggle between the houses of Lancaster and York, the so-called 'Wars of the Roses', which lasted for over sixty years. The Marcher lords, including the Stanley family, lords of Mold, were deeply involved in this struggle. Despite these turbulent events, these years in Wales saw the beginning of the golden century as the country began to recover its confidence and, in a time of economic prosperity, a new Welsh land-owning class emerged who became the officials of a new council set up by the English king to control the royal lordships along the border shires. Although Mold was not a royal lordship, evidence from an account of 1477 clearly shows that Lord Stanley's officials belonged to this new Welsh gentry.

Edward I made known his policy for the political future of Wales on 19 March 1284 in the Statute of Rhuddlan which displayed his determination as 'the Conqueror of the Welsh' for a lasting peace between the two nations. On the whole, apart from minor revolts and one major rebellion led by Owain Glyndŵr at the beginning of the fifteenth century, the Welsh lived peacefully under the government of the English. During this time the town of Mold remained virtually untroubled by any hostilities until the English Civil War in the 1640s. On his victory in 1282, Edward I imagined himself as King Arthur and held a lavish 'round table' event and tournament at Nefyn on the Llŷn peninsula for English and foreign knights and summoned Welsh minstrels to Overton in Maelor Saesneg on the eve of a triumphant progress through Wales.[1]

The pacification of the Welsh was secured by constructing a ring of strategically sited castles around the territories of the Crown. Edward spent an enormous sum of money building magnificent new castles at Flint, Rhuddlan, Conwy and Harlech. At Caernarfon, in the former stronghold of Llywelyn ap Gruffudd, he erected a castle of imperial design, in the style of the emperor Constantine, and on the turret of one of the towers displayed three imperial eagles. Other castles were built by the barons whom the king enriched by the gift of newly-created lordships: Roger Mortimer at Chirk, Reginald Grey at Ruthin, John de Warrene at Holt and Henry Lacey at Denbigh. There is no record of any repairs or reinforcements being carried out to the castle in Mold and, perhaps like the nearby castle at Hopedale, it was allowed to fall into disuse. Although it must be noted that in official documents Mold is called 'the town and castle of Monte Alto.' A new county of Flint

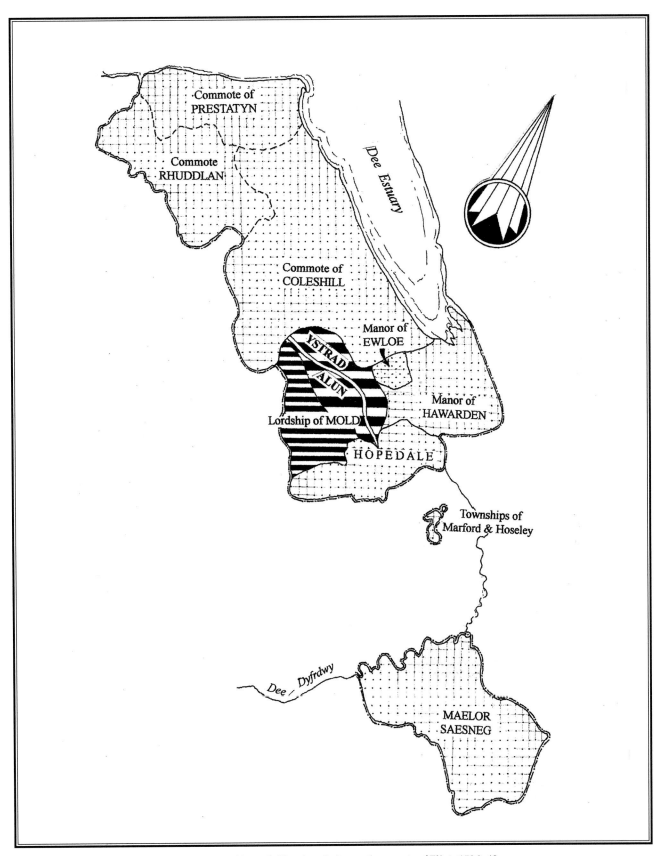

The location of Ystrad Alun in relation to the county of Flint, 1536–42.

was created by the amalgamation of Tegeingl, Hopedale and Maelor Saesneg. Finally, the Norman lordships of Mold and Hawarden were permanently restored to the de Mohaut barons who retained them until their male heirs died out in 1329.

Wales remained an occupied country under the Crown of England and the native Welsh living along the borders were subjected to the rule of the king or his barons. Moldsdale was one of about forty lordships into which almost two-thirds of Wales was fragmented, and was not included in the neighbouring county of Flint. These lordships, both old and new, were virtually petty kingdoms, although for most of the time their lords were absentees and deputed their authority to English or Welsh stewards and constables who later emerged as the gentry in a new society.

Edward I combined the role of lawmaker with that of conqueror. In the settlement of 1284, he set out to acknowledge that he had a respect for Welsh nationality and its laws, customs and language. In most respects these continued to be recognised, particularly the law of gavelkind, the dividing of inheritances into equal parts between the heirs. But in reality, Welshmen suffered severe restrictions and the English were granted a special position and privilege in the courts where there were separate English and Welsh juries for appropriate cases. The Act of Settlement was a deliberate attempt to encourage assimilation between the Welsh and English, a policy which was on the whole successful and for the 250 years which separated the Conquest of 1284 from the Act of Union in 1536, the Welsh and English learned to co-exist peacefully.

Very few documents have survived for the lordship of Mold or its neighbours at Hawarden and Hopedale. We are, however, fortunate to have two short documents from the two lordships dated 1474 and 1477.[2] Within a radius of twenty miles, there were other lordships created by Edward I in 1284: Bromfield and Iâl; Holt; Chirkland; the Honour of Denbigh and others where the records have survived. These were small lordships, made up of planted boroughs with castles, market places and with a mixed population of Welsh natives and English settlers, who faced the same challenges as those of Moldsdale. By examining these and the documents from Mold and Hawarden, we can build up some sort of picture of the way of life in Mold during the late medieval period.

These records are detailed surveys or extents of lordships which were undertaken when they changed hands. The information available was collected by professional servants, usually educated clerics, whose purpose was to inform the new lord of the value of his lordship. This involved a survey of land, rent and customary payments made to the lord as well as such details as the garrisoning and provisioning of the castle (and its use as an office for the treasurer, as a law court and a gaol) and the rents collected from both English and Welsh tenants in the borough and surrounding townships (including the customary payments made by tenants to the lord which were formerly paid to the Welsh prince).

As already noted, the town of Mold and its surrounding district was a lordship granted by the earl of Chester, Hugh d'Avranches, to the de Mohaut family, along with the neighbouring lordship and manor of Hawarden. They remained in control until 1329 and were succeeded by William de Montacute, earl of Salisbury in 1338 whose heirs held them until 1397. In the fifteenth century the Crown held the lordship until the Stanleys (who had briefly held it at the beginning of the century) came into possession of it from 1437 and retained it until 1651.

The same officials appear in lordships throughout the Welsh Marches. The constable was originally the chief military officer of the lordship and was in charge of the castle. It was his responsibility to see that there were sufficient men to defend it and that they were supplied with adequate provisions of food and ammunition. He was in charge of prisoners held in the gaol and the courts where they were tried. In return for these duties he received fees for the prisoners in his custody, fines for impounded cattle, a supply of hay for horses as well as fuel and quarters in the castle. His subordinates were a doorkeeper and deputy porter who looked after the prisoners. The post of constable was closed to the Welsh. The charters of some boroughs in north Wales laid down that the constable must also be mayor of the borough.

The officer at the head of the financial administration was the receiver who was responsible for collection and administration of revenues. He was assisted in their collection by English and Welsh bailiffs (also called *rhingyll*). The bailiff was elected and, together with the mayor, presided over the borough court. He was responsible for collecting monies and rents from the market, bridges, mills and common oven.

Another elected officer was the coroner whose duties were to investigate sudden deaths in suspicious circumstances; the slain, drowned and accidentally killed. In these circumstances he would collect deodand, the instrument which caused the person's death, and hold an inquisition into the cause of death.

There were other officers of the lordship such as foresters and parkers who were there to protect the lord's demesne (personal land) and to control and prevent straying beasts (estrays), the unlawful collection of timber, and assarting (the clearing of timber).[3] There would also be an escheator[4] whose duty was to transfer land without heirs to the Crown.

In the late Middle Ages, the remains of the great forest of Swerdewod still impinged on the northern edges of the lordship of Mold and was recognised as the lord's wood in several townships such as Bistre, Gwysaney and Treuddyn. Roger de Mohaut had formed a deer park in Ewloe in 1241, an enterprise which may have been repeated in the neighbouring lordships in later centuries. Some revenue was received from the sale of wood which was invaluable for the repair and construction of houses, bridges and mills.

The Welsh natives of Moldsdale appear to have got along quite well with the English colonists who had

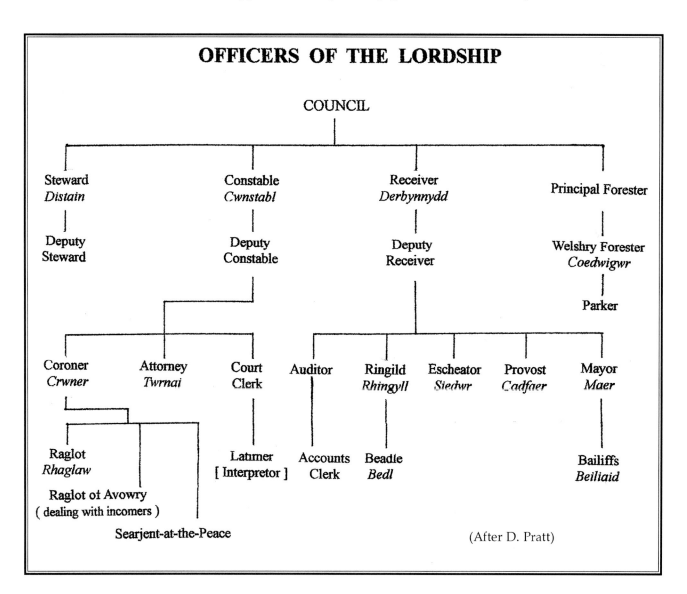

OFFICERS OF THE LORDSHIP

(After D. Pratt)

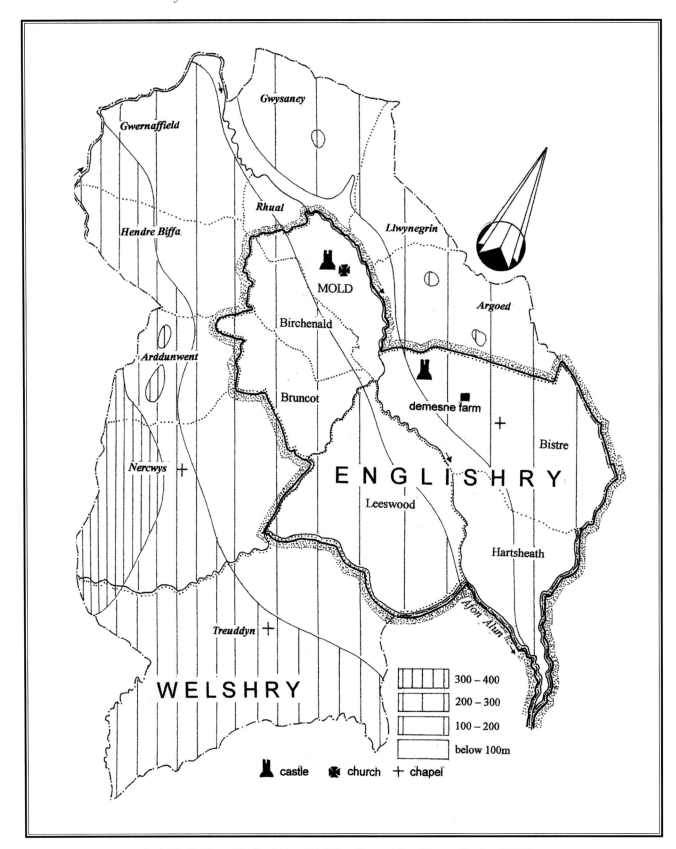

Probable division of the Lordship of Mold into lowland Englishry and upland Welshry.

conquered them and occupied their lands. In a way, this problem of peaceful co-existence had been resolved by the two racial groups occupying separate parts of the lordship. The English, the foreigners, lived in the 'Englishry' in the lowland areas of the Alun valley, where the best land was to be found, and in the town or borough where they built their houses in the vicinity of the castle. The remainder of the lordship, the more hilly land, such as in Treuddyn or Arddunwent, was known as the 'Welshry' where the Welsh descendants of the ancient clans lived in scattered homesteads according to their own customs, speaking their own language. The customary payments they had previously made to their Welsh princes were now transferred to their English lord. In 1334, in a Survey of the Honour of Denbigh[5] for Lord Montacute, the incoming lord, the feudal customs of Denbigh were outlined and these would almost certainly have applied equally to Moldsdale. According to this, the feudal aspect of lordship extended from the King to the lord of the manor and then to his tenants. The lordship would have been granted as a reward for some service to the Crown and both donor and recipient would have wanted to know its worth. The lord would have been anxious to know where his income came from and if he was receiving the full revenue to which he was entitled. Consequently, the lordship would have been regularly surveyed and its value assessed. Many of the payments made by tenants in Marcher lordships originated in the time of native princes and may have taken the form of customary payments in kind – Gruffydd ap Cynan had received honey, bread and ale when he came to Bistre. These payments were later commuted to a fixed sum of money which continued to be received by the lord of the manor into the twentieth century. Originally the economy of the manor and provision of agricultural labourers were dependent upon the services of the tenants. All these various arrangements were known as the common customs of the manor.[6]

The area known by the Welsh as Ystrad Alun was known as the manor of Bistre from the time of its award to Hugh d'Avranches. The earl then granted the manor to his tenant Hugh Fitz Norman who effectively succeeded the Mercian Earl Edwin, who had obtained it after the defeat of the Welsh king of Gwynedd in 1063. Although there was usually more than one manor in each lordship, in Moldsdale there was only one which was made up of fifteen townships.

The manor was different to the lordship, being established not for defence but agriculture. The Normans had introduced the English model of open-field agriculture into Wales. Great open fields were created, called the town fields (*maesydd y dref*). People worked them together, with the fields divided into separate strips, quillets and seilions. The lord's tenants, in return for their holdings, paid him rent in either money or kind and performed a fixed seasonal rota of services: ploughing, harrowing and harvesting. The work in the open fields had to be organized on a seasonal basis by joint decision in the court of the manor.

The lord of the manor retained part of the land, called the demesne, for his own use while the rest was tenanted or used for common waste. The manorial system proved beneficial to the whole of the lordship and its townships because it facilitated the advance of cultivation and pastoralism. Gradually the manor broke up into individual farms of unequal size and eventually the newly-emerging Welsh gentry (*uchelwyr*) began to accumulate land and build up their own estates. This was happening in all the townships of Mold, although many of these individuals were still technically tenants of the lord of the manor.

By the end of the fifteenth century, Thomas Stanley was one of the richest and most powerful of the king's subjects. Part of his wealth came from the possession of over 100 manors, many of them in the north-west of England, hence the soubriquet 'King in Lancashire'. During the troubled years of the Wars of the Roses, he maintained his own private army to defend his estates and support him in the frequent and bloody military engagements. Much of the money which financed his power base, the recruiting ground for his private army, was generated from the profits he made from his manors. Stanley's principal residence was the manor of Latham in Lancashire but from time to time he would reside in north-east Wales, during the summer for hunting or at Christmas time. On these excursions he normally chose to live at Hawarden Castle where he had his demesne. The castle was conveniently nearer to both Lancashire and the city of Chester (in the latter he had a magnificent town house, appropriately known as Stanley Palace). He also had a demesne at Tyddyn in Mold and later in Argoed township. Such visits gave him an opportunity to inspect his estates, meet the officials in charge during his absence, look at their accounts and make recommendations about repairs and future policy to prevent loss and to increase profit.

An invaluable account roll and estate correspondence dating from 1477 shows how the manors of Mold and Hawarden were being managed together to make a profit. The official responsible for drawing up the roll was Robert Lloyd, Thomas Stanley's receiver, whose office was the exchequer at Hawarden Castle. His assistant at Hawarden was Richard Huxley. Money that had been collected from the burgesses of Mold or raised from the agricultural management of both manors, was paid into the exchequer. In addition to being the receiver of Hawarden, Robert Lloyd was also the mayor of Mold and the account roll shows that he had paid 32s for his appointment to the office. The men who oversaw the supervision of the lord's manor, the reeves, were directly responsible to the mayor, and the town bailiffs (*ringilds),* Llywelyn ap David ap Ednyfed and Jankyn ap Hywel, were also under his supervision. The lord's mills were under his charge. Other identified officials in charge of business and administration in the manors were Peter Dutton, who was the steward of both lordships and manors, and Thomas Coverham, the lord's clerk. In Moldsdale, Robert Lloyd worked closely with Nicholas ap Dicus who was a representative of the rising gentry and the grandfather of John Eyton of Leeswood. Nicholas, who had previously held the office of receiver, now held the position of escheator which gave him responsibility for ensuring that the property of any tenant who had been convicted of a felony, or one who had died without adult heirs, reverted to the lord. In the 1470s, Nicholas was buying up tenancies for Lord Stanley. In 1474 he bought three waste tenements and buildings, along with ten acres of land and their appurtenances in the towns and fields of Mold, from Bleddyn ab Einion ap Meilyr. Another identified official was the constable, Thomas Coney, the gaoler at Hawarden Castle who was responsible for the custody of criminals from both manors. The co-operation between the folk of Hawarden and Moldsdale is shown by an incident that occurred in 1474 when there was a hue and cry by eighty persons of the demesne which resulted in the capture of five thieves in Moldsdale. The members of the posse were rewarded with bread and ale. Once captured, the prisoners were watched over by three guards for twelve nights and one, Gwyn ap Gruffudd ap Madog ap Owain, died whilst in prison.

Both manors were run as major agricultural units with most of the workforce farming the land, although there were some distinctions between them. Moldsdale had an urban centre, the Norman borough of Mold, inhabited by burgesses who held their tenancies from the lord of the manor to whom they paid small rents for their burgage plots. In 1477, these burgesses paid 67s 9½d to the lord of the manor on 11 November, the feast day of St Martin. From the Welshry in Moldsdale, 75s was received 'for all the Welsh rents' and the names of the Welsh inhabitants were recorded separately and subjected to separate legal process as the entry from the 1477 account reveals '2s 1d for 2 inquisitions held to settle a dispute between the lord and John ab Ithel as appears in the Welsh Court roll there.'

From time immemorial, the demesne lands were for the sustenance of the lord and his household. The tenants of the manor, formerly both free and bonded, performed services on the demesne and cultivated their own plots for subsistence. Later, many lords found it more profitable to enter into a contract with a cultivator and rent out the demesne for a period of time for a fixed sum of money. This arrangement was called a 'farm' and the 'farmer' was a collector of taxes who paid the lord an agreed sum and made a profit on the collection. In Moldsdale and Hawarden, the 1474 account shows that Lord Stanley had demesne land in both manors and that his residence in Hawarden was recorded as including the manor 'house' and manor farm as well as numerous houses and cottages. The whole enterprise of farming the demesne was dependant on the co-operation of the personnel involved. This team consisted of bailiffs, swineherd and hayward (who had charge of the meadows). There was joint organization of seasonal work: ploughing, sowing, harrowing, manuring and reaping. Sheep rearing in the manor was an important aspect of demesne life, both for the supply of the household at the castle and the general revenue of the manor. Unfortunately, there are few references to Mold in the 1474 account. One records that the pinfold (a pound for stray animals) in Moldsdale was farmed out to Llywelyn ap Grono ap Madog who paid 10s 'for the farm of the lesser pound.'

It was clearly the responsibility of Stanley's receivers, Robert Lloyd, and Nicholas ap Dicus, to ensure that the manor of Mold yielded as much revenue as possible from its major resources. The assessed rents of fifteen townships and all the Welsh rents in the lordship are recorded. A variety of agricultural resources were farmed out and if there was any land that was not being used, a tenant was sought: '£8 11s 10d for the fields of the town. 10s 1d for two buildings and one waste empty tenement and 10 acres of land in the town of Mold and in the fields there let to Blethyn ab Einion ap Meilyr.' Income was received from many sources: '46s 8d for property let Gr[uffudd?] ap Ll[ywelyn?] for 10 years, viz 20s for Gretemadowe, 10s for Middle meadowe, 13s 4d for Kalbmedowe, 5s for one small piece of pasture and 2s 4d for one parcel of land appurtenant to the office of harvest overseer.' 23s 4d for each caracute (originally the amount of land that a team of eight oxen could plough each year, usually about 120 acres) was received for the farming out of ploughing of the tenants within the lordship. 20s was received for the pasture of Padeswood held by Edward Lloyd and Robert his younger brother. Woodland was a diminishing source of income and the great forest of Swerdewood, which once stretched from the outskirts of Chester as far as Conwy, was rapidly being destroyed although some income was being derived from it: '10s for the forest of Buckley let to Robert Ll.[wyd?] 20s for the farm of the forest of Treuddyn held by Ithell Gwyn'; '100s for the farm of the forest of Garth Brewodoyd – not received at the time of this account as no profit was made from it.' A further 8s was received for 'the farm of waifs and strays within the lordship.' Stray animals were kept in the pinfold or in fields set apart for them and their owners paid a fine for their redemption. A swine tax, a fee for feeding pigs in woodland, yielded 5s 10d. The account of the manor in 1686 shows that not much had changed in two hundred years

> Adde more for Estrayes & Tolls in these fower yeares. These [a] ram & in very few sheepe and most of those were challanged (After they had byn long kept in grasse) and sworne out by the owners, and for Tolls we had no sale for Cattle soe the whole proffitts made of these in the last fower yeares charges deducted both for grasse & gathering them together. There Remains to be accounted for the sum of 06:04:00.[7]

The availability of a mill for the grinding of corn was important. The lord of the manor generally tried to ensure that he had a monopoly on the use of the mill which would have been expensive to build and maintain and everyone using the mill had to contribute a certain proportion of his grain to the manor. This tax was known as 'multure.' The mills in the manor of Mold, and their annual fee farm rents, which belonged to Lord Stanley in 1477 were listed in the account:

> 46s 8d for Colyford corn mill let to Thomas Cockerham and Griff[udd?] ap Ll[ywelyn?] ap David ap Grono for 10 years.
> £6 for another mill called Sclatmill let to the above persons for 10 years.
> 13s 4d additional farm for these 2 mills, the lord having spent £6 repairing them at the start of the term, £4 of which was shown in the account of Nicholas ap Dicus, Receiver in 1475 and Robert Lloyd the next year.
> 40s for a fulling mill (for the manufacture of cloth) adjacent to the above mills which had previously been in the lord's hands and produced nothing for want of repairs whilst it was being rebuilt by Richard Huxley, Receiver of Hawarden that year.
> 26s 8d for a new year mill near Mold let to Nicholas ap Dicus and Robert Lloyd the elder for 21 years paying 26s 8d for the first year and 40s each year thereafter. 40s was received from the lord for overseeing the renovation of this mill.

Mention of the above mills and their lessees occur frequently in the sixteenth and seventeenth centuries and will be referred to below

The repair of the court house in Mold has been a frequent item of expenditure throughout the centuries. By 1477 it had been transferred from the castle where it had fallen out of use and in that year the record shows that 3d had been spent on '… repairing 3 windows in Mold court house the previous year.' In the records it was known as *le Courhous in villa de Molde* (the courthouse for the town of Mold) and the courtroom was used separately by the English and Welsh in order that they might settle their disputes according to their own laws and customs. Significant changes were made in 1536 when English law was introduced throughout Wales, and Welsh customary law ceased to be used. The Act of Union introduced the Court of Great Sessions which assembled twice yearly at various centres in each shire, one of which was Mold. But, in spite of this major change, the manorial courts continued to meet here. By the nineteenth century the court was described as 'a barn-like crazy old building appearing better calculated to receive, on an emergency, a set of strolling players, than for the solemnity of a court of justice.'[8] An account of 1686 describes some work carried out on the building:

> Payd for slaters worke and for lime & other Materialls to take itt down and make up again & the slated part of the Hall or Court House att Mould wch was Ruinous and lett in Raine to Rott the Timber of the Roofe. 02:08:11.

> Payd more for 25 Thraves of wheat straw & for ye drawing and preparing itt for Thatch to cover upper part of the Hall for Thatchers work & other labour about itt and for a New lock and boards & nails to Amend ye doore of the Court House as by a particular note appears.

In the manorial courts, the lord of the manor was given certain powers to run his estate and control his tenants. They met regularly and the freemen of the manor, presided over by the steward, made important decisions that everyone understood and accepted in an orderly manner.

Another type of court was the Court Baron, which also dealt with the land of the manor. It normally met every three weeks to confirm and register important decisions. The members of the court were the freeholders of the manor, who acted as judges, and the steward of the manor served as the registrar or recorder. Included in the matters dealt with by this court were the agreements between the lord and his tenants. The tenant was given a piece of parchment which confirmed the agreement and which was a copy of the entry in the court roll – hence the tenant became known as a copyholder. The Court Baron also dealt with the transfer of this land upon inheritance or sale. The main business of this court was to record the deaths of tenants and enabled the estates of the deceased to be either surrendered or regranted by copyhold.

Tenants of a manor had a number of important rights, known as the customs of the manor. They were entitled to share some of the resources of the manor that, in a very practical way, improved their living standards. One example of a customary right was the right of estover whereby a tenant could take wood and other growing things for building, fencing or fuel, and gorse, heather, ferns and bracken to be used as litter for animals. Another valuable manorial custom was turbary, the right to dig turf or peat for fuel.

A second manorial court which was held in the court house in Mold was the Court Leet to which tenants could be summoned to answer for any misdemeanours they were alleged to have committed. The bailiff brought in offenders, and the steward of the manor was judge of the court whose main business was to deal with petty crimes, law and order and the administration of communal agricultural obligations.

The lords of Mold

The labourers toiling in the fields of Ystrad Alun helped to maintain the lords of Mold in, as described in 1284, 'the dignity of their honour'. The wealth and estates of the last of the de Mohaut barons were substantial, having grown and accumulated from the produce and rents of a multitude of manors throughout England and the Marches. To the barons of England, the possession of lordships and manors was an investment to be tended and nursed by their villeins, the agricultural labourers. As far as the baron's overall income was concerned, the revenue from Moldesdale was small. Before 1284, the de Mohaut barons enjoyed their lordships in north-east Wales only intermittently because for most of the thirteenth century, they were constantly plagued by the persistence and irascibility of the princes of Gwynedd. It was unfortunate for them that, when peace eventually came to the region, their line was almost at an end and in 1329 Moldsdale became a royal lordship, a piece of property which the kings of England manipulated for a variety of purposes. The recipient of the monarch's bounty was invariably a member of the nobility who would have been only too aware that royal favour could quickly turn to displeasure and lead to the scaffold.

Two years before he died, Robert de Mohaut IV, having no heirs, came to an agreement with Edward II about the future of the lordship of Moldsdale and his other vast estates. The baron's proposal was to dispose of them to the Crown and thereby raise a pension for his wife, Emma. Edward II agreed to this arrangement and paid Robert IV and his wife Emma 10,000 marks (£6,666 6s 8d) for their estates. It was decided that on Edward's death the de Mohaut estates would revert to his wife Queen Isabella, for her lifetime and then to his second son, John of Eltham, who died in 1336. Two years, later Queen Isabella made an exchange of her life interest in the de Mohaut estates with William de Montacute, first earl of Salisbury. For this transaction, the Queen received 1,000 marks from the revenue of tin mines in Cornwall.

The de Montacutes (or Montagus as they became known) became the first subjects of the Crown outside the Royal circle to receive the gift of the Lordships of Mold and Hawarden after the failure of the de Mohaut male heirs. The first of the Montagu lords of Mold and Hawarden was William, first earl of Salisbury, who held it from 1338 until his death in 1344. Amongst the surviving records of this period is a letter from Salisbury to the king and his council, complaining of the unlawful behaviour of his tenants who were taking advantage of their new owner by trespass and damage, particularly to the great forest.

In this lordship of Mohunteseale [Moldsdale] he [the earl] has a forest called Garthbriddok [Garth Brewodoyd or Swerdewod] adjoining the County of Flynt and the people of the county came there forcibly and continually, by night and day, crop and cut his grass there growing, put to fire and flame the remainder of the underwoods as forage of war, and so threaten his foresters that they dare not come there.[11]

The first earl was succeeded as Lord of Mold by his son, William Montagu (d. 1397), second earl of Salisbury and it is very likely that troops and archers from Flintshire and Mold fought under his command at Poitiers in France in 1356. When he died in 1397 his lands were taken into the custody of King Richard II (1377–99).

In 1397, John Montagu, third earl, succeeded his uncle to his title and estates. This was a time of great unrest and King Richard II was arrested at Flint Castle in 1399 and deposed by his nobles, led by Henry Bolingbroke, duke of Lancaster, who became King Henry IV. Amongst those on the wrong side in this dispute was the Earl of Salisbury, who was beheaded on 7 January 1399 and his estates forfeited to the new king. However, Elizabeth, the widow of the second earl seems to have retained some of the land following an appeal.

The beginning of a new century and succession of a new royal dynasty began a long period of political unrest between rival royal claimants for the Crown of England. The nobility was in the dangerous position of having to make a choice of which side to support in what turned into a long drawn-out conflict which decimated their ranks and lordships were one of the prizes awarded for support and loyalty.

At this time, another family, the Stanleys, became involved with the lordship of Mold. Sir John Stanley[12] was born in Cheshire *c.*1340 and carved out a successful career for himself, laying the foundations of land and power for a family which 100 years later counted the king of England as one of its relatives. Stanley chose the path of royal service and achieved

The Eagle and Child, part of the heraldic arms of the Stanley family, displayed in Mold Parish Church.

King Richard II at Flint Castle, 1399. The king is dressed in what appears to be a monk's habit and the earl of Salibusry is kneeling before him.

eminence as a soldier in Ireland and was appointed steward of the household of Henry IV, having defected from Richard II. Chief amongst the enemies of the new king were the Welshman, Owain Glyndŵr, and the son of the duke of Northumberland, Henry Hotspur, an alliance which Shakespeare dramatically displayed in his history plays. As a reward for his loyalty Sir John was granted the lordships of Mold and Hope.[13] He was also granted the lordship of Man, with the hereditary title of 'King of Man.' After the death of Sir John in 1414 whilst serving as lord lieutenant in Ireland, the lordships of Hawarden and Mold again reverted to the Crown. Henry V then gave them to his brother Thomas, duke of Clarence. He was killed in France in 1421 when the lordships passed to the widowed Queen Katherine as part of her dowry.

Sir Thomas, the first baron Stanley (1406–59), displayed the same political ability and self interest as other members of his family and received considerable reward for the support he gave to King Henry VI, including the lordship of Mold. He was appointed constable of Chester Castle in 1437 and chamberlain of north Wales in 1443. Under his leadership the family became the greatest landowners in the north-west of England with great influence at court and with close connections to the nobility. Sir Thomas's final prizes were being elevated to the peerage in 1456 as Baron Stanley and, the following year, being admitted to the Order of the Garter. The Letters Patent granting the lordship in 1437 recited that:

> Whereas We of our special grace, for the good and acceptable service which our beloved and faithful Knight THOMAS STANLEY, Controller of our Household, has bestowed upon us, and daily does not cease to bestow, and for certain causes US specially moving, have given and granted to the same THOMAS the Castle, lordships, and manors of HAWARDYN and MOHANDES-DALE, with the rents, services, meadows, feedlings, pastures, mines of coal, and advowsons of Churches to have and to hold to the same THOMAS and his heirs male lawfully begotten for ever …

The first Lord Stanley died in February 1459, leaving his son and heir Thomas (*c.*1433–1504) to steer the family successfully through the greatest crisis it was yet to face. By the time of his death he was one of the most powerful of the subjects of the new Tudor monarchy. He was created first earl of Derby, a position he achieved in so spectacular a manner that William Shakespeare made it the climax of his play *Richard III*, re-enacting the last great battle of the Wars of the Roses, Bosworth Field, fought in August 1485. Stanley is the character Shakespeare chose to make the symbolic gesture of placing the crown on the head of the first Tudor monarch, Henry VII, the initiation into a new age. Due to his remarkable ability to survive disaster, Thomas Stanley was described by his contemporaries as the 'wily fox.' In the first part of his political career, he attached himself to the Yorkist faction, married Eleanor sister of Warwick 'the king maker' and became Lord Steward of the household of the Yorkist king Edward IV. His second wife, Margaret Beaufort, was the widow of the Lancastrian earl of Richmond and the mother of Henry Tudor, a claimant to the throne. When Edward IV died in 1483, Thomas supported the claim of his brother Richard III who, as a reward for his loyalty, gave him the manor and lordship of Hope in September 1484. The year before, Margaret Beaufort had been attained for treason and only saved by 'the good and faithful service' of her husband. In 1485, Henry Tudor landed from France at Milford Haven and gathered troops to oppose Richard III. As security for his continued loyalty, King Richard required Stanley to surrender his own son, George, Lord Strange, as a hostage. Thomas and his brother, Sir William Stanley, were summoned by Richard to bring troops to his support as he moved against the usurper. Seemingly obedient to the royal command, they arrived at Bosworth where they carefully remained on the sidelines until, in the midst of battle, moved to support the victorious Henry Tudor. For this support the new King created Thomas the first earl of Derby. The triumph was even greater for Margaret Beaufort and she now insisted on being addressed as 'the King's Mother.' Sir William Stanley, less wise and patient than his brother, was disappointed at not being made earl of Chester and entered into a conspiracy with the supporters of the impostor Perkin Warbeck, who claimed to be Richard IV, and was executed for treason in 1495.

Sometime after the accession of Henry Tudor to the throne, a remarkable and unprecedented phase of church building in north-east Wales took place when the parish churches at Wrexham, Gresford, Holt, Hope and Mold and a new chapel and crypt at St Winefride's Well at Holywell, were begun. A strong tradition has it that Thomas Stanley and Margaret Beaufort were joint patrons and benefactors of this magnificent group of buildings, erected in the perpendicular style, and known as the 'Stanley Churches'.[14] They display similar marks of achievement and craftsmanship to those seen in Henry VII's Chapel in Westminster Abbey where Lady Margaret Beaufort was eventually laid to rest.

The Mold parish church was in decay when the Stanleys obtained the lordship of Mold. Peace, prosperity and the last flowering of medieval art added splendour to a flurry of church building in Wales and the wealth of Thomas Stanley and Margaret Beaufort enabled them to express their devotion and piety as patrons in their own territory. Their connections with the Tudor Court gave them the opportunity to engage the best masons, carvers and other craftsmen to undertake this new architectural work. It is therefore especially intriguing when examining the proposal for the new church at Mold *c.*1490 to consider what influence there may have been from the marriage alliance between Thomas Stanley and Margaret Beaufort on its design and execution.

Sadly, there is nothing in either the Beaufort or Stanley archives which mentions work on parish churches in north-east Wales.[15] Instead, the whole tradition of the family's patronage is founded on statements made by eighteenth-century antiquarians and the presence of their heraldic badges in churches built at the end of

Left: Lady Margaret Beaufort, countess of Richmond and Derby, mother of Henry VII.

Right: Thomas Stanley, first earl of Derby, the fourth husband of Margaret Beaufort.

Stanley insignia, the Legs of Man, in the window of Mold Parish Church.

the fifteenth and beginning of the sixteenth centuries. Thomas Hearne in 1732/3 attributed the building over St Winefride's well at Holywell to Margaret Beaufort and 'that the workmen were the same that built King Henry VII's chappell at Westminster … and they built Wrexham [Church] Tower.'[16] Thomas Pennant reasserted Hearne's statement of Stanley involvement at Holywell, writing that it had risen 'from the piety of that great house.'[17] The architectural evidence for Stanley patronage at Mold has been acknowledged as overwhelming as 'few churches are as crowded with heraldry and badges of a single family as Mold.'[18] Unfortunately, their intention to erect a new church around 1500, on the site of the existing Church of Mary's, remained incomplete at their deaths in the first decade of the sixteenth century. It is a tragedy that where omissions in the building work occurred, they convey such a great sense of architectural loss. What is most obvious is that the absence of a clerestory. To the purist there is obviously a layer missing, as if a lid has been placed upon a box and pressed down. Whereas the clerestory should have soared high above the magnificent arcades it is not there. The progress of building the church in the sixteenth century was rather like that of a ship being built upon the stocks before her launch. It received its main shape and although launched, was not properly fitted out. A simple plan will show how far the aspirations of its patrons at the beginning of the century were fulfilled a hundred years later. The skeleton of the ground plan shows the failure to build a new tower at the west end where the old steeple was to remain until the 1760s, and the cessation of the building at the chancel arch which was not extended eastwards until the 1850s. A vertical cross-section of the nave clearly reveals the absence of an intended clerestory, or the main roof as it was originally envisaged.

But what was completed during the lifetime of Thomas Stanley and Margaret Beaufort was of the finest workmanship in the late perpendicular style. The nave is divided from the aisles by arcades of seven bays each and, above the apex of the arches, there is a hollow string enriched with small animals similar to that upon the exterior. The chapels at the east end of the aisles have fine canopied niches on their eastern walls.

The interior of Mold Parish Church.

Sculpture of the Virgin and Child in a niche where once stood the' Living Image' and a medieval stone carving of the same subject in Mold Parish Church.

In the north chapel is a beautiful niche decorated with a vine trail, with David above playing the harp with six small angels playing musical instruments and bearing scrolls. The canopy head is crowned, not with the pelican, but with the Lathom crest, the eagle and child, under which was placed *Y Ddelw Fyw* (the living image) of the wonder-working Blessed Virgin Mary. Everywhere the stonework is magnificent and nowhere else in north-east Wales is there a finer display of religious and heraldic medieval carving. Mold Church is the Stanley church *par excellence* in its display of heraldry and badges; a mixture of aristocratic pride and dignity which does not draw back from employing angels as attendants bearing their family arms and endorsing their achievements.

The heraldry and badges of the Stanleys are seen in profusion, repeated throughout the church upon the walls, in the roof, and in the glass: the Legs of Man, the eagle's claw, the wolf's head, the stag's head. In addition, are the arms of Henry VII and most of the families to whom the Stanleys were allied. High above the easternmost arches of the nave, north and south, are twelve carved panels with emblems of the Passion.[19]

If we are looking for evidence of who met the cost of the new building at Mold we cannot find an absolute answer. In the absence of such information, however, we may speculate with a fair degree of certainty, that it was paid for not only by the Stanley family, but also by local gentry. There is for example a bequest by 'John Davyes' of Gwysaney in 1558, of 'a couple of Oxen that I bought last year to the building of Mold church where I dwell.'

When the old Norman church was taken down *c*.1490 there were probably no reservations in paying for a new one. It is most likely that for a number of years local monies were set aside in a building fund by the church guild and pious church-goers. Most of all patron, parish priest and townsfolk would have been convinced that the cost of building could be raised, while the work proceeded, from offerings of pilgrims. The assurance for this was that Mold Church possessed an object of special

Edward Stanley, third earl of Derby.

Arms of Bishop Robert Wharton on his memorial in Mold Parish Church.

devotion to those who followed the pilgrimage routes across England and Wales from one sacred shrine to another. Here they had a star attraction in *Y Ddelw Fyw*, praised by the Welsh and held in awe by the English. This was probably a mechanical representation of the rood, crucifix or possibly the Blessed Virgin Mary, to whom the parish church was dedicated. It gained a reputation amongst fifteenth-century bards as an object of adoration and power, not only for its lifelike appearance but also for its response to the intercession of those in need.

A major factor in financing and commissioning the church building was the attitude and responsibility of Bisham Priory. The monks had been in possession of income from the rectorial tithes since 1338, when William Montacute, earl of Salisbury was lord of Mold and Hawarden, and as such were responsible for the repair and upkeep of the chancel, choir and sanctuary of the church. By the time this part of the church was due to be built, both Thomas Stanley (second earl of Derby) and Margaret Beaufort had died and Edward, successor as earl of Derby, was a minor and ward of Cardinal Wolsey. It is believed that the prior of Bisham refused to complete the work and, at the dissolution of the abbey, the rectorial tithes came into lay hands. The final involvement of the Stanley family in the building work at Mold Church is marked by the dedication of the great east window to the memory of Edward, earl of Derby in 1572. This was probably the limit of Stanley patronage at Mold. As far as they were concerned, the work at the east end was literally at a closure with the erection of a window barring further progress eastwards. The Protestant climate of the 1570s did not countenance a rood screen, and there was no liturgical use for a medieval high altar when an Elizabethan communion table would suffice.

Some historians have speculated that some assistance in carrying on the work of building may have been given by two sixteenth-century bishops of St Asaph. The first was Robert Wharton (or Parfew), bishop of Asaph (1536–54), a former abbot of Bermondsey who on the dissolution exchanged his cell for a bishop's palace and a pension of £336 6s. Wharton's coat of arms can be seen in the South Chapel.[20] The other bishop was William Hughes (1573–1600) whose claim stems from the inscription '*Fundamentum Ecclesiae Christus, 1597, W. As. Eps.*'[21]

Medieval decorative stonework in Mold Parish Church.

Notes

1. R.R. Davies, *The Age of Conquest Wales 1063–1415,* Oxford, 1987, p.335.
2. W.B. Jones 'Hawarden Deeds', *Flintshire Historical Society Publications,* vol 7, pp.32–45, and FRO D/DM/426 An Account Roll of Thomas Stanley, 1477, and a report on the manuscript by R.K. Matthais, Clwyd Record Office Annual Report, 1974. I am grateful to Miss Elizabeth Pettit for her transcription of the document.
3. Nibbling away at the edges of the forest by stealth. Converting woodland to cultivation.
4. To collect forfeit lands.
5. *Survey of the Honour of Denbigh 1334,* ed P. Vinogradoff and F. Morgan, 1914.
6. One of the customary duties of freemen and bondmen was to provide for the maintenance, for one day and night, of a stallion and groom belonging to the lord. The same tenants were liable to payments of a penny towards the construction and repair of the hall and buildings of the lord. If the lord came to the commote on a visit, all the Welsh tenants were bound to give his officers first refusal of all foodstuffs, excepting cheese and butter which were marketable during the previous fortnight. All bondsmen who made or repaired fences paid one penny to the lord on a certain day (e.g. 1 May). Other customary payments involved changes in the personal circumstances of the tenant.

The son of a free tenant paid relief of 10s *heriot* to the lord when he succeeded his father. This was still collected in the Manor of Mold in the 18th century from the incoming freeholder. The daughters of freemen paid to the lord on marriage or conviction for fornication 10s – merchet, *letherwyte*. If the wife of a freeman was guilty of adultery, her husband paid 10s to the lord. The daughters of bondmen, *amober*. All the goods and chattels of Welshmen dying intestate were declared to be the property of the lord with the exception of his wife's. These customary duties are listed and discussed in edited publications of extents and surveys made in the fourteenth and fifteenth centuries in lordships in east Wales: Bromfield and Iâl, Chirk, Denbigh, Holt, Ruthin etc. Those made for Hawarden and Mold are lost but it may be assumed that they would be similar and therefore a pointer to what was happening in these Lordships.

7. NLW Wigfair, 2146, 1686.
8. Edward Pugh, *Cambria Depicta,* 1816.
9. Wigfair *op. cit.*
10. *op. cit.*
11. *Calendar of Ancient Petitions relating to Wales,* UW Press Hist. and William Rees, no. 28, 1975. p.208 [125] no. 6208 – 1338–44 AD.
12. Information in *New Oxford Dictionary of National Biography,* 2004, on members of the Stanley family.
13. Sir John Stanley (d. 1414) was granted Lordships of Mold and Hope by King Henry IV in 1399.
14. As this book is arranged as a chronological narrative Mold Parish Church is discussed in the appropriate chapters.
15. See for example M.K. Jones and M.G. Underwood, *The King's Mother,* Cambridge, 1992, p.296.
16. W. Salter, ed., *Remarks and Collections of Thomas Hearne,* Oxford, 1921, vol 79, p.149.
17. T. Pennant, *Tours in Wales, vol 1,* London, 1778, pp.28–31.
18. F.H. Crossley, Rhyl Report, *Archaeologia Cambrensis,* 1947, pp.339–45.
19. These include: the Cock, St Andrew's Cross, the Five Wounds, the Ladder, Cross and Four Nails, the Veronica or Holy Cloth, the Chalice, the Bleeding Heart, the Crown of Thorns, Pincers, etc.
20. D.R. Thomas, *The History of The Diocese of St Asaph,* Oswestry, 1908–1913, 3 vols, vol 2, p.409.
21. ibid from the inscription *Fundamentum Ecclesiae Christus,* 1597.

4: Sixteenth and seventeenth century Moldsdale:
union, strife and change

The sixteenth and seventeenth centuries cover the transition from medieval to modern society, the period of the Tudor and Stuart monarchies. Moldsdale, as a geographical part of Wales, became part of county of Flint following the passing of the Laws in Wales Acts (generally known as the Acts of Union) of 1536 and 1543. For the first time, Wales and Welshmen were given an equal share in government. The Acts abolished the independent lordships and Welsh counties and boroughs were henceforth represented in Parliament. The principality was given its own Council in the Marches, a new judiciary system, the Great Sessions, and was joined with the Chester Circuit for purposes of Assizes and Quarter Sessions. Parliamentary legislation was enforced by the appointment of justices of the peace, meeting in Quarter Sessions, and at the lowest level, by the parish vestry.

The Reformation caused major religious divisions in nation states throughout Europe. In England and Wales it began in the 1530s, the same decade as the Acts of Union, and continued throughout the period under consideration. A new Church in England was created which broke with Roman papal authority. The monarch became head of the Church and both the Bible and Prayer Book were eventually translated into Welsh. Strife and persecution occurred during the reigns of the son and two daughters of Henry VIII who each made significant alterations to the existing Religious Settlement. Edward VI (1547–53) was more Protestant than his father Henry VIII; Mary I (1553–58) was devoted to Catholicism and Elizabeth I (1558–1603) was more tolerant, but attempted to enforce uniformity of worship, and during a long reign had to confront a Jesuit Catholic mission and an attempted invasion by Spain. The Stanley family, lords of the manors of Mold and Hawarden, although conforming to the state religion, were sympathetic to their Catholic tenants. The strife caused by these religious divisions eventually erupted into civil war in the 1640s and a major constitutional upheaval in the 1680s.

There are very few documents from which to assess the effect of these changes on the earls of Derby from the time of the death of Earl Thomas in 1504, to the execution of James, the seventh earl, in 1651. Until this latter date the Stanleys were the focus of power in north-east Wales by right of the lordship and the actions of their agents in Moldsdale and elsewhere. Fortunately there are a handful of extant documents which enable us to see major changes which occurred in the town of Mold and the surrounding countryside of Moldsdale. During this period the countryside first experienced the enclosure of land through population pressure and the growth of new estates and mineral resources were exploited by adventurers and local landowners seeking to add to their income in an inflationary economy. The English Civil War not only divided the allegiance of the nobility and gentry, but also affected the whole of the population, including that of Hawarden and Moldsdale.

The lords of Mold
The five earls detailed below had demesne property in the lordship of Mold and wherever possible administered both Mold and Hawarden through the same officials, the local gentry being usually engaged to look after their interests.

Thomas, the second earl of Derby (1504–21), was a grandson of the first earl, and son of George, Lord Strange, who had been a hostage of Richard III. He spent most of his time at court in attendance on the young Henry VIII, but incurred the king's displeasure for his 'excessive self-assertion in Lancashire.' This potentially dangerous situation was removed by his sudden death.

Edward, the third Earl of Derby (1521–72), succeeded his father at the age of twelve years and became a ward of Cardinal Wolsey who despoiled some of the young earl's manors and took £5,000 out of his rents. He married Dorothy, daughter of Thomas Howard, duke of Norfolk, and was thus the uncle to two of Henry VIII's Queens, Anne Boleyn and Catherine Howard. With the inherited ability of the Stanleys to steer their way through dangerous waters, he survived the religious changes of the English Reformation by supporting the religious policy of Elizabeth I and exercising a policy of tolerance to Catholics in Lancashire. He lived in great splendour and was noted for his hospitality, and is said to have fed sixty poor people every day and 2,700 on Good Friday. Six hundred mourners attended his funeral at Ormskirk in Lancashire, which was conducted with almost Royal pomp. A memorial window was placed in the chancel of Mold Parish Church in 1572.

Henry, fourth earl of Derby (1572–93), the son of the third earl, was one of the young lords educated with Edward VI, the only legitimate son of Henry VIII. He did not share his father's Catholicism and was later an active member of Elizabeth I's Council of the North. He lived in some grandeur with a household staff of nearly 150 and was a spendthrift, a weakness shared by his wife, Margaret, and they separated *c*.1570. Henry then entered into a common-law marriage with Jane Haswall of Knowsley. The earl maintained a second family of four more children at Hawarden Castle and incurred more debt than he could manage. He was a noted patron of drama and had his own company of actors called 'Derby's Men' that performed before the Queen on 14 February 1580. His house in Chester, Stanley Palace, is near the High Cross where he patronised the mystery plays performed at Whitsuntide and Midsummer festivals. Other works took place in his honour at Chester, Lathom, and Knowsley. His daughter (by Jane Haswall), Ursula Stanley, married Sir John Salusbury of Lleweni in *c*.1587.[1]

Ferdinando, fifth earl of Derby (1593–94), son of the fourth earl, spent part of his boyhood as a page to Elizabeth I. He was highly regarded and was the most distinguished patron of poetry and drama of his day. His troupe, Lord Strange's Company of Players, was the foremost in the country and performed many of Shakespeare's plays. Ferdinando was earl for less than a year and was allegedly poisoned. On his deathbed he left the vast Derby estates to his widow, Countess Alice, and their three daughters. This action led to a disputed inheritance which was not finally resolved until 1610. Part of Alice's dowry was an annual revenue of £263 from the lordships of Hawarden, Hope and Moldsdale.

William, sixth earl of Derby (1594–1642), brother of the fifth earl, was aged thirty-three when he succeeded his brother. The next thirty years were spent rebuilding the Stanley fortunes and by 1626, having achieved this objective, he handed over his affairs to his heir, James Stanley, and retired to Chester and Bidston Hall, preferring to live as a recluse in his later years. The earl had travelled

Henry Stanley, fourth earl of Derby.

The Stanley arms in Mold Parish Church.

extensively abroad as a young man and having returned to England by the 1590s, supported his own company of players, Derby's Men, and wrote comedies for public performance. He was a friend of the earl of Southampton and some have made the claim that he was the author of Shakespeare's plays.

Mold and Moldsdale

The first information relating to the town of any length, apart from mention of its name, is given in 1477, in the account of Thomas, Lord Stanley. In the midst of the momentous changes of the 1530s, Henry VIII commissioned his chaplain, John Leland, to travel through the realm to search and survey all libraries of monasteries and colleges and report on what he found. In addition, Leland decided to record 'a whole of thynges very memorable.' He did this when he came to Moldsdale.

Leland informed the king that Mold was called in Welsh 'Wriothegrig' (not a bad effort for an English parson), but commonly 'Molesdales.' The town had a mayor, two fairs, but the weekly market was 'decayed.' At the north end of Bailey Street there appeared ditches and hills 'yn token of an ancient Castle or Building there.' Perhaps he saw some remnants of the motte and bailey castle with its stone keep and a 'fair spring' near it. He reported that a great number of houses were almost destroyed and that there were 'in all scarce forty houses.' There were two streets, Bailey Street and Street *Dadleudy* (Court House Street), and other little lanes. He noted that there was some trade: 'wood from Robert Edwardses carried to Chester, coal pits three quarters a mile from Molesdale town.' He was impressed by its 'very good corne' and agricultural land and observed 'that most of the parish is meately level ground and well served of water and of divers other good things. … With a number of rivers – Alyn, Avon Terrig, and other small rivulets, springs, rills/streams, and brooks.' Leland does not mention the lord of the manor, Edward, earl of Derby, but does record the names of some of the gentry, the new governors of Moldsdale – 'Robert Edwards, gentleman dwelleth on the side of the Alun, Ellis Griffith at Llynegrin, John Wenne (Wynn) dwelleth at Broncoit, alias Regnaultes Tower a square building,'[2] most of whom appear to be of Welsh lineage. If Leland is correct in estimating that there were 'scarce forty houses,' then the town appears to have grown significantly by 1699 when, in answer to a query from Edward Lhuyd,[3] it was estimated that Mold town 'contains about 6 score [120] houses betwixt houses and huts.'

There are only a few references in the sixteenth century records that relate to life in the lordship. An unusual entry survives in the state papers which reflects the efficiency and vigilance of Henry VIII's watchdogs and the rough and ready methods employed by the manorial officials of Mold. In March 1538, an incident took place in Mold which was reported by Bishop Roland Lee, president of the Council in Wales, to Thomas Cromwell, Henry VIII's secretary. It was the record of the suspicious utterance of Edward ap Dafydd ap Rice of Moldesdale, beadle or *rhingyll* of Mold, who had been 'examined about words which were spoken in the afternoon of 16 March' in the company of five others named. Apparently the beadle was under the influence of ale and had a great wound in his head. These worthy town officials had sent for Griffith Ellice, clerk (vicar?) of Moldsdale to join them in their carousing. The vicar later informed the bishop's officers that he heard the beadle declare in Welsh 'I am heir of all the lands in Wales and I ought to rule it and I will rule it.' The drinking bout had been accompanied by an attempt to remove towns-folk from their houses in order that they might be repossessed. In response to his accusers, the beadle declared that 'he had acted under orders from the earl

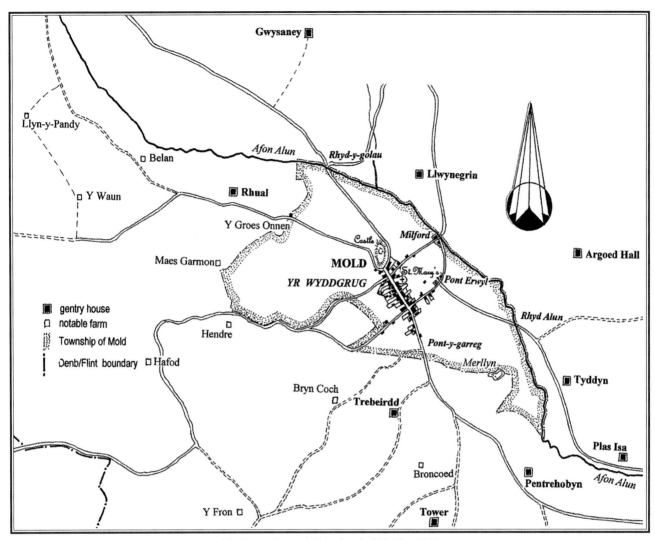

The immediate neighbourhood of Mold, c.1650.

of Derby, lord of Moldsdale.'[4] Although petty in content, it is obvious that Cromwell was looking for information to implicate the earl of Derby and the duke of Norfolk in treasonable activity.

Changes in the law of inheritance laid out in the Act of Union of 1536 made it easier for individuals to create landed estates on the same basis as those that had been developed in England for centuries. The ancient law of gavelkind, whereby a unit of land was equally divided among the sons upon the death of their father, was abolished and replaced by primogeniture, inheritance of everything by the first born. As a result of this small estates were no longer broken up with the passing of each generation as had been the case previously, and a new, land-owning class emerged throughout Wales which was of the same social standing as the gentry in England. These prosperous individuals married well and acquired more property and were quickly in a position to assume the responsibility and leadership of the country. This was certainly true in Moldsdale where many of the families that had acted as officials and agents for the lords of Mold from the fourteenth century onwards, look substantial steps up both the economic and social ladders. With the loss of the lordship of Mold by the Derby family after the English Civil War, an opportunity arose for a take-over of the extensive manorial estate of 18,000 acres that was spread over fifteen townships.

Gentry families dominated Moldsdale between *c.*1650 and 1914. There were between a dozen and twenty of these families at the height of their influence, each proudly claiming similar origins through pedigrees traceable to members of leading kindred groups belonging to the five royal tribes of Wales and the fifteen noble tribes of Gwynedd. Their roots went back to at least the twelfth century, and often predated the arrival of the Normans. Many of their ancestors had held office under the native princes before 1282, and afterwards under the English Crown. These were the families of *uchelwyr* who had lived in the same tribal territories in north Wales for centuries and intermarried to form alliances with other families who settled in Wales from the fourteenth century onwards.

As a social class, the gentry were distinguished by pedigree. The making of pedigrees and keeping them up to date was the responsibility of the bards who wrote 'praise poems' in their honour. Tower, Broncoed is a fifteenth-century survivor of a gentry house. Gwysaney was built at the end of the sixteenth century, and others in the early seventeenth century, Rhual (1634) and Nerquis Hall (1637–8). In the eighteenth century, Sir George Wynne of Leeswood employed Francis Smith of Warwick to build an extravagant palace-like mansion, with a garden designed by Switzer and notable gates by the Davies brothers of Croes Newydd, Wrexham, whilst other country houses were improved and town houses erected.

From the sixteenth century onwards the story of Moldsdale becomes more personalised through the availability of family records which outlined the activities of the gentry, each country house and its family contributing to the story.

Tower

Tower, in the township of Broncoed, is a fortified house built by Rheinallt Gruffydd ap Bleddyn in the mid-fifteenth century. Broncoed (woody hill crest) is mentioned in the Domesday survey, when it was the home of Warmund the Hunter who also farmed the land and pastured sheep. Nothing is known about Tower until 1445 when Rheinallt built a fortified house here. Architecturally there are two parts to the building, the tower and the substantial house to the east. The tower is about forty feet in height and was built for defence. It originally had a narrow embattled wall-walk, from which attackers could be repulsed, and there is a vaulted chamber on the ground floor over a vaulted basement; on the first floor there is a fifteenth-century room, a simple chamber approximately forty feet by thirteen feet which was later divided into two. Part of the building contained a medieval minstrel gallery. The present house of the seventeenth and eighteenth centuries replaced this fifteenth-century hall.

The fame of Tower was established in the fifteenth century by the patriotism of its builder, Rheinallt ap Gruffydd whose bravery and prowess won the admiration of Welsh poets. Hywel Cilan praised 'the fair tower' as a 'fortress twenty fathoms high' and the hospitality of Rheinallt who provided 'his three tables … not without wine.' Rheinallt was a mighty fighter, a Lancastrian leader in Wales during the Wars of the Roses who achieved fame as one of the men of Harlech. His most famous deed is reported by Thomas Pennant.

Tower, Nercwys.

In the lower store of Tower ... still remains a staple in the ceiling; a memorial of the rudeness of the times. During the wars between the houses of York and Lancaster ... Rheinallt and his people were in continual feud with the citizens of Chester. In 1465, a considerable number of the latter came to Mold fair; a fray ensued between the two parties; a dreadful slaughter was made on both sides: but Rheinallt got the victory, took prisoner Robert Byrne linen-draper, and mayor of Chester in 1461, whom he led to his tower, and hung on the staple in the great hall. An attempt was made afterwards to seize Rheinallt; and two hundred tall men sallied from Chester for that purpose. He retired from his house to a neighbouring wood, permitted part of his enemies to enter the building; then rushing from cover fastened the door; and setting fire to the place, burnt them without mercy; he then attacked the rest, pursued them to the sea-side, where those who escaped perished in the channel. Rheinallt received his pardon from Thomas Lord Stanley, Lord of the Council of Wales, and was confirmed under the great seal by Edward IV.[5]

Heraldic arms of David Wynne of Tower, displayed in Mold Parish Church.

In *c.*1539 Leland reported that 'Mr Winne ap Roberts dwellid at stone tower caull'd Broncoit alias Reynaultes Tower'. The next notice we have of Tower concerns the exploits of Piers Wynne, who fought with Sir William Stanley in the Low Countries in 1586. The name Wynne had, by this time, become regularised as the family's surname and memorials to them appear in the parish church in Mold.

Gwysaney[6]

The Davies-Cooke family claim a pedigree that takes them back to Rhodri Mawr, king of all Wales, in the middle of the ninth century, and thence through the royal house of Powys. Their family arms are those of Cynric Efell, lord of Eglwys Eglwyseg, who was living about 1200, and was a cadet of the royal line; on the death of his father, he succeeded to, amongst other land, a part of Ystrad Alun known as Uwch [upper or higher] Gwysaney and from him there is an unbroken descent in the male line down to 1785, when the inheritance devolved upon female heirs.

A great-grandson of Cynwrig Efell, Meilyr ap Grono of Sychdyn, served Prince Dafydd ap Gruffudd in 1277. In the fourteenth century, his descendant, Cynwrig ab Einion, held land in the townships of Gwysaney and Arddunwent and the first extant will is that of Llywelyn ap Dafydd which was proved in 1467.

It is not until the end of the fifteenth century, in the time of John ap David, that the family began to outstrip its neighbours. He was the first of the Davies family to benefit after the Act of Union, becoming High Sheriff of Flintshire in 1550 and serving the Crown under Edward VI as General Woodward and Keeper of the King's Woods in North Wales at a reward of 100s per annum for life.

The patronymic Davies was first assumed by John ap David, who married Jane, widow of Richard Mostyn and daughter of Thomas Salisbury of Leadbrook, Flintshire. His will dated, 16 May 1558, 'bequeathed his soul to Almightie God and to our blessed lady Saint Mary'... and directed that his body shall be buried in the minister of Chester ...' Further I leave and bequeath a couple of oxen that I bought last year to the building of Mold Church where I dwell; also I bequeath a bullock unto the mending of the highway betwixt my house and Mold.' He was succeeded by his son.

Robert Davies I (suc. 1558–1603) married (1) Catherine daughter of George Ravenscroft of Bretton, who bore him three sons. Thomas Davies (d. 1655), his second son, became a lieutenant-colonel and was a great

Gwysaney by Moses Griffith.

support to the next generation of the family in difficult times. (2) Elizabeth Haynes. The young Robert Davies received support from his uncle Robert Davies, Sergeant of Arms of the Yeomen of the Guard as evidenced by his protection of the family interest in Mold Parish Church. Seats and kneeling places in parish churches were regarded as family possessions, the place where descendants would be interred and a mark of the family's place in the local social hierarchy. The acquisition and right of use of these sacred spaces were often confirmed through litigation and in some cases by violent clashes between family retainers. A clash over such rights in 1583, between Robert Davies and John Wynne of Tower, was settled by articles of agreements 'for the final settlement of a controversy respecting the right and title to seats and burial places in the church of Mold' made at Hawarden through the mediation of his uncle and other 'esquires.' The Davies family consolidated their 'territory' by later acquiring the use of 'one bench or pew in the middle of the south side of the church adjoining or lying upon the fourth stone pillar of the same.' The memorial to Robert Davies I, dated February 1602/3, is on a monumental brass in the area of the church he claimed for the family. He was succeeded by his son, Robert Davies II, who graduated at Christ Church, Oxford and served the office of High Sheriff for Flintshire, of which county he was also a justice of the peace and deputy lieutenant.

Robert Davies I and II, whose period as squires of Gwysaney spanned the reigns of Elizabeth I and James I, spent their lives busily involved in building up their estates and occupying various Crown offices in north Wales. Like their kinsmen, the Mostyns, they had an interest in the coal pits in Bagillt and were familiar with

Memorial inscription to Robert Davies, on a monumental brass dated 1602, south aisle Mold Church Translated, it reads: For the death of Robert Davies the elder, Esquire, who died February 1st A.D. 1602, aged 47. His funeral song shall run: Esquire Robert, this tomb contains thy bones, which shall the last day give back whole, even though they perish, Thy lively frame, which time nor carping envy will have the strength to destroy, flies round the world. Religion and the piety of souls are transformed in heaven. Therefore farewell: may thy bright offspring remain in this place.

those at Ewloe. The presence of members of the family in military and royal service in London alerted them to any advantage which might come from this quarter. Moreover, their careful husbandry in Flintshire enabled them to scrape together the necessary cash if a bargain appeared. In 1599, Robert Davies I, and his kinsman Thomas Ravenscroft, purchased lands from the earl of Derby. Ravenscroft's acquisition was in the three Stanley lordships of Mold, Hope and Hawarden and Davies's in the lordship of Mold. In 1606, Robert Davies II and John Eyton of Leeswood acted in an enquiry on behalf of the Crown into the rents of the manor of Ewloe. Its value lay in two water mills, coal mines and pasture in Buckley 'of no certain profit to his majesty.' There was ample evidence of the encroachment of freeholders and restlessness of tenants who were illegally digging coal and taking away timber. In these circumstances the existing leaseholder was prepared to relinquish the manor which King Charles I was prepared to sell. Colonel Thomas Davies bought it in his own name for £300. The manor, approximately 2,000 acres in extent, came to the Gwysaney family on 4 November 1633[7] shortly after the death of Robert Davies II, aged 52 years. His heir, Robert Davies III (suc. 1633–66), was aged 17 years, and two years earlier had married Ann the daughter and sole heiress of the judge Sir Peter Mutton of Llannerch.

A new house was built at Gwysaney around the end of the sixteenth century. Hubbard[8] refers to a date of 1603 in a first-floor room. A valuation made for the Crown in 1634 puts the total acreage of the estate at 1,751 acres, of which 650 were arable, 160 meadowland, 750 pasture, 115 wood and 76 moorland. In addition, the Gwysaney estate had recently acquired the 2,000-acre manor of Ewloe. The Llanerch estate was surveyed on Sir Peter Mutton's death in 1637 when it comprised 2,190 acres in Denbighshire and the vale of Clwyd, of which 160 acres was woodland, 220 acres mountain pasture, 400 acres rough heath and bruery and only 140 acres arable. In addition, the estate included six mills and the tithes of a number of Flintshire parishes.[9] These valuation surveys were made in the decade before the Civil War. When the conflict came, the Davies family, along with other gentry families throughout the troubled kingdom, were forced to take up arms against each other in the struggle between the Crown and Parliament.

Rhual

No work of fiction could have invented a family history as various, unexpected, full of twists and tragedies, and at times as non-conformist, as its members as that of Rhual. Although generally limited at the beginning, the family papers grow in volume from the seventeenth century and enable us to throw further light on the rise of the gentry in Moldsdale on the eve of and during the Civil War.[10] This growth of extant documentation continues into the eighteenth century with an abundance of family records of the most delightful nature. Diaries and letters illuminate country and town life in terms of the adventures, comforts and camaraderie of an élite group of gentlemen.

An examination of the Edwards family of Rhual as an example of the rise of the gentry in Moldsdale provides us with a slightly different perspective to that of their neighbours, the Davies family of Gwysaney. They shared a pedigree with their near neighbours, the Lloyds of Pentrehobyn. The deputy herald at arms, Lewys Dwnn (*c.*1550–1616), traced their descent back

Rhual – an early twentieth-century view
[David Rowe collection, donor
the late Basil Heaton].

through Edwin ap Goronwy, prince of Tegeingl (d. 1073), to Hywel Dda. Other kinsmen resided at Leeswood and the antiquary noted that in *c*.1539, 'Robert Edwards, a gentleman, dwelleth at Rhual on the north side of the Alen yn Moldsdale having plenty of wood and goodly meadow by Alenside.'

Evan Edwards (*c*.1594–1670) owed his advancement to his own talents as an attorney and the connections he made in twenty years of service (*c*.1612–32) to Richard Sackville, third earl of Dorset. On 20 May 1620, Edwards married Joan, eldest daughter of Simon Thelwall of Woodford in Essex. In 1625, his heir, Thomas, was born and Evan was appointed clerk or baron of the exchequer of the county palatine of Chester for life. A deputy undertook this work and Edwards postponed his residence in the north. The death of the earl of Dorset in 1624 had opened up further opportunities as Edwards was appointed secretary to the fourth earl who was appointed to the Privy Council in 1626. Thus Evan Edwards, albeit as an observer, found himself close to the centre of government and was pushed into the House of Commons in February 1628 as member of parliament for Camelford in Cornwall. In the Commons, he witnessed efforts to impeach the duke of Buckingham, the King's favourite, and experienced the angry mood of members who openly defied Charles I in defence of their liberties. By 1632, he had left the earl's service and returned to reside at Rhual. Two years later he began to transform the small house he had inherited into a manor house with a brick addition of three coped and finialed gables, in the execution of which he made use of ideas and money he had garnered over the last score of years. Rhual became one of a number of gentry houses in Moldsdale noted for their architectural quality and the arrangement of the gardens.

In 1639, Edwards was made Comptroller of Customs for the ports of the City of Chester and of Beaumaris and Liverpool. In 1642, on the eve of the Civil War, he leased for three lives the coal and lead mines in the lordships of Hawarden, Hope and Mold, following the example of his neighbours at Gwysaney.

When Civil War broke out, Evan Edward, with his experience under the Sackvilles, and his previous connections with Royalist supporters in the House of Commons, suggested that he held strong Royalist sympathies which were shared by his neighbours at Gwysaney and Leeswood. Furthermore, Evan Edwards and his son Thomas were both closely involved in the Royalist cause as commissioners of array.

The English Civil War

War broke out in 1642 and lasted for six years, gradually engulfing most of England and Wales. After a time of unforgettable upheaval, misery and violence, the king was captured and eventually put on trial and executed in January 1649. The monarchy was then abolished, along with the house of bishops. In their place, Parliament set up a Committee for the Propagation of the Gospel to appoint and remove clergy and, in an atmosphere of unprecedented religious freedom, new sects began to flourish and the celebration of Christmas was outlawed. Refusing to accept the crown offered to him, Oliver Cromwell was recognised as Lord Protector until his death in 1658. Growing unrest and discontent with the experiment of the Commonwealth and a successful intervention by the army brought back Parliament which restored the monarchy in 1660, with Charles II as king.

Colonel Thomas Davies of Gwysaney.

The Civil War had a devastating effect on the country with many people being killed, injured or made homeless, whilst others were subjected to large fines and deprived of their estates. The town of Mold was never at the centre of events and there was no great battle or prolonged siege in Moldsdale, but this did not mean that it did not suffer. Mold was a place which the opposing armies passed through *en route* to an existing scene of strife at Hawarden, Chester, the Midlands and the north of England, or further into Wales to Ruthin, Denbigh and Conwy. On their passage through Moldsdale, Parliamentarian soldiers were tempted to loot the homes of local Royalist gentry and sometimes those of their own supporters on the excuse of raising supplies.

Once again, north-east Wales was the corridor used by opposing armies as they advanced by land from Chester and Wrexham or by sea from the coast to besiege royalist castles.[11] The Parliamentarian general, Sir William Brereton, regarded the principality of Wales as the source from whence 'all his Majesty's provisions of victuals and men doe proceed.'[12] The local gentry were almost unanimous in their support for the ill-fated Charles I, and Wales was called the 'nursery of the King's infantry' and 'a royal fortress.' In one way or another, the gentry families of the area became involved in the complex and fragmentary military campaigns between 1642–6. Upon the defeat of the king, his supporters suffered heavy fines and some, like Robert Davies, of Gwysaney were imprisoned.

Colonel Sir Roger Mostyn (1624–90).

At the beginning of the war Charles had appointed Colonels Thomas Davies of Gwysaney and young Roger Mostyn to lead his forces in Flintshire. Two major campaigns were fought in the area by Parliamentarian forces, during which Hawarden Castle was under siege three times. In November 1643, the Parliamentarians, led by Sir Thomas Myddelton of Chirk, and Sir William Brereton crossed over Holt Bridge into Wales arriving at Hawarden Castle on 9 November. To their surprise, the gates were opened to them by the erstwhile Royalist governor and his Hawarden neighbour John Aldersley. In the first week in December the Parliamentarians were forced by Colonels Davies and Mostyn to surrender. During their stay at Hawarden the extreme Puritan soldiers took the opportunity to visit the parish church where they smashed the stained-glass windows, broke up altar rails and tore pages from the Bible. Throughout the parish, they tumbled church crosses in their iconoclastic rampage.

The second campaign in the area occurred in 1645. It opened in February when Brereton and Myddelton crossed the Dee with 2,000 men and again besieged the castle at Hawarden, but abandoned it on hearing of the presence in the area of Royalist troops. The Parliamentarians returned in April when Brereton attempted to intercept an ammunition convoy on its way from Anglesey to Chester. The Royalist convoy slipped into Hawarden Castle to take refuge and were besieged by Parliamentarians until relieved by Royalist forces on 19 May.

By the summer of 1645, time was running out for Charles I. His forces were no match for the generalship of Cromwell and his new Model Army which showed its mettle at Naseby in June when the 'Ironsides' annihilated the King's main army. On 24 September, the king observed from the city walls of Chester his forces cut down at Rowton Heath and he left the city the next morning: '1645 Thursday Sept 25. About 9 and

King Charles I leaving Chester for Hawarden September 25 1645. Stained-glass panel, west window, St John's Church, Chester.

10 in the morning the king left Chester and went to Harding (Hawarden) Castle, governed by Sir Wm. Neale, stayed 3 hours, and that night to Denbigh Castle.'

At the beginning of 1646, Hawarden Castle was again under siege. Its fate was sealed by the surrender of Chester in February and on 16 March the governor, after receiving the written permission of the king, marched out with his colours flying. The local gentry were

Hawarden Castle and park. Line engraving by W H. Thoms after T. Badeslade, 1740. This image clearly shows the damage inflicted upon the castle during the period of the Civil War.

involved in the siege of Denbigh Castle, which lasted from April until the middle of October. On the inevitable surrender, the vanquished garrison was permitted to leave with honour and amongst the royalist defenders fined for delinquency in arms by the Parliamentary Committee, were Colonel Thomas Davies, John Eyton of Leeswood, and his son, John Eyton junior, and Edward Lloyd, Hartsheath.

In April 1645, the Parliamentarian forces re-entered Wales and plundered 'all that countrey to Gosana (Gwysaney) viz Aston, Shotton, Hawarden, Mould, Northrop etc'. Amongst the incidents was the news that Sir William Brereton had captured Gwysaney 'which,' he reported, 'I took from them and therein the Governor a Captain' (probably Robert Davies III) and 27 prisoners more, amongst which officers.' In the house with the garrison was the 11-year-old Mutton Davies who would forever be reminded of this escapade when he used the patched up front door battered and scarred by troopers' muskets. For five or six weeks, beginning on Good Friday, Mold troops policing the parish kept people indoors. There were few burials and baptisms and the vicar wrote in his register after recording four entries for May and June, 'I baptiz'd no more this year '45, neither buried any, being constrained to absent myselfe in regard of the violence us'd in these parts.'

The Parliamentarian troops busied themselves in terrorising the houses of the Royalist gentry. One of their first actions was the visit to Gwysaney reported above which was followed by another mission to Rhual. There was no Royalist garrison there and Baron Edwards had recently given aid and advice to the Parliamentarians in the reduction of Hawarden Castle. The raiding party of Yorkshire soldiers must have been ignorant of the fact that the owner of the manor was the elder brother of William Edwards, High Sheriff of Chester, a prominent Puritan merchant who in October became mayor and whom the citizens returned a few weeks later as their member to Parliament. Edwards was away from home when Rhual received its visit from an unruly troop of horse and, on his return, reported the violence of their intrusion which he regarded as a case of assault and blatant daylight robbery. He complained bitterly that his house had been stripped and plundered by Captains Coltham and Viner's men, his wife 'stript out of her clothes by ye Yorkshire men, a box of Jewels taken.' As a result, the colonel of the regiment, Michael Jones, admitted that a box of jewels had been taken but he valued them at £500, considerably less than the value of £7,000 placed on them by Edwards.

Edward's collaboration and Puritan connections were either insufficient or too late to win for him a reprieve for his delinquency as a Royalist, although his reported good conduct during the siege of Hawarden Castle reduced the fine to £157.

His plight was fairly typical of the sufferings of the local Royalist gentry. His pocket was affected by his fine and loss of his offices as baron of the exchequer and customer of the ports of Chester. However desperate the consequences of the Civil War was for their fortune, the Edwards of Rhual, like most of the Royalist gentry families, recovered their status at the Restoration. With their income based on land, they had the long term opportunity to replenish their resources through increased rents, renewed leases, tithes, and the farming of coal.

Plague made no distinction between Royalist or Parliamentarian, civilian and soldier. It came to Chester and the vicinity between 22 June 1647 and 20 April 1648, when there were 2,099 victims.[13] Joan, the wife of Baron Edwards kept her husband informed of the news of the district whilst he attempted to salvage his political fortunes in London. She informed him that:

> … the plague has visited Chester, the parish of Estin (Hope), and many other towns, although the inhabitants will not have it said that it was anything but a fever, except on occasions when soldiers came to them to be quartered; one person at Estyn told such soldiers who entered his house that one of his children who he had ordered to lie under a blanket in a corner of a room, had died of the plague, and all soldiers quartered in the district were moved to Mold where they remained about five weeks but have now gone towards the waterside; Peter Winne, who has the chief place in the 'siniogog,' [synagogue]. [The local committee of Round heads] rules all men in the parish, and will do the recipient all the ill offices he can, for he rails against Commissioners of Array; whether she and the recipient if they can therewith be content; Eithel Parry of Hope would like to know whether his brother in London is making the proper use of the money sent him, 21 May 1647.[14]

Plas Teg[15] was another gentry house which suffered from the rough and ready behaviour of the Yorkshire Roundheads during the first week of April 1645. General Sir William Brereton, angered by their conduct, wrote to Captain Hugh Cullham. 'Your soldiers have plundered Sir John Trevor's house, Plas Teg … without warrant or authority … We therefore require you to bring all such persons under your command as did plunder or take away any of the goods.' The stolen goods included bed sheets, blankets, boulsters, pillows, curtains, carpets, '1 Fair Bible, 1 Crossbow, 1 fowling gunne, 3 powndes in money, the Cabinet, one old horse besides such provisions as they found in ye house.'[16]

Plas Teg, built in 1610 for Sir John Trevor.
Watercolour by John Ingleby.

On discovering the identity of the culprits, Brereton had four of them executed. The complaint against the culprits, their apprehension and execution reflected not particularly the enormity of the crime (the goods stolen from Plas Teg were not as valuable as the Rhual jewels), but the prestige and position of the victim, Sir John Trevor II (1596–1673). He was at the centre of power as a leading Parliamentarian who served several times on the Council of State and was elected to many Welsh committees. His father had built Plas Teg in 1610 out of a fortune made as Secretary to the Navy. His son, Sir John Trevor III (d. 1672), was married to a daughter of John Hampden and was related to Oliver Cromwell. Plas Teg is in the lordship of Hopedale and not more than half a mile from Hartsheath.

James Stanley, seventh earl of Derby, succeeded his father a few weeks after the outbreak of the Civil War in 1642. It is doubtful if he visited his three manors and lordships of Hawarden, Hope and Moldsdale after he succeeded to the earldom. During his father's lifetime, he had been entrusted with the administration of the family's estates and pursued a policy aimed at bringing financial stability to the vast Derby possessions which were then overburdened by debts and a disputed inheritance.

James Stanley, seventh earl of Derby, executed 1651.

His loyalty to the Stuart monarchy was unquestioned and at the beginning of the Civil War he met with mixed success against the Parliamentarian forces in Lancashire before being ordered to the Isle of Man to secure it against a possible Scottish invasion. Returning to England in March 1644, he fought alongside Prince Rupert who was accused of the massacre of at least 1,000 soldiers and civilians at Bolton in May 1644. Stanley returned to the Isle of Man in September but would not meet the demand of the Parliamentarians to surrender the island and consequently they refused to negotiate with him about his estates and forced the trustees of the Commonwealth to sell them. The earl remained on the island until August 1651 when his wife, Countess Charlotte, goaded him to join Charles II who was then *en route* from Scotland. She told him to 'pull off the breeches and she would put them on and lead them on.' The earl assisted Charles II to escape after his defeat at the battle of Worcester and then gave himself up to the Parliamentarians at Newport in Shropshire. Refused clemency, he was executed at Bolton, the scene of the massacre of 1644. He was the last member of the Stanley family to own the manor of Mold, although his son Charles, the eighth earl, managed to regain the Argoed estate in 1668.

The lordships of Mold and Hope were conveyed by the eighth earl of Derby, to Captain Andrew Ellis, Sir John Trevor II and Colonel George Twistleton. It was agreed that Sir John Trevor should 'divide and set out of the said manors and premises into three equal parts or allotments to the best of his understanding.' Lots drawn by Ellis and

Sir John Glynne of Hawarden (1603-66), Lord Chief Justice.

Twistleton before witnesses at the Red Lion in Wrexham in September 1657, decided the division of the manor and who should have first and second choices. Sir John Trevor's share was the manor of Hope, and a portion of lands in Mold. Captain Ellis had for his share the manor of Mold and a portion of the land there and therefore was recognised as lord of the manor. Colonel Twistleton had the remainder of the lands in Mold. The mineral rights of the lordship were divided equally between these three portioners and their successors who became known as the lords of Mold. The eighth earl persisted in claiming the restoration of his lost manors and received prospect of success on 6 February 1662 when the House of Lords sent down to the Commons a Bill for 'restoring of Charles Earl of Derby to the Manors of Molesdale and Hopesdale.' The Commons passed the Bill on 17 March, but Charles II refused his assent. Instead, he appointed arbitrators who, in July 1663, arranged that Derby should compulsorily repurchase Mold and Hope by 26 March 1664. If he failed to do so, the King ordered the holders to keep the property as their own. Legal attempts by the earls of Derby to repossess the lordships of Mold and Hawarden continued unsuccessfully until the end of the seventeenth century. The astute legal arrangements made by Lord Justice John Glynne made the transaction for the sale of the lordship of Hawarden irreversible but, after lengthy proceedings the eighth earl of Derby was eventually successful in permanently regaining the lordship of Hope on a legal technicality.

Oliver Cromwell, Lord Protector of England, died in 1658 and was succeeded by his son Richard who was ineffectual and had no desire to be head of state and resigned in 1660. The people of Mold, in common with the nation at large, were relieved to welcome the return of Charles II from exile. Evidence of this anticipation of the restoration of bishops and the king is seen in a slim volume of Mold Churchwardens' Accounts dated 1654–63, the first volume of such accounts that has survived for the parish. From the selection of entries given below we sense a return to normalcy. After years of neglect and misuse the parish church was repaired and records kept.

> Payd for 10 horse loads of Lyme to mend ye churchyard wall, 0 – 9 – 11
> Payd for a Register Book for ye Church, 0 – 5 – 0
> For 12 foote of board & for nayles and hinges and making it
> into a box to keep ye Church Book & other things, 0 – 2 – 1
> Payd Richard for his journey to Wigan to enquire for ye Bellfounders, 0 – 7 – 0
> 1659 Pd a Glazier of Hawarden for mending ye windows, 0 – 15 – 06
> 1660 Pd Hugh Roberts for fetching of ye Kings Arms frame, 0 – 1 – 0
> 1660 Griffith Hughes for drawing of ye Kings Arms frame, 2 – 10 – 4
> A new Register book, 0 – 8 – 0
> and this book of Accompts and a copy of Will ap Grono's will in parchment
> and a box to keep these writings in
> For 3½ yards of greene cloth for the Communion table carpet, 2 – 2 – 0
> For bread and wyne for the Communion at Whitsuntide 1654, 0 – 3 –8I
> For cords to lengthen the bell ropes & for a lb of soape & goose grease, 0 – 2 – 7
> To the Joyner for mending the Comon Seates, 0 – 4 – 9.

The forty years between 1660 and 1700 is an arbitrary period.[17] The use of the word 'Restoration' to describe the events of 1660 is an accurate description of the political recall of the Stuart monarchy and reinstatement of the gentry. However, we can see a gradual change in the circumstances of the gentry in terms of wealth and leadership. The replacement of the Stanley family as lords of Mold by new men was one important indicator of this change, reflecting the triumph of Parliament in the Civil War. That Moldsdale was a big prize to win is clearly reflected in a survey of the lordship carried out in the 1650s. This period of change may be compared with a cold spring. The buds were slow to open and blossom; the green shoots began to appear, but were hard to identify and agonisingly slow to start growing. This in some way is what happened with the exploitation of mineral resources and the slow beginnings of agricultural change. The final forty years of the seventeenth century were a prelude, a preparation for further change. The Restoration settlement of 1660

The Rhual Baptistry, c.1685.

presented the gentry families, yeomen, artisans and traders of Moldsdale with the opportunity of change which in the next century would lead to improvement.

The loyal parishioners of Mold confirmed their allegiance to Charles II with the erection of a framed board displaying the King's Arms and announced it with a peal of bells. The religious situation in 1660 was exceedingly delicate as the Presbyterians were in power in the Convention Parliament, and for the Church of England to be re-established, then episcopacy and the book of Common Prayer would have to be restored. A new House of Commons packed with gentry churchmen achieved both objects.

George Griffith was consecrated bishop of St Asaph in October 1660 in place of bishop John Owen, who died in 1651. During the Civil War, George Roberts had been vicar of Mold in 1643 and he was replaced by the Puritan Thomas Price. He resigned at the Restoration when he was appointed bishop of Kildare. Price had begun life as a Royalist and was serving as chaplain to Sir Robert Byron's regiment when he was taken prisoner by Parliamentary forces in Liverpool and was eventually appointed by them to the living of Mold. On the eve of his consecration as bishop of Kildare, he wrote to Robert Davies of Gwysaney 'My constant prayers are for yor whole family … I doe remember all my parishioners wth true affection giveing them a place in my dayly prayers. God keepe us …'[18]

In spite of attempts by the earl of Clarendon and the Cavalier Parliament to uproot the 'green shoots' of religious difference, they were not entirely destroyed and at Rhual Thomas Edwards (1649–1700), an Independent and member of a dissenting congregation, built a baptistry.

In 1660, most of the gentry regained the power they had held before the Civil War and resumed occupancy of the traditional offices of responsibility at parish, county and national level. They were back in power through the variety of positions they shared amongst their families, as members of Parliament (for county or borough), high sheriff, on the Commission of Peace as justices, and as churchwardens. Their social position was distinguished usually by the appellation of knight, esquire and gentleman. In Moldsdale after 1660 these families were: the Davieses of Gwysaney; the Eytons of Leeswood; the Wynnes of Tower, Nercwys and Argoed; the Pennants of Mold; the Bithells of Llwynegyin; the Lloyds of Pentrehobyn and Hartsheath; the Williamses of Arddunwent; the Edwardses of Rhual. These are the principal names, although others occur in the church records and there is a list of about fifty names for the townships of Mold of the names of houses of note and their residents in 1699.[19] The name of Mutton Davies of Gwysaney appears as a member of Parliament elected for the county in 1678, and members of the Commission of Peace in 1680 include Robert Davies, William Lloyd, John Langley and Peter Wynn.

Just before the Restoration, the sale of the manor of Mold,[20] which was the title to be used from this time onwards, was probably the major event in the history of landholding in the area and was the basis of future revolutions in agriculture, and industry. As noted above, after the purchase, the manor of Mold was divided into three portions and the conveyances by which the partition was completed were executed in January 1658. The three purchasers, known collectively as 'the Lords of Mold' were new names in the history of the area.

Captain Andrew Ellis, descended from an ancient Welsh lineage that had been long established at Althrey, near Bangor-is-y-coed,[21] had served with the Parliamentary forces in Wales and was appointed to the Commission for the Propagation of the Gospel in Wales. In 1650, he was charged with the stewardship of the Welsh estates sequestrated from delinquent Royalists. He was appointed registrar for Flintshire and governor of Hawarden Castle and replaced Roger Hanmer as steward to the Commission for the Compounding of Delinquents in North Wales. He was in the strongest possible position to realise that the sale of the former Flintshire manors of the earl of Derby was a prize worth having and pursued the sale of these lands with two other interested supporters of the Commonwealth. The Ellis portion of the manor of Mold was described in April 1791 as containing: 'with appurtenances and 80 messuages, 50 cottages, 2 dove-houses, 5 tofts, 1 water corn mill, 80 gardens, 50 orchards, 500 acres of pasture, 200 acres of wood, 10,000 acres of furze and heath, 20 acres of land covered with water and all usual rents, rights and courts.'[22]

Colonel George Twistleton of Barley Hall, Yorkshire, had married Ellis's sister-in-law. He too had served with General Mytton's army in Cheshire and north Wales and was appointed governor of Denbigh Castle in 1647. Although a member of the court assembled for the trial of Charles I at Whitehall in 1649, he did not sign the death warrant and therefore escaped punishment as a regicide. During the Commonwealth, he served as a member of Parliament. He later married Mary Glynne, of Lleuer in Caernarfonshire. The Twistleton portion was described in 1815 as having:

> 50 messuages,10 cottages, 20 tofts, 6 water grist corn mills, 10 dove houses, 50 curtilages, 50 gardens, 50 orchards, 600 acres of land, 200 acres of meadow, 700 acres of pasture, 50 acres of wood, 100 acres of furze and heath, 50 acres of marsh, 100 acres of land covered with water, common of pasture for all manner of cattle, common of turbary and piscary … with the appurtenances in the several parishes of Mold, Northop and Flint.[23]

The third purchaser, Sir John Trevor (1596–1673), spent his public life in London and had succeeded to two estates in north Wales, his uncle's at Trefalun and his father's at Plas Teg. He served on the side of Parliament in the Long Parliament elected in 1640. He was father-in-law to John Hampden's daughter, Ruth. Trevor's own daughter, Mary, married the Sussex Parliamentarian, Colonel Morley of Glynde. The Commonwealth government regarded him as the mouthpiece for north Wales' affairs and as such, he became a member of the Council of State 1651 and 1652–3 and served on several committees. Sir John Trevor's Plas Teg lands gave him a personal interest in the neighbouring Derby lands and he eventually paid £2,209 12s 8d for the manor of Hope. John Peck, his agent in north Wales, out-manoeuvred Captain Ellis's bid as a candidate in the Flintshire Parliamentary election contest in 1654, turning up at Mold on the day of the election with hundreds of supporters for Sir John's son, who was duly returned for the county.[24]

The Trevor purchase of the lordship of Hope was eventually returned to the Derby family by order of the courts because of a legal nicety. As a result of this, only a small portion in the manor of Mold was retained by the Trevors whilst the Ellis portion, the largest, descended through the marriage of his only daughter Cecill, to the Langley family (see below). George Twistleton's (1618–67) share, not as large as that of Ellis, was divided by his widow into six parts and left to her children. By the time of his death in 1711, Edward Lloyd of Tyddyn, Mold had bought up and re-consolidated the six shares and they eventually descended to John Lloyd of Wigfair (d. 1815).

Captain Andrew Ellis married Frances, daughter of the Honorable James Fiennes of Shutford, Oxfordshire. Their only daughter, Cecill, married Sir Richard Langley who died in February 1677, aged only 29, and left all his estates to his father Alderman Langley of London. Sir Richard's widow was not mentioned in his will and later married William Fiennes, Esq, the elder brother of Laurence, fifth viscount of Saye and Sele. She died without issue on 23 July 1715.

The other children of Alderman Langley were: John (alderman of London, his daughter, Elizabeth, married Sir Hans Sloane, founder of the British Museum); Andrew; Martha; Elizabeth and Samuel (also an alderman of the City of London).[25] The lordship of Mold passed to Andrew and then to his nephew Anthony Swymmer (d. 1729). Both Andrew and his sister, Martha, were in Jamaica in January 1689–90, where the family amassed a substantial estate of sugar plantations.

The mineral rights of the manor of Mold were shared equally between the owners of the three portions and was described as '… one undivided 3rd part or share, the whole into 3 equal parts or shares to be divided of and in all mines, quarries, ores, minerals, metals, and coals of and in 500 mine pits, 200 lead mine pits, 50 copper mine pits, 100 mine pits of calamine, 50 mine pits of ores of zinc and 100 coal pits and of and in all other mines, quarries and mine pits of what nature or kind soever with the appurtenances in the manor of Mold in the parish of Mold or in either of them in the said county of Flint.'

A survey, dated 15 July 1652,[26] was made to determine the boundaries of the manor and took the form of a perambulation walked by witnesses. They left a description beginning 'the Mannor of Mould is bounded & lieth … Eastward from the River Alyn about two Roods before Hartsheath Mill …' The description of boundaries then continue until the witnesses return to the same place. A copy of this was obtained from the Court of the Exchequer at the time of the boundary dispute in the eighteenth century and it distinguishes the extent of the manor of Mold from its neighbours, the manor of Hope and the lordship of Bromfield and Yale.

The 1653 survey of the manor[27] is different from the one of the previous year in that it is much longer, running to forty-one folios. It was made by 'a Commission Founded upon an Act of Parliament' to sell off the estates of 'James late earl of Derby.' The survey gives general details and a list of property, names of tenants, their leases and rents. The purpose of the survey was to estimate the value of the manor by recording its property and rents so as to enable the commissioners to obtain a fair market price for it. The document is an inventory, an extent, a record prepared for a transfer of property which protects the interests of tenants and buyers.

The introduction to the 1653 survey gives general information relating to the ordering of the manor such as the Court Baron, the Court Leet, the district bailiffs, details of two fairs, their tolls and value to the lord of the manor,[28] as well as incidental descriptions such as 'another piece of wasteland in Mold called Bailey Hill charged upon the inhabitants of Mold from the Great Oak standing in the midst of the Town to the said hill.' It lists the rents that were due to the lord of the manor. These customary rents go back to the founding of the town of Mold. They are burgage and other rents, descending from lands originally granted to the lord's tenants and based on feudal tenure when the property carried an obligation to perform military service. These were called chief rents. Other land was known as charter land (i.e. a grant confirmed by deed); hence 'charter' rents were paid which were an important part of the lord's income and the lease established the date when the rent was payable (usually in cash for the amount agreed in the lease) at midsummer (24 June) or Martinmas (11 November). Burgage rents were paid by seventeen gentry (for lands belonging to Tower and for burgages relating to Pentrehobyn) who included Robert Lloyd of Mold, Kenrick Williams, Peter Williams, John Evans of Llwynegryn.

An important part of the survey provided details of existing leases made between the tenants and the lord of the manor. These details were recorded on the manorial court rolls (which do not appear to have survived). It was important for all concerned that they should be aware of the true facts and one place where they could be found was in the survey. Special care was taken to do this in the form of a memorandum recording recent agreements. The Commonwealth commissioners relied on the goodwill of the local population, particularly upon those tenants whose loyalty was to a former owner.

In the 1630s William, the sixth earl of Derby, abdicated the responsibility for the management of his estates to his heir James, Lord Strange, known in the survey as Sir James Stanley. In 1638–9, he conducted a policy of improving the value of the lordship by making new contracts with his tenants which included an additional annual rent charge for enclosures and improvements of waste land. By this means, the rental value of the lordship was increased tenfold, from £122 16s 8d to £1,320 16s 2d. John Baker, the surveyor general, estimated 'ye whole improved value of the lordship as £1,528. 4s. 2d.' Many of the leases in the survey refer to his negotiation with the tenants in the 1630s when the Derby estate was recovering from the great dispute between Countess Alice (widow of the fifth earl) and her brother-in-law, William, the sixth earl. Part of the income for her dower was from the lordship of Mold. The survey hints at the activities of Peter Wynne of Argoed who acted as a Derby official in the manor and at the time of the survey was resident at Argoed. He was not popular with his fellow gentry and appears not to be trusted by the commissioners for the Commonwealth.

One of the leases in the survey is typical of the information recorded by the commissioners. It is dated 20 May 1638 and was made between Griffith Edwards of Gwernaffield and Sir James Stanley. In the lease, the term 'Surrender for a sum of £59 8s 4d – 13½ acres large measure' refers to the renewal of the lease and the payment made by the tenant to the landowner to enable him to have security of tenure for a fixed period. In this instance, for the lives of Griffith Edwards, Catherine, his wife and Edward Griffith, his son. By 1652, Griffith was 46 years, Edward *c.*17 years, and Catherine was dead. A rent of 6s 8d was payable at midsummer and Martinmas, and one capon yearly at Easter. The landowner made his return on the property at the surrender. On the death of a tenant, his heir paid a heriot, a fee or death duty, to enable him to resume the tenancy. This payment often took the form of the best beast or was commuted to a money payment, in this case 50s.

The survey carefully recorded the timber in the lordship. The number of trees in Argoed and Bistre were counted as 587 timber trees, 1,057 pollards and saplings at 3s each. There is no record of tenants being required to plant trees.

Another interesting part of the survey is the reference to water mills in the manor where the grain crops were ground into flour.

Herseth mill. One under shott Mill in the tenure of Edward Lloyd in Herseth worth per ann £6– Memorandum that by Indenture 20 June 1638 Sir James Stanley in Consideration of £335 paid, & secured, demised the then last rated premises unto Henry Lloyd … late in occupation of John ap Reece ap Evan. Leeswood Mill.

'Memorandum: that by Indenture 20 May 1638, Sir James Stanley in consideration of £129 paid & secured demised unto Peter Wynne by the name of all the Water Corne Mill Situated in Mold called *Y Felin Berfedd* – and one parcel of land and one parcel of land near adjoining the mill at yearly rent £5

' and another Water Corn Mill at Bronkoed called *Y Felin Fychan* and a small parcel of ground adjoining, rent 26s 8d.

'A water corn mill in Trythin & one messuage and tenement with appurtenances in Trythin containing about 1 acre 2 roods of the large measure, rent 26s 8d. for the lives of John, Richard, and Robert sons of Peter Winne & the survivor of them rent payable at Midsummer & Martinmas: 2 fat capons at Easter and 2 at Martinmas.

'One undershot water corn grist mill in Bistre commonly called discus Millne with the Toll multure x£ thereto belonging in the possession of John Eyton Esq xv£.

The surveyor was careful about accepting the statements of witnesses he suspected as being biased by local loyalties and self-interest, and on occasion records his doubts and suspicions. An example of this appears in the right of tenancy of Robert Davies, Esq, of Mold Mill, a shot water corn mill in Mold 'in the present possession of Robert Davies, esquire, Gwysaney.' In a contract, dated 20 June 1638, Sir James Stanley, for a consideration of £41 17s 6d, transferred the premises – except the mill of which there was a dispute about the tenancy. Alderman William Bennett of Chester claimed to be the next tenant, under the hand of William late earl of Derby, in support of whom Peter Wynne of Leeswood gave evidence. In a memorandum dated 7 May 1652, Wynne made an oath in writing that 'the mill was to be in reversion after the decease of Alice Countess of Derby who was then seized of all the said estate in the Lordship of Mold for life'. After her death, Earl William was reported as directing that 'the said lease should be altered and made to be for three lives viz. for life of Mr Henry Smith and Margaret (his late wife) now wife of William Bennet[t] Alderman of Chester'. Wynne's statement was questioned by the commissioner who cautiously noted 'wch makes me apprehend that neither Smyth nor Ald Bennet have any legal right it yet I conceive but with submission that Ald Bennet who married Mr Smith's widow may have some time set him to make good his Title if he have any.'

Charles, eighth earl of Derby, did not allow the purchasers of the three Flintshire lordships to rest. His vindictiveness and persistence were not confined to those who he alleged had tricked him into surrendering his family estates in the difficult years of the Commonwealth, when money was not available to buy them back and circumstances prevented him from keeping his promises. Before his death in 1672 he engaged in a relentless campaign, challenging the right of the new purchasers to surrender their gains. Although on occasion he met with some support in Parliament he failed to move Charles II who refused to assent to a Bill

Pentrehobyn.

passed in Parliament directing the return of his Flintshire lordships. Earl Charles never forgave the king whose life had been saved by his father, James, after the Battle of Worcester and as a consequence of which, suffered 'martyrdom' at the hands of his enemies the Parliamentarians who now lived off the fat of the land of what was once his patrimony. But he did achieve some satisfaction and redress by having the lordship and manor of Hope returned to him by Sir John Trevor. The ingenuity of the earl's advisers knew no bounds and they were prepared to pursue the Derby claims in whatever court they could obtain a hearing.

The case against Peter Wynne (*c*.1591–1653) was only of minor consequence in the business of mending the family fortunes, but it was a victory which gave Derby the confidence that some, if not all, of his enemies could be scattered and brought to justice. Cromwell's commissioners had regarded Wynne as a 'dodgy character' as did the Derby tenants in Moldsdale whom the earl addressed as 'my trusted and noble loved friends.' They came from Gwysaney, Leeswood, Tower, Rhual, Hartsheath and other houses, and included his father's chaplain, Dr Christopher Pashley, recently removed by the Puritans from the rectorship of Hawarden. It is not surprising therefore that the misdemeanours of the Derby agents in the lordships came to his notice.

Peter Wynne was the second son of John Wynne of Tower and, as early as 1628, had acted with George Ravenscroft as an agent for the earl who instructed them to purchase land in what later became the Argoed estate.[29] Peter Wynne used the earl's money to gain possession of Argoed and, with the help of William Lloyd, evicted three sitting tenants and then began improvements and repairs to it.

With the outbreak of the Civil War and the reversal of the fortunes and execution of James, earl of Derby, Wynne may have felt secure in his possession of Argoed, which passed on his death to his son John. Wynne's luck and judgement deserted him towards the end of his life, his having overspent on rebuilding Argoed by at least £800, most of it borrowed from his kinsmen, Evan Edwards of Rhual and Edward Lloyd of Pentrehobyn. Eventually he was sent to Flint gaol as a debtor, with ample time to meditate on his change of fortune. He never came out alive. It was recorded that 'Peter Wynne of Argoed, beinge in prison, fell sick of a feaver and died.'

After the Restoration the new earl re-opened chancery proceedings and succeeded in evicting Wynne's grandsons from the estate in 1668. It had over 400 acres of land with a handful of farms. The next year, bishop Isaac Barrow was appointed to the diocese of Asaph from Sodor and Man, where he had been governor since 1663 and his patron, the earl of Derby, provided Argoed Hall for his grace and favour. In 1715, the earl of Derby sold the Argoed estate to Charles Roberts, a gentleman of Denbigh.

Charles Stanley, eighth earl of Derby.

The appearance of new lords of Mold did not appear to affect the balance of power in the area or cause any diminution in the influence exerted by gentry families who were well entrenched in the locality. The Trevors had been on the scene at Plas Teg throughout the sixteenth century and eventually migrated to Glynde in Sussex, although the family retained their interest in the lordships through their share of the mineral rights. Andrew Ellis's position as lord of the manor of Mold passed, through marriage, to the Langleys who, although their main interest was in Jamaican sugar estates, managed the manor and mineral rights by the employment of a member of the local gentry as agents. The Twistleton share of the lordship was bought back through the enterprise of the Lloyds of Tyddyn. In other words, there was a process of assimilation and integration. Amongst the circle of gentry, families were knitted together through marriage, mutual society, politics and religion. There were, however, fluctuating shifts in leadership. After the Restoration, the Davies family, through the example of sacrifice and leadership in the Civil War, and fortified by an increase in their estates through marriage to the heiress of Llannerch and purchase of the manor of Ewloe, found themselves representing the county in the House of Commons. The respect which they enjoyed in Mold was reiterated by Charles II when meeting Mutton Davies in 1679, 'the king said he knew Mr Davies to be an honest man …'[30]

The Edwards family of Rhual indicated a change of direction in their religious views shortly after the Restoration. Thomas (d. 1664), son of Evan Edwards, predeceased his father by six years. He had married Elizabeth the daughter of Edward Lloyd of Pentrehobyn and they had eleven children. Thomas was succeeded by his son, also named Thomas (1649–1700), who married Jane, the daughter of Robert Davies of Gwysaney; they had no children. He was a member of a dissenting congregation although it was not until 1695 that he severed his ties with the Anglican Church. During his lifetime, Rhual was a haven for dissenting ministers, including Vavasor Powell and John Williams, the Independent minister of Denbigh and later of Wrexham. Thomas Edwards' sisters married dissenters: Mary, the elder and heiress of the Rhual estate, married Walter Griffith, a member of a dissenting family from Llanfyllin, Montgomeryshire in 1683; Ann, the younger, married the Reverend William Harwood. Walter Griffith died in 1702 and Mary and her four children returned to Rhual. Two of them, Nehemiah and Thomas, kept diaries from which it has been possible to reconstruct the history which appears in the next chapter.

In 1597, Edward Lloyd of Pentrehobyn granted the lease of a lead smelting mill and a small plot of ground called *Y Ddol*, 'the meadow' (the site is in the vicinity of Milford Street, Mold), on his estate to William Ratcliffe, citizen and haberdasher of London and his partner William Chaloner. It was sold four years later to Richard Grosvenor of Eaton. The mining and smelting of lead in Flintshire and Denbighshire were to be a significant factor in the subsequent fortunes of the Grosvenors. The smelting mill flourished, with 90% of the pig lead from Mold being shipped to London. The mill was improved in the 1660s and continued to operate until 1683, when smelting there ceased because of cheaper production costs on Deeside from where there was a direct line from ore mining at Halkyn to smelting at Gadlys and shipment by sea to London from Flint and Chester. The industry did not return to the Mold area until the end of the eighteenth century.[31]

Coalmines at Nant Mawr in Bistre township were amongst those worked by the partnership of Evan Edwards and John Eyton in the three Stanley lordships on the eve of the Civil War. On the sequestration of the Stanley estates in 1651, the mines were taken over by Robert Coytmore, Secretary to the Navy in Cromwell's Protectorate and resident at Plas Onn in Nercwys township. In 1651, he claimed that the coal mines at Nant Mawr had been destroyed by the enemy [Royalists] and he paid for their repair in 1657. At the sale of the manor and lordship of Mold they continued to be part of the mineral rights shared between the three new lords. They were still productive when Walker made his survey in 1791.

The Civil War gave an impetus to the digging for clay and the infant pottery industry on Buckley Mountain when the siege of Chester cut off the supply of tobacco pipes from the city. At this time, Brookhill pottery was producing clay pipes, bestiary ware and simple decorated slip-trailed pottery.

Notes

 1. T. Lloyd Roberts, 'Bard of Llywenni; Shakespeare's Welsh Connection, *The New Welsh Review*, vol. vi, no.3, 1993–4.
 2. L. T. Smith (ed), *Leland's Itinerary in Wales, 1536–9,*1906–10.
 3. E. Lhwyd, *Parochalia 1699, Archaeologia Cambrensis supplement,* 1909–11, p.891.
 4. *Letters & Papers Domestic Henry VIII,* vol 13, pt i, 1538.
 5. Thomas Pennant, *Tours in Wales,* vol i, pp.427–8.
 6. G. A. Usher, *Gwysaney and Owston,* Denbigh, 1950.
 7. T. W. Pritchard, *The Making of Buckley and District,* Wrexham, 2006, p 46*f*.
 8. E. Hubbard, *The Buildings of Wales Clwyd (Denbighshire and Flintshire),* London, 1986, p.399.
 9. Usher, op cit, p.47.
10. B. E. Howells (ed), *A Calendar of Letters relating to North Wales,* Cardiff, 1967.
11. See K. Lloyd Gruffydd, The sieges of Hawarden Castle during the first Civil War, 1642–6, Buckley, 2004, pp.3–16, and N Tucker, *North Wales in the Civil War*, Wrexham, 1992.
12. R. Morris, 'The Siege of Chester and North Wales', *Chester and North Wales Archaeological and History Society Journal*, xxv, 1923, p.42.
13. J. Morris (ed), *The Impact of the Civil War,* London, 1991, p.20.
14. FRO D/HE/468.
15. M. Baker, *Plas Teg A Jacobean Country House, Pontblyddyn, Mold,* Ruthin, 2006, p.28.
16. ibid.
17. From the 1660s for Flintshire there is an increase in the number and variety of records available at the County Record Office – Civil, Ecclesiastical, and Estate. These are the source of information for this chapter and the next.
18. Usher, op cit, p.78.
19. E. Lhwyd, ibid.
20. See FRO schedules especially Mostyn, and Keene & Kelly, and Henry Taylor, 'The Lords of Mold,' *Publications of the Flintshire Historical Society*, vol 6.
21. One of his ancestors it is said was a standard bearer to Prince Owain Gwynedd d. 1170. Andrew Ellis married Frances, second daughter of the second viscount of Saye and Sele.
22. FRO D/M/68.
23. Denbighshire Record Office Ruthin, DD/HB/1226.
24. D. G. Evans, *History of the Lordship of Hope [Flintshire]*, unpublished, in FRO.
25. Calendar of the Coleman Deeds and Documents, vol.1 (Nos 1238, 19 Oct 1658; 1269, 28 June 1677), National Library of Wales, edited for the Flintshire Historical Society Records series, No. 1, G.J.G. Edwards, 1924.
26. NLW Wigfair Ms 1214.
27. FRO D/KK/263.
28. Described in ch. 3.
29. I. M. Read, 'Argoed Hall', *Clwyd Historian*, no. 26.
30. Usher, ibid, p.94.
31. See J. N. Rhodes, 'The Lead Mills at Mold,' *Flintshire Historical Society Publications,* vol 25, pp.21–30.

5: Eighteenth-century Mold:
evidence of the gentry

The recipe for telling the history of eighteenth-century Mold is made up of the richest ingredients. It is as if rationing restrictions were lifted and, for the first time, the historian has a greater choice of source materials to draw upon. We have for example two separate diaries from Nehemiah and Thomas Griffith, members of the gentry family of Rhual. They demonstrate that the diary of an intelligent, well-placed individual, not meant for publication, is one of the best methods of throwing light on contemporary events. Thomas Griffith was the personal physician to, and either the acquaintance or relative of, gentry families in a radius of twenty miles from Mold. Unusually for the time and as a member of the gentry, he was a practising dissenter. Another voice we hear for nearly thirty years is that of a clergyman of the Church of England, the Reverend Hugh Lloyd, vicar of Mold, a member of the gentry who was well connected, highly educated and a pluralist, holding the livings of both Mold in the diocese of St Asaph, and Llangynhafal (near Ruthin) in the diocese of Bangor. Although Parson Lloyd speaks primarily through his columns of accounts, his witness is invaluable and never dull. He spends money in the markets in Mold, Ruthin and Chester on food, wine, paying his curate, clothing the poor and in generous support of young scholars. Lloyd is an affectionate relative of the artist Richard Wilson and shows his concern for his welfare, together with the painter's uncle, Sir George Wynne of Leeswood. Both parson and physician were intimates of Sir George and the vicar, the former was his brother-in-law. Lloyd's father sheltered him in his youth, and the future baronet married his daughter.

In the eighteenth century we hear not only the voices of the gentry, but we also see them in their portraits. The bewigged and waist-coated men-folk, with their ample figures, and their ladies, equally generous in their elegant proportions, betray the confidence of those born to rule. The mansion in the park, set in a fashionable garden, the decorative ironwork of the gates, the lodges at the entrance, the drive which sweeps over bridge and past lake and folly, to the big house were their ideal. They shaped the landscape in order to express such perfection, and the creation of such paradise gardens in Moldsdale is retained in the watercolours and prints of Moses Griffith.

Of course, there are other voices to be heard in this hierarchical society. The gentry were found in the middle rank between the nobility and common people. With the departure from Moldsdale of the earls of Derby, no member of the nobility owned estates in the manor and parish of Mold. The three new lords of Mold were members of the gentry, a group which made up only a small fraction of the community, estimated as one twentieth or one twenty-fifth of the local population. The gentry were divided into three degrees or layers. At the top were knights, followed by esquires and below them, gentlemen. The poll tax imposed in 1660 was graduated according to rank: an 'ordinary person', the bulk of the population, paid only 6d a year, but a gentleman paid £5, an esquire £10, a knight £20, a baronet £30, a viscount £50, an earl £60 and a duke £100.

Below the gentry in the social scale were the 'commonalty,' classified as yeomen, merchants, artificers, tradesmen, mariners and all others getting their 'livelihood after a Mechanic Way,' the skilled workers, many of whom had attained their positions and occupations through serving an apprenticeship.

The ordinary people were at the bottom of the hierarchy, at the base of the pyramid. This group were often known in the eighteenth century as 'the poor' or 'the labouring poor,' descriptions which showed that even when in work, many struggled to survive. The 'poor' did not all live in poverty, but made up that part of society that was vulnerable through age, sickness and lack of a regular income. It was estimated that around more than 15% of the population were in receipt of some sort of charitable aid at some time or other. There was always the fear that, if not controlled, the so-called able-bodied poor would riot, steal or as 'the mob' take the law into their own hands. The gentry saw their own estate as a community, providing employment and care. Both former and contemporary servants were part of the household and regarded as tenants. As such, when they became elderly, fell ill or found themselves in reduced circumstances with large families, they occasionally benefited from reductions in farm rents and charitable donations. Within the bounds of the parish and beyond, across the county, the gentry regarded it as their duty to control and provide for the poor. The law of the land laid down how many hours in the day common men should work and how little they should rest. In 1563, the Statute of Artificers had made it the responsibility of the judges at the County Assizes (with the gentry justices of the peace in the same court-room) to inquire whether there were workers who 'do not continue from Five of the Clock in the Morning till Seven at Night in the Summer and from Seven till Five in the Winter.'

How do we distinguish the gentry of Mold in the eighteenth century? We recognised their rise in the last chapter as a group of people whose families went back several centuries, descendants of Welsh princely houses and aristocracy who proved this lineage through elaborate pedigrees, recorded and authenticated by bards and heralds visitations. These pedigrees and armorial bearings were the hallmark of their 'quality' and position in society. The heraldry was no longer displayed for recognition as in battle on shields or surcoats but now, in more peaceful times, decorated entrance gates, carriage doors, church pews and funeral hatchments. The gentry had no difficulty in recognising who they were and identified with their own class, even when, as often happened, the circumstances of some were reduced by poverty. In the summer of 1670, the heralds of the College of Arms had summoned a number of the gentry from each township in Mold to attend a visitation where they recorded each family's pedigree before visiting the parish church to note the heraldic inscriptions and badges displayed there.[1]

The gentry have been defined as:

> … basically a class whose superior incomes made possible a certain kind of education, a standard of comfort, and degree of leisure and a common interest in ways of spending it, which marked them off from those whose incomes, perhaps as great or greater in money terms, could only be obtained by constant attention to some form of business.'[2]

Leeswood, built by Sir George Wynne, Bart. This painting by Moses Griffith shows the entrance over a bridge through the park.

Their income was usually derived from the rents of farms belonging to their landed estates.

In a study of the gentry in eighteenth century Moldsdale, it is assumed that they were usually of long residence in the neighbourhood and had lived in the same township for generations, usually in the same house. From time to time, a family would erect a new mansion, as did George Wynne at Leeswood in the 1720s, when his income over a score of years was above £20,000 per annum. Wherever they lived, their estates became little spheres of influence which were at the centre of power. Wherever they exercised leadership, they generally acted in unison with their fellow gentry. Notable exceptions when they might experience disharmony, were parliamentary elections. If the election was contested then the electorate took sides with all the enthusiasm, violence and corruption for which eighteenth-century hustings were a byword. At these times the gentry looked further afield for support from the people who mattered most, the electors, the freeholders – men aged between the ages of twenty-one and seventy, with freehold property worth at least forty shillings a year – who could vote at parliamentary elections and generally formed the backbone of members of the parish vestry. It was they who set the rate and allocated the money for relief of the poor, church repair and other objects.[3]

Sir George Wynne of Leeswood 1700-1756.
Line engraving after J. Vanderbank.

The supremacy of the gentry in the affairs of Moldsdale in the eighteenth century is seen in every sphere. As justices of the peace they were involved in the work of the Quarter Sessions, as members of the church vestry they were responsible for poor relief, regularly concerned with repairing the church, re-siting the pews, erecting a gallery, renewing the clock, recasting the bells, re-glazing the windows and building the new west tower. As lovers of liberty, the gentry were against the tyranny of taxation. Generally supporters of the Church of England, they were loyal to the Hanoverian monarchs, although some of them indulged in Jacobite protest as members of the Cycle of the White Rose. At the end of the eighteenth century, in wars against Napoleonic France, they expressed their loyalty to the flag and served the crown as officers in the local militia.

Some of their charitable work was outside the Church vestry; a notable example of this being the apprenticing of teenagers which was arranged through their dining club which met regularly.

The main sources of entertainment were visits to the houses of other local gentry for family gatherings, friendship, courtship, dining, drinking sessions and sick visiting. Purposes of such visits included gaining information about mining adventures, advice about horses and dogs, and the organisation of coursing, hunting and fishing. It was the custom either to deliver personally, but more often to send with a servant, presents of fruit, venison and salmon. Local inns and town houses were centres for meetings, balls, and suppers. In the 1770s, some of the local gentry flocked to Wynnstay to take part in the theatricals.[4]

The vicars of Mold and other clergy from the parish, such as the Reverend Dr William Wynne of Tower and the Williams dynasty from Fron Hall, added the distinction of scholarship to their ranks and welcomed the public support of their brethren in the affairs of the parish. The Reverend Hugh Lloyd promoted the building and endowment of a charity school.

After the turmoil and division of seventeenth-century politics which culminated in the Glorious Revolution of 1688, the nation benefited from peace, stability and an increase in prosperity. The time to 1815 is often called 'the long eighteenth century', an age in which the gentry fulfilled their responsibilities of office and leadership and contributed to the growth and enrichment of Moldsdale. They initiated the changes that took place and controlled the local population by reason of their social position. They intermarried with their own class and were dependent upon one another for mutual support. The gentry class had resilience and self-assurance, were generally comfortably wealthy and incessantly gregarious. Their rank produced examples of ability, eccentricity, admiration and very rarely pity. The gentry's involvement in eighteenth-century enterprises such as mining, industry and agricultural improvement will be dealt with in another chapter.

The Rhual diaries

The personal papers of the Griffith family resident at Rhual provide a commentary on over 300 years of the life in their household, locality and further afield. The names and activities of the Moldsdale gentry are well represented in the archive[5] and provide the source material for any study of their social class in the first part of the eighteenth century.

The Griffith family were dissenters and selections of diary entries are chiefly taken from the personal diaries of the brothers Nehemiah (1691–1738) and Thomas Griffith (1695–1740), who were two of four children of Mary, elder daughter and heiress of Thomas Edwards (1649–1700), the grandson of Baron Evan Edwards (*c.*1590–1670). Mary's younger sister Ann married the Reverend William Harwood of Broad Marston on the Worcestershire/Gloucestershire border. Mary's father, Thomas Edwards, changed from being an Anglican and broke away from the state church towards the end of his life to worship as a member of a dissenting congregation. During his lifetime, Rhual was a haven for renowned dissenting ministers along the Welsh border, including Vavasour Powell and John Williams, Independent minister of Denbigh. The connection with dissenters was further strengthened by the marriage in 1683 of Mary, the heiress, to Walter Griffith a dissenter from Llanfyllin in Montgomeryshire. On her husband's death in 1702, Mary returned to Rhual with her four children at which time Nehemiah was aged eleven and Thomas seven.

A brief note on the religious and political background will give some understanding of the peculiar position of the Griffith brothers as dissenters. During the period of the Reformation, the Edwards family had, in common with surrounding gentry, accepted the establishment of the Anglican Church. The Civil War in the middle of the seventeenth century saw an outburst of religious freedom and the establishment of a multitude of different sects. The religious temper of the Commonwealth was forcibly directed towards freedom of worship, but against Roman Catholic authority, ritual and ornament and the rejection of the Anglican Church. This led to the execution of its head, King Charles I, and the removal of bishops and many of the clergy. Puritans and other dissenting groups controlled religion through the Committee for the Propagation of the Gospel. Evan Edward's brother, William, was a Puritan but there is no suggestion that he was a dissenter. At the Restoration in 1660, it was assumed that King Charles II and his parliament would exercise some toleration in worship towards Protestant dissenters. This did not happen, however, and over 2,000 members of the clergy left the Church of England in 1662. Dissenters, Protestants who worshipped outside the communion of the established church, increased in numbers and established their own congregations from amongst Presbyterians, Independents, Baptists and Quakers. In 1685, James II, a Roman Catholic, succeeded his brother Charles II to the throne and attempted to introduce religious toleration, which would give freedom to both Roman Catholics and dissenters. The bishops of the Church of England refused to endorse this prospective alliance and seven of them were imprisoned in the Tower of London. The birth of an heir to the throne in 1688 led Parliament to invite the Protestant William III and Mary to accept the crown of England. James II abdicated and fled to France. Parliament upheld the Protestant succession and passed the Toleration Act in 1689. Its effect on the Griffith family of Rhual was to separate them from their fellow gentry in religious worship and subject them to legal disabilities. They were excluded from holding public office, whilst still being required to pay tithes and other parochial dues. Undergraduate entrance to the universities of Oxford and Cambridge was subject to a religious test which forced Thomas Griffith to obtain medical qualifications from the University of Leyden in the Netherlands.

The abdication of James II in 1688 drove the House of Stuart into permanent exile in France from where, with their followers in Britain, the Jacobites, they plotted to regain their lost throne by force. The first attempt occurred in 1715, following the death of Queen Anne, sister of Queen Mary and daughter of James II, the previous year. The succession to the British throne had devolved to the Protestant German prince, George, elector of Hanover. Many of the Flintshire and Denbighshire gentry were members of a Jacobite society called the Cycle of the White Rose, which met every three weeks in a rota (cycle) of venues. Although the nation prided itself that the change of dynasty that occurred in 1688 was a bloodless revolution, many of the Tory gentry secretly wished for the return of a Stuart monarch.

Political supporters were divided, either in support of the Tory party (which had thrived in the time of Queen Anne) or the Whig party, which supported the Hanoverians and the Protestant succession to the throne. The Whig ministry, led by Sir Robert Walpole, lasted from 1721 to 1742 and was reviled generally by the Tory gentry of Moldsdale, although George Wynne of Leeswood was an exception. Thomas Griffith campaigned for the Whigs and his diary reports Wynne's unsuccessful election campaign in 1727. At the next contest Wynne triumphed and represented the borough of Flint in Parliament from 1734–41.

Thomas Griffith, perhaps because he was a dissenter and a second son, qualified as a physician in 1725. As a doctor of medicine he was much in demand and earned the respect and esteem of the gentry of Moldsdale. He used his diary indiscriminately, both as a medical daybook to remind himself of visits to patients and what he had prescribed for them, and as a record of social engagements. From the pages of his diary he reveals himself as an intelligent, hardworking country squire who was not averse to joining in the frequent roistering at social gatherings in the town of Mold. The following 'prayers,' found on a loose sheet in the diary, express his religious position and philosophy of living.

> *Good God, Save me from a bankrupt Citizen*
> *And from one set up afresh*
> *Save me from the Power of Priests, from*
> *Apothecaries drugs; From him that hears Prayers*
> *Twice in a Morning and from him that*
> *Swears by his conscience*

> *The Prayer of Piovane*
> *The Prayer of the Author of Religion will*
> *Bless me in this life with peace of my*
> *Conscience, command of my affections*
> *The love of sufficient Friends, and I*
> *Shall be happy enough to pity Caesar*

Nehemiah Griffith was the elder of the diarist brothers and was living at Rhual with his mother. He wrote the first of his entries in 1715, at the age of twenty-four, when his mother was alive. He never married, although he had planned to do so, his courtship being cruelly ended by the accidental death of his intended, Miss Eliza Lloyd of Denbigh. He died aged forty-seven in 1738 and was buried in the family vault in Mold churchyard. He has been described as 'a man of taste and education, and to have decided literary tendencies, for he composed a poem *The Leek*.' Nehemiah was a churchman and was responsible for erecting the well-known obelisk which marks the site of the Hallelujah victory in 429 AD, on the field of Maes Garmon on his estate.

The accession of George, elector of Hanover (1660–1727) to the throne in 1714 was a peaceful transition from one regime to another, noted by one observer with the words: 'there appears not a dog to move his tongue against the Protestant succession.'[7] Although acknowledging political differences within the nation, verses copied by Nehemiah Griffith expressed his support for the Hanoverians and a desire for peace and unity.

Let the glass run over the Brim
Though Anna is gone
Think of her no more, think of her no more boys,
Great George is now come,
Toss away your bumpers to him.
Though the Feuds be so big

Twixt the Tory and Whig
And the mischief pursuing
Proves almost our ruin
We've a King will unite
Both High Church and Low.

Few gentry in Mold or in England and Wales shared his support for the German princes but it was left to Scottish Jacobites to rise up in support of the Old Pretender, James Stuart who admitted in September 1715 that 'I must confess my affairs have a very melancholy prospect.' Nehemiah had journeyed to visit his aunt in Broad Marston, Gloucestershire in July, before the rebel Jacobites crossed the border into England. He noticed that the Midland trained bands of militia were bracing themselves in preparation for the conflict.

When the Scottish Jacobite forces (joined by the few English supporters they could muster) reached Preston they were defeated and surrendered on 13 November. The diary entries of Nehemiah Griffith record the prevalence of rumours about the rebellion and reactions to its eventual outcome.

16 July My Aunt went to Wrexham.
17 July Returned with account of the Riot, and demolition of both Meeting Houses.
21 July Birmingham – the Warwickshire Trained Bands in Town.
20 Aug Jon Quarrel came with account of the Meeting House demolished at Llanfyllin.
26 Oct At Chester. The City Train'd Bands up.
12 Nov At Waen midnight this neighbourhood (Mold) was affrighted with the discharge of Canon which
    proved to be at Liverpool for General Will's surrounding the Rebels in Preston in Lancashire.

This was the night before the surrender and impatient to learn the outcome Nehemiah went to the scene of the action accompanied by Whig party members.

18 Nov. went to Preston arrived on 19. 'The rabble shift'd into the Church, mostly Highlanders. The Leaders in
    several houses(number of prisoners 1489).
20 Nov. About 200 marched under a guard to London …

County business, as well as national danger, occupied his attention in 1715, the year that his friend and neighbour, Mr Wynne of Tower, was to serve the office of High Sheriff. Nehemiah, with other gentlemen of the county, found himself waiting upon the judges and, in preparation for the event, went to Chester to purchase a sword, belt, spurs and a hat which he wore on 5 April at the spring Assizes.

5 April 'Waited on the Sheriff, a handsome appearance, between 20 and 30 gentlemen besides Clergy. The Judge dyned with Mr. Williams of Nerquis, 'Sherriff of Denbighshire'.

In September, he served on the grand jury and dined with them at the Red. On 18 October he was at the autumn Leet Court at Mold, possibly acting as agent to the lord of the manor. As always, the year had its quota of memorable events such as:

22 April The Great Eclipse.
23 April Went to Flint. Saw two Fellows Hanged, one of Newmarket for murdering his brother, the other of Nant Mawr for stealing; the former gibbetted.
16 June Went with Br and Sistrs to see the Engine (a 'Fire-Engine' for pumping water from mines).

Other activities recorded included coursing about Mold and Chester Races (23 April) and Fair (24 June). The diary ends on 5 December with a short list of 'Books Lent To Coz: Baker amongst which were 'Tale of a Tub', Rabelais 3d pt. of the 'Armours of French Kings.' To Mrs Lloyd of Pentrehobin Dryden's' Virgil'. To Mr Wm Brock, Archb of Dublin's Serm and Ans, and 'German Doctors'.

In 1726 Nehemiah was 35 and his brother, Thomas, 31, their sister Elizabeth had died in 1720. Nehemiah was chiefly resident at Broad Marston and Thomas at Rhual with his mother, Mary, sister, Anne, and aunt, M. Lloyd. Nehemiah chose to live at Broad Marston possibly to be a little nearer to London and Oxford, although this did not deter him from making long visits to Rhual. The brothers made up for their separation by regular correspondence and visits to each other. These extracts from Nehemiah's diary record his presence at Rhual for about thirty days in 1726, spread throughout the months from May to November. The purpose of these visits was to enable him to fulfil his familial duties to his mother and siblings and to attend to affairs relating to the Rhual estate. His amiable personality was always welcomed by gentry and clergy on his return to Moldsdale. Amongst the latter were the incumbents of Hawarden, Llanferres and Northop. When in residence at Rhual, Nehemiah appeared to go about as much as possible, his chief companions on these jaunts being his brother Thomas, the Wynnes of Leeswood and Tower and the Conways of Soughton. His sister was friendly with the wife and mother of vicar Hugh Lloyd and nearly always accompanied him to Mold vicarage or to his Lloyd cousins at Pentrehobyn. He recorded the visits and the preaching of Independent minister and author Thomas Baddy of Wrexham whom he said was 'always fashionably dressed and well mounted' and to whom the Rhual family paid a salary of £6 per annum.

Nehemiah was always involved in 'business interests' and on occasion acted as the agent for the Langley-Symmer family, absentee lords of the manor of Mold. On his visit in 1726, he took the opportunity to arrange 'taking a lease for mines of the Lords [of Mold who shared the mineral rights] enclosed lands admitting myself and if they please the other Agents Partners.' He was guest of the partners of the Gadlys Lead Smelting Company at Bagillt. Leisure activities he reported were as varied as 'Mr Brock of Broncoed here dressed for Cocking at Mold' on 2 July and, before his return to Broad Marston in November, participation in a raffle 'At Mold Red for Jane Jones's pound of Coffee.'

When Nehemiah Griffith died 17 May 1738, his sister Anne said of him, 'He was a person of great excellencies, had few faults. Sure never man died more regretted by all who knew him.'

By far the longest extent of the diary extracts of the Griffith brothers covered almost the whole of the calendar year of 1727. Written by Thomas Griffith,[9] the diary is a brief almost daily account of his activities. As a result of his financial independence he was free to indulge his fancies. The diary shows the author practising as a physician and, in the company of his merry companions, experiencing to the full what the town of Mold had to offer in a search for conviviality and fun. The diary combines this jolly portrait with one much more serious, that of the practice of a dedicated doctor whose first duty was to his patients' welfare. Dr Griffith's relative success was achieved by a mixture of earning their trust, his medical skill, social graces and acquaintance with the many foibles of his patients, most of whom he would have known all his life. A pattern of activity emerges which presents a fascinating glimpse of the opportunities available to him.

Thomas Griffith was a founder member of the Lion Club in Mold.[10]

January 24 Mr Wynne of Tower coz Ben Conway, and Mr Hugh Jones of Llanverres, din'd here, after dinner we went to the first meeting of our Club at the Red Lyon, wr. the following persons subscrib'd to the Articles. Mr John Wynne of Tower, cozn Jn Lloyd junior of Pentrehobin, Mr Jn Wynn of Leeswood, Mr Benj Conway of Souchton [Vicar of Northop], Mr Hugh Lloyd Vicar of Mold, Mr Hugh Jones Rector Llanverras & my self, I was appointed the

The Black Lion in Mold High Street, one of the inns where the Lion Club held its meetings.

Steward for the first month. The same night also enter'd Mr Robert Curate of Trythin & Mr Rawlins the Excise man.

This club was seen by Thomas and his companions as a way of enabling the gentlemen of the town to meet together regularly without imposing on their own households the burden to cater regularly for such large gatherings. Three of the founder members were young gentlemen about town and the others local clergy who welcomed the opportunity of conversing and dining within their own social group. The articles of association drawn up at the beginning laid down rules generally adhered to for the next twenty years. Members met every Tuesday from the end of September until the end of March from 2–6 p.m. and the rest of the year from 3–7 p.m. It was laid down that the meetings should take place at The Red, White and Black Lion to which was later added the Golden Lion and the dwelling houses of the parish clerk and local barber. The articles imposed rules which prevented members using it as a drinking and gaming club.

The club minutes are useful for providing the names of members. All local country gentlemen and clergy are listed but this did not inhibit the election of Mold tradesmen such as Walter Cahoun, apothecary; Rob Parry, sadler; Evan Evans, officer of excise; and others.

It would seem that from the outset, one of the purposes of the club was to arrange the apprenticing of poor boys. A list exists of apprentices nominated by members and the payment of stamp duty of £4 for each indenture paid out of club funds, money accumulated from fines and forfeitures. Between 1727 and 1740, the club enabled fifty-four poor boys to serve a seven-year term of apprenticeship to local tradesmen. The first boy recorded in the list was Thomas Griffith, who had been apprenticed to a tailor, but who was now disabled, having had his right hand cut off by reason of a mortification. He received three pounds towards setting himself up as a stocking merchant. The young man 'was nominated by the whole Club'. The following February, Dr Griffith and Mr John Wynne nominated 'Griffith Edwards (the son of Edward Griffith Pierce of Mold lately deceased, aged ten years)'. He was bound as an apprentice to the tailor John Hughes for seven years, commencing from 2 February 1727/8 as recorded on his indentures which were delivered to him on 4 February 1734/5. On this occasion, the sum of money laid out was £4.

Thomas and his family made visits to Chester at least twice a year to attend the races, inns and theatres. The city was the local metropolis and political centre for the Grosvenors and other families and a reputable provincial market for goods brought by sea from London and Ireland. It had its own assay office which may well have been supplied during this period with silver from George Wynne's mine at Halkyn. His entries for his visit there in the last week of April give some idea of their pleasures.

24   Mr Jn Wynne, Mr Roger Wynne, coz Jn Lloyd & I set for Chester Race. We Inn'd at the White Bear and stay'd there till Fryday noon … we liv'd merrily.

25   Mr George Wynne treated us all day. A large company of us at the Plume of Feathers wn the Company broke up – Mr George Wynne, Mr Brock, Jack Wynn, Jack Lloyd & I went to the Rose, drank one bottle then went to the White Lyon & drank 3 bowls of Arrack Punch. Mr Richard Wms, Mr Wm Wynne & one & Mr Wm Griffith there.

26   we went in the Evening to the Play – the Spanish Friar was acted. Jack Lloyd found a young fellow among the actors he knew at Oxford where he had taken his Bachelors Degree but upon a quarrel with his father left and married one of the Players.

27   we went in a body to Mr Brock's when we drank hard of punch.

28   we came towards home call'd at Harding then at Daniel's Ash. Then to Northop where we din'd drank a bowl of Punch so returned home.

The merry company returned to the city in November for the annual St Cecelia's day concert and ball.

22   Went to Leeswood about noon the Squire (George Wynne), Will Wynne, Jack Wynne, Jack Lloyd & myself set out for Chester, call'd at Broughton House – Inn'd at the Feathers, thence to the Assembly Room where the Consort & Ball were performed in honour of St Cecelia – Thence to their entertainment at Kemps – Sir Harry Bunbury & Mr Clark were stewards – that Night Sir Harry deliver'd his wand to Mr George Wynne ye Steward for the following year. There was a handsome appearance of Ladies & Gentlemen.

The entry for 26 May records the merriment of Thomas Griffiths and his companions.

With Mr J. Wynne & cozn Lloyd & Mr Roger Wynne I went to the Mill dam. We took abt 14 dozen trout but many very small. After we had din'd and walked with them to the Town took a glass at the Clerks were there came a queer Dog whom we persuaded to strip & run stark naked thro' the Town which he did for ½ a dozen of ale.

The next entry records the visit of Mr Baddy, the dissenting Minister from Wrexham to Rhual, who preached there.

The diary indicates that Thomas Griffith was a great lover of country sports, coursing, setting and hunting which he enjoyed all the year round in the company of his companions the Wynnes from Leeswood, Tower, and the clergy of Mold and Llanferres. He was fond of his dogs 'Ap 15 I had Colonel brought me from Leeswood, about a month old.' Whose pedigree is noted as 'Cupid the Dog (Mr Richard Williams) & Tiffy the Bitch (Mr John Wynne's Flora).'

The persons who command our attention most in the 1727 diary are George Wynne of Leeswood and his wife Margaret Lloyd. During this year Thomas Griffith's most frequent contacts, outside his own small family circle, were with the Wynnes at Leeswood. He was their physician and by the time the diary closes Mistress Margaret Wynne is the mother of six children, all under eight years of age. Three of these children died the following year 1728/9. In the year 1727, when she was pregnant with her sixth child, the diary entries reflect her concern for the health of her small children who were often sickly. Another important aspect of the friendship between Thomas Griffith and George Wynne is that the 'Squire' (the title by which the diarist refers to George Wynne in his entries) is attempting to embark on a political career and the doctor is chosen to act as one of his chief supporters. The appreciation of the Squire and his wife for the professionalism and friendship of the physician is referred to in the diary where he records their gifts and fees. The Squire could afford to be generous because of the income he was enjoying from a lead-mine in Halkyn which brought him undreamt of riches. This lead-mine was the horn of plenty, which made George Wynne a legendary figure for extravagance; it also brought him a treasure of inestimable worth, his bride Margaret Lloyd.

George was the elder son of John Wynne of Leeswood (who lived at Rhydycleifion in Nercwys, or quite often, in prison),[11] and of Jane, daughter of Humphrey Jones of Flint. George's mother died when he was an infant, bequeathing him the land on which the rich lode was later discovered. His widowed father remarried and his paternal grandmother, Elinor Wynne, arranged for George and his siblings to be made wards of Evan Lloyd of Lygan-y-Wern, Halkyn where George Wynne was raised with the Lloyd children, including his future wife, Margaret, and her brother, Hugh (1683–1749), vicar of Mold 1718–49. George's father, the cantankerous and litigious John Wynne, had sisters who enter the story as well. One of these, Alice, was the mother of the artist Richard Wilson (1713–82) and another was the mother of Catherine Jones of Colomendy who gave her cousin shelter in his last years. In a small field in Halkyn was discovered a rich lead lode which over a period of more than twenty years, made George Wynne richer by £300,00–£400,000.

The diary also records national events and their effect upon the local society in Mold.

22 June [1727] I went in the Morning to Souchton thence with Mr Ben Conway to Lygan y Wern and to the Lyon. King George II proclaimed at Northop.

30 June Receiv'd King George the II's first speech to his Parliament everything good.

George I had died unexpectedly on 11 June, aged 67, whilst on a visit to Hanover. The accession of his son George II has been described as a non-event and, as one historian put it, 'the corridors of power echoed with the heavy shoes of continuity.'[12] The continuity of the rule of Walpole was endorsed by the electorate in the customary general election which took place on a new accession to the throne. Elections for borough and county seats were the principal business in August and September when Sir Robert Walpole's party the Whigs were returned to power. Amongst those who sought to tread the corridors of power at Westminster was George Wynne of Leeswood.[13] Thomas Griffith gave the following account in his diary as he saw events unfold and hopes for victory rise and fall in the Summer campaign.

10 August Met Mr George Wynne at the Red Lyon in Mold betimes in the Morning from whence he, Mr Eyton, Mr Whittal, Mr Foulkes, Mr Robert Grosvenor, Mr Brock, Jack Lloyd, Jack Wynn, Dick Wynne & self went to Holywell wr there was a General Meeting of Gentlemen to fix upon their men for the ensuing election Sir Rogers's (Mostyn) Party at the Star, and Mr Puleston's at the Chester Arms. Sir Roger Mostyn and Mr George Wynne were declar'd on one side for the County & Borough and Mr Puleston of Emral & Lloyd of Leprog on the other. Tom Whitley of Aston drew his sword upon Mostyn of Maesmynnan. I stay'd in Town all night, went with Jack Wynn, Jack Lloyd, David Ffoulkes &c. to the Play –

25 August [electioneering] I went in the morning to Souchton and had a cold welcome by the Esqr. Went round Flint Wood, got all the votes we could. Thence to Flint. Went round some of the houses that night. We went to the house where Mrs Virginia Lloyd was and drank a bottle of wine with her Ladyship. I lay with Mr Wynne at the George.

26 August Went round the Town making interest (i. e. canvassing) Mr Edd & Jn Pennant, Mr Tom Hughes, Jack Pennant & myself set out – it was light by Jack Hughes in Northop, thence to Leeswood, & at 4 next morning set out for Wrexham found Mr Watkin Williams (the Tory Jacobite from Wynnstay) at the George and settled some affairs there. Thence to Gwersillt drank a bottle with Mr Shakerley – thence to Caergwryle. Mr Wynne & Mr David Pennant went to Bryn Yorkin & din'd there with Mr Salisbury Lloyd (the opposition candidate). Made what Interest we could at Caergwrley thence all home.

28 August In the morning set out to join Mr George Wynne which we did on Souchton Mountain. Thence in a very large Body to Flint where the Poll began about noon which continued with great heat & violence till the Thursday – Mr Wynne Introduc'd me to Sir Roger Mostyn who was extremely obliging &c

Thursday August 31st The Poll was closed at Flint and Stood thus

George Wynne Esqr – 675
Salisbury Lloyd Esqr – 313

Notwithstanding which vast majority one of the Bailiffs influenc'd by promises & Threats of the Party had the impudence to return Mr Lloyd as duly Elected & the other return'd Mr Wynne. The pretence was that Mr Lloyd had a Majority of Resident Burgesses but even that was false being out poll'd in them some scores.[14] I came that Night to Leeswood, the Monday Night I lodged at Llygan y wern, Tuesday Night at Halkin, Wednesday Night at Flint , Thursday night at Leeswood.

At the beginning of September Thomas was busy canvassing for Sir Roger Mostyn in the election for the county member of Parliament.

5 September
Mr Wynne, of Tower came to us, to Leeswood in the morning – The Esqr. , &c I set out about the parish to gather

Votes for Sir Roger Mostyn. Went round Nerquis, Trythin, Beestree & Argoed, came last to Mr Whitmore where we drank a bottle, & thence to our Club at Mold.

6 September
Mr G Wynne to Mr Wynne of Tower – breakfasted with me; we set out visited Gwernafield, Gwysaney &c I thence to Souchton & thence to Llwynegrin, saw Mr Evan Lloyd there – took Mr Whitmores case ... refused a Fee – & came to Leeswood

7 September
In the afternoon I set out with Esqr G. W. & Mr Richd Wynne for Denbigh – just call'd & took one Dram here, then over the Mountain & lay at the Crown in Denbigh that night.

12 September
In the morning set out wth Mr Geo Wynne went & spoke again to several voters.

13 September
In the morning went to Mold where a larger Company Met & accompany'd Mr Geo Wynne to the Election at Flint which this day began between Sir Roger Mostyn Bart. & Thos Puleston Esqr I came home at Night call'd at Bryncoed.

16 September
The Election at Flint ended thus: Sir Roger Mostyn – 431, Mr Puleston – 301.

With the end of the borough and county elections, life returned to normal – '19 September Went a Coursing with Mr Brock & Mr Roger but one Hare killed'.

On Monday the 2/3 of October the Court Leet was held at Mold. My Brother by reason of his Indisposition was not there for which reason I was Manager. Mr George Wynne & his Brother, Jack Lloyd, Mr Wynne of Tower, Mr Brock, Mr Edward Jones, Clomendu, Mr Foulkes, Jack Hughes, Mr Lewis Jnr, Mr Roberts, Mr Thos Wynne &c were there.

4 October

Tŷ Mawr (the tall building on the right), High Street, Mold, the town house of Sir George Wynne, now demolished.

In the morning went to Leeswood din'd there – In Afternoon Mr G W came along with me to Broncoed. The old Gentleman of Tower came with us when we All got drunk.

10 October

I spoke to Mr G W about the Coronation that he should celebrate it at Mold. The which he agreed & order'd Matters accordingly that night.

11 October

Went betimes to Town thence to Leeswood engag'd the Ladies to appear at the Ball where Mr George Wynne entertained most of the Parish Gentlemen & others with a Dinner. In the Evening to the Ball at his new large house in Mold [Tŷ Mawr] were there was a handsome appearance of Ladies – Mrs Wynne, Mrs Ann Wynne Senr & Junr, Mist. Jane Lloyd, Mist. Let & Betty Eyton, Miss Peg & Nancy Brock, Miss Betty Foulkes, Miss Doll Lloyd &c we danced all night.

11 December

I breakfasted & dined at Leeswood Mst Wynne fell in labour and abt 2 o'clock in the afternoon was brought to bed of a son (the child was baptised Lloyd 26 December and buried 3 Jan. 1728/9). I came with Jack Wynne to Tower Went to the Vicarage and Thence to the Black Lyon [16] My brother came home.

19 December

Went in the morning wth Brother to the Black Lyon in Mold were several met at Mr G. Wynne's Invitation & concerted matters relating to his late Election &c.

There is no mention of Christmas although the diary entries continue to the end of December.

Many entries in the diary of Thomas Griffith concern his patients and reveal his care and treatment for them at Rhuallt or in their own homes.

January

7 one Robt Price of Trythin came to consult me – prescribed medicines.

12 ordered Jn Price to take his vomit wch work'd well

15 sent for to old Mrs Lloyd of the Vicarage who was much indisposed. Made up some things

16 Call'd a.m. Vicarage old Lady better.

19 Gave J. W[ynne] old lady recover'd pretty well.

February

3 Souchton Mst K. Lloyd much better – went to Bryn Griffith found Tony Williams very weak & bad of a cold.

13 At vicarage old Lady pretty much out of order prescribed paid a guinea.

17 Order'd a physick for Mist K. Lloyd.

March

2   In the morn went to with Mr Coitmore to Skiviog to his sister who was not well din'd with his mother an old woman of 100 yrs age perfect in all her senses feed 10s. 22 Mrs Lloyd of Vicarage died, She went off very unexpected – went to Tower left 2 purgings for Mr Wm Jones – I went to Wain found Mr Thos Wynne in great torture & willing to take something to ease him, prescribed. 29 Northop saw Robt Edds order'd him some things.

April

1   Between 10 & 11 at night their servant [from Suchton] came with an acct. that Mist Mary Lloyd was taken very ill. I went there found her extremely bad, shrieked out & complained much of an intolerable anxiety &c I endeavoured to bleed her but failed. Laudanum was the only thing that seem'd to have any effect. I stay'd there that night & almost all the Sunday. Fee'd 2 guinea he visited her again on 2,3,5,7 – Mr Matthews visited Thomas Griffith who prescribed.

10   Mr Wynne of Leeswood feed me 2 guineas pt I had prescribed his brother & old John Price – I was sent for to Margt. Tower but found her too bad to prescribe anything to the purpose.

12   Went to Plas Onn Mrs Coitmore not at all well ordered her a purge.

19   Went to Plas Isa prescribed.

30   Att noon I was sent for to Tower where I found Mr Wynn indisposed I gave him a vomit.

May

1   Went in the morning to Leeswood saw Tom Lloyd who was but so – his case seems to be Decay after long Debauch. I ordered him a purge.

13   At one Edd. Evans at Herseth were his sister Mary Evans was very far with the dropsy prescribed. Fee'd. 27 Sister was bled in the foot.

June

5   Was sent for to Mr Wynne of Leeswood.

6   Summoned to Leeswood were Dr Hall came. I had made up a compressing … at Leeswood 6, 7, 8, 10.

15   In the Morning Jes of Caisey came here to consult abt his boy yt was violently taken with a fever.

28   At Tower; went to Trythin Mr Roger Wynn with me to see a sick woman.

July

15   I was sent for from whence to the Fron were I found Miss Kathy Williams seiz'd with a fever. I bled here & gave her some drops of laudanum.

16   Miss Kath somewhat better.

August

5   At Souchton Mrs K Lloyds all most well. Mst M Lloyd bad with Hystericks.

7   Sent for to Leeswood where I found Mr Jackey and Miss Peggy both seiz'd sharply with some fever – I first apprehended it to be the small pox but found it after to be an intermittently fever. Mr Jones Apothecary from Denbigh was there who I order'd to bleed 'em both.

9   While I was at dinner in the vicarage messages came for me to go to Leeswood where the children were bad. Miss Peggy was extremely sick with a pain in her side which happily was soon remov'd with a fomentation of Vinegar & laudanum.

11   Leeswood where I found Mrs Wynne just arrived from Buxton & in great distress abt the children – I stay'd there all night and most of next day.

15   Leeswood – I was for to Llwynegrin were Robt Williams & his wife were both sick of the distemper

18   I was fetch'd by Mr Wm Barker of Gadlys to his brother Mr Thos Barker where I went and found him very much out of order, particularly with a violent pain in his face &c order'd him a vomit &c stay'd there all night order'd him what I thought proper next day, was fee'd 2 5s piece & came away.

October

28   In the evening I was sent for to Plas Isa gave Mr Foulkes a Glyster & order'd a prescription for the Gravel with which he was much afflicted.

December

2   About 6 I gave an emetic to Mr George Wynne. It lay above 2 hours in his stomach but afterward work'd very well. I lay there that night.

10   I was sent for to Leeswood I gave Mr Wynne another Puke & stayed there.

29   I was sent for to Leeswood to Mr George Wynne who I found a little Feverish only presumed occasion'd by his Teeth and a severe cold.

Thomas Griffith's diary is full of prescriptions which he prepared and administered himself. The medicines he gave to his patients were made up of potions flavoured with conserve of red roses, honey, lavender water and other concoctions. Often used were liquorice, marshmallow, parsley, comfrey and rhubarb. Some of the most active ingredients came from South America e.g. Jalap root – a violent purgative which caused considerable pain. Impecanuana, a small plant from Brazil, was given to George Wynne as a 'puke'. Other ingredients were mineral derivatives such as dilute hydrochloric acid, and calomel (mercurous chloride). Other treatments included bleeding, the application of leeches and blistering.

The third diary which contributes to our understanding of the history of the town of Mold is the day-book of Reverend Hugh Lloyd (1688–1749).[15] This is a middle-sized book of nearly 300 pages in which he entered his personal accounts. He was an ordained priest of the Church of England and served as the vicar of Mold. As already noted, he was something of a pluralist and his income was therefore above average for a Welsh clergyman. Although he did not pay his curates in Mold more than £20 a year, his own income from clerical offices, parochial tithes and surplice fees was in the region of £300. His day-book reveals that he received other income from his own property, the sale of his garden produce and from interest on money he lent. One item even records his purchase of a lottery ticket. Later in life, he managed the family estate at Halkyn and there is also a record of money from the parish of Somerford (in Cheshire?) which may refer to income from tithes.

Hugh Lloyd's background was typical of many eighteenth century Church of England parsons. He was the second son of Evan Lloyd, JP (1656–1724), of Lygan-y-lan. 'My father dyed at Rhewl, November 21 1724' and his wife, Elizabeth Hughes, 'My mother dyed March 27 1727.' Hugh's family were of the minor gentry and of sufficient standing for his elder brother to be High Sheriff of Flintshire in 1720. The family were fortunate enough to become financially comfortable through the exploitation of lead mines in the area. Hugh went up to Christ Church Oxford, matriculated in 1709, graduated in 1712 and received his masters degree in 1716. After a year as the incumbent of Llanasa, he moved to Mold in 1717/8 where he remained until his death in 1749.

The account book begins in 1728 and continues in some detail until 1744. Naturally his record of events and personalities is presented differently from that contained in the diary of Thomas Griffith. The advantage of Hugh Lloyd's record is that it covers a longer period and is more informative of life in Mold. The book does not deal with the day-to-day household accounts of Mold vicarage. If such a ledger ever existed, the accounts would have been entered into it by the mistress of the house, Lucy Lloyd, whom Hugh married in 1720 when he was 32 and she was over 40. No child of the marriage survived, although one son, John, was baptised in Mold on 14 March 1721/2 and buried on 19 May 1722. The account book contains no expression of personal feelings and these were probably recorded in papers long lost. Hugh Lloyd does however enliven his accounts with miscellaneous memoranda of a more masculine nature, for he was a man of business who loved to be in his counting house recording, calculating and speculating. In his ledger, there are pages of detail on the contents and arrangement of his cellar and brew-house, the collection of tithes, the payment for the repair and maintenance of old buildings and the erection of new ones.

Although these observations may give the impression that he was hard and miserly, the opposite is probably true. There are countless examples of his generosity and concern for friends and family. In order to perform these acts of kindness he would have pleaded that he was a careful manager. The account book contains a variety of memoranda of visits to gentry houses in Mold and elsewhere in Flintshire and Denbighshire, and Hugh Lloyd's affection for and loyalty to various individuals amongst whom was the family of the landscape painter Richard Wilson. In addition, he provides incidental information on life in Mold in the first half of the eighteenth century which is not available elsewhere.

The extracts given below are selected from the account book and other documents to illustrate his life as a member of a gentry family in Moldsdale and his own special connections to members of his own profession, the clergy of the dioceses of St Asaph and Bangor, and his parishioners at Mold.

> 1716 March 5th Memorandum: That upon this day, being the 5th of March, 1716 A. D. I Hugh Lloyd was instituted in the Vicarage of Mold. I found in the vicarage house at Mold 2 bedsteads, 1 oval table, 6 wainscot chairs, 2 little square tables, 1 settle, a grate in the kitchen, a grate in the parlour, in the kitchen chamber, a stillage in the cellar, a dresser and 3 shelves.

The terrier of 1710[16] provides additional information stating that, this furniture was 'freely bestowed upon the Vicarage of Mold when it was built in 1684 at the sole cost and charge of Mrs Anne Davies relict of Robert Davies, Esq. , formerly of Gwysaney. It measured 'twelve yard in length within, from one end to the other, and six yards in breadth …' Another terrier of 1732 displays Hugh Lloyd's passion for building and describes the vicarage as, 'One mansion house well slated consisting of four bays of buildings one of which containing a brew house a parlour a lodging room & garret was built by ye present Vicar as was also a little buttery & closet & coal house in the year 1719'.

In 1726, Hugh Lloyd added a bay of farm buildings in addition to those erected by the Reverend Morgan Jones (1691–1706). Also recorded in the terrier were 'Two gardens and an orchard containing one statute acre formerly called Croft y Vicar.'

> 1730 28 Sept Pd the miner for sinking the well 6 days.
> 1740 10 March Planted 444 plant in 6 asparagus beds joyning the orchard.

Another programme of unspecified building and repairs to the vicarage is itemised in the accounts for 1732/3. Over 100,000 bricks and 4,000 slates were used. The brew house was probably slated and possibly enlarged and installed with a 'furnace in the new brew house' with vaults. The management of this brew house has a prominent place in the account book which is used as a record of the contents of the cellar and dates and additions of the stock of beer, cider, wines and spirits, rum, brandy. He notes gifts from friends and his brewing activities. A furnace, water butt, bottles, flasks, casks, baskets, barrels bings and stills all find their place in old and new cellars and the brewing and bottling of beer 'elder wine by cosn Lan 1734 – pink raisin wine – maligo raisin wine 20 gallon cask and supplies were sent to Llangynhafal.'

Details of the engagement of servants are noted although it is more than likely that more were employed and that Mrs Lloyd would have had her own servants.

> 1729 Margaret Jerman began her service at £3 a year. She was in service from 27 May 1729 to 27 May1736.
> 1733 5 Jan. Betty began her service at £1:15s a year and received an increase of 5s. a year in 1738.
> 1733 15 Oct. John Wms began his service at £3 pr ann. & 'old cloaths.'
> 1736 22 May. Edward Peter began his service at £3. 10 0 & old cloaths he received an increase of 10s in March 1736/7.

Hugh Lloyd took advantage of his visits to Chester, London and elsewhere to purchase fashionable household goods similar to those of the neighbouring gentry.

> 1726 May eight blew & white tea cups & a bowl from London
> 1728/9 6 Jan for 6 Tea dishes & saucers 2s. 6d.
> 1729/30 For 2 gross of pipes 4s.
> 1731 For 12 yds of China for the screen.
> 1732 2 Sep for ½ tobacco, 8 pipes 2s carriage from Chester 6s
> 1733 17 Nov for a hive of bees from Lanverres 5s.'

The income of most clergy depended to a great extent on the produce of the land by way of tithes and farming of the glebe (land which attached to the parish for the benefit of the clergy). Lists of crops and tithes are given in some detail and include wheat, barley, oats, 'pease', mixed corn.

> 1728 28 May The Black cow went to the bull.
> 1728 10 Aug sowed turnips after a good crop of bean.
> 1728 29 Oct The grey filly came here. Got by Mr Peter Whitely's grey horse; foaled May 21st 1728; measured 14 hands.
> 1728 3 Nov Sold at Chester three turkeys at 1s 10d, four at 1s 8d one at 1s. 6d.
> 1728 6 Dec set two quarts of beans in the rent plot in ye upper garden.

The usual place to find details of parish life are in the minutes of the vestry and churchwardens accounts. Another source is the returns made to the bishop and rural dean on the occasion of their visitations. Hugh Lloyd, however, appeared to use his account book to record miscellaneous transactions and events for which he was responsible.

1732 25 Dec Gave the 3 lads yt sang the carol in Church even 1s.

1732/3 Jan 1 Gave the Ringers 1s Gave the Bellman & Fidler 2s.

1734 July 7 Pay'd Mr Harrison singing master to this day & 1s over £1 1s.

1735–44 The buying of flannel for making clothes for the poor

1730/1 20 Jan To the 17 prisoners whipt att the new market att Mold 4s.

1731 21 May At Fire engine at Hardin 6s. att Potter 6s. for Potts 2s.

1733 31 July Confirmation at Mold Bp Tanner.[17] Candidates came from the parishes of Eastyn (Hope), Llanarmon, Llanverrres, Halkyn, Northop parishes. The number confirmed 521. The Bishop gave a Guinea to the poor & half a guinea to the singers.

Before regular census returns began in 1801, the clergy made returns to the diocese in answer to specific queries made by the bishop.

1738 15 July It was computed that there was of families in the townships of Mold 150, Fron 018, Leeswood 044, Broncoed 011, Herseth 024, Argoed 030, Lwynegrin 020, Brychainllt & Trebeirdd 006, Gwernaffield 060, Bistre 055, Hendrebissa 012, Gwysaney 034. [total 464 families]

Expulsion from the offices of the Church was the ultimate penalty imposed upon those who persisted in acting contrary to its rules – fornication being the most frequent offence. The penalty banned the offender from receiving communion, being buried in church ground, or having their will proved in the Church court. An example recorded in his day-book by Hugh Lloyd is: '1733 Dec 12, John Wms, Eliz Hughes, Mary Edds, Mary Parry, Mary Pulford under a decree of Excommunication as by General process a Court held at Wrexham May 5 at St Asaph Sunday May 17 1733.'

Hugh Lloyd was one of the leading clerics of the diocese of St Asaph, a member of the cathedral body known as the chapter. Its members were canons who occupied stalls in the chancel. Leading members of the chapter had further ancient offices conferred upon them and in 1725, Lloyd was appointed prebendary of Meifod and sacristan of St Asaph Cathedral.[18] The cathedral chapter met regularly in the Chapter House to administer its affairs and when necessary played their traditional role in approving the nomination of a new diocesan bishop. Hugh Lloyd was rewarded with a stipend of £74 per annum for life for holding the office of prebendary of Meifod. Of equal financial benefit was his enjoyment of the parish of Llangynhafal, in the vale of Clwyd. In order to qualify to hold simultaneously the livings of Mold and Llangynhafal, he had to reside part of the year in each parish. It was his custom to go to Llangynhafal for four months of the year in the spring and early summer and return to Mold for the rest of the year. It was therefore necessary to employ assistant curates in both places. He may have held another clerical office at Somerford, possibly through the influence of his friend, George Shakerley, archdeacon of Wells. If this was correct, his annual income form clerical stipends and tithes may have been *c.*£500.

Extracts from the account book.

1729 6 July at Bishop Sherlock's primary Visitation at Denbigh Procuraters for Llangynhafal 6s. 8d.

1729 17 July at St Asaph first visit to Bishop Hares. Butler 1s. Footman 1s others 6. 2s. 6d

1730 18 Dec Mr Lewis inducted to Halkyn by me.

1731 16 Dec St Asaph Chapter choosing Dr Thos Tanner Bp. 2s. 6d.

1730/1 16 Jan For making my cassock & trimmings David Tailor 4s.

1729 Aug 17 We were both at Somerford

1736 Due from Somerford Chapel Lady Day 1736 £150

1738 From Mr Shakerley Somerford Stipend (Lady Day) £210.

1738 17 March from Somerford chapel by Mr Ed Parkington £200.

1728 4 July Pd Mr Jones the Curate for the Qtr due Midsum £2 10s. (There were 2 curates Roger Jones and John Jones.)

1730/1 24 Dec Pd ¾ Qtr Salary to the Curate of Llangynhafal £15
1740 5 Jan Lent Mr Rogers upon his note £20.

Hugh Lloyd is chiefly remembered for building and endowing the charity school at Mold. In the visitation returns of 1731 he informed the bishop that 'our curate did keep School, but is now disabled being lame of his right hand that he can't write.' The situation had improved in 1738 when the vicar acknowledged that 'there is no Public or charity school endow'd but there are children taught to read & write & are instructed in the Principles of the Christian Religion.' Hugh Lloyd decided that it was time to remedy the situation and at a vestry held in the parish church 5 August 1739 'it was agreed and consented with the approbation of the bishop of Asaph that the Rev Mr Hugh Lloyd, Vicar of Mold, shall have the liberty to build and erect a Charity School in a waste place 45 feet, in length and 30 foot in breadth in the north-west side of the Churchyard next to the garden of the Vicarage.'

The foundation stone was laid on 21 September and the account book records a total cost of £116 11s 4d and the entry, '1739 Sept 21 Recd from my wife towards school house £10.'

In his report to the bishop in 1745, Lloyd presented a summary of his achievement

There is a Charity School house built & thirty poor children taught to read, mostly at the expense of the Vicar, who endowed it with eleven pounds a year for ever paid quarterly. Towards the erecting of the said schoolhouse & purchasing the rent charge the Vicar paid £390. Private benefactions £53. The children are instructed in the Principles of the Church of England & are duly brought to Church upon Sundays, Wednesdays, Fridays & Saturdays. The offertory money by the consent & order of Bishop Maddox is laid out quarterly towards their clothing.[19]

In 1744, Lloyd took the opportunity of purchasing the house called Trefriew from the brothers John and Anthony Barker, trustees of their late brother Thomas. The Barker brothers were agents to the Smelting Company at Gadlys, Bagillt and well acquainted with Hugh Lloyd. He bought it to secure an endowment of £11 a year for the charity school and to add to and consolidate land already owned by the church in the vicinity. Although when purchased Trefriew was a small house, it was enlarged and occupied by him although he did not buy it to replace the vicarage that had been built by Anne Davies in 1684. In 1847 Trefriew was sold to the church to become the vicarage. On Lloyd's death, Robert Wynne of Garthewin came to live there.

Hugh Lloyd knew the parents of Richard Wilson (1712/3–82), the landscape painter, whose father, John Wilson (d. 1728), was a clergyman in Montgomeryshire, and his mother, Alice Wynne of Leeswood (1684–1756), returned to live in Mold. Alice Wilson's nephew, George Wynne of Leeswood, was a churchwarden. Alice Wilson chose to live close to the church at Pendre, and was thus able to renew her acquaintance with Hugh Lloyd who was just four years her junior. It was only natural that he sought to assist her in making provision for her children and directing them into suitable occupations. The impression given by entries in the account book is that Hugh Lloyd, who was often absent from Mold, looked upon Alice Wilson as a kind of unofficial curate or church-warden. His wife is barely mentioned in the daybook, and

Richard Wilson, line engraving from a portrait by Anton Raphael Mengs c.1752–6.

was clearly not involved in day-to-day church matters. It was Alice Wilson whom he trusted with his business affairs.[20] No doubt Hugh Lloyd, together with George Wynne, was included in a family conference when the future career of young Richard Wilson was discussed. His talent and inclination had suggested to them his ability to pursue an artistic career. One of his first works is dated in 1728, before he went up to London, and is a portrait of his father. An early source observed that 'the walls of his father's house … were covered with rude attempts in outline: a burnt stick was his pencil.' It was decided that the young Richard should go to London to be apprenticed to the artist Thomas Wright for six years. Hugh Lloyd kept in touch with him and visited him in the metropolis whenever he was there. Sir George Wynne had more than one London house in which to entertain his kinsman. The account book records the following entries relating to the Wilson family:

> 5 Feb 1729. Dick Wilson went to Mr Wright to London.
> 17 Oct 1731. Delivered to Mr Wright to give Dick Wilson 5s.
> 1731. Pd Dr Griffith my subscription to Mr Wright's Prints 10s. 6d.
> 1731 7 Nov. a letter from Mr Vaughan & Mr Dick Wilson 9d.
> 1732 9 Jan. Mr John Wilson [Richard's brother who later lived at Llanferres] was ordered supernumerary to Wales Middle Collector [excise].
> 1739 9 Oct. Gave Mr Dick Wilson by Mrs Wright 10s 6d.
> 1736. Pd Mrs Wilson Clergymen's Sons Charity £5 (The Sons of Clergy?)
> 1736 3 Oct. To Mr Rich. Wilson at Bedford Coffee House Covent Garden
> 1737 25 Nov. for a letter from D. Wilson £1. 1s.
> 1737. Recd a letter from Mr R. Wilson with a bill upon Sir G Wynne for £2 15s.

After minor success as a portrait painter, Richard Wilson went to Italy and developed an excellent reputation as a landscape painter. Amongst his patrons was the young Sir Watkin Williams Wynne (1749–89), fourth baronet of Wynnstay. On his return from Italy, Wilson was appointed librarian to the Royal Academy. His health declined in the 1770s and he returned to live with his cousin Miss Catherine Jones at Colomendy, close to his brother John. He died in 1782 and was buried in Mold churchyard where he is commemorated.

Vicar Hugh Lloyd was twelve years older than his brother-in-law George Wynn who had married his sister Margaret Lloyd in 1720. Relations were cordial and there are numerous references to George Wynne in the account book.

> 1728 16 July To Mr Wynne's Coachman yt brought the Salmon 2s.
> 1732 3 Aug At Leeswood (eating of venison) 3s.
> 1732 Sir George Wynne's Summer House finished & six pictures put up each £100: Lady Moreland, Nel Gwyn, Lady St John, Mol Travers, Lady Bellairs, Mrs Mag Hughes.

Unfortunately, Hugh Lloyd does not mention the large mansion house, attributed to Francis Smith of Warwick, which had probably been completed *c.*1724–6 before the grounds had been laid out under the influence of Stephen Switzer. The architectural historian Hubbard describes it as being 'of eleven bays, with a third storey above the main cornice. There were moreover, side wings of no fewer than thirteen bays each, with cupolas and three-bay pediments.' Moses Griffith sketched the house and grounds *c.*1770 before the mansion was drastically reduced in 1798.

The magnificent white gates, 100 feet in length, are attributed to Robert Davies of Croes Foel, Esclusham, near Wrexham, and date from about 1726. They survive in situ, but the black gates were removed and now form the entrance to Tower. The pleasure grounds, laid out by Switzer, had features such as the summer house mentioned by Hugh Lloyd, a garden pavilion, grotto, ice house, kitchen garden, ornamental water garden, round ponds, movable menagerie, statue, sundial, drives, paths, bridges and the river Terrig.[21]

All this display of wealth and splendour came to an end in the space of a few years. Lady Margaret Wynne

Wrought iron gates, Leeswood, erected by Sir George Wynne, painting by Moses Griffith.

died in 1743 and Sir George Wynne died an undischarged bankrupt in 1756.

Hugh Lloyd displayed more restraint and discretion in his spending habits and what he accumulated he used wisely. His account book shows that he fitted into the more modest social life of his neighbours. He went 'to John Jones's cocking,' and regularly paid his dues at the Lion Club, and as well as visiting the Wynne's of Leeswood, he went to Rhual on occasions. He noted in his account book the secrecy of the marriage of Dr Thomas Griffith with the widow Jane Mostyn of Cilcain.

4 June 1731 At Hartsheath giving the servant to my ladydship 3s. 6d. (Lady Gwyllym)
10 June 1731 At Rhual fishing 3s. 6d.
21 April 1733 Dr Griffith own'd his wedding & appeared with his Lady at Mold Church
17 July 1733 Dr Griffith's son born at Kilken.

The Black Gates and lodge at Leeswood. These gates now are now located at the entrance to Tower.

Memorial to William Wynne of Tower by Rysbrack in Mold Parish Church.

Lloyd was particularly close to 'Mr William Wynne (of Tower) who was a fellow of All Souls 1722,' the chaplain to Bishop Tanner and rector of Llanfechain (1735–76), a friend of Thomas Pennant and the author of his own epitaph.

Lloyd was also a frequent visitor to Gwersyllt Isa in the parish of Gresford, the home of Geoffrey Shakerley, Esq., the son of Sir Geoffrey Shackerley of Hulme, Cheshire, who had bought Gwersyllt in order to live near his old Royalist comrade-in-arms, Colonel John Robinson of Gwersyllt Hall. In 1723, Geoffrey Shackerley had been a member of the Cycle of the White Rose alongside Thomas Eyton of Leeswood. In 1748, Frances Shackerley married Sir Watkin Williams Wynn of Wynnstay, the leader of the Welsh Jacobites. The Reverend Geoffrey Shackerley, a contemporary, was archdeacon of Wells, and Hugh acknowledged his long friendship in his will by the bequest of 'my Gold Tompin watch and gold chain and seal and my two large silver cups and cover and all the china dishes and plate given my by his father and the silver half pint the gift of his Aunt Jones to my wife.'

Anne Shackerley daughter of George Shackerley was born at Gwersyllt May 12 1710.
1729 A great sheep came from Mr Geof Shakerley.
8 Dec 1729 Both Mr Shakerley's pictures came here from Mr Fellows.
24 April 1731 sat the last time to Mr Fellows for my Picture to Mr Geoff Shackerley.
16 Jan 1723 Mr Shakerley made a present of the repeating clock.
31 March 1732 Miss Anne Shackerley was born.
20 Sept 1733 at Winstay.

Hugh Lloyd's closest friend was Dr Robert Wynne (d. 1743) of Garthewin, in the parish of Llanfair Talhaearn, a descendant of a Civil War Royalist family and Jacobite sympathisers. He wrote a 'Discourse on the Martyrdom of King Charles I.' Wynne was a competent lawyer and became a fellow of Jesus College Oxford, chancellor of the diocese of St Asaph (1690–1743) and rector of Gresford. His son, Robert Wynne (1698–1771), was a barrister and executor of the will of Hugh Lloyd. His grandson, Robert Wynne (1732–98), was a favourite of Hugh Lloyd's, as was his sister, Diana, to whom he left his largest silver coffee pot. The grandson Robert wrote an entertaining diary (now lost) 'which was in some ways startling, for scarcely a death was noted which was not attributed to hard drinking! The diarist recorded banquets, baptisms and funerals with equal gusto and seems to have been a great frequenter of all three, often when attending the latter taking particular note of the weight of the coffin!'[22] In his will, Hugh Lloyd stipulated that Robert Wynne and his successors should live at Trefriew on condition that the rent charge of £11 per annum was paid to the charity school.

Jan 1729/30 Jan At Leeswood wth Csn. Wynne's Garthewin 5s.
6 Sept 1731 at Garthewin to Mrs Davies housekeeper 3s. Butler 2s. Groom 2s. Chamber maid 2s. 6d. Kitchen maid 5s. at Llanerch maid & man 2s.
11 July 1734 for ninepin's to Garthewin's boy 1s.
1740 Memorandum let Garthewin house at seven pd year rent clear of all taxes to Thomas Jones Joyner to enter May Day 1741 Recd. 6d earnest.

Hugh Lloyd made his will on 10 February 1747[23] which was witnessed by his curates, William Rogers and John Williams, and his physician, Nathaniel Cahoun, of Mold. After his death in 1748/9 he was interred on 19 March in accordance with his instructions 'to be buried in the most private manner between the hours of one and three in the morning and not before the fourth day after my decease and carried by my tenants to the Church and Vault under the Charity School in the Church yard of Mold.' His will, which was proved in the Prerogative Court of Canterbury, 30 December 1749, revealed that he had property in the parish of Bury in Sussex, land in Towyn (Abergele) and a house and land in Gresford. In Mold, in addition to Trefriew, he owned houses and gardens in Bedlam and others which were in the tenure and occupation of Mrs Wilson and the one adjoining it where dwelt the barber, Robert Griffith, as well as other holdings. His beneficiaries included his brother Richard Lloyd, sister Mary and nieces and nephews of himself and wife Lucy. His serving-maid, Margaret Jerman, received an annual pension of £4 10. He left instructions that his executor was to discharge 'the sum of two hundred pounds towards clearing and discharging the present incumbrance upon the estate of Carreg Lwyd in the parish of Mold purchased for the use of the Free school of Ruthin with the right of nomination of one boy descended from the family of the Lloyd's of Segroit or Lloyd's of Llanynys.' He also left the sum of £20 each to the incumbent and churchwardens of the parishes of Llanasa, Llangynhafal and Gresford with which they were to purchase lands from which the rents and profits were to be 'paid yearly to a schoolmaster or schoolmistress for teaching the poor children to read and repeat the Church Catechism etc.' His wife Lucy died and was buried in Mold 24 June 1746.

Notes

1. Michael Powell Siddons (ed) 'Visitations by the Herald in Wales', *The Harleian Society,* new series, vol 14, 1996.
2. D.W. Howell, *Patriarchs and Parasites: The Gentry of South-West Wales in the eighteenth century,* Cardiff, 1986.
3. For list of Mold freeholders in 1701, see FRO D/DM/3–4.
4. C. Price, *The English Theatre in Wales*, Cardiff, 1948, pp.62–3.
5. FRO D/HE.
6. The Diary of Nehemiah Griffith, Esq., for the years 1715, *Chester Archaeological and Historic Society,* new series, vol xix–xv, 1908–9, FRO D/HE/430.
7. A. Crichton (ed), *The Life and Dairy of Lieut. Col. J. Blackadder*, Edinburgh, 1824, p.449.
8. The Diary of Nehemiah Griffith of Broad Marston, Campden, Gloucestershire for the year 1720. FRO D/HE/431.
9. The Diary of Thomas Griffith of Rhual, 1729, FRO D/HE/433.
10. Q.R.H. Dodd, The Lions Club of Mold, 1726–*c.*1742, Ystrad Alun pp.1–14, and 'Minutes of Club Meetings …' FRO MF/404/1, copy from Cardiff City Library.
11. Rosa Baker, 'Brief Lives: Margaret Wynne of Leeswood and Her Children' *Clwyd Historian/Hanes Bro Clwyd* 2003, Spring 2–6.
12. J. Hoppit, *A Land of Liberty England 1689–1727,* Oxford, 2000.
13. H. Taylor, 'Sir George Wynne, Baronet, MP, Flint District Boroughs 1727–41, *Flintshire Historical Society Publications,* vol ix, 1922, and P.D.G. Thomas, 'Sir George Wynne and the Flint Borough Elections of 1727–41, *FHSP,* vol xx, 1962.
14. P.D.G. Thomas, *Politics in Eighteenth-Century Wales,* Cardiff, 1984, p.41.'Lloyd had property in Flint town, but Wynne controlled the borough machinery, and his electoral preparations included the admission of several non-resident burgess there … At the close of the poll, Wynne had a majority of 685 to 312, but 397 had been queried as non-resident, 335 of them from Flint. The two Flint bailiffs sent in separate returns one for each candidate, and the case went to the Committee of Elections, which made its report on 21 May 1728 and deprived Wynne of the seat.'
15. 'The Account Book of the Reverend Hugh Lloyd, vicar of Mold, NLW, Ms 598E in FRO M/F 982.
16. A Terrier: an inventory of church property made by the incumbent cleric and churchwardens at the request of the diocesan bishop. Those for Mold are dated 1710, 1732, 1749, 1791 and 1856, and a modern log-book and inventory compiled *c.*1995.
17. Glebe, 'land farmed or leased out by an Incumbent.'
18. Prebendary an ancient ecclesiastical office whose holder occupied a prebend or bench in the Cathedral and received an income from tithes customarily allocated for the purpose.
19. NLW SA/QA/3/1745.
20. See Rosa Baker, The Family of Richard Wilson, RA, and its Welsh Connections, Rosa Baker, *Flintshire Historical Society Journal,* vol 35, p.92.
21. See Jane Furse and David L. Jaques, *Report for the Garden History Society of the Historical Interest of the Garden and Grounds of Leeswood Hall, Flintshire. June 1981.*
22. R.O.F. Wynne, The Wynne Family of Melai and Garthewin, *Denbighshire Historical Society Transactions,* vol 5, 1956 p.82.
23. FRO D/LE/3760.

6: The activities of the gentry in eighteenth-century Mold

The eighteenth century was a time when the gentry held an undisputed position in local society. In Wales, they exercised this from the time of the Act of Union in 1536 until the Local Government Act of 1888 appointed elected county councils. As members of the significant local families, they exercised their authority as justices of the peace and as members of the Commission of the Peace for the county, to which in the seventeenth and eighteenth centuries, lesser gentry were added. Sessions of the justices were required by statute to be held four times a year:[1] around Epiphany in early January; at Easter, normally around the beginning of April; at the time of the Translation of St Thomas the Martyr, in early July; and Michaelmas in late September. In the eighteenth century, the Quarter Sessions met in rotation in Flintshire at the towns of Flint, Holywell and Mold, and usually adjourned to a local inn. In Mold, the inns frequented were the Red Lion, the Griffin, the Black Lion and the Leeswood Arms.

Keeping order was only one of the functions of a country justice. In his own district he was effectively the chief of police, the tax collector, the recruiting officer, the magistrate, a government spy, the censor of morals, the supervisor of welfare services, the treasurer, the inquisitor, the licenser of ale-houses, a detective and even sometimes in the company of his fellow justices, a legislator.[2] Two satirical verses sum up the work of the justices and the nature of their business at Quarter Sessions.

The Country Justice[3]

The social Laws from Insult to protect	To aid and bring her Rover to her heart
To cherish Peace, to cultivate Respect	Wild Riot's Voice with Dignity to quell
The rich from wanton Cruelty restrain	Forbid unpeaceful Passions to rebel.
To smooth the bed of Penury and Pain;	Wrest from Revenge the meditated Harm,
The hapless Vagrant to his Rest restore,	For this fair JUSTICE raised her sacred Arm;
The maze of Fraud, the Haunts of Theft explore	For this the rural Magistrate, of Yore
The thoughtless Maiden, when subdu' by Art,	Thy Honours, Edward, to his Mansion bore.

The business of a Country Quarter Sessions[3]

Three or four Parsons, three or four Squires,	Three or four Bulls, three or four Cows,
Three or four Layers, three or four Lyars.	Three or four Orders, three or four Bows,
Three or four Parishes bringing Appeals,	Three or four Statutes not understood,
Three or Four Hands, three or four Seals,	Three or four Paupers praying for Food,
Three or four Bastards, three or four Whores,	Three or Four Roads that never were mended,
Tag, Rag, and Bobtail, three or four Scores	Three or four Scolds, – and the Session's ended.

If these lines bore any semblance to reality, the work of the justices was unending. They were assisted in their duty by local officialdom, distinguished by dress and badges of office: a gold-laced coat, a full-bottomed wig and three-cornered hat. Some of the appointments were annual, most of them unpaid. Many who served in these offices felt that they were serving a sentence of community service, others enjoyed the petty power which they exercised with maximum authoritarianism. The court was filled with amateur officialdom.

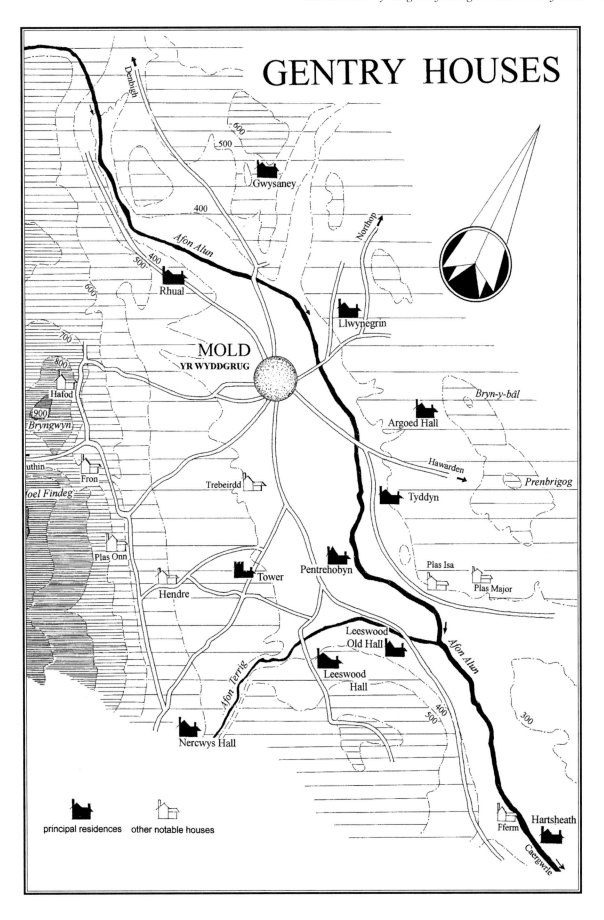

The High Sheriff served in the office unpaid for the term of a year. Most of the Mold gentry served in this office in their turn and, although generally regarded as an expensive nuisance, it gave the office holder status in the local community. The High Sheriff was responsible for the judges when they were on business in the county, he summoned various officials to court and organised the custody of prisoners and their court appearance. He also regulated the bailiff, constables and petty constables from each of the fifteen townships in Moldsdale. These officials were responsible for the collection of fines, crown revenues and the execution of writs and precepts and the serving of summonses. Other important officials were the ten constables of the peace or high constables, two from each of the five hundreds of the county of Flintshire. This was one of the obligatory unpaid offices of the county, imposed upon yeomen and minor gentry. They were the underlings to the justices and were expected, together with petty constables, to keep the peace, apprehend criminals, control vagrants and make sure roads and bridges were maintained in good repair. The overseers of the poor were expected to ensure that the county and township rate was levied on the value of the property and the poor given relief according to the resolution of the vestry.

The Clerk of the Peace[4] until 1888 was appointed by the *custos rotulorum*, the Lord Lieutenant of the county. Chosen from the ranks of local attorneys and solicitors, he generally had his own private practice with his own assistants. To be successful in carrying out his duties he needed to be experienced, efficient and honest. His duties were to advise the court on procedure, to record its decisions and see that they were fully implemented. The clerk in Flintshire was unsalaried and was allowed a nominal sum of £10 by the justices, but was entitled to fees and expenses. In the eighteenth century, the clerks appointed a deputy – in 1749 this was Thomas Owen, steward of the manor of Mold.

No records for the Flintshire Quarter Sessions[5] exist until the eighteenth century. Minute books date from 1720 and give a summary of the business of the courts and the names of and attendance of justices. The documents relating to the business of each session were rolled up together into a roll. The Quarter Sessions was an administrative body which dealt with a wide range of matters including the repair of roads and bridges, the enforcement of the Poor Law and other parliamentary legislation. It was also a court of law for the punishment of crimes such as assault, felony and theft. Justices would sit in whichever court they had been summoned to, irrespective of their place of residence, as they were nominated for the whole county and not for the hundred. At sometime or other, all the leading gentry families of Moldsdale were represented in the court of Quarter Sessions, described as 'a local parliament held in a noisy and informal atmosphere in Welsh county towns.' These included the Davieses of Gwysaney; the Griffith family of Rhual, the Lloyds of Pentrehobyn, the Eytons and Wynnes of Leeswood, the Wynnes of Tower, the Hydes of Nercwys, the Wykes of Llwynegryn, the Gwyllyms of Heartsheath, the Williamses of Fron and the Revd Hugh Lloyd of Mold.

Numerous references are made in the court records to matters relating to Mold:

[Sacrament certificate] October 1740 'Evan Lloyd and Edward Ellis having this day made due proof of their having received the Sacrament of the Lords Super and having also taken and subscribed the Oaths of Allegiance and Supremacy. It is ordered that their certificates be enrolled'. Note: The Test Act of 1673 excluded from civil or military employment all except members of the Church of England who had to produce a certificate of proof.

[Cryer] 1731 'That Humfry Millington Cryer of this Court be fined thirteen shillings & fourpence for his non-attendance'

[Gaoler's negligence] April 1740 'William Pritchard who was fined last Quarter Sessions for suffering Edward Kynaston a prisoner to escape out of his custody shew cause at the next Quarter Sessions why his fine should not be levied.'

[Cattle distemper] 6 April 1749 'County of Flint the grand jurors at the quarter sessions … resolv'd that neither bull, ox, heifer, steer or cow shall be driven from any part of the County Palatine of Chester to the said town of Mold … as long as the said contagious distemper shall reign in the said County Palatine of Chester.'

[Cattle distemper] 1750 October 'That the sum of two pounds and one shilling be assessed and charged on ye Inhabitants of this County to pay Mr Adams printer for printing Certificates on account of ye Distemper of cattle. That a sum of twenty pounds be assessed and levied on ye inhabitants of this County to pay ye several

Inspectors and all other charges relating to ye distemper amongst ye horned cattle in this County'.

[bridges] April 1729 'it was Order'd that the sum of £142 8s 1d be assessed upon the County to repair the Lead Mill Bridge & Pentre Bridge and that Richard Lloyd, George Wynne & Thomas Eyton be appointed Overseers thereof & that they bring an Account of their expenses therein into the next General Quarter Sessions.'

Expenditure at Rhygoli bridge on the Mold to Denbigh road included payments to a paver in 1757 and unspecified work on the main bridge and four small bridges in 1767.

The River Terrig caused particular problems described in 1776 as 'a very rapid and dangerous stream.' Apparently a wall had been washed away at Terrig Bridge between Mold and Treuddyn and money had to be spent in 1777 and 1779 rebuilding its foundations. The River Terrig also caused problems lower down, flooding at Llong Mill Bridge in 1771 necessitating work on watercourses in fields towards Pontblyddyn and Pentrehobyn, from Cae Rhedyn to the smithy at Llong Bridge in 1787, through land belonging to John Hope Wynne Eyton of Leeswood Hall. In 1770 Felin Blwm (Lead Mill Bridge) on the road from Mold to Northop was described as being too narrow for two carriages to pass, but no action was taken.

[Highway] April 1720 'Ordered that any sum not exceeding sixpence in ye pound be assessed and levied of ye freeholders & landowners and Inhabitants of the township of Bryncoed for the repair of the Highways there.'

1721 April 'The sum of £20 to be levyed and assessed upon ye freeholders, landowners and Inhabitants of ye Parish of Mould for ye Repaire of yt part of ye High-Way in ye township of Beestre which overflowed by ye River Allen and yt. ye same time be paid into ye hands Thomas Eyton Esq and Mr Edward ffoulkes to be laid out for yt. purpose.'

[Pinfold] October 1730 'That the sum of ten pounds eight shillings five pence half penny to be levyd on the Inhabitants of the Township of Leeswood to reimburse George Wynne & Robert Ellis their bill of Repaires for making a Pinfold'.

[Nuisance] October 1725 'Ordered that the Inhabitants of the town of Mould be fined ten pound for not repairing and cleansing ye Causey and Streets in ye town of Mold.'

[Poor Relief] July 1724 ' Ordered yt five pounds pr. Anno be Assessed and Levyed on ye parishioners of ye Parish of Moulde to maintaine Robert Griffith a poor distracted person now in Gaol yt the same be paid to the hands of John Venables of Gwysaney to be laid out for that purpose'.

[Abandoned child chargeable] 10 Dec 1757 'The Churchwardens and Overseers of Mold complain that Thomas Morris, Turner & his wife Jane have lately absconded from the parish and gone to the Parish of Ruthin and left their Daughter Anne (about 15 months old)…the child becoming troublesome to the p'sh.'

[Cost of Removal] Epiphany 1775 'Removal of Dorothy Evans from Northop to Mold cost £4 10s 2d. of which the attorney William of Mold received £1. 1s. 0d. for attendance at Quarter Session and a meeting with the Overseer of Mold parish a further 6s. 8d.'

[Conveyance of Vagrants] October 1730 'Payments to Petty Constables – include Robert Jones Llwynegrin 15s, Edward Lloyd Bistre £4 2s1d. & Edward Davies Pentrehobin 15s 7d.'

[Whipping of Vagrants] 1730 'That the following persons stand Committed to the House of Correction for a week and be whipt (the men at cart tails) the three ensuing Market Days between the hours of two & three o'clock on the sd. days at Caerwys, Mold & Holywell vizt. Thomas Bailey, Henry Bailey and Rosamund his wife, Mary Parry, Anne Smith, Lucy Buckley, Enoch Wood Etc. and then Conveyed to their respective places of Settlement.'

[Stealing] April 1740 'Whereas Owen Parry was this day tried and convicted of the felonious taking and carrying away a cock of the goods and chattels of one William Lewis. It is therefore ordered by this Court that the said Owen Parry be whipt on Saturday next between the hours of ten and twelve from the Black Lyon to the Red Lyon in Mold.'

[bound over to keep the peace] April 1742 'Ordered that Alice the wife of John Thomas of Mold stand committed till she find bail for her good behaviour for saying she would take out the Gutts of Jane Griffiths of Rhual widow.' [possibly the widow of Dr Thomas Griffith the diarist d. 1740]

[Illegal sale of ale – unlicensed ale house] Summer 1758 'Information of Edward Hughes, Innkeeper of Mold…who says that last Easter Monday he was in the dwelling house of one William Webb in the town of Mold wherein he did see the said William Webb's wife sell & retail a considerable quantity of Ale to him…& to several other

People there drinking & tippling…and he doth believe that William Webb was not then lawfully licensed.'
[Convicted]

[Fortune Telling] Epiphany 1762 'Janet otherwise Shoned the wife of Evan Hughes of the sd. Town of Mold Shoemaker is a woman of ill fame & bad character and maketh a practice of telling fortunes, & using Subtil craft by the cutting of cards & tea grounds in order to deceive and impose upon his Majesty's Subjects and that the sd. Janet otherwise Shoned hath often told this informt. (Richard Edwards of Mold) that she used to make a custom & practice of telling fortunes by cutting of cards & Tea Grounds.'

[Theft of lead ore] Mid-Summer 1772 'Examination of William Jones, miner, says on oath that Thomas Williams, miner of Mold, came to his home and asked him if he would 'go with him to steal some lead ore from a place called Cat Hole upon Mold Mountain?' Jones went with him but got cold feet and refused to go any further. Williams told him to stay where he was while he did the thieving, which he did. Jones was given a 50lb bag of ore to carry to Fron (Arddunwent) where he did mix it with some other ore which they had washed at Fron aforesaid … which they sold to Mr Joseph Birks smelter of Pentrehobin in the parish of Hawarden. On 22 April 1772 they met at Mold before proceeding to their work at Fron where they 'saw somebody at the Hillocks; upon which Thomas Williams said to this Examinant that he was afraid that persons he saw there would discover some bags of lead ore which he the said Thomas Williams had stolen and hid there the night before.'

[shooting a pig] Midsummer 1795 'The Jurors for our Lord the King upon their oath present that John Jones the Younger late of the Parish of Mold in the County of Flint miner being an ill designing and disorderly person of a wicked and malicious mind on the 17th day of December in the 35th year of the reign King George III with force of arms at the Parish aforesaid unlawfully, wilfully, and maliciously Did with a certain engine called a Gun shoot at and wound and maim a certain Pig (the same then being the property of John Ithel) and which said Pig afterwards to wit on the 20th day of December … by means of such maiming and wounding died against the Peace of our said Lord the King his Crown and Dignity'.

Caring for the bodily needs of the population as well as saving the souls of its inhabitants were two main challenges that had confronted countless sixteenth-century parliaments. A means of salvation that was acceptable to the consciences of most citizens was almost achieved by the end of the reign of Elizabeth I. This spiritual provision was enacted by parliamentary statute which included the Act of Uniformity which imposed compulsory attendance at the local parish church. The second object of feeding the hungry, clothing the naked, visiting the sick, caring for widows, orphans and the destitute – the biblical works of mercy – were also made compulsory by parliament and grew quickly into an ever-increasing body of legislation, the Elizabethan Poor Law.[6] This was the substitute for acts of charity formerly depicted in wall paintings in churches and now obliterated by iconoclastic whitewash.

New angels of mercy, the churchwardens and overseers, were appointed guardians of the poor by the parish vestry, presided over by the vicar, under the influence of the local gentry. The seventeenth century was an age of philanthropy. Grammar schools and almshouses were endowed and apprenticeships became available. Voluntary acts of piety, lists of charitable gifts left to the poor, were placed on boards on the walls of the church for the poor to read by flickering candlelight and to be encouraged that someone cared. On the alms board in the parish church of Mold was written: 'A Catalogue of such worthy piously charitably disposed Persons who have contributed towards the Ornament of the Church or maintenance of the poor of Mould Parish.' The first benefaction read:

Ap 1 1641 'Wm David ab Gronow of (Llstynhunedd) left forty pound, the yearly interest of which is to buy eight grey or Russet Prize Gowns to be distributed by the Vicar & Churchwardens att Xmas to the poorest of Mould.' 'Robert Williams of Llwynegrin left pr. Ann to buy 15 hats Xmas Eve yearly to be distributed by the Vicar to the poorest of the parish £05. 00. 00.

A prayer that must have lain in the hearts of many arthritic old women as they struggled up the hill to St Mary's was a plea that they would be chosen by the vestry to receive a prize gown.

The parish vestry was the last resort for those in need and the only people who could help the poor were its members. The Elizabethan parliament had seen that the parish unit was the best means of controlling poverty and a more efficient agent than the religious houses dissolved sixty years previously. By this time, the justices of the peace, whose ranks were filled from the gentry class, had proved themselves the ideal instrument for controlling unrest in the localities. As major beneficiaries of the dissolution of the monasteries, it was an opportunity for them to show their loyalty, gratitude and usefulness to the state which had rewarded them.

The Tudor approach was logical. It treated the poor according to their needs. The phrase 'the deserving poor' applied to the impotent: infants, aged, invalids, lunatics and others who were unable to support themselves financially. They were to be helped, given poor relief, by the parish of their birth upon whom they had a moral and legal claim for a minimal maintenance. This financial assistance, or dole, was to be paid by local landowners from a rate levied upon all occupiers of land. The freeholders and squires of Mold were responsible for supporting those in their townships who were unable to support themselves. They could also relieve the potential burden of excessive demands by refusing to give to the able-bodied vagrants who were to be sent packing and returned to their place of birth. Quarter Sessions could order that they be whipped and returned to their parish of birth. In this way, bands of sturdy vagrants were prevented from eating the bread of the poor and the able-bodied poor were set to work in the fields and later in workhouses.

1716 Paid Edward Roberts Constable for giving notice to yea Strange people to meet yea Justice of yea Peace 6d.
1718 Pd to Edward Jones the constable for removing yea peddlers. 00. 00. 04.

The vestry acted as the parochial executive, its membership comprised the minister, churchwardens and leading parishioners, who were either co-opted or elected. In Mold, the parish raised money for the upkeep of the poor by levies, or rates, charged separately upon each of the fifteen townships. The vestry decided how this money was to be spent. It decided whose case was worthy to be relieved and, through knowledge of the applicants' needs, advised accordingly. The Mold vestry accounts and minutes are recorded in large books and ledgers of quarto size which contain pages of applications for relief, giving ample evidence of an increasing population and imposing an impossible burden on the parishioners. In the 1820s, the relief bill for Mold Parish exceeded £4,000 per annum. A similar situation was prevalent throughout the country at the beginning of the nineteenth century when it was acknowledged that the old Poor Law could no longer provide adequate relief for the poor.

As the burden of poor relief increased during the eighteenth century the vestry met more frequently and elected special officers as overseers of the poor. These usually came from among the yeomen, husbandmen and craftsmen, rather than labourers or cottagers. Their names were submitted to the justices of the peace for approval. At first they received no payment but, around 1800, because of an increased workload and the volume of money they were responsible for, they received yearly payment of around £100 each. Their growing responsibility included recommending relief, making payments to individuals, checking the validity of requests for relief, the removal of incomers liable to be a burden on the parish to their place of legal settlement. Also amongst their responsibilities was the apprenticing of poor orphans to local tradesmen and households. The extent of their business is seen in the large number of surviving records of their work.[7] Most of the examples given below show the demand for poor relief in Mold during the second half of the eighteenth century. They illustrate the nature of applications received by the vestry and the variety of relief prescribed. Eighteenth-century parish officers were not trained social workers, but had a great deal of familiarity with the lives of the poor and probably knew the individual circumstances of the applicants and their dependants. They were usually experienced enough to assess whether the application was genuine and there were enough informers to advise them to the contrary. The cases were dealt with according to normal procedure and there is evidence to show that the parish of Mold adopted new rules when necessary. Some relief is given by means of regular payments and others in kind, to assist the specific needs of the recipient or to enable them to follow their occupation and support themselves.

At a vestry meeting held at the parish church of Mold on Sunday, 21 June 1767, amongst the applicants for relief were:

> Mrs Williams of Carreglwyd. Widow Bellis having 6d a week apply'd for further Relief and was allow'd 12d a week till further order. The disabled Thos Williams apply'd for Relief being lame and John Hughes apply'd for relief for his child. The destitute Margaret Rowlands of Gwysaney apply'd for ye Rent and Esther Richards hoping to make ends meet apply'd for two shillings to mend her wheel. In alleviation of their distress the Vestry ordered the overseer John Hughes to supply Mrs Williams of Carreglwyd with 3 pounds of Flax from time to time and 6d. a week till further orders. It allow'd John Hughes for his child 15d. a week to commence from the first instant June but denied Margaret Edwards her rent by reason of her brother being her landlord. Margaret Williams received 12d. a week as before. It ordered William the Miller be paid 12d to redeem his goods at Neston and for Thomas Williams to be provided by Edwd Williams Overseer as he thinks his necessity to Require till his leg gets better. It then dealt with the means of caring for the young. John Jones another of the parish overseers was ordered to bring Edward Hughes Butchers Girl to Thos Gibbons being allotted to him an apprentice and that no further allowance be given her mother but that John Jones to bring the rest of the Children to be Boarded with Jane Williams of Bistree and to agree with her for the same till further order to the contrary. The vestry further instructed that the said John Jones make no further allowance to Mary Jones of Llwynegrin till she brings her daughter to be Deliver'd to Edward Jones she being Balloted to him as an apprentice but that in the meantime he Provides according to his Discretion for the other Infant Children about and apart from their Mother.

The vestry was attempting the impossible in their allocation of resources to make sure that needy petitioners benefited and became less of a burden on the parish. The minutes were signed by the overseers, Math Griffith, John Jones and Edward Williams.

> 6 July 1768. [it was] … order'd & agreed upon that Mr Wynne Attorney be employ'd to Prosecute Thos Lewis of Hope for inveigling his two Daughters, Apprentices of the Revd Mr Lewis & Edward Jones from their said Services contrary to Law the same to be done at the Parish Expense at the next Qtr. Sessions to be holden in Holywell …
> 5 Nov 1768. Memorandum that John Jones Overseer of the Poor for Mold Allotment paid the sum of one pound seventeen shillings and sixpence to Redeem Deborah Davies's bed the same being taken by Distraint of her Landlord Mr William Lloyd for two years Rent, and charged in taking and keeping the same and the said John Jones caused the bed and the Bolster be now lent to the said Deborah Davies till such time as her or his Successor overseer shall think Proper to demand the same as the Right of the said Parish (Bed and Bolster 32 pounds in weight).
> July 19 1769. Order'd that a cow be Bought for David Williams late of Bistree widow at the Expense of the Parish to enable her to maintain herself and Family.

The Poor Law Act of 1601 had given authority to churchwardens and overseers to apprentice poor children to employers, as they thought proper. Apprentices were of two classes – those apprenticed by voluntary consent without the intervention of the parish officers, and parish apprentices bound by parish authorities. By the eighteenth century, the pauper apprentice system had become open to abuse. Jonas Hanaway described it as 'Orphans who are in a vagabond state, or the illegitimate children of the poorest kind of people are said to be sold, that is their service for seven years is disposed of for twenty or thirty shillings.'[8] As a result of these abuses, other remedies were tried on a local basis. In Mold in the 1730s and '40s, the gentlemen of the Lions Club were responsible for apprentices being bound and legally indentured to tradesmen for the usual term of seven years. By the 1770s, parish records show that the Mold vestry was following the course followed elsewhere in the country; apprenticeship was no longer a voluntary agreement between parent and master but had become a system of imposing children upon employers by the system of balloting. If the employer did not take the child allotted to him by ballot he was liable to be fined. In June 1770, at a vestry meeting held in the parish church of Mold, the following paupers were balloted as parish apprentices:

Rice Williams to Edward Roberts Arddunwent; Jno Jones Son of Edwd. Jones Labr. Mold to John Matthews of Gwysaney; John Hughes to Edward Edwards Mold; David Davies to Geo Johnson.

The under mentioned Persons chose as under:
Edward Longford chose [—] a child of Ithel Davies's without any consideration. He received no payment from the Vestry for clothing the child.

Edward Williams Dolphin chose Robt. Powell a child of David Powell's of Mold without any consideration.

Thomas Longford chose Mary Jones Child of Edward Jones Labr of Mold with Twenty Shillings.

Mary Owen Kilken to have Mary Griffith with a child of the late James Griffith Mold with the Consideration of Two pounds allow'd her also a pair of shoes.

To James 5s as assistance till he recovers of his illness.

4 Feb 1770 ordered that John Eubale be given £1 1s to buy him a fiddle. Also that from this date no Paupers have any more flax to spin on account of the Parish.

At a Vestry held in the Parish Church of Mold on Wednesday June the 8th. 1774.

Agreed that the Brick now in making & intended for Building a Workhouse be made at the Parish expense and consequently deemed their Property.

Jan 20 1771 Allow'd Thos Jones Weaver as assistance till he is able to work.

June 2 1771 Order'd that the Overseers of the Poor Pay them their Allowance every Wednesday Morning.

Ordered that Edwd Hughes's children be properly cloathed in case they find Services N.B. they are to have £2 the (Clothes) equivalent in Value to that sum to be distributed by Mr Smith.

March 1st 1772. To David Wms of Bistre 9s. to buy corn & 2s. a week during his wife's illness.

Nov 1st 1772 Also that from this date the Parish will allow but 3s. 6d. for delivering any woman troubling the Parish.

Febry 7th 1773 To Thos Jones of Rhyd y mwyn's widow straw for the repair of her House not exceeding 10s at the discretion of Abel Jones. Febry 7th 1773 Ordered that from this date no Pauper shall at their funerals have but a Plain Coffin without Paint or Trimmings a Decent Shroud and a Passing Bell in a Particular Manner. Also no Pauper be suffer'd to offer or Permit others to offer at such funerals.

June 30 1773 Ordered that every Pauper belonging to this Parish have no further allowance from the Parish if they appear without a badge. [Under an Act of 1697 those in receipt of poor relief were supposed to have a letter p. and the initial of the parish sewn on their clothes. This was abolished in 1782].

May 5 1775 Robert the Cobbler of New Street have 10s. towards repairing his house.

July 6 1774 Ordered that Mr Roger Jones of Caie be allowed Eight shillings being Expenses he paid at Chester taking a Plan of the House of Industry there, four persons having been there for that Purpose

From the seventeenth century onwards, parishes began to establish workhouses as places where they could send the able-bodied who were in need of poor relief. It was anathema that 'the sturdy beggar' be allowed to remain idle and instead, they were supervised and forced to live and work in special premises erected by parish authorities for this purpose. Workhouses became one of the major features of the Poor Law Amendment Act of 1834 when Mold became part of the Holywell Union where a workhouse was built in 1840. There is no evidence of an eighteenth-century workhouse being erected in the parish of Mold.

The Church
In the Summer of 1749, the rural dean, Hugh Jones, friend of Hugh Lloyd inspected Mold Parish Church. His report to the bishop was brief and to the point.

1726	Mr Lloyd Vicar of Mold Gave Plate for ye use of Sick comunicant	8	4
1727	Mr Thomas Wynne of Waen Left by will yearly & forever	1	
1729	Robert Williams of Llwynegrin Left by will yearly & forever	1	
1729	Lady Wynne of Leeswood Gave a Velvet Covering for the Comunion Table and two Stools		
1729	Griffith Jones of Mertyn Left by will yearly & forever	8	
1730	Mrs Pennant of Pen y garth Widow Left by deed (paid in 1741)	20	
1732	Mrs Margaret Lloyd of Waen Left by will	20	
1734	Thomas Williams of Gwysaney Left by will	5	
1734	Evan Ambrose of Hawerden Parish Left by will	20	
1735	Gave fine Linnen for ye Comunion table		
1737	Mrs Wynne of Leeswood Widow Left by will	20	
1741	Mrs Lloyd of Pentrehobyn Widow Left by will	30	
1742	Mr Hugh Lloyd Vicar of Mold Built a Charity School houseland towards the Endowment of it Gave	120 267	
1742	John Evans of Gwysaney Gave towards ye Endowment of it	40	
1742	Gave towards the Endowment of it	10	
1742	Gave towards Buying Books	3	
1744	Mary Jones of Nerquis Widow Gave towards the Endowment	10	
1742	Richard Lloyd of Hartsheath Esqr Left by will to bex payd 1745	10	
1745	Thomas Jones of Argoed Left by will	50	

Part of the benefaction and alms board, south wall, Mold Parish Church.

The Church is a stately building consisting of three large Isles with light Pillars, all of free stone, but with a very poor steeple. The Roof of the middle Isle is in bad order, and stands some part of it upon props; where has been lately a collection for the repair of it … the seats are all uniform and regular …

Vicar Hugh Lloyd had struggled for over thirty years to keep on top of the endless task of maintaining the building and, whenever possible, improving it. The rural dean was familiar with the problems and the excellent response of Hugh Lloyd and was aware that the vicar and churchwardens had much more to do. 'The very poor steeple' had to be taken down and replaced, and the props supporting the roof removed. It took another fifty years, until the end of the eighteenth century, for things to be put right.

When Hugh Lloyd came to the parish in 1717 he viewed with sorrow the 'stately building' and saw it as a decrepit old lady, lame in several joints. He realised that his predecessors had had an uphill task to maintain the church fabric which appeared to be in a condition of decay and unable to meet the demands of unfavourable weather. In the 120 years since the church building was acknowledged to have been 'finished', successive vicars had found themselves responsible for an unfinished architectural masterpiece. The church building had begun its life with all the mystery and splendour of high Catholic design and was now allowed, in the 'age of enlightenment', to stand neglected and incomplete. It was all too obvious to the discerning that interior work at the eastern end had been abruptly terminated by blocking the chancel arch with a stained glass window for 400 years. From an exterior view, the pre-perpendicular gothic tower at the west end gave the building the impression of wearing outdated clothes. The failure to add the clerestory (the upper storey of the nave) reduced the height of the building and amount of daylight that was let into the building.

Bishops ordered regular reports to be made on church buildings and clergy and churchwardens were required to make returns and appear before senior officials to justify their replies. In this way parishes were brought to task and obliged to remedy any defect in church fabric. Throughout the eighteenth century the parish was fortunate in having clergy who gave long service to the parish: Hugh Lloyd 1717–49; Robert Lewis 1749–92; and Hope Wynne Eyton 1792–1825.

During the eighteenth century the architectural style of new church buildings was generally classical. But

Mold was in no sense a classical church. However, the fact that the sixteenth century perpendicular church had remained incomplete was, to some extent, an advantage for those wishing to make changes. It allowed the church authorities to introduce some elements which were peculiarly eighteenth century. This was probably done more for reasons of convenience and necessity than adherence to a definite plan. There appears to have been no architect employed for general repairs. However, the tower replaced by Joseph Turner in 1768–73 suggests that there was a conscious attempt made to replace the gothic steeple with one in keeping with a perpendicular-style church. The square-like shape of the interior, with its almost flat ceilings, was ideal for use as an auditory church[9] without any structural changes and this was achieved unobtrusively by the addition of a gallery and the gradual introduction of a regulated seating plan. The gentry were also given licence to introduce church monuments in the Baroque style. The best examples of this are the life-sized standing figure of Robert Davies of Gwysaney 1728, sculpted by Sir Henry Cheere (1703–81) and a wall monument to William Wynne 1757, signed by Rysbrack. There are also several classical wall tablets.

Monument to Robert Davies of Gwysaney by Sir Henry Cheere, Mold Parish Church.

Innovation walked hand-in-hand with decay and new seating was introduced and a new gallery erected whilst the roofs of the aisles were propped up. Recognising this anomalous state the vicar and churchwardens desperately sought a remedy. The rules of the Church made it clear that churchwardens were responsible for all repairs to the buildings.

> The Churchwardens or questmen shall take care and provide that the churches be well and sufficiently repaired, and so from time to time kept and maintained that windows be well glazed, and that the floors be kept paved, plain and even, and all things there in such an orderly and decent sort, without dust, or anything that may be either noisome or unseemly, as best becometh the House of God … The like care they shall take, that churchyards be well and sufficiently repaired … [canon 85, 1604][10]

If individuals wanted to make an alteration or improvement to the fabric of a church, or introduce a sitting, kneeling or burial place within the church, the applicant had to receive permission from the vestry and final approval from the vicar general who acted as diocesan chancellor. The process opened with a general proclamation of the work to be done in the parish church and then passed to the chancellor for licence to make the improvement or, if there was any objection, to the consistory court. On these occasions the petitioner, usually a member of the gentry, was charged a fee for the privilege of making his application.

Money for repairs and improvements could be raised by a church rate levied by the vestry on the amount of owned or leased land and was collected in the townships. This was done annually. On the repair of church bells or other specific work, such as the purchase of a new clock, the vestry generally entered into a contract with the tradesmen involved.

On rare occasions vestries found it difficult to contemplate how they could find large sums of money in order to carry out exceptional work. This dilemma confronted the churchwardens of Mold in the period from 1740–70 when, in order to make the church building viable for the future, they had to repair the roof and windows and take down the old decayed tower and replace it with a new one. It was necessary to resort to an appeal for assistance beyond the townships of Mold and pockets of the local gentry. They applied for a brief, or royal mandate, for a collection in churches throughout the kingdom. The first step was to obtain a certificate from the Quarter Sessions and then publicise the work to be done in the brief and hope that the parishes where it was read would respond.

The Reverend Peter Williams (vicar 1706–17), a native of Mold, decided to embark on a course of action not previously pursued by the parishioners. In 1709 an application was made for (King's) Letters Patent, a brief for the purpose of making a collection for a charitable purpose, in this instance the repair of Mold Church. He and his churchwardens set about carefully preparing a list of the works needed to finish and repair the church and the costings involved. The information they presented was circulated and read in 10,000 churches throughout England and Wales, with a request for donations to be sent to the churchwardens in Mold.

The applicants pointed out that the church had not been completed in accordance with the plans of the founders and that the building was in danger of being ruined and raising the money necessary was beyond their means hence their appeal to the charity of other parishes.[11] They had engaged the services of Peter Whitehead, Thomas Roberts and Edward Jones to provide an estimate of the work to be presented with the petition. Whitehead was instructed to 'draw a model of Mold Steeple and Chancel in order to get a brief to build upon.' This 'model' is lost and may refer to either a drawing or three-dimensional object. The most celebrated model, that of St Paul's Cathedral (1673–4), is 21-feet long. Whitehead's for Mold would probably only have been a simple wooden one. In addition, Roberts, Whitehead and Jones provided an estimate:[12]

Imprimis for 150 Tun of Timber £490; For Carriage £75; Workmanship £200: Casting of Bells; 500; Iron Work £2915; Glaziers £50; Lead work £100; For Stone Carriage Lime, Sand &c and workmanship £1500 – Total £ 2975: 00: 00.

The following documents were prepared for submission to the justices at the Flint Sessions of 1709:

Draft petition for a brief. Petition for the Churchwardens, Gentlemen and other Inhabitants of the Parish of Mould als Mon: Alto — Humbly Sheweth That the parish Church Steeple and Chancel of Mould als Mont Alto were not finished according to the Moddell of the Pious founders reason whereof as well as by reason of the Bleak situation the same is become ruinous and farr out of Repaire tho' your Petitioners have from time to time continued to the utmost of their ability towards the repair and finishing of the sd Fabrick that yr Petitioners are in no way able to repaire and finish the same.

   Minister and Churchwardens have expended the sum of £300 and upwards to the repair of the said Church. The parishioners have a further charge of sending for experienced workmen to view the condition of our church where they have at a moderate computation Drawn up an Estimate of one thousand five hundred and 20 pound and upwards before the said Church can be truly repaired and finished.[13]

The justices allowed the petition, which was recommended to Lord Cowper, Baron of Wingham, High Chancellor of Great Britain for permission to receive the Letters Patent for the Brief. There is no more extant information about the outcome of the 1709 appeal but the parish would have appeared to have been unsuccessful as the construction of a steeple had to wait another sixty years and the completion of the chancel another 150 years.

The 1709 petition did not mention the state of the church roof, the major maintenance problem for the churchwardens in the eighteenth century. The large area and low elevation of the roofs of three aisles made care of lead work a major priority. In 1674, an agreement had been made between John Austin, a plumber of Ellesmere, and the churchwardens 'to make a good and durable cover of the roof.' The sum agreed for the work was £17. The churchwardens were to pay for timber work and Austin was engaged at 20s a year to keep

Mold Parish Church, Joseph Turner architect.

and maintain this work in sufficient repair.[14] Thirty years later, a new agreement was made between churchwardens John Lloyd and William Brock, and Nathaniel Wright, a Wrexham plumber, to roof the church with lead for £75 (except the south aisle) the terms being £15 in hand and £10 per annum for six years and, in addition, made a new arrangement which was still in place in 1732.

1704 Articles of Agreement made between the churchwardens John Lloyd, Esq., William Brock, Esq., and Nathaniel Wright of Wrexham Plumber. Wright entered into a bond of £50 to roof the church with lead for £75 (except the south aisle), the terms being £15 in hand and £10 a year annually for 6 years and in addition 'for the time of his natural life for 5s a year he was to repair the lead on the church'. The church wardens were to arrange to have the lead 'all ready upon the top or roof of that part of the church' needing attention. Wright was actually only paid £28 between 1704 and 1732 (when the agreement was still in place). Major problems with the roof were to re-appear some ten years later.

In order to avoid disputes amongst the gentry the Reverend Hugh Lloyd, together with the churchwardens, pursued a firm policy in the allocation of church seating.[15] In reality, what the applicants were seeking was a title deed, the right of ownership of a space in the church in which they would isolate themselves and their families by means of a box pew. The parish and diocesan records from the 1720s[16] contain many applications from the parishoners of Mold for new seats in the church during which time most of the names of the local gentry appear in the records, an example of which is the permission given to John Lloyd of Pentrehobyn on 1 November 1725:

Licence to Erect a seat or pew in a vacant place in the room of two common Benches situate in the north side… to the north passage or alley six foot and in Breadth from the Pew or seat of Mr Hugh Pennant of Mold Clerk 5'5' – where a seat may be erected.

In 1719, Hugh Lloyd had a reading seat for the clerk placed under the pulpit. In order to accomplish this re-ordering, arrangements were made for a voluntary exchanges of seats[17] and the poor were set apart and other seats, 'the common seats,' increased in number,

1734. Thomas Williams bill for erecting seven new common seats and the Churchwardens and overseers seats 36. 01. 09.

1743. Work done for the Parish of Mold by David Davies Painter of Ruthin.

For painting 26 Common Seats and the Churchwardens names and the Churchwardens seats, Overseers seats and Sexton Seat being in all 282 letters at 3d. a hundred £0-8-7½.

Perhaps to demonstrate his great good fortune, George Wynne of Leeswood applied to the diocesan court for a faculty to erect a gallery at the west end of the middle aisle. It measured 25 feet across, from north to south, and 16½ feet deep, from the belfry, extending into the church with a convenient staircase. The new gallery was to be shared with Richard Lloyd of Herseth and Thomas Eyton of Leeswood, who were to pay him £20 for a quarter part between them. George Wynne was to have half and the right to dispose of the remaining quarter part when it was constructed.

A ring of six bells[18] was made for Mold Church by Abraham Rudhall of the Gloucester Foundry with the name of the founder on the third bell; Hugh Lloyd, the vicar, on the fourth; Edward Jones & Edward Williams on the fifth; and the traditional greetings on the first and second of 'Peace and Good Neighbourhood,' and 'Prosperity to this Parish.' The new bells were frequently used for both religious and secular events.

Recd of Thomas Peters one of the Churchwardens the sum of four shillings upon Account of the defeat of the Rebels [Jacobites] to Drink among the Ringers of Bells in Mold by me Peter Price in 1746.

Mr Jones Clerk Bill paid £3 9s. Feb 26 1744 included for ringing the 29th of May, the 11th of June, the 30th October, the 5th of November.' He was paid ten shillings on each occasion.

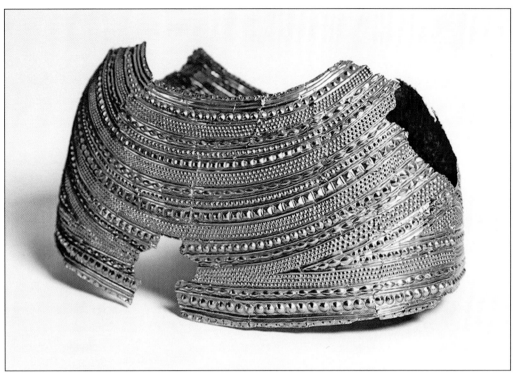

1. *The Mold Cape (as reproduced in Mold Museum)*

2. *Heraldic arms of the Stanley family in Mold Parish Church.*

3. *Heraldic arms of David Wynne, of Tower, 1636. Displayed in Mold Parish Church.*

4. Llyn-y-Pandy (or the Black Valley) by John Ingleby.
5. Pen-y-Vron by John Ingleby.

6. The view from Loggerheads, near Carreg Carn March Arthur by John Ingleby.

7. Carreg Carn March Arthur by Edward Pugh.

8. Mold, with the Parish Church and Bailey Hill in the distance and the Cotton Mill in the centre by John Ingleby.

9. Mold Parish Church from the garden of Trefriew by John Ingleby.
10. Nerquis Hall (with Miss Giffard in the garden).

11. *The Cotton Factory near Mold by John Ingleby.*

12. *Portrait of Daniel Owen (1836–95) by Charles Marston.*

13. *Mould in Flintshire by the Reverend J. Breedon, 1785.*

14. *View of Mold in the Vale of Ystrad Alun with Bailey Hill, watercolour by J. Warwick Smith.*

The churchwardens reported on 27 December 1742 that the roof of middle & south aisle were 'most decayed & in a dangerous condition & that the expense of repairing them … [would be] very considerable & above what the inhabitants can bear.' They again agreed that a petition should be drawn up and presented at the next Quarter Sessions with the intention of obtaining a brief. This new application was more detailed than that of 1709 and was endorsed in 1746 and headed 'Mount Alto Church in Com' Flint. Charge, £1,959 and upwards to be collected from House to House in the Counties of Flint, Denbigh, and Radnorshire in Wales.' On this occasion the appeal was limited to raising funds for the repair of the roof and no mention was made of replacing the steeple and finishing the chancel.

> That the Parish Church of Mold … is a magnificent Fabrick, in Length One hundred and nine Foot, and in Breadth Seventy Foot, consisting of Three large Isles, supported by Thirty two Pillars and Arches curiously wrought, and adorned with fine Carvings, both in Stone and Timber, built for the Service of Almighty God; but that the Roofs of the South and Middle Isles are, by Length of Time, and the Bleakness of the Situation, become so ruinous and decayed, that it cannot any longer be repaired, most of the large Beams in the said Roof being crack'd, and for many years last past cramped with Irons; and although the Parishioners have annually assessed and raised amongst themselves Large Sums of Money to support their said church, yet the Roofs of the said Isles are now in so dangerous a Condition, that they must be taken off and rebuilt.
>   That the Truth of the Premises hath been made to appear to Our said Justices in their open Sessions upon the oaths of the Minister, Churchwardens, Inhabitants and several able and experienced Workman have made an estimate of the charge of taking down and rebuilding the Roofs and raising the Battlements to preserve the Middle Isle which when rebuilt will amount to the sum of £1959 and upwards.

This appeal and a local house-to-house collection raised about £150, leaving a substantial shortfall. Payments of £325 for roof repairs are recorded to Hugh Wilkinson and John Sneyd, a master builder, in the summer of 1751 and, in order to make up the deficit, money had been loaned by the Poor of Mold Parishes fund which was charged at 4% and was to be repaid over three years. It took nine years to complete the repairs, although it is evident that further significant work on the roof became necessary before the end of the century.

> 1753 Sept 5 Ordered that the parts of the south Isle of the Church wanting repair be sufficiently repaired and that Edward Edwards be employed.'
>   The security was the Poor's money of £95 and various sums of a £50 bequest, £36. 13-4 held by the Vicar. The balance of £113-6-8 had to be borrowed at 4% for 4 years.
> 1777. North Isle of the Church be new leaded.
> 1799 May 11 Ceiling of the middle Isle of Church be taken down.

At the same time as the work was being carried out on the roof, moves were again made to repair the tower of the church. Instead, a decision was made to completely rebuild the tower and the design brief was given to Joseph Turner from Hawarden in 1754, a member of a local family of respected architects, who probably had a good understanding with George Berks, churchwarden and smelter of Pentrehobyn.[19] Together with the vicar, they formed a useful and experienced team, well suited to tackle the long delayed challenge. A watercolour by Moses Griffith shows the church shortly after the tower was built, capturing its successful blending with the rest of the sixteenth-century exterior. The only suviving document relating to this work manages to convey some information relating to the magnitude of the undertaking.[20]

> An Account relating to the repairs of Mold Steeple, 1768–70 Mold Steeple Acct begun 1768
> 8 July 1762[21] Advertizing Meetings 18s.
> Peter Price &c. Clearing Maes Garmon Quarry 2. 10
> Taking Down of Old Steeple & Cutting foundation 18-8-7
> To cash pd on Acct of Maes garmon Quarry by John Hughes 15-17-0

Mold Parish Church, south view.

John Hughes superintending labourers at Quarry
To William Meredith for laying foundation of the New Steeple 18-15-0
To Willm Evans for getting stone 45-9-7 & 23-19-3
To Mrs Anne Wynne for liberty to Raise Stone in ye Quarry 20-0-0
To Stone Cutters Bill to July ye 8th 1769 232-12-0
To a Bill Mr Turners Board & for his horse Jul 1st 1768 to July 9th 1769
Total Acct. £737-12-5 carried to July 27th £795-4-7

From this we can see that most of the stone work was completed within two years with probably only the bell-chamber and the re-hanging of the bells left to a future date. In December 1771, a final appeal was made for £200 'for the purpose of building up and finishing the steeple.'[22] Five years later, the finishing touches were made when the order was placed that '… Four Fanes [sic] be bought at the Expense of the Parish to be erected upon the Pinnacles at each Corner of the Steeple'.

During the demolition of the old steeple *Y Ddelw Fyw*, the Living Image, the icon that had played such an important role in the medieval church, was discovered hidden in the tower.[23] It was considered superstitious and idolatrous that such a relic from the popish past should be permitted to survive and the vicar ordered its destruction.

The Reverend Hope Wynne Eyton (1754–1825) became vicar of Mold in 1792 and rural dean in 1793. He recorded that,

Upon the death of the Reverend Robert Lewis Vicar of Mold I was instituted to the vacant living by Lewis Bishop of St Asaph. I trust in God I shall have grace to execute the duties of this scared office with integrity and that I shall be industrious in my vocation make amends for any deficiency in other respects.

The Parish is extensive, and populous and likely to increase in the latter as an extensive Cotton mill has been erected near Rhyd Goli [Rhydgoleu]… The mine works and Llwyn-y-pandy are now worked with great Spirit by Mr John Wilkinson of Bersham …

The name of the new vicar confirmed his family relationship to the local gentry – the Hopes of Broughton, Hawarden; the Eytons of Old Leeswood, the Davieses of Gwysaney and the Wynnes of Tower. A few years later, he bought the former estate of Sir George Wynne and reduced the mansion to a manageable size where, with the bishop's permission, he took up residence.[24] At the time of his appointment, Wynne Eyton observed that the 1790s were a period of economic change. He noted the diversity of the district, with a cotton factory in Mold and the enterprises of the iron master John Wilkinson at Bersham. In his first months as vicar, he became involved in the promotion of agricultural change: 'Walked the Boundaries by the Parish of Mold with Messrs Potts, Calvely, and Mathewes, Commissioners for inclosing the Lordship which is the same Boundary.'[25] Two years later he made his own personal perambulation of the parish.

> 1794 December 26. began this day to perambulate the Parish to visit every dwelling expecting by this means to be better acquainted with the Persons & dispositions of those committed to my care and during the course of my visits to make such observations as may be useful & beneficial to myself & them.

He noted that in the township of Leeswood, 'The land is mostly of a strong clay nature which grows good wheat & oats' and 'there is a considerable Body of Coal in this neighbourhood and that Messrs Wardle, Parry Goodriche have erected an expensive fire engine near Pontblyddyn for a trial of coal. Kennel (cannel coal) has been found here & sold for a moderate price these last two years on Plas Onn Estate.'[26]

In 1793 Wynne Eyton became rural dean which meant that one of his principal duties was to inspect parishes within the rural deanery and present a written report to the bishop. This task encouraged his enthusiasm for church improvements. As we have seen during the previous seventy years Hugh Lloyd and Robert Lewis had carried out major improvements to the fabric of the church in Mold. The task of providing the necessary finishing touches now fell upon their successor who began by raising funds and creating extra seating to meet the needs of an increasing population. In July 1796, he persuaded the vestry to sell off vacant seats at the west end and put the money raised into the hands of trustees. A few months later, he received a letter from Bishop Lewis intimating that he wished to be informed concerning the proposed erection of new pews in Mold Church, and that care was being taken during the work not to damage the 'beauty and uniformity of your church.'[27] In 1799, twenty-nine new seats were made by contract and sold to the highest bidder at an auction held on 11 March. The bishop, who was in London for the parliamentary session, was kept informed of his prospective changes and wrote advising him of what he considered to be the priorities.

> 2 April I rejoice with you on the success of the Plan of your Church, and am much obliged to you for informing me of the scheme for further improvements in consequence, it appears to me that of making the ceiling of the middle aisle more suitable to the rest of the beautiful Fabrick is the most desirable – an organ would entail a great deal of future expence on the parish – and as the church is at present large enough I see no advantage that would be gained by building a chancel – This is what occurs to me from what you state – you are on the spot and can collect the sense and wishes of your most intelligent neighbours who will best be able to judge what is fittest to be done…[28]

The building of the chancel was again postponed and it was over fifty years later before the work was funded by his son in his father's memory.

Music, particularly psalm singing, played an important role in church services throughout the eighteenth century as is evidenced by numerous entries in the records

> 1703 paid Mr Oliver Jenkins for teaching poor children to sing Psalms 12s.
> 1736 Apr 26 Order'd that twelve Singing Books be bought for the use of the Singers of Psalms.

1737 April 11 12 Compleat Melody £1 14s. rec'd in full.

1746 Rec'd then of Richard Williams Churchwarden the sum of two pounds: being for Instructing the boys to sing Psalms &c William Webb £2.

1749 to October ye 26 1750 William Webb.

1751 May Rec'd sum of Twenty Shillings, being for Instructing the Boys to Sing Psalms from October ye 26.

1764 Pd Jno Jones Singing Master 3-0-0.

1787 Psalm Singers Ale at the Black Lyon 18s 6d – Reeds for the Bassoon 6s – Books for Psalm Singers 17s.

1788 Psalm Singers and Treble Boys £1.

1791 Reeds & pitch pipe 0-12-0.

1811–12 Music Books & Hymns 4-3-0.

In the first years of the nineteenth century, contrary to the advice of the bishop, steps were taken to install an organ.

1805 May 8

To consider the expediency of erecting an Organ in the church of Mold and as many of the Parishioners are divided with regard to what kind of Organ should be put up. It is to be wished they would all attend to deliver their sentiments, as by what means all subject of future complaint would be avoided and the business carried on with a greater probability of its speedy accomplishment.

   Resolved that: 'it is in the opinion of this Vestry that a finger Organ be erected in the Parish Church of Mold. That the Allowance now paid the singers be applied towards an Organist's Salary and that a further sum of Twenty Pounds be paid out of the Poor's Ley in addition to the above allowance.

1807 July 27

Thomas Valentine appointed organist and manager of the organ of the parish church of Mold – annual salary of £30.

Wynne Eyton's tenure of office as vicar of Mold were momentous years of transition and, as a typical example of a clergyman from the ranks of the gentry, he played a leading role in the local community. In time of war he raised a regiment of militia, in time of peace he founded a savings bank and National school. In an age of political revolution throughout Europe he served as a magistrate and dealt with enclosure riots at Hope, corn riots in Flintshire and trades union strikes on the coalfields. As a landowner, he benefited from the Mold enclosure award and the general agricultural change and prosperity caused by the wars with France. The Industrial Revolution and its effects were evident on his doorstep in the coal mining, lead smelting and cotton spinning townships of Flintshire and they must have had a significant effect on his ministry.

Notes

1. M. Bevan-Evans, *Guide to the Flintshire Record Office,* 1953, p.63.

2. Quoted p. 62 by M. Bevan-Evans, see note above, from *The Country Justice* by John Langhorne, 1774.

3. Lines from the *Ladies Magazine,* 15 December 1750.

4. For the careers of clerks of the peace in Mold in the eighteenth century, see Quentin Dodd, *The Practice,* Wrexham, 2003.

5. See M. Bevan-Evans, op cit.; A.G. Veysey, *Guide to the Flintshire Record Office,* 1974 and FRO Source guide no 10; *A Calendar of the Flintshire Quarter Sessions Rolls,* D. Pratt, Ruthin, 1983; Bryn Ellis, 'Quarter Sessions Records for Hawarden and Mold 1747–99, *Buckley Magazine,* vol 21; and items generously given to the author by Mr K. Lloyd Gruffydd.

6. For a general history see D. W. Howell, *The Rural Poor in Eighteenth-Century Wales,* Cardiff, 2000, and W.E. Tate, *The Parish Chest,* Cambridge, 1st ed, 1946. See Mold Parish Records FRO P/40 and Keene and Kelly ms D/KK/ c.1640 to the twentieth century.

8. Jonas Hanaway, governor of the Foundling Hospital, London.

9. In many places of worship ordered after the Reformation emphasis was on the ministry of the word with the lectern, reading seat, and pulpit taking pride of place. Hearing the word of God was emphasised at the expense of ritual.

10. There were 140 canons of the Church of England, revised in 1604 and 1969.

11. Letters patent authorising a collection for charitable purposes.

12. FRO D/LE/949–50, 953–4.

13. Ibid.

14. D/KK/11.
15. Hugh Lloyd worked in collaboration with his friend Robert Wynne of Garthewin, vicar general of the St Asaph diocese.
16. See NLW SA/FB/1–2, and Mold Parish Records D/KK 113–116.
17. D/KK/Vestry Minutes 1714–28.
18. The FRO for 1678–1733, see D/KK/117 correspondence from Abraham Rudhall for ring of six bells, also Coulson, 'The Church Bells of Flintshire', *Archaeologia Cambrensis,* 1951, p.14.
19. D/KK/15.
20. D/LE/954.
21. Some sources give a sum of £1,047 as the total for cost of the tower built by Joseph Turner. This figure is vague. The expense by 1770 was £795 and on 16 Dec 1771 (D/KK/114) it was ordered that another £200 be raised for finishing the Mold Church tower.
22. D/KK/114.
23. See earlier discussion.
24. Thomas Eyton (1682–1757) married Elizabeth, daughter of Robert Davies of Gwysaney and Llannerch. Their son, John Eyton married Penelope Gray Hope, and their son Hope (the vicar) married Margaret, niece and heiress of Robert Wynne of Tower. Hope Wynne Eyton came into possession, through marriage, of Old Leeswood (Eyton) and Tower (Wynne), and through purchase, Leeswood Hall (Sir George Wynne's heirs).
25. D/LE/839.
26. D/LE/825.
27. D/LE/961
28. D/LE/966.

View of Mold in the Vale of Ystrad Alun with Bailey Hill, watercolour by J. Warwick Smith (c.1790).

7: Enterprise, industry and agriculture, 1750–1820

From the eighteenth century onwards, as a result of large industrial enterprise and agricultural improvements, the landscape of Moldsdale was changed dramatically on a scale not previously experienced.

In 1800, the process of land enclosure which had continued in a piecemeal manner since the sixteenth century, finally reached completion through concerted action by the gentry of the parish who successfully saw the relevant legislation through parliament. By this means, 4,000 acres of 'wastes and commons' in the fifteen townships of the parish were fenced off into allotments and shared out between the chief landowners, which enabled them to carry out 'improvements' in accordance with current agricultural ideas. Coincident with the enclosure award of *c.*1800 was the sale of the manor of Mold by the colourful Thomas Swymmer Champneys (later Mostyn-Champneys) which released 'new land' onto the market. An interesting and detailed survey of the manor had been carried out in 1791 by him on his impending marriage to Charlotte Mostyn.[1]

The countryside of Moldsdale, as shaped by the enclosure commissioners in 1800, remains generally the same today. At lower levels, this takes the form of fairly small fields, meadows and pasture, divided by hedgerows and trees and distinguished at the end of narrow lanes by farmsteads and cottages. On higher ground, climbing to over 1,000 feet, are the long, stone walls of sheep pasture and the abandoned *ffridd* settlements.

Minerals had been mined in Flintshire since Roman times and, in the middle of the seventeenth century, new lords of Mold, aided by English adventurers, began to exploit minerals throughout the lordship. From an agreement made when the manor was sold in the 1650s, the three purchasers divided the mineral royalties equally. For industrial development and the promotion of mining interests, the gentry usually relied on the skills and enterprise of entrepreneurs. Lead, coal and clay were extracted wherever it was practical to do so and estate records provide an account, not only of the location of industrial sites and leases, but also of a long drawn out legal dispute (*c.*1732–63) to determine the boundary of the lordship of Mold upon which depended the claim for considerable mining royalties. The records of this dispute give a good insight into lead mining on the boundary near Loggerheads. In the 1790s, a cotton spinning factory, dependent on water-power, achieved some success in Mold.

Part of the work of the enclosure commissioners had been to arrange for the construction of new roads across the so-called 'wastes and commons'. These distinctive highways are the basis of the existing rural pattern of boundaries and roads. The change in landscape was therefore two-fold. Industrial activities were exploitative – extracting minerals above ground by means of quarries, open-cast working and adits, whilst coal and lead extraction took place at a greater depth as water-pumping technology developed. But the extraction of minerals inevitably damaged the landscape, causing dereliction through spoil heaps, water pollution and other degradation of the surface soil. Industrial townships were dependent on new settlements, some of which eventually became separate ecclesiastical units and no longer part of the mother parish. The majority of the fifteen townships during the next two hundred years were subjected to explorations for minerals on a random and speculative scale, many of which were abandoned before they had the opportunity to create a permanent settlement.

The Lead Industry

In the eighteenth century, the land to the east of the river Alun in the parish and manor of Mold flourished as a lead producing area. It shared its prosperity with its neighbouring communities at Holywell, Halkyn and Llanarmon. The industry was enhanced by lead smelting at Bagillt and Pentrehobyn in the parish of Hawarden and by the shipping facilities that were available at Chester and in creeks of the Dee estuary. The lead industry was always speculative and reliant on merchant adventurers (usually speculative investors from the City of London and other financial centres) and investment by local gentry. This appetite for lead was satisfied to some extent by a half-dozen major mineral veins running roughly east to west which were all worked both before and after the eighteenth century.

Towards the end of the sixteenth century, the connections of the Mold area with the lead industry were being redeveloped and by the 1700s lead mining on Mold Mountain and along the boundaries of the lordships of the manor of Mold and its neighbour Bromfield and Iâl, was becoming noted for controversy rather than rich yields.

Details have already been given of a lead smelting mill at Mold which was let by Edward Lloyd to William Ratcliffe and William Chaloner, speculators from London. In 1601, the mill was sold to Richard Grosvenor of Eaton and, later in the seventeenth century, was owned jointly by the Grosvenors and the Myddletons of Chirk. Extracts from a sales book of 1681 show that the majority of the pigs of lead produced in Mold were sold to Alderman George Mainwaring, a Chester merchant, with smaller quantities going to a Liverpool merchant. Other purchasers were locally-based craftsmen and gentry.[2] The Mold mill continued to smelt until 1683 but then ceased operating due to cheaper competition from mills on Deeside and from Gadlys, as well as a shortage of charcoal and skilled labour and ever-increasing drainage costs.

In the 1660s, Evan Edwards of Rhual and John Eyton of Leeswood had been given an opportunity to repair their fortunes at the end of the Commonwealth period and were beginning to take advantage of the demand for lead.

Lead mining in Moldsdale and along its boundaries was disturbed in the years *c*.1732–63 by a long running dispute between the lords of the manor of Mold and the Grosvenor family.[3] In particular, the southern boundary at Loggerheads was violently contested because of a rich cluster of lead-bearing veins.

In the 1650s, the mineral rights of the manor of Mold had been equally divided between its three purchasers and by 1737, were owned by John Trevor (of Glynde in Sussex), Edward Lloyd (of Tyddyn) and Anthony Langley Swymmer, an infant under the guardianship of his uncles, William and Henry Swymmer, Bristol merchants who traded in West Indian sugar. To the south-west, across the county boundary into Denbighshire, the mineral rights of the lordship of Bromfield and Iâl had belonged to the Grosvenors of Eaton Hall in Cheshire since 1601. The third dominant mineral owner in the Mold area was the Davies (later Davies-Cooke) family of Gwysaney, who held a large tract of land, including the whole of the Bryn Celyn vein, enclosed by the loop in the course of the river Alun near Rhydymwyn.

Although a detailed survey of the manor of Mold in 1652 makes no mention of mines, and a rental of Ellis's part of the manor in 1657 enters 'lead mines' under 'small rents', there is no shortage of evidence from the beginning of the eighteenth century relating to the extraction of lead ore from the veins along the southern boundary of the parishes of Mold and Llanferres. Detailed maps showing a number of mine workings were produced as evidence to prove the boundary and name the sites operated by leases on occasions when the dispute was brought to court from the 1730s to the 1760s. The prospect of stumbling on a rich vein such as that discovered by Sir George Wynne in Halkyn was a constant spur to a continual procession of entrepreneurs.

The boundary was then unenclosed waste land known as Mold Mountain which adjoined the waste of the Denbighshire parish of Llanferres at Cathole (Cadole). It was alleged that the boundary between the two lordships was not clearly defined, although parishioners of both parishes regularly walked it on their customary Rogationtide perambulations. It was noted in evidence presented to the boundary dispute inquiry

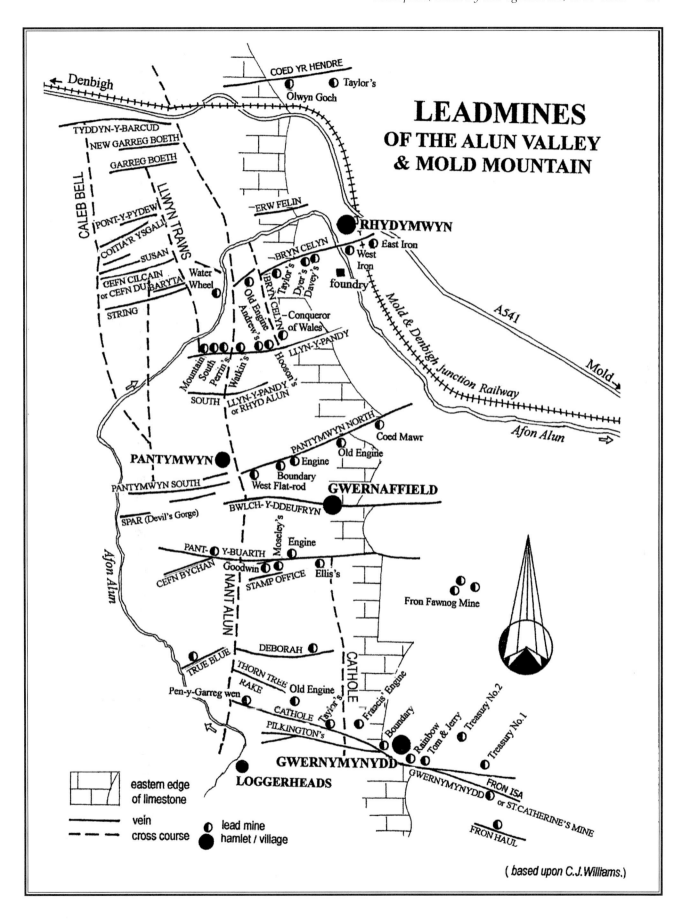

LEADMINES
OF THE ALUN VALLEY & MOLD MOUNTAIN

(*based upon C.J.Williams.*)

that in the 1690s there were areas described as 'ancient remains of two leadworks one called *Twn Rake* and another *Y Rake Vechan* where lead was picked up and sold to the Buckley potters.' From at least 1706, this part of the waste of the manor had been leased for lead mining, one lease, for a period of thirty-one years, was made by the lords of Mold to Chester merchant Daniel Peck, mineral agent to the Mostyns, who owned three smelting mills on the Dee. His activities ceased when he became bankrupt and in 1718 his mines were taken over by a group of four men known as the Derbyshire Company. Shareholders in this enterprise included a member of the Thornhill family from Derbyshire and two Chester men, Jonathan Robinson and James Comberbach. Most of their ore came from the Pant-y-Buarth mine. About the same time, the lords of Mold granted a take note (an agreement for letting) for Thorntree Rake, situated at the west end of the Cathole vein near Loggerheads, to William Brock. Brock is an example of the involvement of the minor gentry in business activities. He had married the daughter of Thomas Williams of Broncoed, the agent of the lords of Mold in 1704 and 1712 is recorded as collecting rents for Edward Lloyd of Tyddyn. His name appears in the diary of Thomas Griffith and as a regular member of the Lion Club.

Sir Richard Grosvenor was encouraged to encroach less than a mile across his lordship boundary by the existence of lucrative lead mining activity at Cathole which was in the next county. He had several allies among the miners and parishioners of Llanferres as well as the support of the rector, Hugh Jones, and his brother, Edward Jones, the squire of Colomendy. Grosvenor gambled on the three lords of Mold taking no action and judged that one of them, Antony Swymmer, due to his absence in Jamaica, was too far away to intervene. As a result, in 1723, Grosvenor began to encroach into the lordship of Mold and leased mines which straddled the lordship and county boundary to Thomas Pilkington of Ashby de la Zouch, therby causing a dispute which was to take forty years to resolve. Ten years later, two of the lords of Mold, Edward Lloyd and John Trevor, lodged a bill of complaint but no proceedings ensued and the Grosvenors continued to lease land for mining on the Flintshire side of the boundary. In 1737 Grosvenor granted a new lease on what had been formerly leased to the Derbyshire Company by the lords of Mold, to Benjamin Perrin. Another man who leased an interest from the Grosvenor estate was Edward Cheney who lived at Loggerheads and Colomendy. He began mining opposite Tŷ Draw at Cathole in the late 1720s and, after taking over the mines leased by Sir Robert Grosvenor to Thomas Pilkington in 1723, claimed that they were in the lordship of Mold, and that he had a lease from the lordship of mines on that part of Mold Mountain not granted to the Derbyshire Company. Two Denbighshire justices were approached but declined to intervene, declaring the mines to be in Flintshire.[4] Not prepared to be thwarted by the impudence of Cheney, the Grosvenor family attempted to recover them but not before the hard-faced Cheney retreated to a Derbyshire manor purchased from the £5,000 he is said to have made from great quantities of ore he had already raised.

In 1752, Sir Robert Grosvenor's lessee at Cathole, Benjamin Perrin, was served with an ejectment order on behalf of Anthony Langley Swymmer, lord of the manor of Mold. The case was heard at Salop Assizes in the summer of 1753, and resulted in a verdict in Swymmer's favour. Sir Robert Grosvenor, however, claimed that many witnesses who could have proved the mines to be in Bromfield and Iâl could not attend at Shrewsbury and legal proceedings continued for another ten years. The evidence for the defendants, the lords of Mold, is preserved in a large number of depositions of witnesses.[5] Their case began with the submission that:

> During the minority of the present defendant Mr Swymmer (his guardians living at Bristol and seldom coming into Wales and being Strangers in the Country) several persons made Encroachments on the Mountain and attempted to Sink Pitts. The Place now in question lyes on the north side of the Boundary between *Carreg Carn March Arthur* and *Pen y Garreg Wen* about [blank] yards within the Boundary on the North Side of the Green path in which place the said Mr Perrin under some lease or Agreement of Sir Robert Grosvenor hath sunk several Pitts or Shafts and thereout Raised and taken great Quantitys of Lead Ore lying within the waste land of the said Manor. A little North of these Pitts there are two others known by the name of Cathole which were sunk 30 years ago … and in a direct line westward are several Pitts known by the name of Thorntree Rake or Cathole Vein.

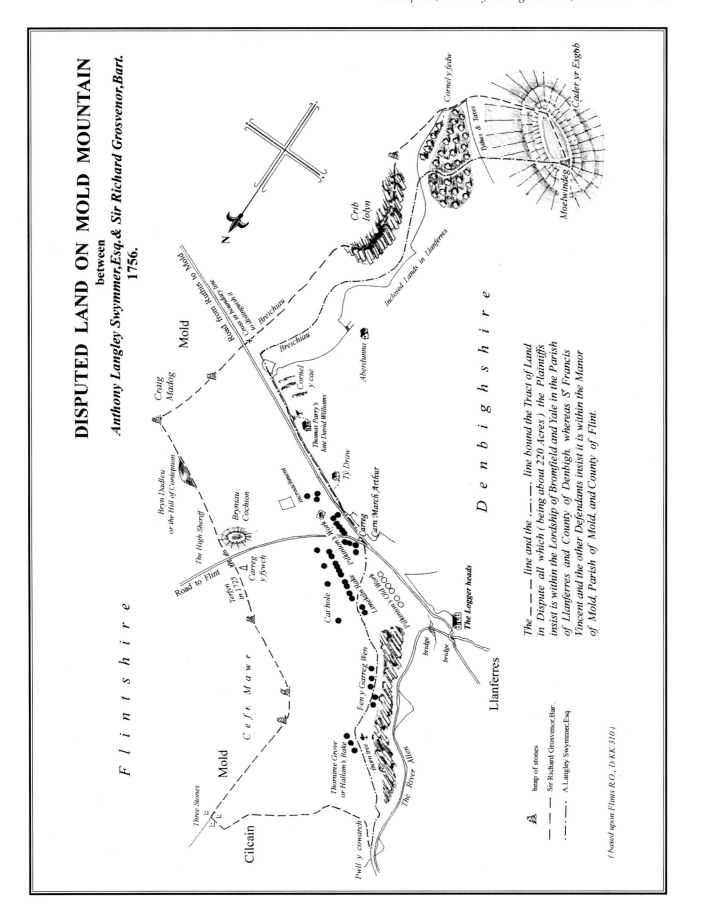

DISPUTED LAND ON MOLD MOUNTAIN
between
Anthony Langley Swymmer, Esq. & Sir Richard Grosvenor, Bart.
1756.

The ——— line and the .—.—. line bound the Tract of Land in Dispute all which (being about 220 Acres) the Plaintiffs insist is within the Lordship of Bromfield and Yale in the Parish of Llanferres and County of Denbigh, whereas S⁺ Francis Vincent and the other Defendants insist it is within the Manor of Mold, Parish of Mold, and County of Flint.

heap of stones
——— Sir Richard Grosvenor, Bar.
.—.—. A. Langley Swymmer, Esq.

(based upon Flints R.O., D KK 310)

The defendants produced witnesses to prove that Grosvenor's boundary had been redefined by the parishioners of Llanferres, alleging that:

> A stone cut of late years by orders of Rev. Mr Hugh Jones Vicar of Llanferres on which was the word *Terfyn* [boundary] as a pretended boundary of the Parish to extend the same out of private view and to promote his own vicarial perquisites or advantages and not as a boundary of the Lordship of Bromfield and Yale but quite foreign thereto.

Hugh Jones, a blacksmith and witness to the making of this illegal boundary marker, testified that:

> … in April 1732 as he was walking across Mold Mountain very Early in the morning about Sun Rising he saw one John Jones Mason one of the sons of the Mr Jones late Rector cut the word *Terfyn* on a large stone called *Carreg y fwch*. He heard that John Jones cut the stone by order of Mr Edward Jones of Colomendy, Attorney at Law and his brother the Rector.

Further evidence that the Llanferres folk had tampered with boundary markers was presented by Thomas Cheney, a local miner, who swore that 'the Parishioners of Llanverres always varied from time to time by encroaching further on the mountain and demolishing their former marks and placing up new ones.' A number of witnesses spoke of the custom of Processions of the Boundary at Rogationtide and the way in which they had been taught never to forget the experience which appeared to be impressed upon their memories as clearly as the footprint of Arthur's horse was on the boundary stone. The evidence of John Edwards, a gentleman, aged 71 years, who had been examined previously at Salop but had since died, had testified that:

> several times he walked the boundary when a boy at school and at such processions they halted & stood a long while at the said Boundary Stone called Carreg Carn March Arthur & threw stones & Horse Nails in the sd. Stone which appeared to be in the form or shape of a Horse-Shoe deriving its name from Arthur's Horse.

Children halting at such a stone or other boundary were generally pinched by the ears or punished in some other manner as one John Jones of Mold testified:

> … one George Leach threw some half-pence into the hole in Carreg Carn March Arthur for children to scramble for where they had their ears pinched and when he attempted to run away from this reminder received a stroke from the whip which hurt him and made him cry.

The experience suffered by Richard Thomas of Rhosesmor when ten years old was more disgusting '… he sat down near the stone and a person came behind him and laid him on his back and urined in his mouth.'

The gathering of stray sheep 'Waifes & estrayes' was a regular occupation in the manor and formed the basis of the evidence of Edward Jones, aged 68 years, who about thirty years previously had rented (for 10 years) 'the Toll Waifes & Estrayes of the Lordship of Mold from Nehemiah Griffith Esq then Agent or Steward to the Lord of the Manor of Mold during which time he carried Waifes & Estrays from within the defendants Boundary without any interruption, threats, claims or molestation whatsoever from the parishioners of Llanverres.'

There were a number of witnesses to prove that Carreg Carn March Arthur was indeed the boundary between Denbighshire and Flintshire, where the Denbighshire sheriff conducted the judges to meet the sheriff of Flint. Here a pole, with a handkerchief tied to it, was put into the hole of the stone to denote the boundary. Others recollected that Mr Jones, rector of Llanferres, 'kneeled down upon Carreg Carn March Arthur and said prayers with all parishioners agreeing the stone to be the boundary.' A former overseer of the highways stated that the parishioners of Llanferres directed that the roads be repaired no further than this stone.

Another witness remembered that 'it was the place where we used to have Ale & Bread & Cheese given.'

The dispute finally ended up in the Court of the Exchequer in 1763 which found in favour of the lords of Mold. A boundary stone,[6] which local legend said bore an impression made when one hoof of Arthur's steed landed on it after jumping from the summit of Moel Famau, about three miles away, was erected beside the Mold to Ruthin road,

The Carreg Carn March Arthur Boundary Stone.

on the spot adjudged to be the boundary. Both stone and monument were moved and re-erected by Denbighshire County Council when the road was widened in 1974.

> The stone underneath this Arch
> CARREG CARN MARCH ARTHUR
> was Adjudged to be the Boundary of the
> Parish and Lordship of Mold in the County
> of Flint and of Llanverras in the County
> of Denbigh by the High Court of Exchequer
> at Westminster 10th November 1763.

In the spring of the following year the lady of the manor of Mold, Dame Arabella Vincent, widow of Anthony Langley Swymmer (who had died in 1759), issued firm instructions to those perambulating the newly confirmed boundary.

> To get a Stile made on Moel Windeg side of the Vedw by leave of the Owner and to perambulate thro' the Vedw. The Tenant of the Vedw be applyed for leave to erect a Stile.
>
> To walk the boundaries in question the next Ascension Day and then to destroy all the Llanverras heaps of stones and pretended boundaries previously giving notice of such intention to Lord Grosvenor's Agent and the Minister and Churchwardens of Llanverras.
>
> Keep an attested copy of the Notice – prevent Llanferras people from Cutting Gorse &c. on disputed ground and take away such gorse &c. as they shall cut. Drive their sheep off the disputed ground. Erect a Pillar near C[arreg] M[arch] Arthur with an inscription denoting that to have been ascertained as the boundary stone at the trial. In the perambulation let a person go over thro' Ty Draw barn. Put a boundary stone or tree in the Green Path between C. M. Arthur and Pen y garreg wen. Clear the Path between Pen y garreg wen and the Troughes of all Rubbish so that the Path may be clear and visible. Continue the Old perambulation up the River from Pwll y cowarth between Mold and Kilkin as heretofore. See if Kilkin people can be prevailed on not to Perambulate from the Circular Stones to Pwll y cowarth.[7]

The verdict of 1763 put an end to further encroachment and allowed the lords of Mold to continue granting mining leases for the lead veins in the wastes of Mold Mountain. In 1737, in the face of Grosvenor encroachment on the southern boundary, they had attempted to combine together to mine lead throughout their territory. An Act of Parliament was obtained to enable the guardians of Anthony Langley Swymmer to join in partnership in making mining leases with the two other lords, John Trevor and Edward Lloyd. There was much at stake, for the 31-year-old lease originally granted to Daniel Peck, was scheduled to expire later that year. The initiative for the partnership came from a proposal of Thomas Griffith of Rhual who had heard rumours that one of the shareholders in the expiring lease, Alderman James Comberbach, had obtained a new one from Langley Swymmer's guardians. Griffith proposed forestalling such a move by obtaining a new lease for shareholders, including himself, the lords of Mold, Sir George Wynne, Simon Yorke of Erddig and others, with a total capital of £4,800. Although the deed of partnership recited a lease from the lords of Mold of the Pant-y-Buarth Mine alone, it is clear from the accounts that the partners worked mines on the whole of Mold Mountain, from Llyn-y-Pandy in the north to Gwernymynydd in the south. They achieved their objective, but, although they did not make an overall loss, their profit from 1738–60 was a meagre £1,820.

The Gwernymynydd (or St Catherine's) Mine[8] was worked by the Mold Mountain Company by means of an adit tunnel which commenced from Bryn Coch, just south of Mold, and ran for about half-a-mile. Ore worth £4,690 was raised between 1738 and 1757. This, along with the Cathole mine, was leased in 1786 to Richard Kirk of Wrexham but was said to be making a loss. D. Walker, in his survey of the manor of Mold in 1791,[9] optimistically reported that:

> Gwernymynydd Mine is nearly due south of the town of Mold and near the road from Mold to Ruthin in which it is suggested the principal lodes of lead ore are found. Because of water and the declivity of the ground a level has been driven of great length through the farm in the occupation of Edward Jones, Broncoed, and part of the commons into the lands of the Revd. Mr Williams of Fron where they now get ore. The level is now within 40 yards of the common and their further or present pit is 90 yards deep. As this level is drove into the heart of the mining country it will of course drain a great extent thereof. The work is undertaken with judgement and in all human probability will be attended with great success.

For sixty years after 1760, when the lease of the Mold Mountains proprietors expired, there is little evidence of mining activity elsewhere, except at Pen-y-Fron and Llwyn-y-Pandy mines situated at Rhydymwyn, north of Mold, in the loop of the river Alun. Both these enterprises captured the notice of topographical artists and the attention in the summer of 1798 of a tourist from Bath, the Reverend Richard Warner.

Sometime around the beginning of the 1780s, a former grocer, Richard Ingleby, invested in the mine known as Pen-y-Fron[10] at the west end of the Bryn Celyn vein. At first he made a great loss but, by the 1790s, was prospering and made his fortune. The mine was drained by a Newcomen engine and three water wheels, and had both a smelting and a rolling mill and was fed by a leat from Halkyn. In 1796, John Ingleby (no relation to Richard) a 'jobbing artist' from Halkyn, painted a water colour of the mine which gives us a good insight into operations on the site and this was supplemented by Richard Warner's report of his visit there two years later.

> [The mine] is drained by a steam engine upon the old construction and a water wheel…Independent of these are two other wheels which raise the water from the lower workings to the main level, communicating with the engine. With all this power, Mr Ingleby is scarcely able to get to the bottom of his work, except the weather be particularly dry. Were he able to effect this completely, his profits would be immense, since the mine is incalculably rich, there being one vein of solid ore two yards and a half in width, besides several other seams. In the few instances where Mr Ingleby has gotten to the bottom no less than seventy tons of ore have been raised per week.[11]

Warner had just visited the Llyn-y-Pandy mine lower down the Alun valley which was also painted by John Ingleby. This mine had been worked intensively earlier in the eighteenth century by Benjamin Perrin and the Mold Mountain proprietors. The famous Bersham iron master, John Wilkinson, took it over in 1791. In the same year, Walker in his survey gave a description of the water engine and observed that 'it will cost the undertakers at a moderate computation £8,000 before they get an ounce of ore. To such Exertions and Spirit of Enterprise this Kingdom owes its superiority to its surrounding Neighbours.' Warner described the site as:

the most considerable lead mining speculation in England [sic] … the property of John Wilkinson Esq., the great Ironmaster, who has, with infinite spirit and perseverance, encountered obstacles in bringing it to its present state, that would have exhausted the patience and resolution as well as the coffers, of most other men. With all his exertions, however, he has not been able to render it complete, the mine even now contains so much water, that he has been under the necessity of erecting four vast engines (of Messrs. Boulton and Watt's construction) upon the premises to drain it … Many thousand tons of lead ore are now in stock upon these premises waiting for a market, the war having almost suspended the demand for lead, and lessened the price to nearly one half of what it formerly sold for. The engines also are quiet, and the works at a stand.'[12]

Before the 1820s, production at the mine has been estimated at 20,000 tons; Wilkinson was probably responsible for most of this, although the mine appears to have been practically abandoned from about the time of his death in 1808.

Coal mining

There is little evidence of coal mining in the lordship of Mold before the nineteenth century when a number of pits were developed in easterly townships. The geological formation of the westerly part of the lordship on Mold Mountain had no coal measures and major faults, providing lead rather than coal. From the medieval period until the twentieth century, coal was extracted further east in the neighbouring lordships of Hawarden and Ewloe. In the eighteenth century, it was the Glynnes of Hawarden, and later the Davies-Cookes of Gwysaney, lords of the Manor of Ewloe, who profited from coal royalties rather than the lords of Mold.[13] John Leland had observed in 1536 that there were 'cole pittes a 3 quarters of a mile from Molesdale towne' probably at Nant Mawr. In the seventeenth century, some of the gentry dug for coal on their own estates; the Trevors of Plas Teg are known to have opened a mine at Coed Talon in 1630.[14] One such pit, between Treuddyn and Pontblyddyn at 'Werne dyvallog' (Gwern Dafolog), was worked by a handful of men with an output of only 235 tons. Other pits were located nearby at Leeswood, from whence cannel coal was sent to Cheshire and the towns of Denbigh and Ruthin. Evan Edwards and Robert Coytmore were mining at Nant Mawr in the 1650s and in 1666, two colliers are known to have drowned in a 'colepit'. In the eighteenth century, coal was carried via Mold, Loggerheads and Ruthin to the vale of Clwyd.

In 1791, the surveyor, Walker, advised Champneys of the potential coal reserves in the townships of Mold, south of the river Alun, where 'there are workable seams of excellent coal under several farms and commons on this side of the estate … and there will be soon a considerable demand for coals not only to burn lime for the improvement of the new inclosures as well as to work the very capital [steam] engines now erecting at the Llyn y pandy mines.' He advised Swymmer to open another colliery nearer the lead mines than Spon of which he spoke well.

The Colliery [Spon] is about 8 miles from Chester … a great part of the Coals are carried there and deemed much preferable to any other coals which come to that City… The thickness of the principal Seams of Coals near 3 yards thick and excellent Coal.

Spon was also benefitting from the employment of two steam engines, one for draining the pits and the other for raising coal.

It was not until after the end of the French wars in 1815, when there was a greater demand for coal to meet the needs of factories and later the railways, that the Mold coalfield was really developed.

The cotton factory[15]

The artist John Ingleby was born on the mountain, half-way between Holywell and Mold. He was given the opportunity to provide the naturalist and writer, Thomas Pennant, with illustrations for his history of Whitford and Holywell in the 1790s. He recorded the copper works and cotton mills of the Greenfield Valley, probably at a time when a cotton mill was being constructed in Mold that was described by a fellow artist,

The Mold Cotton Mill, watercolour by J. Ingleby. The mill building can be seen in the centre distance.

Edward Pugh, as 'A handsome and stupendous cotton factory, close to the town …' Ingleby produced a watercolour of the 'Mold Cotton Mill' in *c.*1795. The Parish Church, visible on the ridge opposite, now had a rival for attention; Jerusalem above and a dark satanic mill in the valley below, although it was not described as such by the new vicar of Mold in 1792, who wrote in his common place book, 'The Parish is extensive, and populous and likely to increase in the latter as an extensive Cotton Mill has been erected near Rhyd y goleu by Messrs Atherton & Hodson.'[16]

More information had been provided the year before in a survey of the manor of Mold which described the premises as a

> Farm and Water Corn Mill let on lease at £120 pa to Peter Atherton Esqr who is now constructing a Capital Cotton Mill and making other Necessary Buildings for a Cotton Manufactory thereon – Rhydygolley Mill consisting of an Overshot Water Corn Mill on an old and bad construction with two water wheels driving separately two pair of stones … lands lying contiguous to the River in the Occupation of the Revd. Mr Edward Parry might at a small expence be converted to a Capital Water Meadow.

The landscape of the old town of Mold was in the process of changing. The fields in the vicinity of the new mill and on the banks of the river Alun were described in 1791 as 'the Town Fields' divided into 'Yokings'. The site was part of the pre-Norman settlement, an area long used for arable and meadowland. They were the fields mentioned in the survey of 1477 as a water corn mill and which had surrounded the seventeenth-century lead mill. Over the centuries, a small settlement had gathered at Maes-y-Dre which was to expand as housing was constructed there for the Lancastrian immigrant workforce. An advert in the *Manchester Mercury in* 1800 supplied details of the mill estate which included stables, barns and sixteen cottages (the latter located at Rhydygoleu, which may previously have housed the lead miners of an earlier venture). The machinery included '4,000 spindles and all the necessary geers, tumbling shafts, water-wheels, &c'.[17]

The lease of the newly-built cotton mill was sold to a group of Manchester manufacturers, the Batemans and Knights, and was eventually run by the brothers Samuel and James Knight as the Mold Cotton Twist Company and must have impressed the people of Mold in 1812 by lighting the building with coal gas, although a distinguished local critic was polite and limited in his praise describing it as 'a handsome building of the sort, and forms a conspicuous object in the vale, although the admirers of rural scenery may not be disposed to consider it has any accession

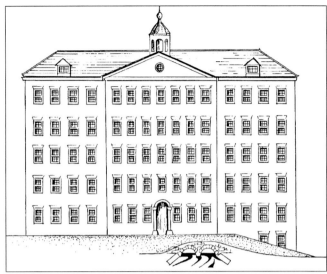
The Mold Cotton Mill.

to its beauty.' In 1815, the Knights bought the premises from Sir Thomas Mostyn (now lord of the manor of Mold) and by 1822 about 300 people were employed and the mill was extended in 1825. The Knights also bought the Rhual estate after the death in action at Waterloo of Major Edwin Griffith, whose heirs sold it for £24,500. They went on to became bankers as well as mill proprietors but were declared bankrupt in December 1831, when Rhual was bought by Field Marshal Sir Alured Clarke, who transferred it to his niece, Mrs Henrietta Maria Philips, sister to the late Major Edwin Griffith.

Agriculture and enclosure

By the eighteenth century, social and economic pressures, driven by an increase in population and a more scientific approach to farming, led to a significant change in the countryside throughout Britain. The most obvious and significant transformation was the enclosure of waste and common land which occurred in Moldsdale at the turn of the nineteenth century.

Two contemporary reports had recommended enclosure in the district. The first was a detailed review and a set of recommendations for the improvement of the manor of Mold prepared in September 1791 by D. Walker of Marylebone Street, London.[18] He had made a careful tour of the manor and produced a 'Survey and Valuation of Thomas Swymmer Champney's Estate in the Parish of Mold' which was full of sound advice to the owner on how he should make use of the industrial potential of the estate and approach obtaining a bill for parliamentary enclosure of land.

A Bill is now soliciting by the almost unanimous consent and approbation of the proprietors of Estates within the Manor for the Inclosure of the extensive Commons and Wastes therein and they have agreed to give the Lord one twelfth part of the Commons in some townships and a sixteenth in others quantity and quality considered as an allotment in lieu of all mineral rights (the Mines excepted besides an Allotment in Common with others and in proportion to the size of his Landed Estate in the respective Townships and reserving to the Lord and others interested therein all Mines and Minerals within the respective Commons to be inclosed ... The great extent of Commons is towards the south side and Mountains between Flintshire and Denbighshire ...' Walker described the nature of the soil, 'under the Commons in the townships of Nerquis, Arddynwent, Hendrebiffa, Gwernaffield &c is a Lime Stone Rock and the soil is better and worse in proportion to the thickness or shallowness of the staple upon the Rocks and where there is any soil produces sweet herbage and there is an extensive and fine tract of sheep Common towards the Inclosures on the North from Mold Mountain and the Summerhouse to Llynpandu Mine and well worth inclosing but part of this great Common towards the south is very rocky. To the westward of the above road from Nerquis to Llanarmon lies the great Lead Mining Country ...

He concluded his long, 54-page report with the observation,

> As this Estate is Capable of great Improvement and the Mines therein likely to produce considerably more than they have hitherto done I would advise it by no means to be sold. The present Rents are near to £1,400 per ann and therefore sufficient security for £20,000 … and to let leases for 21 years for the best and most improveable rents … particularly for the Mines and New Inclosures.

A much shorter report was made in 1794 for the recently founded Board of Agriculture by George Kay, a Scotsman, who briefly reviewed the parish in *A General View of the Agriculture of Flintshire*. Kay made his short report when the process of the enclosure of common land by Act of Parliament was just beginning and observed,

> Although some small portions of the waste lands have lately been divided and inclosed, yet there are many thousand acres of the waste lands still left in their original state, which are very capable of being converted into arable and pasture land.

Kay saw what was happening on the commons in the surrounding areas around the farms and the wastes on the mountain with sheep, black cattle, horses and asses grazing at will and in an 'almost starved state,' that 'can never improve.' His comments on the state of farms in Flintshire were generalised,

> Where the farms are large, the tenants are very well supplied with housing; but the smaller ones, that rent from £20 to £50 a year, of which there are a greater proportion, are very ill accommodated. They are in want of farmyards and sheds for cattle …

This observation may well have offended 'improving land lords', such as the Giffards of Nerquis Hall, who had capitalised their estates with improvements.

Walker's survey had reported that, on the whole, the land was well farmed and the buildings in good repair. For example, 'A substantial and convenient farm house of stone and thatch had recently been erected at *Rhyd-y-goleu* with chambers above and a lean to abutting with a stable, cowhouse, and cart lodge.' The Revd Edward Parry at Town Field farm had a similar house and buildings, with a detached buttery stone and slated.[19] Three notebooks compiled in 1795 for the townships of Bistre, Argoed and Treuddyn provide further information on landowners, tenants and holdings, as well as recording the field names and acreages.

Between 1750 and 1850, over 4,000 Acts of Parliament were passed to promote the enclosure of land, affecting over six million acres. An Enclosure Act made it possible to enclose commons, wastes and open fields and conferred legal sanctity and finality on the arrangements made. This course of action was taken to make farms more compact, larger and easier to work. It resulted in a better balance between arable and pasture land and allowed for the better care of animals.Waste and common land became profitable by improvement such as ploughing, rotation of crops and the application of marl and manure. More land was brought under regular cultivation and in some instances, tithes were got rid of in exchange for enclosed allotments.[20] The Enclosure Act for Mold was passed in 1792 following the presentation to Parliament of a Bill drawn up by local landowners. The Act appointed commissioners to supervise the enclosure and gave them power to act.[21] The purpose of the Mold Enclosure Act was embodied in its title and preamble.

> An Act for Dividing and Allotting the Common Lands in Mold Parish 1792.
> AND WHEREAS THE SAID COMMONS AND WASTE LANDS are in their present state of little value, but if divided and enclosed may be very considerably improved to the advantage of the several persons interested therein: but such division cannot be made without the aid of Parliament.[22]

The Act contained information relating to the land that was to be enclosed, the making of roads, the duties of the commissioners appointed to supervise the work and the means used to meet expenses and inform the interested parties which included proprietors, commoners and prospective purchasers.

The Act showed the total area of the common land to be 4,044 acres, more than six square miles. It named the chief landowners as being: 'Thomas Swymmer Champneys, of Penton Lodge, in the Co. of Southampton, Lord of the Manor and of the soil of the said commons and Owner and Proprietor of divers Messuages, Lands &c within the Manor of Mold'; the vicar of Mold, the Reverend Robert Lewis, who was entitled to certain glebe lands within the parish, as was Hugh Mason, the curate of Nercwys and Treuddyn; Lord Dacre, Grace Trevor and George Boscawen, three descendants of Sir John Trevor (one of the three purchasers of the lordship in the 1650s); John Lloyd of Wigfair (head of the family which had bought up Colonel Twistleton's share of the lordship); Mary Puleston, widow, of Gwysaney; Catherine Wardle and Gwyllym Lloyd Wardle of Hartsheath; John Giffard of Nerquis Hall; Richard Hill Waring of Leeswood Hall; Hope Wynne Eyton, of Tower and Coed y llai. Others were also named as entitled to the right of common and waste within the manor and the lords of Mold, Thomas Swymmer Champneys, Lord Dacre, Grace Trevor, George Boscawen and John Lloyd were entitled to all the

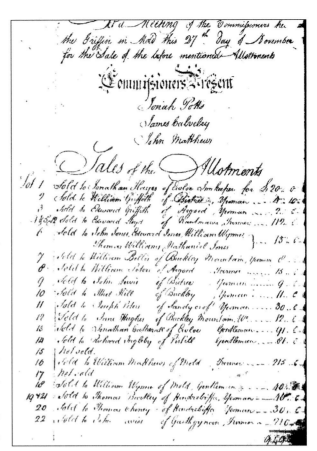

Sale of enclosure allotments by the commissioners.

mines and minerals located under and upon the commons and waste lands within the manor.

The manorial rights of the lord of the manor were to be preserved: 'Six statute acres in total allotted to the Lord of the Manor and Proprietors of Estates within the Manor for the purposes of getting lime stones, building stones, gravel, sand earth, and marl, and clay to make bricks to be used upon lands in the said Manor or in the repair of the highway and private roads.'

The appointed enclosure commissioners were: Samuel Wyatt, of Burton on Trent, Staffordshire (later replaced by Josiah Boydell of Rossett); Josiah Potts of Ollerton, Cheshire; John Calveley of Huntingdon, Cheshire and John Matthews of Newmarket, Flintshire. They were to ascertain the boundaries of the manor of Mold and the commons.

> The said Commissioners, or any three of them shall together with Thomas Swymmer Champneys, or his steward, Agent, or Bailiff, and all other persons entitled to Rights of Commons or Waste Lands shall openly and publickly, and in the day time ride or perambulate the limits or out boundaries. Notice to be given in both Chester Newspapers and written notices to be affixed upon the principal doors of the Parish Church of Mold and on the south doors of the Chapels of Nerquis and Tryddyn … Hope, Llanarmon, Llanverras, Kilken, Northop and Hawarden.

To defray the expenses of the Act, the commissioners were given power to dispose by public auction of any new allotments, cottages or encroachments which had been made within the last twenty years and which were deemed to be common, some of which were the homes of potters at Buckley and lead miners at the Loggerheads. In all, the commissioners disposed of about 584 acres of commons and wastes by auction and obtained the sum of £5,500 towards the expenses of surveying, passing and carrying out the Act. The commissioners were also required to set out all necessary public and private roads for carriages and horses, as well as footpaths, ditches, fences, watercourses, bridges, banks, drains, sluices, gates and stiles. Carriage roads were to be at least 40 feet broad (exclusive of ditches).

Anyone receiving an allotment in the enclosure was to be rated for a year for the purpose of making all the new roads and paths which were to be kept in repair by the inhabitants and occupiers of lands in the townships. Fences were to be repaired by the owner but no gates could be erected across any carriage road nor could they plant trees in hedges at less than fifty yards apart. All springs, wells, ponds, pits and watering places were reserved for occupiers of the land.

A further enclosure award was made in 1800 which covered Buckley and Treuddyn.[23] In this instance the commissioners divided 2,848 acres among 93 claimants of which 1,823 acres were given to seven large proprietors in allotments each amounting to more than 100 acres. The lord of the manor, Thomas Swymmer Champneys, was the largest beneficiary receiving over 469 acres. John Lloyd of Wigfair received allotments amounting to 253 acres; John Giffard of Nerquis Hall gained 258 acres; the Reverend Hope Wynne Eyton 186 acres; Trevor Lloyd of Pentrehobyn and Trevor Hall 194 acres; Gwyllym Lloyd Wardle of Hartsheath 190 acres; Mrs Catherine Wardle, 18 acres.[24] A further thirty one proprietors were given lots of between 2 and 10 acres, and twenty eight proprietors shared 29 acres.

Throughout the country, parliamentary enclosures brought forth protests from country people and poets like John Clare lamented the peasant's loss of freedom and the destruction of the old landscape.

> Unbounded freedom ruled the wandering scene
> Nor fence of ownership crept in between
> To hide the prospect of the following eye
> Its only bondage was the circling sky …
> 'Fence now meets fence in owners little bounds
> Of field and meadow large as garden grounds
> In little parcels little minds to please
> With men and flocks imprisoned ill at ease[25]

The enclosure awards not only reshaped the pattern of rural areas and destroyed the silence and isolation of moorland, they deprived country people of what they regarded as their right. The enclosing of wastes and commons extinguished common rights of grazing, the right to cut and take wood, reeds, heather and bracken, and the right to dig turf or peat for fuel. These rights related to natural produce, not to crops or the commercial exploitation of the land. In many instances, cottages which had been built on the commons were either pulled down or became the property of the person allotted the land. These changes were resisted in some places and, although there is no record of a violent reaction to the Mold enclosure, there was a vigorous protest against the work of commissioners in the neighbouring parish of Hope which turned into a riot.[26] A labourer called Thomas Jones was arrested for pulling down enclosure fences and put in Flint prison from where, at the demand of 200 men from Pontblyddyn, he was forcibly released and triumphantly returned to Hope. Troops were sent to the area, the culprits arrested and tried at the Great Sessions in Mold in August and found guilty. The local gentry, particularly the Reverend Hope Wynne Eyton, who was both a magistrate and beneficiary of awards from both parishes, were disquieted at the prospect of general rural discontent spreading to Mold and had no desire to create martyrs. It was therefore thought prudent to approach the Attorney General who, given certain reassurances, obtained a pardon for those convicted.

We have seen how the manor of Mold had originated in Saxon and Norman times and been adapted and used by Welsh Princes for the same purpose as tightly self-subsistent agricultural units and how it was transformed from the eleventh-century manor of Bistre, becoming the dominant unit in the local economy. By 1800, it appeared to be no more than a status symbol with little economic advantage. Although the manor retained its medieval prerequisites of rents, tolls, courts and customs, these had little effect on the people of Mold. The powers of the Court Leet and Court Baron served only as a means of controlling nuisances on the highway and in the market place, and other powers, such as the appointment of constables, were about to become the responsibility of local authorities. Any remaining economic advantages were vested, not in the manor but in the lordship and these were not to be broken up or alienated when the manor was put up for sale in 1801. The lords of Mold were to retain their rights to the minerals of the lordship at a time when these assets were to become particularly valuable.

The manor, part of the medieval lordship which had been bought by three purchasers from the eighth earl of Derby in the 1650s, had become the property of Andrew Ellis of Althrey Flintshire (d. *c.*1660) from whom it passed to his daughter and, in less than twenty years, to the Langley family in whose hands it remained, descending by marriage through the female line from the 1670s onwards, until its sale at the beginning of the nineteenth century to Sir Thomas Mostyn, whose heirs became lords of the manor of Mold.

The Langleys were an Essex family who at the end of the seventeenth century had developed links with the West Indian island of Jamaica where they developed sugar plantations in the parishes of Vere and St Thomas. John Langley is mentioned as having a house in Mold in 1698.[27]

Colonel Anthony Swymmer, a nephew of Andrew Langley, inherited the manor in 1710. The Swymmers were Bristol merchants and members of a family trading in Jamaican sugar and slaves and Colonel Swymmer was a member of His Majesty's Council in Jamaica and a man of some wealth and importance on the island. In his will, dated 20 January 1729, he named two of his children. The eldest, Jane Langley Swymmer, was left £4,000 on attaining the age of 21 years or marriage. She married Richard Chaundler Champneys, a widowed wealthy merchant from Fareham in Hampshire, who had a large estate in Somerset.

Colonel Swymmer's second child, Anthony Langley Swymmer, succeeded his father in 1729 when barely four years old. His rentals in Mold were in the care of John Lloyd, gentleman. An Act of 1737 (when he was aged 12 years) enabled his guardians, William and Henry Swymmer, to issue leases for certain mines in Flintshire.[28] Anthony was married at St James's, Westminster, on 5 January 1748 to Arabella Astley, daughter of Sir John Astley. He became a member of Parliament for Southampton and was resident at Longwood House near Winchester whilst earning a substantial income from his estates in Jamaica where he owned 8,278 acres, divided into at least half a dozen plantations. He devised the manor of Mold to his wife for her life and after her decease, to his nephew Thomas Champneys, the only surviving son of Jane Langley Swymmer.

Thomas Champneys was created a baronet in 1767 and his memorial in the parish church at Orchardleigh in Somerset sums up the startling career of the first Champneys, later lords of the manor of Mold, and the reason for its inevitable sale.

The late Sir Thomas served the office of High Sheriff with great splendour in the year 1775. Was a magistrate and deputy lieutenant of the same, he inherited very considerable estates from his father and uncle in the several counties of Somerset, Hants, Wilts, Flint and Gloster, but from mismanagement by his guardians during his minority and too easy and liberal a disposition through life no less than six entire manors with other property was alienated from the family estates and Manors of Orchardleigh and Frome Selwood, and certain estates attached thereto alone remained with the plantations in Jamaica at his decease. Sir Thomas departed this life… July 21 1821 aged 76.[29]

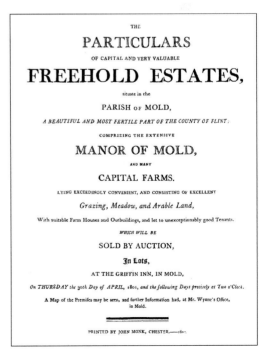

THE
PARTICULARS
OF CAPITAL AND VERY VALUABLE
FREEHOLD ESTATES,
situate in the
PARISH OF MOLD,
A BEAUTIFUL AND MOST FERTILE PART OF THE COUNTY OF FLINT;
COMPRIZING THE EXTENSIVE
MANOR OF MOLD,
AND MANY
CAPITAL FARMS.
LYING EXCEEDINGLY CONVENIENT, AND CONSISTING OF EXCELLENT
Grazing, Meadow, and Arable Land,
With suitable Farm Houses and Outbuildings, and let to unexceptionably good Tenants.
WHICH WILL BE
SOLD BY AUCTION,
In Lots,
AT THE GRIFFIN INN, IN MOLD,
On *THURSDAY* the 30th Day of *APRIL*, 1801, and the following Days precisely at Two o'Clock.
A Map of the Premises may be seen, and further Information had, at Mr. Wynne's Office, in Mold.

PRINTED BY JOHN MONK, CHESTER.——1801.

Sale catalogue of Thomas Swymmer Champney's estate in Mold.

*Portrait of Thomas Swymmer Champneys
with his sister.*

The extravagance, exhibitionism and eccentricity of the son exceeded that of the father. Thomas Swymmer Mostyn-Champneys (who later became the second baronet) led a life of irresponsible and needless expenditure becoming heavily involved in litigation. Despite this, he retained the support and loyalty of his wife, Charlotte Margaret Mostyn, second daughter of Sir Roger Mostyn, whom he married in 1792, when the manor of Mold was settled on him by his father. During the early years of their marriage, they made some attempt to rid their estates of debt[30] and finally, in 1809, Sir Thomas Mostyn paid £15,000 for the manor and lordship of Mold.'[31] Despite this, Thomas Champney was unable to contain the cascade of funds to creditors and eventually, after the death of his father, ended up in the insolvent debtor's court which declared his liabilities to be upwards of £429,000 (£18 million at today's values). The whole estate was placed in Chancery and Champneys was sent, first to Ilchester gaol and afterwards to Winchester prison for debt. He was later again imprisoned for debt until Lady Charlotte cleared them from an inheritance she had received. Even then,

He could not resist the temptation of more magnifence, however for his homecoming was staged magnificently. He had a procession to meet him on his arrival from gaol. In a carriage were eight daughters of farmers dressed in white, with white straw bonnets trimmed with blue ribbons, and carrying baskets of flowers. His tenant farmers' sons he got to dress in short smock frocks, white straw hats and more blue ribbons, and with the bells ringing in the Church of Frome Sir Thomas came home from prison. He gave a dinner at the George to 100 persons and then at Orchardleigh Park there was a bonfire of six hundred faggot, with a high pole in the centre, at the top of which was a leg of mutton. Unlimited beer was given away to wind up the whole event. After this he lived a quieter life. When he died in 1839 his love of show was reflected in his funeral arrangements. His coffin was so magnificent that it was on display in a window in the Market Place for some days and many people went to see it. Soon after his death Lady Champneys paid off every one of his creditors in full. Those who lived in Frome set the church bells ringing once more to express their joy.[32]

The details of the sale of the manor of Mold are complicated by the fact that initially (in 1801) it failed to find a buyer and had to be auctioned again in 1809.[33] On both occasions, details were advertised in the sale catalogue and local newspapers:

THE PARTICULARS of Capital and very valuable FREEHOLD ESTATES Situate in the Parish of MOLD
A beautiful and most fertile part of the County of Flint Comprising the Extensive MANOR OF MOLD and many Capital Farms lying exceedingly convenient, and consisting of excellent Grazing, Meadow, and Arable Land with suitable Farm Houses and Outbuildings, and let to exceptionally good Tenants
    Which will be Sold by Auction in Lots At the Griffin Inn, in Mold, on Thursday the 30th Day of April, 1801, and the following Days precisely at Two O'clock' A Map [missing] of the Premises may be seen, and further Information had, at Mr Wynne's Office in Mold.

The twenty-five lots were divided between the townships of Argoed, Bistre, Nercwys, Leeswood and Treuddyn, and the second part of estates in the several townships of Arddynwent, Hendrebiffa, Broncoed, Gwernaffield, Gwysaney and Mold. Although made ten years earlier, Walker's survey of the manor provides an interesting background to both the properties sold and the purchasers, and a pencilled catalogue indicates some results of the auction. Three important lots failed to realise their asking price and were bought in. This was the fate of Lot 53 which advertised as,

> The MANOR and LORDSHIP of MOLD, with the Court-house, Tolls of Mold Market, and all other Rights, Royalties, Privileges, Members and Appurtenances, together with ONE THIRD part of the Royalty of Lead, Coal, and other Mines therein …

These lead mines were leased to Evans and Kirk of Catherine's Mine (expiring 1808); Pant-y-Buarth Mine (expiring in 1813), and Llyn-y-Pandy Mine to John Wilkinson, (expiring in 1813). The lease of Lixwm-green Colliery was let to Mr Nathaniel Jones and others.[34]

Lot 54, Mold castle, 'MONTE ALTO, with the Plantations, Cottages and Lands inclosed with a strong and high wall, adjoining to the town of Mold' was withdrawn. Walker had included a description of it in 1791 under the heading, 'Observations respecting the Town of Mold.'

> The Bailey Hill or Monte Alto situate at the West End of Mold appears to have been the Site of an Ancient Castle the present proprietor has enclosed the same with a Substantial Stone Wall and is now planting the whole Hill or Mount with forest Trees, this will contribute much to improve and beautify the Town.

Walker had recommended that development could take place on the ground

> … opposite thereto adjoining the Road to Flint and of the Ground in New Street. Tenants would be found who would Erect in the stead of the shabby cottages therein neat and uniform houses to be occupied by Manufacturers and such as will be concerned or employed in the Cotton Manufactory, establishing there. The approach from the Ruthin Turnpike Road might be made through New Street.[35]

Lot 55, the Black Boy public house located near to the court-house was bought as was lot 75, the recently built cotton mill, standing in 38 acres of land in the holding of Robert Hodson and partners. The catalogue also indicated that Thomas Swymmer Mostyn-Champneys was already disposing of allotments recently awarded him by the commissioners adjacent to existing holdings, e.g. lot 26 in Arddunwent had been made up to 61 acres with 'the old inclosure' of 1 acre 3 rood 26 perch and lot 34, the Summer House,[36] surrounded by allotments of common land containing 129a 2r 1p, had grown from the mere 8 acres reported by Walker in 1791:

> The Summer House on the Top of Mold Mountain with the Plantations surrounding the same inclosed by a stone wall lately erected. It is built with stone, stuccoed and slated, and contains on the ground 8 acre. It has a floor, a Family kitchen, small parlour, Octagon Tea Room and lean to woodhouse &c behind the House. On the first floor: three bed chambers and closets with a lead flat over part of the Octagon Room which commands a prospect of vast Extent over the Chester and Liverpool River and Surrounding Country.

The sale catalogue revealed that some town development was happening, and lots 58–9 were advertised as groups of newly-erected dwelling houses with another lot of four cottages and gardens. However, no effort was made by the vendor to use the catalogue to publicise any potential urban or industrial growth in Mold. Seventeen of the lots sold in the first half of the sale were in the townships of Argoed and Bistre, and totalled 595 acres, two thirds of which was land Mostyn-Champneys had received from the enclosure award. The sizes of the lots varied, seven were of less than 6 acres, 4 between 10 and 30 acres, one of 42 acres and five between 78 and 105 acres. Some were not sold. Amongst the purchasers were William Hancock (13 acres) and the vicar of Mold, the Reverend Eyton.

The main purchaser at the sale was Sir Thomas Mostyn, sixth baronet, the brother-in-law of Thomas Mostyn-Champneys. Amongst the lots he acquired were:

Lot 66 several parcels of land of 9 acre 3 rood 2 perch for £630; Lot 67 another six parcels total acreage 35a 0r 12p for £1520. Lot 71 Maes y dre farm[37] 71a 1r 35p for £2,120 let to the Revd. Edward Parry.

The Town Field and four following fields are fine level land lying between the Town of Mold and the River Allen it is the intention of the present tenant to turn most part of them to meadow and a great part of them might be converted to capital water meadows at no great expense … Mr Parry appears to spare neither labour nor expense to improve his lands and tho' not professionally a farmer he may not withstanding be considered to be a tolerably good one.

Lot 73 close to the town of Mold was a group of holdings in the tenancy of Mr Parry (a surgeon), Mr W. Wynne and the Reverend Edward Parry. Lot 74 was a similar combination of holdings, one of which was 'the Alders wet land' of 11 acres. In 1791, Walker had recorded that this field had '… been drained and improved by the present tenant Mr Leach at considerable expense. There is peat earth in some parts of it to a considerable depth and which if cut dried and burnt as fuel in heaps when dry and the ashes sown early in the spring on clover or meadow land would greatly improve them and produce fine crops of clover and grass …' Lot 79, comprising of parcels of land totalling 34a 0r 32p in the township of Broncoed, let to Robert Ennion, was bought for £1,630. Ennion had succeeded in restoring 'an impoverished farm' and had been commended by Walker 'as an industrious man and a good farmer who has brought most of his land into a proper state of cultivation.'

The 61-acre old battlefield of Maes Garmon was tenanted by John Jones and bought by Edward Morgan, for £2,000. Walker had made the comment ten years earlier that 'this farm is not so well managed as it ought to be. The land is much over run with thistles and kept in a very slovenly state. The land is in general good and capable of considerable improvement and needs draining.'

Another purchaser at the sale was William Wynne (1771–1820), treasurer, Clerk of the Peace of the county of Flintshire and agent of the lord of the manor of Mold, who practised as an attorney and had acted as secretary to the enclosure commissioners. Wynne spent £2,500 on the purchase of 40 acres of land near the town. As years went by, he became over confident and, having speculated with clients' money, eventually took his own life.[38]

An improving land owner

An examination of the account book[39] of Miss Elizabeth Giffard of Nerquis Hall provides a unique picture of the early years of the nineteenth century as a period of transition. In her daily record, written between 1811 and 1834, she provides us with a cameo of the energetic life and achievements of a gentlewoman in charge of an ancient estate, a story which is a fitting climax to the activities of the gentry of Moldsdale, but which is unusual as the record of a wealthy heiress indulging her passion for building, gardening and developing the resources of an estate at a time of industrial growth and agricultural improvement. A generation earlier, the naturalist Thomas Pennant would have been delighted to visit her garden and hot-houses and Miss Giffard would have approved of the ambitious architectural ventures of Sir George Wynne at neighbouring Leeswood a hundred years before.

Miss Giffard's personality, hospitality and the constant changes taking place at Nerquis drew a stream of visitors to her door. Year after year, she received the local gentry – the Ravenscrofts, Mr Wardle of Tower, the Garmons of Colomendy, Mrs Crew of Hawarden, the Glynne family and many others. In return, she, invariably accompanied in her earlier years by her sister Mary Eleanor, sallied forth in her carriage to Tower, Fron, Plas Isa, Rhual and elsewhere. It was unusual if no-one visited her – '1830 Jan 13, Old New Year's Day. Nobody came.' Roman Catholic bishops and priests stopped off there on the way to Ireland and she entertained the bishop and dean of St Asaph and the vicar of Mold.

Her father, John Bonaventura Giffard (d. 1791), was a member of an old Catholic family from Blackladies and Chillingford in Staffordshire. He had met with violent opposition from his mother-in-law about the future religious allegiance of his young daughters. The eldest, Elizabeth, was baptised into the Church of

England but John Giffard prevented this from happening to her sister, Mary Eleanor, by taking her to be educated by nuns in Paris until they were driven home by the French Revolution. By the time the account book begins, Elizabeth Giffard's close family had died. Elizabeth Hyde, her formidable Protestant grandmother, and her Catholic father both rested in the family vault in Nerquis churchyard. The inscriptions to both made no judgement on their life-long beliefs. Of the former it was said: 'her good works have established her memory on earth and will intitle her to eternal reward in the mansions of the blessed,' and of her father that 'he was religious, just and charitable, affectionate to his relatives, kindly to his dependants, affable and accomplished in his manner.' Elizabeth's mother had died in 1805 and her younger sister in 1808, leaving her, a spinster, alone in charge of the ancient estate.

Nerquis Hall was built of stone by John Wynne between 1637 and 1640 and is contemporary with Rhual which is of brick. It was originally known as Plas Newydd and replaced an adjacent house. The family had lived in Nerquis township for generations and were descended in the female line from the twelfth noble tribe of north Wales, that of Edwin of Tegeingl. In the sixteenth and seventeenth centuries the Wynnes intermarried with emerging gentry families of Moldsdale such as the Lloyds of Hartsheath. The estate passed in the eighteenth century through the female line to the families of Pyndar and Williams and, in 1737, to Elizabeth, the niece of Paul Williams who married Robert Hyde (d. 1747) and eventually to her granddaughter, Elizabeth Giffard.

The architectural historian, Hubbard, described the alterations which were made to the house at the turn of the nineteenth century.

> In 1797 elephantine Gothic wings, Jacobean in style on the garden front were added either-end, and somewhat later, a more delicate Gothic porch, the latter probably by Benjamin Gummow … Similar in style to the wings, battlemented, with Gothic touches, are screen walls and a gatehouse belonging to the stables.[40]

Miss Giffard romantically also added a folly, Tŷ Castell, to the north of the house to catch the eye of visitors before they entered the iron gates at the entrance to the driveway with a semi-octagonal gothic orangery within the grounds to the right of the driveway. She also had built what amounted to a model home farm below the hall. Here was a complex of buildings which included a chaff house, loose-house, calf cote, cow house, stables, dog kennel, turkey house and an extensive poultry court, the whole of which was skirted by a dung walk leading to the pasture.

Nerquis Hall as extended by the Wrexham architect, Benjamin Gummow c.1815. The right-hand side of the building was demolished during the 1960s.

Miss Elizabeth Giffard seated in the garden at the rear of Nerquis Hall.

The gardens were originally planned and developed by Sir Paul Pyndar (d. *c*.1730) and were brought to fruition by the brothers Sir Paul and Edward Williams. In his will Sir Paul expressed the desire that 'when my debts and my mother's debts are paid that the Garden and Cannal at Nerquis may be made according to the draught or platform Robert Lawton has drawn and which my agent has to produce … ' By 1734, the canal was in position and, by the time of his death in 1797, John Giffard had probably added the pond and the ha-ha which defines the west part of the garden.

The account book beginning in 1811 shows a significant expenditure on the garden: '1811 Mr Jordan for Green house windows etc. £341 8s 6d'; '1812 Mr Shepherd for Plants Engine for Washing Trees etc., £45 5s 1d'; 1815 'Mr Hunter for plants £35 12s 0d.' The proud mistress of the house, presiding at her table, was often delighted to serve and record her own produce, as for example in 1816: 'Feb 23 first French beans to-day at dinner; March 10 first mushrooms at supper tonight; March 12 first potatoes at supper tonight; March 31 A cucumber at Dinner to-day.' Her horticultural and agricultural successes were recognised and applauded, '1820 August 10 Mr Boydell dined here & presented to me the Medal awarded by the Flintshire Agricultural Society' – in recognition of which she gave them a donation of £12.

Some of the plants collected by a generation of flower hunters inspired by Sir Joseph Banks and the botanists at Kew found a place at Nerquis. When she died the following advert appeared.

Rare Exotics to be sold at Nerquis Hall in the County of Flint.
The following collection of Rare and Valuable Plants, carefully selected for the late Mrs E . Giffard deceased from the East and West Indies, New South Wales, Ceylon, Peru, Africa and various other countries … The Plants have had the care of a very superior Gardener … 19th December 1842 and continue during the week.

A frequent visitor to Nerquis was Chester physician Dr William Makepeace Thackeray, cousin of the famous author, who had received a gold medal from the Society of Arts for planting a variety of trees. It has been estimated that he raised over 500,000 mature trees in north Wales of which 135,000 of oak, beech, ash, elm, sycamore, scotch fir and larch were on Nercwys Mountain on unproductive pasture.[41]

> 1825 Febry 8 wages of children who assisted at Plantations 4s 2d.
> 1827 March 19 Wages to children who helped to plant trees £2 10s.'

Although agriculture and horticulture were her interest Miss Giffard saw the opportunity of raising coal – '1806 Mr Jones Jnr of Wrexham came this morning to settle respective Leeswood Coal Works.' She did make some money from these collieries and in 1816 her share of Leeswood Coal Money was £93 18s and the next year she received £203. The mines were still operating in the 1830s.

Elizabeth Giffard was described as 'the old type of gentlewoman' by Miss Fanny Fletcher. 'She lived among her people in great state, keeping up the customs of her ancestors, and dispensing her charity and hospitality in a most lavish style. Her gardens and collections of foreign plants were one of the sights of the neighbourhood.'

An important feature of her life in the neighbourhood was the patronage she extended to the local tradesmen, the chief of which appeared to be the wine merchant. Her accounts of 1830 include bills from the gunsmith, chandler, clock-maker, saddler, line-man, milliner, newsagent, farmer, surgeon, mason, slater, rat-catcher, shepherd, druggist, shoe maker, thatcher, butcher, horse-breaker, book seller, horse doctor, draper, upholsterer, confectioner, glazier, wheelwright, bricklayer, mercer, plasterer, blacksmith, joiner, almanac maker, and for livery – including hats, lace and shoes. She also went further afield and bought beds from Mr Gillow the London cabinet maker.

The cost of such patronage and architectural enhancement of the ancient house was difficult for the estate to carry. On average, during the years of building, she was spending about £10,000 a year. To make up the deficit of the rental on her estates, *c*.£7,500, she sold land and Hendre Ucha for £5,000 in 1819, as well as diamonds for £890. From the rents, she established a sinking fund which would eventually clear her debts and rid her heirs of liability.

Notes

1. Charlotte Mostyn-Champneys was the sister of Sir Thomas Mostyn (died 1831).
2. W.J. Lewis, *Lead Mining in Wales,* Cardiff, 1967, p.63.
3. C.J. Williams, 'The Lead Mines of the Alyn Valley', *Flintshire Historical Society Publications,* vol 29, 1979–80, pp.5–39.
4. ibid p. 11.
5. FRO D/KK/294 and other papers in the same collection.
6. J. Barrel, 'Edward Pugh at Carreg Carn March Arthur', *Denbighshire Historical Society Transactions,* vol 58, 2010, pp.23–55.
7. NLW Wigfair 2198.
8. Williams op cit p.64.
9. D/KK/267.
10. Williams, op cit, p.65f.
11. R. Warner, *A Second Tour Through Wales August/September 1798,* pp.252–3.
12. ibid, pp.249–52.
13. T.W. Pritchard, *The Making of Buckley and District,* Wrexham, 2006, p.87f.
14. K. Lloyd Gruffydd, 'Coal Mining in Flintshire during the early modern period 1509–1737', *Flintshire Historical Society Journal,* vol 38, 2010, p.19f.
15. D.J.P. Johnson, 'Mold Cotton Mill', *Ystrad Alun,* 4, 2003, and E. Foulkes 'The Cotton Spinning Factories of Flintshire, 1777–1886, *Flintshire Historical Society Publications,* vol 21, 1964, p.91.
16. D/LE/825, p. 62.
17. Foulkes, op. cit., 95.
18. D/KK/267.
19. D/GW/433–5.
20. J. D. Chambers & G. E. Mingay, *The Agricultural Revolution 1750–80,* Blandford Forum, 1966, chapter 4, Enclosure, pp.77–105.
21. FRO The main documents for Mold Enclosure are the Act D/GW/B/652 – Commissioners Minutes 1792 D/KK/273 and the Enclosure Award 1800 QS/DE/Mold.
22. 32 Geo III, *c*.54.
23. 34 Geo III, c. 14, 1784

24. FRO QS/DE/Mold.

25. John Clare poem 'The Mores.'

26. D.G. Evans 'The Hope Enclosure Act of 1791', *Flintshire Historical Society Journal,* vol 31, 1983–4, p.161f.

27. NLW 4998 E/2.

28. D/KK/274.

29. From his memorial tablet in St Mary's Church, Orchardleigh, Frome, Somerset.

30. D/M/3996, Abstract of title of Sir Thomas Mostyn to lands purchased from the Trustees of the Champney's estate in Mold, 6 Oct 1710–26 Aug 1801.

31. D/M/683 in 1809 Sir Thomas Mostyn paid £15,000 to release into his possession 'All that ye said Manor and Lordship of Mold.'

32. J. Lewis 'The Church and Manor of Orchardleigh. Historical Survey.' I am grateful to Alistair MacLeay and Michael McGarvie for their assistance with the Champney family.

33. FRO D/KK/269 and 271.

34. Known as Lexham Green Colliery, 'Old Coppa' was acquired by Jonathan Catherall in 1798.

35. Walker ibid.

36. This is probably Hafod in Gwernymynydd.

37. Walker, p.12 referred to it as the Town Field.

38. Q. Dodd, op cit, p.21.

39. FRO D/NH/1272, The Account Book and Diaries of Elizabeth Giffard.

40. E. Hubbard, op cit, p.406.

41. T. W. Pritchard and N. Evans, *Ein Pentref,* op cit, pp.53–55.

8: The nineteenth century

The first part of the nineteenth century, sometimes known as 'the Age of Elegance', was for the majority of the population of England and Wales a very different experience, one that was shared by the people of Mold. For them, the first four decades might be summarised as the '3 Rs' – revolt, repression and reform. In the first part of this period, the years 1793–1815, Britain was engaged in a series of European wars against the forces and allies of revolutionary and Napoleonic France. This total commitment brought both sacrifice (amongst those who suffered were the Griffith family of Rhual, whose heir was killed at Waterloo) and prosperity. The newly enclosed acres of Moldsdale yielded quick returns to their owners who benefited from the improvements in agriculture and the rapidly growing demand for coal, iron and lead.

From 1801 onwards, at intervals of ten years, a population census was conducted. Although the information first gathered was limited, it provided reliable figures showing a significant rise in the birth rate and confirming the migration of families from rural areas to find work in the factories and mines. The restoration of peace in 1815 brought with it a stagnation in industry, bankruptcy, unemployment, unrest and revolution. The government reacted by a series of repressive parliamentary statutes. Economic slump and wage reduction brought the first signs of organised industrial action. Strikes and large demonstrations by workers occurred in mining and textile districts, which led to the reading of the Riot Act, and intervention by magistrates, regular troops and local yeomanry cavalry. Poverty, deprivation, lack of political representation and a sense of injustice found expression in a new literature of protest and revolution, all part of the making of the working classes. Regarded with equal suspicion and alarm were the signs of growth of religious dissent and the appearance of newly-licensed meeting houses in the thoroughfares of country towns and on the fringes of new settlements.

This is the background to the story of Mold in the nineteenth century. These first four decades cover almost precisely the years before the accession of Victoria to the throne. They are also the years immediately before the birth of Daniel Owen, the Mold novelist whose portrayal of Nonconformist society in books such as *Y Dreflan* and *Rhys Lewis* is unparalleled in Welsh literature.

Apart from brief periods of peace in 1802–3 and 1814–15, Britain was at war with France on land and sea for a period of twenty-three years. Generally speaking, these were years of prosperity and full employment for those engaged in the industries of war supplying manufacturers with iron, lead and coal. Newly enclosed land was cultivated and, when harvests produced good yields, there was, despite a continental blockade of Britain, sufficient food to feed an ever-increasing population. It was in years of shortage, when harvests failed and grain supplies were insufficient, that a high price was created for basic foodstuffs. Bread was a main item in the diet of the poor and when rising prices outpaced increase in wages, corn riots regularly disturbed Wales between 1793 and 1801. The magistrates of Moldsdale desperately attempted to feed the starving whilst at the same time preventing the mob from taking the law into their own hands. The leading townsfolk and clergy gave notice that they would prosecute anyone committing burglary or caught stealing food and livestock.

In 1795, a large and angry mob assembled in Mold to protest about the high price of corn. When magistrates failed to restrain them they succeeded in breaking open the warehouse of a dealer who exported corn to Chester and Lancashire and forced him to sell it at something under the market price. It was found necessary

Mould in Flintshire, watercolour by the Reverend John Breedon, 1785.

to call the troops. The magistrate, Thomas Griffith of Rhual, reported the incident to the Secretary of War. 'At present,' he wrote, 'there are none [troops] in this Country or near it, and should the numerous body of Colliers and Miners again assemble, the property of the whole country might be laid waste and destroy'd before Assistance could be procured.' Such was the desire of the Home Office and local magistrates to prevent insurrection in the town that three Bow Street Runners were said to have served in Mold during the 1800s.[1]

In March 1801, because of the scarcity of grain, the overseers of the poor were ordered 'to procure some herrings and make Enquiry for other articles to save the consumption of Bread corn.' Wynne Eyton, vicar of Mold, organised bread and beef to be distributed to 97 people at a cost of £12 1s 6d[2] and continued to do so throughout the war when necessary. The year 1813 was a bad one and a number of 'self-denying' measures were drawn up by middle-class townspeople and gentry, designed to help, … the poor of Mold during these times of distress.' They explained

> … that our poorer neighbours having behaved in the most exemplary manner during the scarcity of bread, suffer in consequence of the exorbitant price of corn, and we are called upon by duty as well as inclination to give them all necessary support during these times of distress. Rather than this assistance be a burden on the rates subscriptions were called for and pledges were made to the effect 'that we pledge members not to use any White Bread fine flour or pastry of any sort in our families except such as is made with rice or potatoes … that all unnecessary consumption of Barley should be stopped for which purpose we pledge ourselves not to brew or buy any ale during the present scarcity and that we will not diminish the number of our labourers during such times'.[3]

The war imposed extra burdens by increased levies and taxation. Parishes had to raise their quota of men to serve in the army or navy. One way of achieving this was to recruit men by means of a ballot, with the payment of an initial bounty and extra parish relief to maintain servicemen and their families. Mold vestry shared in a nationwide rise in parochial expenditure which included a massive growth in the payment of weekly and occasional relief, house rent, funerals and other basics such as 'necessary clothing' and 'emergencies.' The largest item was that spent on weekly paupers. This financial liability by the authorities in Mold showed an annual increase and expenditure by 1813/14 was £2,477, which rose each year to £2,931 by 1817/18 and reached an even higher figure in the 1820s under the burden of post-war problems.

The first years of peace saw economic depression and radical agitation highlighted by the Peterloo 'massacre' in Manchester and the Cato Street Conspiracy in London.[4] Such events caused nationwide alarm and increased local vigilance. There were, however, positive signs to promote the welfare of the poor and provide them with an opportunity of self-help and improvement such as the opening of the Mold Provident Institution for Savings, established on 16 March 1818 which owed its foundation to the energy of the Reverend Hope Wynne Eyton. Backed by the vestry and the support of Sir Thomas Mostyn, the bank's first premises were located in the school-room in the parish churchyard. It was open to customers for two hours on Saturday afternoons. An appeal made to local

Cartoon satiring the 'Peterloo Massacre' of 16 August 1819.

gentry and property owners for subscriptions raised £65. Sir Thomas Mostyn was elected president and Hope Wynn Eyton, Richard Garnons of Colomendy and James Knight, of Rhual, were elected trustees. Every subscriber of £1 served as a manager 'with the duty of attending in rotation alphabetically' to be present during opening hours and attend to the business of the bank. The subscription of managers was later increased to £100 which provided further capital. The curate of Mold, the Reverend Charles Butler Clough, was appointed treasurer, a position he held for thirty-six years until he was appointed president in 1856, by which time he had become dean of Asaph.[5]

The original rules of the Savings Bank show that it was established to encourage small savings from the poorer classes. Its first object resolved,

> That an Institution be established and maintained in the nature of a Bank to receive deposits of money from those who are inclined to save from their earnings in the Parish of Mold and neighbourhood to accumulate the same for their benefit and secure such investments in Government securities without risk of loss, and they may wish to deposit at Interest leaving them at Liberty to withdraw the whole with the accumulations or any part thereof whenever they require it.

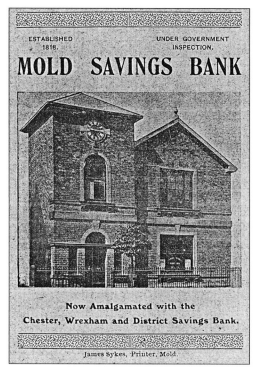

Mold Savings Bank.

Deposits were limited to £100 in the first year, and not more than £50 in any subsequent year. Minimum deposits of one shilling and upwards were received, which earned an interest of 4% when the sum deposited reached 12s 6d. The founders aimed to encourage thrift and did not replicate the objectives of friendly societies which aimed to protect their members in times of unemployment, sickness and bereavement. Whatever safeguards the trustees and managers introduced to protect their own interests and those of the customers, there was a weak link which exposed them to financial loss. The minutes of the bank show this occurred on two occasions, at a time when the failure of private banks was a common occurrence. The Mold Savings Bank takings were held in a local bank from where they were transferred on their behalf to the National Debt Office. When Knight's Bank in Mold stopped payment in 1828, £250 was lost because of a delay in transferring the funds to London. A greater loss occurred in 1818 which was not made good until 1855 when it was resolved that the treasurer, Butler Clough,

> … having lost in 1818 about £300 by the bankruptcy of Messrs Douglas & Co, Bankers Mold in whose hands £626 of the Savings Banks money had in consequence of the Treasurers unavoidable absence from home been placed by the Secretary to the Treasurer's private Account for which he has no legal remedy against the Bank be paid a gratuity from the surplus fund of £1,000.

It was possible for members of the middle classes to survive loss in the post-war period, but the only alternative for most day labourers and their families was to protest

Five Pound note, Mold Bank.

before they starved. The initial reaction of the local colliers to their distressed circumstances and conditions was to seek redress for their grievances. Eventually, they began to combine in their protest through the organisation of trades unions. In some instances, there was violence when they were adjudged to be taking the law into their own hands. On these occasions, the marching miners were viewed with fear by the populace and the Riot Act was read, ringleaders arrested and the military employed as peace keepers. Mold colliers were involved in periodic protests across a coalfield which extended from Deeside to Chirk.

Flintshire had its own regiment of mobile peacekeepers who could be directed across the county whenever trouble occurred.[6] On 15 May 1794, at a meeting at the St Alban's Tavern in London, some Flintshire gentlemen first recommended the raising of a troop of volunteer horse. Three years later, at a meeting held in Mold, it was resolved to form an armed association for the purpose of local defence which would consist of both infantry and a troop of thirty horse and men armed with pistols and swords. Thomas Griffith of Rhual was elected captain of what was termed the Mold troop of Volunteer Cavalry which would serve anywhere in the north-western district (of England and Wales). In August 1803, a second troop was raised in the Hawarden district. The establishment of the corps was then fixed at two captains, two lieutenants, two cornets, two quartermasters, two sergeants, two corporals, two trumpeters and ninety troopers. Thomas Griffith was appointed captain commandant of the expanded unit, now known as the Mold Yeomanry Cavalry, and served until 1811 when ill-health brought about his resignation and he was succeeded by Sir Stephen Glynne of Hawarden when the Mold troop was led by Captain John Wynne Eyton. In January 1814, the Mold Yeomanry volunteered to serve anywhere in England or Wales. The unit remained in service after the peace of 1815 and was active in the localities in 1819, 1825 and 1826 when unrest amongst colliers in Flintshire culminated in civil disturbance and disorder. In September 1827, the corps was stood down and disbanded. However, three years later when there was again trouble across the coalfield, the Mold Troop was reformed as part of the Flintshire Yeomanry Cavalry at a meeting of some gentlemen at Hawarden Castle on 30 December 1830. It went immediately into action and a few months later in July, it was employed in keeping the town of Mold quiet.[7]

In 1826, despite the Flintshire Yeomanry Cavalry being garrisoned at Mold, rioting broke out there following an attempt by local pit managers to introduce the so-called Cornish shift system of working eight hours in sixteen (as opposed to six hours in eighteen) which had caused considerable trouble in nearby Halkyn. The colliers of the Bromfield and other pits in the Mold area responded with a demand for an unprecedented six-hour-a-day shift pattern and, when it became apparent that the management would not make any concessions, they rioted. On 6 March, the town's yeomanry were sent to suppress the riots, but they became so widespread and severe that the authorities had to send for reinforcements from Holywell and two troops of the Royal Maylor Cavalry. The disturbances in and around Mold were described as 'most serious rioting' and must have been quite bloody, for the cavalrymen were out on patrol for twelve days, on four of which they were involved in clashes with rioters, and there were still ructions going on as late as 26 March. Indeed, during April and May of 1826, Northumbrian colliers employed at the nearby Coed Talon pit went on strike and rioted, and once more the cavalry had to ride out to crush the disturbance. As a result of this unrest, the leading inhabitants of Mold requested, and received, a reinforced garrison for the town, and this enlarged military force was retained until 1827 to deter the malcontents of Flintshire from undertaking further rioting.[8] But, in January of the following year, fire attacks on farm buildings occurred across the county.[9]

A decline in trade in 1829 led to a fall in the demand for coal, reduced prices, lower wages and unrest and protest across the coalfield. In 1824 and 1825 the colliers took advantage of the repeal of the Combination Acts of 1799 and 1800, which made collective action and the right to withhold labour legal, and trade unions sprang into prominence. A branch of the Friendly Association of Coal Miners Union Society in Lancashire was established in Bagillt in 1830.

Over Christmas and New Year 1830/31, colliers throughout Flintshire and Denbighshire demonstrated

Yeomanry cavalry officer and trooper, 1803.

their strength by a strike which spread across the coalfield from Hawarden to Chirk. Sir Stephen Glynne sent to Chester for support from the military. On Christmas Day the strikers, in a menacing mood, had visited Leeswood Hall near Mold and made clear their grievances to Wynne Eyton. From there, they had continued their progress and crossed into the Denbighshire coalfield by way of Coed Talon and Brymbo, and marched on the colliery villages between Wrexham and Chirk. At Rhosllannerchrugog and Ruabon, they were confronted by the Denbighshire Yeomanry, led by Sir Watkin Williams Wynn, who arrested three of the ringleaders who immediately escaped. On the 30 December, the colliers attacked the Wynnstay Arms at Ruabon and later their representatives presented Sir Watkin with a list of grievances which included poor housing conditions, defective machinery and the unregulated method of assessing the amount of coal raised. An agreement was reached on a wage rate with the proviso that it was accepted by all other coal masters. In order to receive this assurance, a section of the strikers proceeded on New Year's morning to Chirk. The men eventually returned to work but were resentful of the fact that six of their ringleaders were under arrest and that a detachment of soldiers had been sent from Chester to Wrexham. Local magistrates were instructed by the Home Office to prosecute the ringleaders. It was an uneasy and unsatisfactory situation with the miners smarting under their treatment and the masters determined to enforce their authority. It was against this background that another incident involving colliers occurred a few months later.

> The first week in July, colliers who normally worked at Bromfield Colliery, near Mold, determined to take action against the blackleg labour imported from Anglesey during the district strike, and, on the 6th, between three and four o'clock in the morning, between two and three hundred colliers led by their Union leaders marched to the colliery demanding that the 'Anglesey pigs' (*Moch Môn*) be dismissed. To this, the agent, Joseph Price demurred. The Anglesey men, were, in due course, rounded up, and with their coats turned inside out, were driven through Mold, Northop and Flint, and supplied with food and money to assist them to their homes across the Menai Straits.[10]

The magistrates, J.M. Eyton and J.B. Hough reported the events to London on 6 July:

> A company of infantry having been stationed at Mold for the last six weeks secured the temporary peace of its vicinity which had previously been much disturbed. Application was made to us last week by the Commanding Officer of the Corps to sanction their withdrawal but we positively refused to do so knowing too well the state of the country. In spite of our remonstrances they were withdrawn, and at a very early hour this morning a Gang of 4 or 500 men from Holywell came thro' the Town of Mold to the great Dread of the Inhabitants and forcibly took away from their Employ a Body of Colliers working peaceably and paraded them thro' the Town to send them to their native County Anglesey. Their fault in the Eyes of these people was their being strangers and not belonging to the Working Union. As this outrage took place at day Break it was totally impossible to organize any force capable of

withstanding such a Multitude for a Moment. Indeed before any magistrate was apprized of it the Riotous assemblage has passed thro' the Town of Mold and were on their road towards Holywell. We have communicated with the commanding officers at Wrexham and Chester the former of whom has signified his readiness to co-operate with us in the apprehension of the ringleaders whom we hope to be able to identify. At the same time we think it our duty to impress on your Lordship that in our opinion the neighbourhood of Mold is now in such a State as absolutely to require a permanent Military Force stationed in that Town for some time.[11]

The Home Secretary, Lord Melbourne, arranged for a military force to be stationed at Mold where they were to establish temporary barracks. The Mold troop of the Flintshire Yeomanry Cavalry was under the command of Captain John Wynne Eyton of Leeswood and the entire regiment, 233 men in all, under the command of Lord Belgrave, marched into Mold for training; mounted drills were held at Leeswood Hall and foot drills in a meadow nearer the town.[12]

Melbourne wanted the trade union leaders of the 1830/1 troubles to be punished, but they were ably defended by barrister John Jervis at the Mold Assizes in August 1831 and, although Judge Bolland directed the jury to bring in a verdict of guilty, they chose to return a verdict of not guilty against all prisoners.[13]

The Flintshire Yeomanry Cavalry, being one of the smaller yeomanry units, was disbanded on 30 July 1838 as part of the government's military economies. Many of the men who had served in the unit then joined the Denbighshire Yeomanry Cavalry which took on the responsibility of protecting both counties from future expressions of civil unrest.

The colliers regarded themselves as being at odds with the coal masters who were obviously hostile to the union because of the nature of their demands. But they also incurred the enmity of religious bodies, the Calvinistic Methodist Association, when at Mold on 29 February and 1 March 1832, excommunicated members,

> … because these Unions are in direct contradiction to the Word of God, and to the laws of the state of which we are citizens, and because their object is to attain the reins of Government, because of the methods used to initiate their members, their secrecy, and victimisation of those who are not members. No-one who is connected with these Unions will be admitted into this religious body in the future.[14]

Another outspoken critic of the colliers was the Reverend John Blackwell. He was born at Ponterwyl and apprenticed to a shoemaker who encouraged his interest in Welsh poetry and history. His ability won him the chair at an eisteddfod in Mold in 1823 and brought him to the notice of a number of gentlemen who contributed the sum of £220 for his education at Jesus College Oxford and his ordination in the Anglican Church. Whilst he was a curate in Holywell (1829–33), he became known in the town as 'The poor man's parson' for his work in establishing a clothing club for the poor and his efforts during the cholera epidemic in 1832. When he left the parish the following year, he was presented with a silver tea service as a 'suitable memorial for the exemplary discharge of his sacred duties while curate'. His political attitudes, however, reflected the views of the gentry who had paid for his Oxford education and he became their spokesman in opposition to the striking miners. The report of a reform meeting at Holywell in January 1831 summarised his position.

> [The Rev J Blackwell] … in a severe philippic against political agitators in general, addressed the meeting at great length, as the organ of those who were opposed to reform altogether, thinking it unnecessary, and calculated to lead to mischievous results, in the present highly excited, unsettled and distressed state of that district.[15]

Words and pictures describing Mold at the end of the eighteenth century emphasise the beauty of the vale and its agricultural communities. Those artists who portrayed industrial scenes show them as picturesque, set in the surrounding valleys, alongside rivers and streams. Moldsdale is shown as a paradise, surrounded by gentry mansions. The townscape was only portrayed in a primitive drawing by Reverend John Breedon,

Reverend John Blackwell.

a touring parson, in 1785. Moses Griffith gives us a rather vague, distant view of a ribbon of humble dwellings, ignored rather than hidden. The poverty of the majority of the population is absent in these pictures and writings, whereas the wealth of the rich is displayed as natural and part of a divine order.

A perambulation through the alleys, courts and back streets of Mold would have revealed a very different scene, one of filth, inequality, destitution and the need for reform. These contrasting views were all too obvious throughout an increasing number of industrial areas in Britain and the odour of inequality was becoming a great stink and brought forth a protest of injustice and a chorus for reform.

Widespread revolt, repression and local riots eventually turned into a parliamentary discussion for reform which became a reality through legislation introduced as a response to radical demands for the abolition of an outdated system of parliamentary representation, a fairer distribution of parliamentary seats and the need to remedy problems brought about as a result of the industrial revolution. There was a need to clean up filth in urban areas which were environmentally unsafe leading to disease and death. The unregulated growth of new towns and the impact of a rapidly expanding population on ancient towns such as Mold threatened a visitation of a new plague, cholera, and political revolution at the hands of a new working class stirred up by mob orators.

Violent revolution was however avoided. The state began very slowly to intervene in the condition of the people, bringing about compulsory improvements through regulation. Gradually, beginning in 1832, measures of electoral reform increased the number of those entitled to vote. It took nearly 100 years before every man and woman was given the vote and there was an even distribution of parliamentary seats throughout the United Kingdom.

The success of a variety of social reforms was dependent upon a partnership being established between national and local government, with action following on from inquiry, report and legislation. Greater opportunity was given to local authorities to borrow money in order to undertake large-scale capital investment in drainage, sewage, education and health.

Reform usually began with a government inquiry, conducted by special commissions, into the working conditions of the men, women and children employed in particular industries. From such revelations of working conditions, parliamentary legislation was framed directly towards the improvement of hours, health and safety in the work-place as well as living conditions. Emphasis was laid on the enforcement of the regulations enshrined in the new legislation. For this purpose, inspectors were appointed to report on conditions in mines and factories to an ever-growing number of civil servants in newly-established government departments. A highly able and efficient group of civil servants, men such as Edwin Chadwick and John Simon, were amongst the architects of a reformed society bringing order to industrialised Britain. The Factory Acts of 1833 and 1844 regulated textile manufacturing, including the Mold cotton mill, and women and children were forbidden from working underground in coal mines in 1842.

The town of Mold profited from the benefits of this reform. With the rest of society, it experienced the establishment of newly-created units of local government to administer and enforce parliamentary legislation, with power devolved into the hands of newly enfranchised and elected representatives. The opportunity to become elected members of such bodies, particularly in urban areas, passed from the landed gentry and professional men into the hands of those of humbler birth, generally of small tradesmen. The shopkeepers and inn keepers of Mold became members of the new boards responsible for the running of the town. By the 1860s, urban affairs and local administration had passed from church vestries to local boards whose membership in Wales reflected the proportionate strength of Nonconformity. This redistribution of power was not lost on the Mold novelist Daniel Owen, who was himself an elected member of the town's local board and first chairman of its successor, the Urban District Council. In his novel, *Y Dreflan*, Owen summed up what had taken place in Mold during his lifetime,

> There are in Dreflan enough Boards to furnish a Palace! There is a Local Board consisting of twelve men, or more, who have prospered in the world, who meet on the first Monday of each month to gaze wisely at each other and to greet one another politely. Their purpose in meeting is to keep dangerous diseases away from the town without the aid of prayer or Providence, and they bring about improvements wherever they can, near to their own homes; they decide on the amount of the rate, and keep on good terms with the Press reporter in order that their grammatical errors may be corrected before their speeches are reported in the Local Press. There is a School Board consisting of respectable men representing the two factions, the Church and Nonconformity; the Churchmen are there to see that the Nonconformists do not get too much of their own way, and likewise the latter keep an eye on the Churchmen. But what does it matter so long as the street Arab receives an education which will start him on his way in life and possibly make him a good scholar and many have profited from its endeavours. Time will not allow me now to mention all the Boards, Companies and clubs, and especially the characters in Dreflan …[16]

Local government was the executive body empowered to implement a continual flow of national legislation, designed to improve the environment and safeguard public health. In pursuit of these objectives a new professional class of local government officers was appointed – surveyors, engineers, sanitation officials, inspectors of nuisances and lodging houses. All these concerns along with regulation of the market place, roads, pavements and housing development were the subjects of an increasing number of by-laws. There was no blueprint for such reform and improvement. In Mold, it became necessary because the primitive living conditions inherited from the eighteenth century could not cope with the overcrowding caused by industrialisation and the growth in the urban population. In the early nineteenth century, this was unplanned and took place with the building of new, cramped accommodation such as Jenkins Court and Griffiths Court, dwellings crowded into spaces carved out of in-fills of medieval burgage strips,

> There are, here, [wrote Daniel Owen] back streets, dark and filthy, where there is poverty, misery, and evil in abundance, which continues from year to year. There are scores here, who spend every penny they can lay their hand, in the taverns, while their wives and children starve in the cold, and are black and blue in the face for want of food.

These filthy enclaves were the last resort of the poor, a refuge for criminals and the drinking dens of the intemperate. Subject to overcrowding and an inadequate water supply, they had no means to dispose of human waste, rubbish and nuisance. They also invariably included a pig sty, a basic necessity in the domestic economy of the poor. In such conditions, there was no hope of preventing disease without the provision of adequate sanitation and cleansing and, in the 1830s, there was no understanding of preventative medicine. The scientific explanation for the spread of infectious disease came following the arrival of a new plague, cholera. 'Nor was the real need for proper sanitation made clear until the discovery of the microbe revealed the hitherto missing link between stinking miasmas and deadly fevers'.[17]

Compulsory and innovative sanitary authorities supplied a mixture of carbolic and quick lime to streets and privies. School boards, managers and inspectors, through drill and discipline, dispelled degradation and the new police forces clamped down on disorder.

The Parliamentary Reform Act of 1832 for 'Amending the representation of the people' was a symbolic watershed, marking the beginning of a new age when Britain led the world in manufacturing and ruled a vast empire. At home, the middle classes emerged to share power and wealth with the landed aristocracy and gentry. Although there was a great deal of noise, debate and protest surrounding the beginning of this age of reform, violence and bloody revolution were avoided. The Act disenfranchised fifty-six so-called rotten boroughs[18] and the vote was given to the middle classes, increasing the electorate from 478,000 to 814,000.

By the Act of 1832, Mold was constituted a contributory borough[19] sharing with Flint, Caergwrle, Caerwys, Holywell, Overton, Rhuddlan and St Asaph in the return of one member of Parliament. The new arrangement lasted until 1918 when Mold returned to the county constituency. As a result of the 1832 Act, the right to vote was vested in 'every male person of full age occupying, either as owner or as tenant under the same landlord, a house or other premises of the annual value of £10 and upwards'. In 1844, the number of such tenements within the limit of the borough, coextensive with the township of Mold, and an area of about 570 acres, was about 150 of which 140 were in the town.[20] For a number of general elections following this increase in the number of voters, the town of Mold experienced fiercely contested polls.

Of more relevance to the pockets of the Mold parish ratepayers was the Poor Law Amendment Act 1834 whereby some 700 units, under elected boards of guardians, replaced 15,000-odd parish units and were centrally controlled by three Poor Law commissioners until the establishment of the Poor Law Board in 1847. The Act established Poor Law Unions, reorganising the old parishes into unions, which would be jointly responsible for the administration of the Poor Law in their area. The parish of Mold was joined with Caerwys, Cilcain, Flint, Gwaenysgor, Halkyn, Holywell, Llanasa, Nannerch, Nercwys, Newmarket, Northop, Whitford and Ysceifiog into one union and a new workhouse was built at Holywell. This provided a cold and uncomfortable blanket of minimum protection for the destitute. The responsibility for the poor was therefore transferred from the parish vestry to a newly constituted Board of Guardians of the Holywell Poor Law Union.[21] This arrangement, however, was regarded as humiliating as Mold did not want to play second fiddle to Holywell, having only recently asserted itself over Flint as the county town.[22] On 22 February 1837, the Mold General Vestry contacted the Poor Law Commissioners 'expressing the sentiments of the Vestry as to the inconvenience of this parish being joined to the Holywell Union.' They objected on the grounds that they had a population of near 9,000, residing 14 miles from Holywell, and that it was of great injury to the trade of the town that 'a considerable portion of the rates raised in this Parish will be abstracted from their natural circulation and will necessarily be expended elsewhere and was above all to the hardship and vexation imposed upon the poor.'[23] Their protest went unheeded and Mold remained in the Holywell Union. The workhouse[24] was built into which paupers were admitted under a rigid system of classification which separated husbands from wives and parents from children.

The Municipal Corporations Act of 1835 established the borough as the primary unit of local government which would later become the body for administering the Public Health Acts and the appointment of police forces under control of local watch committees.

The most important social crusade of central government in mid-Victorian Britain was its effort to improve the nation's health. Two reports 1844/5 of the Royal Commission on the Health of Towns made inquiries with regard to the health of the working population throughout England and Wales and reached the conclusion that the annual loss of life from filth and bad ventilation was greater than wounds or death in war. Epidemic and endemic diseases generated by decomposed animal and vegetable substances, damp, filth, overcrowded dwellings and defective water supplies were judged 'to produce an adult population, short-lived, improvident, reckless and intemperate, and with habitual avidity for sexual gratifications.' There is ample evidence that Mold was not spared these social evils.

The leader of the war against dirt in the 1840s was the civil servant Edwin Chadwick. He advocated an improvement in the living conditions of the labouring classes through the provision of pure water, drainage, cleansing and the removal of refuse from dwellings, streets and roads. He advocated that sanitary reform and public works should be undertaken by responsible and qualified officers, equipped with knowledge of

Mold High Street mid nineteenth century.

science and civil engineering. This strategy was initiated by Chadwick in the Public Health Act of 1848 and reinforced by a further act ten years later when the Mold Board of Health was established.

The pattern of the Mold Board of Health's business and responsibility was established from the beginning. Fifteen local citizens were elected by ratepayers to clean up the town as efficiently and cheaply as possible through the appointment of a corps of local sanitation officers consisting of a surveyor, an inspector of nuisances, a legally qualified medical officer of health, with a treasurer and clerk. The local board was the manager of all sewers, with the responsiblity for cleansing and emptying them. It became illegal to erect a house without drains or a sufficient water closet or privy or ash-pit. All streets and pavements had to be properly cleaned and watered. Slaughter houses and common lodging houses were to be registered and offensive trades regulated. Chadwick put the engineers in charge of the environment.

On 24 February 1859, Mold's 'sanitation army' went into action with the first meeting of the newly-elected Board. They met in the Grand Jury Room in County Hall where their business was conducted on the first Thursday of every month. Their orders were to make and enforce regulations, to protect the health and property of ratepayers, to appoint paid officials to operate under supervision of government inspectors and to be careful with the public purse. All that they had previously learnt about business and human nature behind their shop counters and in the chapel *seiat* was put to good use. Under cover of agendas, minutes, reports, standing orders and press reports, they learned discretion, formal politeness and the powers of delegation. Through their joint influence as members of the Board, they became an effective instrument of change. Like all joint bodies they developed a sense of collective responsibility and were spurred on by an awareness of answerability that was of more consequence than the day of judgement, when the electorate was more likely to show revenge than mercy and the mighty would be brought low. Members of the Mold Board of Health were elected to create a new Jerusalem and, as they walked round the town and market place, attended their place of worship on the Lord's Day or confronted their customers across the counter, they were in a position to know the ultimate truth, that of public opinion.

It was appropriate that the first officer appointed by the board had a reputation for issuing commands and expecting to be obeyed. Sergeant-Major Kenmair was appointed surveyor at a wage of £1 a week, for which he was expected to perform the duties of collector of rates, inspector of nuisances and common lodging houses, and look after the fire-engine and highways. His job description was to be found in the by-laws

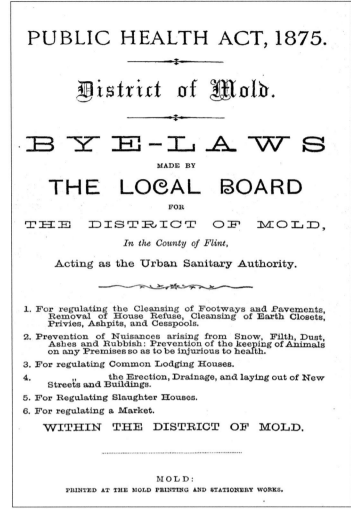

Mold Bye-laws, 1875.

approved by the Secretary of State and circulated to all ratepayers throughout the district. The fire-engine received special attention. It was placed in the charge of a fire brigade consisting of ten men who were paid a shilling each for going out to exercise it (and the horses) for a space of at least two hours once a month. It appeared to be the ambition of the Board to persuade the local militia to take on this responsibility.

Often overlooked, but of great importance, was the Board's actions in drawing up an accurate plan of the town and its drains, naming its streets, lighting them by gas and having the main thoroughfares paved with brick and the lesser roads watered in the dry season.

In 1866, Mold was visited by the cholera epidemic which prompted a flurry of activity by the Board. In September, they issued local inhabitants with a printed circular of the precautions then in use in Chester. These recommended the use of quick lime, carbolic acid, whitewash brushes and the burning of infected articles. In October, the Board appointed Dr Alfred Jones as medical officer, with instructions to combat nuisances. Within a few days, he reported back that the areas of nuisance were:

The Slaughter House at the back of the Griffin and Bank and the pig sty at the back of the Feathers. Also the rag and bone warehouse on the Griffin Yard and that he consider all to be nuisances injurious to the Public Health and had served notices to the tenants to abate the nuisances.

The doctor's exertions were recognised by the Board and rewarded when his appointment was confirmed with a salary of £10 *per annum*. The Inspector of Nuisances was paid £2 for his extra services during the visitation of the cholera.

A further Public Health Act, passed in 1875, the architect of which was John Simons, was a comprehensive and consolidating piece of legislation[25] under the direction of the Local Government Board which had been set up in 1871. The Medical Officer of Health, together with his fellow officer, the Inspector of Nuisances, was still a sanitarian, involved chiefly with the town environment.

In Mold, local legislation and regulation continued at an increasing pace. The Local Board formed a sanitary committee and made an application to borrow £5,000 for general improvements to the sewage and drainage in the town.[26]

By the frequency with which they were mentioned, pigs appeared to be the most common and conspicuous of animals in Mold. An attempt was made to control the local pig population in *cytia moch* 'swine huts', erected on land allotted for the purpose in order that dwellings with no space for a pig sty in their back-yard could have access to an alternative site.[27] Local legislation attempted to further control the keeping of pigs in the town:

1871 Sept 7th That the Inspector of Nuisances take proceedings against the persons keeping pigs within six yard of their dwelling houses.

1874 July 30 The plan of houses intended to be built at the Lead Mill by Mold Argoed Colliery be allowed on condition that the ash pits be covered and no pig stys be erected.

1877 October 3rd 'A memorial from the inhabitants of Alun Terrace,' requesting the Board to allow them to 'keep Pigs to eat the bad potatoes' that were expected to be gathered in consequence of the bad harvest was considered and refused.

A pig sty – 'the poor man's bank'.

It was recognised that Mold markets and fairs were an important part of the town's economy and the Board's minutes contain notices of their regulation of them e.g. in August 1859 it was decided that the corn market would in future be held in the Upper Market Hall (also known as Eyton's Market) and that the 'streets be cleared of stalls & things set up between March and September before 11 p.m. and for the rest of the year at 10 p.m., that the contract for cleansing of streets on Market & Fair Days be £7 a year'; in July 1877 the inspector gave 'notice to the Earthenware and General Dealers at Fairs and Markets that they must cease to create any noise otherwise their stalls will be refused'; in August 1861, 100 posters were printed to regulate the fairs and the police were requested to assist the surveyor in enforcing the new rules.

The Board's acquisition of the Bailey Hill in 1870 was one of its early successes. For the members, it was a diplomatic triumph, proof to the ratepayers that perhaps the Board did have the interests of the town at heart. The negotiations were conducted in a grand manner:

1870 17 May

To the Hon. The Lady Augusta Mostyn – The Humble Memorial of the Mold Local Board of Health under their Common Seal. Sheweth:-

That your memorialists have heard with extreme regret that it is your Ladyship's intention to dispose of that interesting and historical property known as the Bailey Hill in the town of Mold.

That your memorialists feel convinced that your Ladyship is not acquainted with the claims the inhabitants of this town have upon it, otherwise they feel assured you would not concur in the proposed sale by auction.

That, as the advertisement of the sale in public prints very properly points out, the Hill 'was formerly a British Fortress and is associated with several interesting and stirring scenes chronicled in early history' – to cut up such a property into lots as it is proposed would indeed be a lamentable proceeding, and will be especially hurtful to the Welsh inhabitants of this district, who naturally feel a strong and deep interest in the preservation of relics connected with the interests of their country.

That in the same advertisement it is also stated that this Hill 'was formerly used as a recreation ground for the inhabitants' – it might have been more correctly stated that a portion of this property had from time immemorial, without the slightest interruption been used and enjoyed by the inhabitants; and it is to this point your memorialists would specially direct your Ladyship's attention. It is felt your Ladyship would not knowingly deprive, or attempt to deprive, this town of its rights and privileges …

On June 13, the minutes recorded '… best thanks of the Board, as the representatives of the Town to tender to the Right Hon. Lady Augusta Mostyn for the aid she has so kindly rendered in securing for Public purposes the Bailey Hill.' The Bailey Hill Committee was formed and the site was soon in regular use and was planted with trees.

In the eighteenth century, there were no hospitals in Flintshire and patients were forced to travel to Chester or Liverpool to receive residential treatment, the cost of which was paid by the parish. In the nineteenth century, with hazardous working conditions in textile mills, deeper coal pits and lead mines, accidents at work became more common and there was a need for residential hospitals to provide treatment for serious illness in every industrial locality. Holywell opened a dispensary in the 1820s, but it was not until fifty years later that the town of Mold was provided with a small cottage hospital near the Bailey Hill. In November 1875, Mold Local Board 'offered no opposition to the Cottage Hospital Committee to take the piece of land' chosen in Gwernaffield Road.

The provision of hospitals at this time was a voluntary activity and not entitled to state aid. Until the National Health Service came into being in 1948, the money for building, equipping and maintaining hospitals was raised in the voluntary sector. The driving philanthropic force in Mold for the building and support of Mold hospital came from the local gentry and industrialists, whose women folk delighted in organising annual bazaars for their support. Apparently they were encouraged by the dedication of a local general practitioner, Dr Alfred Trubshaw, whose experience of accidents in the workplace identified the necessity for a hospital. The Mold Cottage Hospital Committee engaged the services of the architect John Douglas of Chester who, at the same time, was engaged on building the church of St John the Evangelist in King Street as a church for the Welsh-speaking Anglicans in the community.

The hospital was built in 1877 at a cost of about £1,200, the monies being entirely raised by voluntary subscriptions. It contained accommodation for about eight patients, with a resident matron; medical services were given gratuitously by local doctors. The opening of the hospital was delayed for a year until £600 was raised to furnish it. A Welsh-speaking nurse from the cottage hospital at Oswestry was engaged.

Amongst the Rules and Regulations of the hospital were:

The Hospital is designed for the accommodation of the Poor when suffering from sickness or accident …

Patients shall be admitted on payment of a weekly sum, the amount of which dependent on their circumstances should be fixed by their employers and friends in conjunction with the Ladies' Committee and Medical Offices, but shall in no case be less than two shillings and sixpence a week …

Patients shall be allowed to see their own Clergyman and those who are not of the Church of England may see their own minister …

Patients will be required to assist as far as circumstances will allow, in housework, needlework, gardening etc …

Patients will be responsible for the washing of their own clothes …

[The Nurse] will read prayers in the wards under the direction of the Ladies Committee.

Mold Cottage Hospital.

Notes

1. T.L. Jones, *Rioting in North East Wales 1536,* Bridge Books, 1997, p.35.
2. FRO D/LE/1130.
3. FRO D/LE/1137.
4. At the 'Peterloo Masssacre' eleven people were killed when cavalry attempted to disperse a crowd of 60,000 that had gathered to listen to the radical orator Henry Hunt on St Peter's Fields, Manchester, in August 1819. The 1820 Cato Street Conspiracy was a plot to assassinate the Prime Minister and the Cabinet and thereby form a new government. Five of those arrested there in February 1820 were executed and others transported.
5. Butler Clough was vicar of Mold 1825–54 and archdeacon of St Asaph. An exemplary cleric supporting the poor and building schools and churches in townships of Mold parish at Gwernaffield, Bistre and Pontblyddyn.
6. Reference to *The Military Historical Society Bulletin*, vol xxv, no. 100, May 1975.
7. This discussion is based on the researches of Emlyn Rogers, 'Trade Unionism in the Coal Mining Industry of North Wales to 1914' edited by R.O. Roberts, *Denbighshire Historical Society Transactions,* vols 12–15. Also T.L. Jones, op cit.
8. T.L. Jones, op cit p. 36 fn 157.
9. Emlyn Rogers, 'Labour Struggles in Flintshire 1830–1850', *Flintshire Historical Society Pub.*, 1953–54, vol 14, p.47.
10. ibid, p.57.
11. ibid, p.58.
12. *Flintshire Historical Society Publications,* vol 13, 1952–3, p.76.
13. ibid, Bevan-Evans's account based on *The Chester Chronicle,* August 12 1831.
14. Emlyn Rogers, ibid, *FHSP,* 14, p.66, fn 69.
15. *The Chester Chronicle,* Jan 14 1831.
16. *Y Dreflan,* Daniel Owen, *c.*1881 in translation in English by Ceiriog Williams 1981 by kind permission of Flintshire Library Service.
17. K.B. Smellie, *History of Local Government,* 1946, p.45.
18. Depopulated borough constituencies in the gift of patrons who continued to send MPs to the Commons until the Reform Act of 1832.
19. A parliamentary constituency whose electorate was made up of a group of small boroughs.
20. S. Lewis, *Topographical Dictionary of Wales,* 3rd ed. 1844.
21. The town of Holywell was nominated by the Poor Law Commissioners to be the centre of a Poor Law Union of a number of parishes jointly to administer the new Poor Law as established by the Poor Law Amendment Act of 1834.
22. Mold was challenging Flint for supremacy and the courts and gaol were removed there at this time.
23. FRO D/KK/155.
24. The workhouse of the Holywell Poor Law Union (architect John Welch) was built to enforce the principle of indoor relief; the inmates were subject to a strict regime of discipline which included the performance of specific tasks. Workhouses quickly acquired a forbidding reputation amongst the poor.
25. Public Health Act, 1875 (343 sections and 5 schedules).
26. This section is based on the minutes of the Local Board 1858–78. See FRO LB/B/1–2.
27. These were situated in the Bryn Garmon and Woodlands Close area.

9: Nineteenth-century Mold: religion

The expression 'cleanliness is next to godliness' found favour amongst the sanitary reformers of the mid-nineteenth century. Advocates of this attitude were responsible for many of the improvements in public health which made the streets and dwellings of the townsfolk of Mold safer from disease and more habitable. An increasingly mixed diet of religion was also thought to further the spiritual well-being of the local population. More people began to live longer and enjoy a slowly rising standard of living. It is not surprising that an increasing number of people in Mold took William Ewart Gladstone, their Hawarden neighbour, to their hearts when, as chancellor of the exchequer, he reduced or abolished duties on essential household goods, as a result of which goods such as tea, sugar, flour and soap found a place in their shopping baskets. Gladstone pursued his policy of improvement further than the market place and corner shop. When he became prime minister, his radical parliamentary programme was aimed at providing compulsory education for all. Through the implementation of this policy, the School Board came to Mold. A reduction in stamp and paper duties increased the number of Welsh Nonconformist books and periodicals that were published and fed an appetite for religious controversy, a debate which was invariably conducted in their own language. The people took pride in this, perceiving it to be their right to converse freely in Welsh, not only to each other, but also with the Almighty.

Gladstone won the admiration of Welsh Nonconformists and was described by the Welsh-language journal

Y Gohebydd as 'the greatest orator of the nineteenth century and no mistake. Really [he] is a most wonderful man.'[1] This identification of Gladstone with the Nonconformist majority of the Welsh population became clear in the public address he gave at the opening of the National Eisteddfod held at Mold in August 1873. He received a rapturous welcome from a crowd of over 3,000 when he entered the eisteddfod pavilion which had been erected near the railway station. The audience listened spellbound to his passionate and emotive support for the culture of the Welsh people and their language. He captivated their attention from the beginning of his address with the admission of his conversion from 'prejudices which prevailed in England with respect to the Welsh language and antiquities, but he had changed his opinions, a series of letters by Mr H. Richards MP, having done a good deal to open his eyes.'[2] He criticised as wrong the policy of the London-based government towards the Gaelic tongue in Scotland and to Erse speakers in Ireland. It was a mistake to attempt 'to change the language, the customs, the traditions and the affections of a people by force.' He spoke of the usefulness of the English

William Ewart Gladstone, photographed in the early 1870s.

language to the Welsh when in England and its promotion in education. In his conclusion he made clear to his Welsh listeners that he believed in their identity as a nation and the integrity of their language and culture.

> Welsh is an ancient language connected with an ancient music and an ancient literature ... If we wish really to promote the progress of civilisation, never let us neglect, never let us undervalue, never let us cease to reverence the past.

He concluded his address by congratulating his Welsh audience on their pride in their culture and told them,

> your laudable and patriotic efforts, as they come to be more understood, will be more respected and regarded by the English people at large, and that prosperity and honour will attend the meetings by which you endeavour to preserve and to commemorate the ancient history, the ancient deeds, and the ancient literature of your country, the Principality of Wales.[3]

These sympathetic sentiments won the hearts and minds of all Welsh men and women. The insults heaped upon the morals, religion, language, ignorance and culture of the ancient nation over the previous quarter of a century were exchanged for generous praise which publicly extolled the integrity, pride and patriotism of the Welsh. Their national identity was formally confirmed and respected. Gladstone's speech had come at a critical time in the progress of a national debate in Wales on language, religion and education. From that moment onwards, the Welsh electorate gave him and his party their full support and for the next fifty years, the Liberal Party was the undisputed people's representative in Wales.

Nonconformity

The first evidence we have for the 'planting' of Nonconformist places of worship in Mold are licences issued by the bishop of St Asaph granting permission to Protestant dissenters to assemble together for worship in dwelling houses. They were literally 'house churches,' meeting houses that were licensed according to law by the authority of Toleration Acts of the seventeenth century and later. In these places, teachers, preachers and congregations could meet for worship. A notable example of this was at Rhual which had became a stronghold of the Anabaptists at the end of the seventeenth century. The early Welsh revivalists were itinerant evangelists seeking conversions from their preaching and attracting migrant workers and other groups. From their ranks emerged the lay leadership and the first Nonconformist ministers. As numbers increased, the original 'house churches' were replaced by simple, purpose-built places of worship, used not only for worship but also for Bible study, prayer meetings, Sunday schools, singing festivals and temperance societies.

The Reverend Thomas Charles of Bala (1755–1814) was the founder of the Sunday school movement in Wales. He saw them as promoting 'the useful practices of learning chapters of the Bible, and being catechised publicly,' and making progress in learning their own language. These Sunday schools went hand in hand with chapels attended by scholars of all ages. The chapels and Sunday schools gave their members a sense of assurance, opportunities for self-expression, self-improvement and experience of leadership. Their religious experience transformed and reformed their lives. Gradually, the combination of Nonconformist membership began to overtake that of the established church in Wales and made them a considerable political force in the principality.

John Wesley came to Mold three times, in 1759, 1760 and 1761, and there was probably a small Methodist society established in the town by 1762. In his journal for 2 May 1759, he recorded

> I rode over to Mould in Flintshire, about 12 miles from Chester. The sun was very hot, and the wind was very cold; but as the place they had chose for me was exposed to the sun and wind, the one balanced the other. And notwithstanding the Chester Races, which had drawn the rich away: and the market day which detained many of the poor; the serious part of whom soon influenced the rest, so that all but two or three remained uncovered, and kneeled down as soon as I began to pray.[4]

Richard Harrison (1743–1830), a weaver from Llanferres, was converted to Wesleyan Methodism and became a member of the Octagon Chapel in Chester. He was also associated with the Calvinistic Methodists at Ponterwyl in Mold and they gave him the option of membership or expulsion, but he chose to remain a member with the Wesleyans. He was a founder of Ferm's Yard Chapel which was granted a bishop's licence on 3 October 1803 and was registered for worship on 25 April 1804. It was described as 'A certain building or meeting house in the Town and Parish of Mold. Named are John Harrison, Thomas Pierce, Edward Griffiths, Thomas James, Richard Harrison and Robert Morris.'[5] The premises used by the Wesleyans proved to be too small and Richard Harrison was responsible for obtaining land at Ferms Yard in Wrexham Street.[6] He obtained a lease (dated 5 June 1802) for land for 63 years on which they built a new chapel. It was opened at Whitsun in 1803, when the preachers were the Reverends Owen Davies, Edward Jones and John Bryan, and Richard Harrison of Northop. The first leader of the cause at Ferms Yard was Thomas James of Abergele. A new chapel was built in 1851 which the religious census of that year showed as being able to accommodate 50 (free) plus 100 others, with 40 attending morning service and 35 in the evening. Ferms Yard Chapel was eventually demolished to make way for Bank's Villa.

In 1828, Welsh-speaking members of the Mold Wesleyan chapel chose to separate and moved to a new site at Pendref, at the foot of Bailey Hill.

Having determined to build a Welsh Chapel, land was leased from Sir Thomas Mostyn at one corner of Bailey Hill 642 yards in extent in the name of Robert Harrison and others. The annual rent in 1849 was £5. 10s. 6d. The building cost £1,600. The opening service took place on 6th–7th July and nine preachers were engaged and they began preaching at 6 a.m. when both chapels were in use. In addition the distinguished Calvinistic Methodist Preacher the Rev. Thomas Jones of Denbigh preached to a crowd of 2,000 on the side of Bailey Hill. It is estimated that 5,000 people were present during the two days' services.

In 1856, the Mostyn estate in Mold was put up for sale and the trustees purchased the lease for £100. In 1876 extensive alterations were carried out at a cost of £1,264. It was re-opened in October 1877. The Schoolroom was opened on the 1st. Dec. 1904.[7]

Pendref Wesleyan Chapel, Mold (now King's Christian Centre).

According to the 1851 religious census, Pendref had 107 worshippers present in the morning, 158 in the evening and 158 attenders at the Sunday school.

The tentative beginnings of the Welsh Calvinistic Methodist cause have been described as follows:

Howel Harris had preached in a gentleman's house near Mold in 1751, and there is an interesting account of the start of Calvinism Methodism in the town. Rumours had spread that the Methodists were devils in the guise of men, and when a preacher arrived there to proclaim the gospel standing on a horse block, he was attacked by a fierce crowd who threw dung and mud at him. He held his ground and delivered his message, but a local publican was of the opinion that it would be worthwhile to teach him a lesson. This publican kept a bear in the tavern and he let the animal loose. However, rather than attacking the preacher, the beast approached him and licked him to the disappointment of the publican and the wonderment of the crowd. The event left a big impression on them, and after that there was less persecution.[8]

By 1762, many worshippers were meeting at the home of a woman called Sara Howel, but afterwards the services were moved to a barn in Glanrafon. As the work flourished, a chapel was built at Ponterwyl in 1794, near the site of the railway station. A licence for a meeting house was granted on 24 October 1795 in the holding or occupation of Sarah Jones, widow. It named Thomas Jones (of Denbigh), George Foulkes, T.C. Williams, Edward Jones, Sarah Jones and Elizabeth Lloyd.[9] There is a memorial stone in the garden by the roadside above the present-day Tesco petrol station denoting the site of this early chapel.

Mold's first Wesleyan Methodist Chapel, Glanrafon.

By 1806, membership had increased to 140 and the chapel was registered as a place of worship in 1807. In 1815, a revival increased the membership, the chapel became too small and it was decided to build a larger chapel in New Street at a cost of £1,000. This opened in 1819 and was named Bethesda.

Proof of the growing strength of Calvinistic Methodism in the area and the facilities of Bethesda, is seen when, in March 1834, it was chosen as the meeting place of the Quarterly Association 'and was more numerously attended than any similar occasion, there being upwards of five thousand persons present. The religious services were kept up during the greater part of the day in a field adjoining the town.'[10] The 1851 religious census showed that the chapel could accommodate 205 (free), 350 others and 120 standing. The attendance figures were 240 (morning, 230 afternoon, 230 (Sunday school), 401 (evenings). A twelve month average showed an attendance of 300 in the mornings and 520 in the evenings.[11]

A licence was granted for an Independent meeting house on 23 December 1808, in 'a house situate in New Street in the occupation of Jonathan Catherall of Hawkesbury House, Buckley.' Those named in the licence were: Thomas Jones, Robert Edwards, Edward Williams, William Jones, Owen Jones and David Morris. Jonathan Catherall, II (1761–1833), built Bethel Chapel on the same site in 1827 and appointed and paid the minister £30 a year. He also built chapels in Holywell and Buckley Mountain Congregational Church in 1811. The 1851 religious census recorded that the chapel could accommodate 213 (free), 400 others and 200 standing. The attendance figures were 140 (plus 60 scholars) in the morning, 195 (plus 127 scholars) in the evening.[12]

The period between 1851 (the year of the Religious Census) and the outbreak of the Great War in 1914 were sixty years of triumph and ascendancy for Welsh Nonconformity before its values and way of life were undermined by secular modernity and industrial depression. A view of these years is taken from the novels of Daniel Owen who died in 1895. By the 1880s, he was lamenting the disappearance of the qualities of the old-style Methodism in Mold. A quiet observer of Mold society throughout his life, he recorded his impressions of both the religious and secular scene. He had been strictly nurtured by his widowed mother in the values of the old cause and in his youth he trained with, and was teased by, his fellow apprentices in Angel Jones's tailor's shop in the town. He missed nothing and learned to think and express his own opinions. Whether at Bethesda Chapel, Bala College, or as a member of the Mold Local Board, he was deceived by neither saint nor sinner. His fictional account of life in the town included not only the closed and intensely religious hothouse of Nonconformity but the work and temptations of the devil incarnate in factory, mine, market place, behind shop counter, public house or present in the squalid dwellings of the poor, feckless and destitute. His compassion extended beyond the narrowness of the elders of his denomination and was broadened by his sympathy with the plight of the poor and the injustices they suffered in the workplace at the hands of unscrupulous owners and managers.

Bethel Independent Chapel, Mold.

Every religious denomination in the nineteenth century sought to provide sufficient accommodation for a growing population. As a result, the building of places of worship became a duty to be entered into with enthusiasm, dedication and not a little competition. The rise in the number of Nonconformist chapels in Wales was phenomenal, an increase which happened periodically over the decades as a result of missionary activity and spectacularly as evangelical campaigns burst into heady religious revivals. These brought thousands of converts through the chapel doors and seats had to be found for all of them. In Mold from the 1850s onwards, another phase of Nonconformist expansion was marked by the opening of new chapels where worship was conducted in both Welsh and English. In the town, there was an *ad hoc* building programme which either replaced existing chapels or provided new ones. Most had schoolrooms attached to them designed to cater for a programme of weekly activities. This expansion during the second half of the nineteenth century is seen in a review of the efforts made by the various denominations to practise their faith according to their traditions and engage in missionary and other activities.

During the seventeenth and early eighteenth centuries, the few members of the Baptist cause in Flintshire found support and protection from the Griffith family at Rhual and ministrations from Wrexham. Thomas Griffith built a baptistry and Rhual became a centre for the Old Cause in Mold, with links to Wrexham, Denbigh and further afield. At the end of the eighteenth century, others came to Mold to keep the cause alive, men such as Evan Evans from Llanfyllin who moved to Northop Hall in 1797 where he influenced John Pritchard (formerly of Ruabon) to become a Baptist. In the absence of a place of worship in the Mold area, Pritchard travelled to Ruthin to worship but by 1805, had decided to establish a place of worship nearer home and for this purpose, rented Tŷ Mawr in High Street for the sum of £5 a year.

The arrival of Baptists in the town was greeted with resentment and persecution and efforts were made by their fellow Christians to drive them away. The Wesleyans are reputed to have physically attacked John Pritchard, and the vicars of Northop and Mold joined in this hostility and refused to bury his unbaptized child. An anonymous letter of this period sent to the vicar Hope Wynne Eyton, informed him of the intention 'of an Itinerant Rascal of a Quack Doctor from Buckley … to baptize a number of people in the River by the Lead Mill,' which he termed the River Jordan.'[13] Events turned nasty when, after the two candidates Robert Gitten and Edward Price had been immersed, John Pritchard was struck by a stone and assaulted with a knife.

Baptist ministers who served in Mold in the nineteenth century included:

1833	Edward Williams of Manchester and Aberystwyth.
1835–7	William Roberts ('Nefydd', 1813–72) came as a Baptist home missionner.
1838	Hugh William Hughes ('Arwyst').
1842	Thomas Williams – John Evans.
1853	Bethabra Chapel was built.
1861	John Jones of Haverfordwest College.
1866	H. Gwerfyl James, Pontypool College – John Roberts.
1876	A new chapel was erected in Wrexham Street at a cost of £860 with Dr Gethin Davies of Llangollen in charge.

1888–91   Thomas Shankland 1858–1927, a distinguished bibliophile and historian with a generous sympathy for the traditions of all churches.

1895   Thomas Morgan.

Ebenezer Baptist Church, Mold.

In the middle of the century, the major Nonconformist denominations in Mold made provision for worship to be conducted in English for those ignorant of the Welsh language by building three churches

The English Presbyterian Church, Tyddyn Street was opened in 1863 at a cost of £3,087.
The English Wesleyan Church, Wrexham Street, the foundation stone of which was laid on 25 May 1868 and the English Congregational, Westminster Road opened in 1869 at a cost of £4,400.[14]

Daniel Owen was a lifelong member of the Calvinistic Methodists which formed the background to his 'autobiographical' work, *Rhys Lewis*. He adopted a light-hearted approach to distinguishing the nuances of the Nonconformist denominations he experienced in Mold. His ecumenical attitude betrayed a broad vision of understanding and tolerance, spiced with irony and amusement, something that was unusual in religious discussion at the time. His first novel, *Y Dreflan*, published in 1881, opened with the observation that,

> The Methodists are not without significance in Dreflan. They have more than one chapel in the town, providing a strong membership with spiritual sustenance, served by a minister and an army of deacons. The minister is a learned, able young man, and a good preacher, or at least that is the opinion of his admirers; but there are those who claim that his preaching is too prosaic, that they would prefer a minister who had been to College.[15]

Although there is an abundance of water here in Dreflan, the Baptist brethren, by comparison, are fewer in number. I know no reason why this should be so unless it be a geographical one, namely that Dreflan is situated too far to the north. The few we have, however, are ardent workers. The Independent and Wesleyan brethren are more Pentecostal than all the other denominations, particularly in one respect, they preach in more than one language. The Independent Chapel minister, a keen, able man, is a poet and an Eisteddfodic zealot. Attached to his chapel is a preacher, a little delicate-looking man, with a peculiarly squeaky voice. He is known throughout the Principality and America, by his bardic pseudonym, 'The Roaring Lion'. The chief characteristic of the minister of the English chapel is that he always wears spectacles, except to read, and he wears a Jim Crow hat and light-coloured trousers on a Sunday. There is considerable likeness between the two Wesleyans, respecting their personalities, and their mode of dressing. They are always neatly and well clad, and are not

Daniel Owen, photograph by F.M. Davies.

strangers to the establishment of Messrs Glenfield and Co. They rarely become involved in public activities in the town, and that presumably because of the great volume of work confronting them, and their stay here is for only two, or possibly three years at the most. They are devoted workers for the Cause and are jealous of the doctrinal beliefs of their denomination; one of them is an ardent temperance worker. As I write these words I see the Catholic priest passing by, quietly and unobtrusively, apparently taking no notice of a living soul; but no doubt, he, in his own way, is as busy as any of these I have mentioned.

But in spite of all the preparation, and the opportunities provided for evangelizing our town, and in spite of all the prayers and exhortations, there are still hundreds here who are as ignorant of the Gospel as if it were the most unfamiliar thing in the world. There are, here, back streets, dark and filthy, where there is poverty, misery, and evil in abundance, which continues from year to year. There are scores here who spend every penny they can lay their hands on, in the taverns, while their wives and children starve in the cold, and are black and blue in the face for want of food. Carry on, brethren, of all denominations! There is still much left undone, and what does it matters who turns the sinner from his evil ways so long as that is achieved.[16]

By the beginning of the nineteenth century, the Nonconformist demands for the disestablishment and disendowment of the Anglican Church in Wales grew more vociferous and a royal commission was established to discover the relevant strengths of all religious bodies. The commission toured the principality, receiving evidence from a large number of witnesses, amongst whom was Thomas Parry, JP, a member of Bethesda Welsh Calvinistic Methodist chapel.[17] Parry was a good choice as a leading member of the new Nonconformist élite which had recently achieved prominence and power in local government. By 1907, he was either a past or present chairman of every influential body in the area, including the Mold Local Board, the Urban District Council, County Council, Flintshire Calvinistic monthly meeting and was a governor of Mold Intermediate School. He was a deacon, a treasurer and a trustee at Bethesda Chapel. The data which follows is strongly based upon his evidence, although it is supplemented with information from other sources.

The first purpose-built chapel at Ponterwyl was occupied by the Calvinistic Methodists from 1794 until 1819 when it was sold to St Mary's Church for use as a National School. The first Bethesda Chapel in New Street was built in 1819 at a cost of £1,023. This was replaced on the same site in 1863 at a cost of £3,500. New classrooms were built in 1894 (at a cost of £637) and in the period between 1819 and 1906, a total of £7,947 was spent on the Bethesda chapels, providing seating accommodation for 890, seating in the large schoolroom for 200 and additional seating in three classrooms of 100. The chapel had 362 communicants, 5 elders and

Bethesda Chapel, New Street, 1864.

600 adherents (including communicants and children).[18]

A feature of Nonconformity was that its activities were not limited to Sunday. Its religious bodies were societies which came together more regularly to practise a wide range of religious observances such as prayer meetings, Bible study, choral singing, etc. All who had been admitted into the chapel community were expected to attend not only on Sundays (at least twice), but to take part in the mid-week meeting, the *seiat*, at which members could be disciplined.

Sunday services were formally conducted around the sermon, the great evangelizing weapon of Nonconformity. Later it became more common for an organ to be introduced into Sunday worship which was initially seen as a difficult innovation but, once accepted, the chapel became not only an auditorium but a concert hall for the performance of oratorio, with the organ used in singing festivals and *eisteddfodau*. In 1906, a two-manual organ was installed at Bethesda at a cost of £500 (shared equally between the Scottish-American philanthropist, Andrew Carnegie, and Peter E. Roberts of Bromfield Hall).[19] The report mentions that 'there has also been in existence for 56 years a musical and literary meeting, known as the eisteddfod, held on Christmas Day, or the day following when Christmas has been on a Sunday. The average attendance in recent years at the afternoon meetings has been about 600, and at the evening meeting about 1,000.'

The library at Bethesda provided an opportunity for chapel members to borrow books, a facility that was no doubt used and appreciated by Daniel Owen. It provided an opportunity for self-improvement and an alternative place for recreation. The books, in both English and Welsh, comprised works of theology, history, biography, science, poetry and fiction, together with several standard books of reference.

Chapel buildings were designed to be shared with their own and other Nonconformist denominations in the promotion of common activities such as temperance, Sunday schools, *eisteddfodau* and singing festivals.

The normal weekly programme at Bethesda Chapel was:

Sundays: 10 a.m., service and sermon; 11.30 a.m., young people's prayer meeting; 2 p.m., school (average attendance 211); 6 p.m., service and sermon, followed by short church meeting; 8 p.m., singing practice.
Communion the last Sunday in each month.
Weekdays: Mondays 6 p.m., two children's Bible-classes under 12 and under 16; during winter, in separate classrooms. Number of members 60; 7 p.m. prayer meeting; 8 p.m. adult's bible-class, during winter, members 15.
Thursday 6 p.m., Band of Hope, during winter, members 60. 6 pm. Young communicants i.e. those in preparation.

In both rural and urban areas of Wales, Nonconformity exerted its influence through evangelization, conversion to the Christian way of life, spreading the word of God, keeping members on the straight and narrow through uncompromising exhortation and strict discipline, and self-examination.

New English Presbyterian Church (architect T.G. Williams) 1892. This was an example of church extension from Bethesda.

The chief means was church extension by establishing new congregations. Pentre Chapel on the outskirts of Mold, Thomas Parry's chapel, was a good example of this but not the only chapel to have emanated from Bethesda. He gave evidence that Bethesda Church had inspired the foundation of religious congregations at nine places in the area.[20]

Thomas Parry gave evidence that the Pentre Mission began in a private house about the year 1852. Eventually a chapel was built in 1874 at a cost of £327.[9] The church was in the charge of the minister of Bethesda and its activities were:[21]

> Sunday Services: 10 a.m., children's service; 2 p.m. School; 6 p.m., service, sermon or prayer meeting. Weekdays: Tuesday, 7. 30 p.m., night school for adults during winter, conducted by Miss Roberts, a member of Bethesda and on alternative weeks conducted by Revverend John Owen, pastor of Bethesda. Wednesday, 7 p.m., Bible classes, children and adults. 7 p.m., Band of Hope. The library and reading room were open every week-night from 7 to 9.30 p.m.

He emphasised the effect of church extension on the life in their communities.

> As one who has worked in connection with Pentre Mission for the last 35 years, I can say that the mission has done much to raise the character of the place. It has also been the means of starting several of the young people on a useful career who have left the district. The present superintendent was brought up in the school, and we have several instances of the same kind.

Parry stated that the Welsh language appeared to be used in Mold as the language of worship. In Bethesda Chapel, all services were in Welsh (English sermons being the exception). At Pentre, although 99% spoke English, they chose to have their services in Welsh as did eight of the nine chapels in the communities 'planted' from Mold. There were no bi-lingual services, but there was no antagonism by Welsh members in attending English services held by other religious bodies. When questioned about the language spoken by children, Parry said that English was principally spoken by those playing in the streets, but most of those attending the public elementary schools 'would speak Welsh at home.'

Ebenezer Chapel, Pentre.

It was natural at a time when Nonconformity was in the ascendancy that the role of its spokesmen became paramount and persuasive. In the nineteenth century, the influence of Welsh Dissenting ministers became as pervasive as that of Catholic priests in rural Ireland. The minister and his acolytes, the elders, directed the hearts and minds of chapel members, probed their consciences, fixed the boundaries of behaviour and dictated moral standards in an atmosphere at times reminiscent of the Spanish Inquisition. The discipline and punishment which they administered in the *seiat* were meant to bring shame and repentance and in the last resort resulted in excommunication. The emphasis was on an outward respectability, summed up by the poet Dylan Thomas in the phrase 'Oh, what will the neighbours say, what will the neighbours say?' Being found out, indulging in intoxicating liquor or carnal temptations, was the greatest shame and many members failed to live up to the high moral standards demanded by Calvinistic theology. It is little wonder that the peace-loving Henry Richard in 1866 described the ministers as the 'unpaid policemen of the countryside.' By the

Angel Jones, tailor, of Castle Street, Mold.

last quarter of the nineteenth century, an increased Nonconformist electorate looked to the minister for guidance as to which way to use their vote and expected him to be on the platform with the candidate of his choice. The political agenda for the Liberal Party in Wales during parliamentary elections became weighted in favour of Nonconformists, with issues such as temperance, removal of inequalities and disestablishment being high on the political agenda.

Human nature led to many Nonconformists failing to meet the moral expectations of chapel society which in turn led to double standards, hypocrisy, injustice and disillusionment. It is this predicament in Welsh society which was sympathetically explored in the writings of Daniel Owen who drew on his own experiences when portraying his own age in an honest and lively manner. He admitted that he never learned much at the Mold schools he attended and that his intellectual development only began in 1851 when, aged fourteen, he was bound as an apprentice for five years to Angel Jones, a tailor in Castle Street (behind the old Market Hall). Jones, a devout Calvinistic Methodist deacon at Bethesda, became the inspiration for the character of Abel Huws in *Rhys Lewis*. On his death in 1860, he was succeeded by his son, John Angel Jones, and the shop moved to the High Street where it was referred to as 'Mold's Parliament.' Owen's eight or nine fellow workers were the ideal company to engage his mind, stimulate his interests and develop his powers of observation and expression. In this atmosphere, he developed a mind of his own and, as long as their work did not suffer, they had the freedom to read magazines, newspapers and the novels of Scott and Dickens and the customers were encouraged to participate. The Reverend J.J. Morgan gave this account of the group.[22]

Edward Williams, well over six feet, straight as a poplar, a fine bass, a zealous Wesleyan; Edward Foulkes, (Foulkes *bach*), short of stature, a proficient literary man, soloist and elocutionist; Xavier (Saphir) Lehmann, a German and a Roman Catholic, a competent organist; Robert Dykins, bird-fancier, singer and an expert in pig-breeding; Ellis Williams, a capital reciter, a humorous raconteur, a merry companion, and a good vocalist; Isaac Jones, a strong Calvinist, with a weak leg, who walked with a crutch, Daniel's friend and admirer for over half a century; John Williams, a pugnacious controversialist, deliberate, sagacious, a local preacher; and David Arthur, who alone remains …

The Reverend Roger Edwards played an influential part in the development of Daniel Owen. He had arrived in Mold in 1835 and pursued a versatile career as secretary of the North Wales Calvinistic Methodist Association, assisting as minister at Bethesda and as editor of the journal, *Y Drysorfa*. His radical principles influenced the development of political liberalism in north Wales, and he established the customary Christmas Day eisteddfod at Mold in 1855. He proved to be the ideal person to encourage the young Daniel Owen, who became a full member

Reverend Roger Edwards.

John Angel Jones with some of his staff. Daniel Owen (third from left) worked here for thirteen years. There were usually eight or nine men working here, most of whom were of 'acute intelligence, wide interests, alert in spirit, ready of speech and enthusiastic in temper. Edward Williams [centre left, front], well over six feet, straight as a poplar, a fine bass, a zealous Wesleyan; Edward Foulkes [Foulkes Bach, extreme left, front], short of stature, a proficient literary man, soloist and elocutionist; Xavier (Saphir) Lehmann, a German and a Roman Catholic, a competent organist; Robert Dykins, a bird fancier, singer and an expert in pig-breeding. Ellis Williams a capital reciter, humourous raconteur, merry companion and a good vocalist. Isaac Jones, a strong Calvinist, with a weak leg, who walked with a crutch, Daniel's friend and admirer for half a century; John Williams a pugnacious controversionalist, deliberate, sagacious, a local preacher; and David Arthur who alone remains.'

of Bethesda in 1859, attended Bala College in 1865–7 (at the same time as his son, Ellis) and published his novel *Y Dreflan* in 1881, extracts from which reflect characters and scenes influenced by his experiences in Mold.

Mrs Price had salted the round of beef days before, had brought out the cutlery, and had polished it until one could see one's face in it. In passing allow me to observe that I see something typically Welsh-Methodism in a round of beef – something suggestive of its strength and Prosperity and therefore very appropriate for the lunch table of the Monthly Meeting, and for that of the General Assembly.[23]

This part of Dreflan [Mold] is known as Jenkins' Yard because most of the dilapidated, dreary-looking, ram-shackled buildings to be there belonged to Jeremiah Jenkins …

Although I was born and bred in Dreflan, and Jenkins' yard was only just off the main street, I must confess that it was as unknown to me as darkest Africa, but I knew from hearsay that there were many living there, and that there were facilities there to house tramps. I had on several occasions, seen loitering about the entrance, samples of the types who stayed there, and from their appearance they were no credit to the town or to mankind …[24]

As we were going through the entrance we met a surly, cross-eyed woman who appeared thoroughly dismal-looking, carrying a jug in her hand. She had such a squint in her eyes that we would never have known that she had seen us had she not hidden the jug under her apron as soon as we came into view. She was not going for water, nor for milk, but for something which was available on Sunday until one o'clock … Although it was the Sabbath I could not keep my mind from off mundane things and I meditated on the Local Board's hygienic standards.

It was a weird experience to wend one's way through Jenkins' Yard on such a night. I knew from Mr Pugh's silence that he was frightened, and I was not surprised, because here in the Yard were some of the worst tramps and local scamps. The heavy rain had done nothing to decrease the odour which was there … It was getting late and I thought everyone in the Yard would have retired to bed, when suddenly we heard sounds of merriment coming from a house with its door partially opened. The room was well-lit and four fierce looking men were sitting round a table on which there was a jug and several glasses. One of the men was shuffling a pack of cards which he manipulated dexterously. Sitting by the fire, smoking a short stemmed pipe, was the dirty cross-eyed woman … So black and filthy was she that I imagine she went in and out of the house by way of the chimney![25]

Anne William's shop … the most honest business in Dreflan…On a square piece of paper, pinned on to the red curtain behind the window he will see written the first two lines of English poetry he may ever have to learn: 'TABLE BEER, SOLD HERE' which indicates the main feature of her business … It is acknowledged that Anne's table beer is the best in Dreflan, and Bass & Co. are no prouder of their product than she is of her temperance drink. Although this was the mainstay of her trade, there are other articles in her shop, such as red-herrings, a variety of sweets, toffee, India Rock, and the like, which had often caused my teeth to water in my childhood … If the visitor has a penny to spare let him patronize the old Lady, because in addition to all her other virtues, she is a zealous Methodist. Let him push open the already partially open door, and the bell connected to it, drooping like a half-withered flower, will ring, and in answer to its call a neatly addressed old lady will appear, smiling through her yellow spectacles. If the visitor chooses, he may get, in addition to a fair amount of toffee for his penny, a pleasant edifying chat. But let him not be disappointed should the large multi-coloured cat, half asleep at one end of the counter appear to ignore him because that is her attitude to everyone.[26]

No one suspected that there would be great poverty and distress. There were few beggars about and few were unemployed apart from those too lazy to work. The government of the day was constantly planning improvements and oiling the machinery of industry and the economy was improving. Everywhere there was work and food. On market days the streets of Dreflan were over-crowded with people and rarely was there a pale face to be seen. The wives of ordinary labourers struggled home under the weight of heavy baskets and many had to procure a conveyance. On Saturday night, the shopkeepers could not close their shops until Sunday morning was upon them, let alone find time to count their money.

But the class which earned most was the miners. The men at the coal face earned two pounds ten shillings to three pounds a week, and sometimes more. So flourishing was industry that it was practically impossible to employ a farm labourer at any price. The term 'labouring class' and 'worker' were so sacred that no one dared to utter any criticism of them without incurring the displeasure of hundreds of people, and even endangering one's life. Men were employed at a large wage, more for their own benefit than that of the workers, to tramp the country making speeches and forming societies to safeguard or in other words to enable them to strike if there was any suggestion of lowering their wages … Trade was booming and Providence was pouring forth her blessings so abundantly that even the lowest grade of collier had become aggressive. Mercifully the more thoughtful class among them especially the religious folk, could see that this abnormal prosperity was only temporary, and they made preparation for the rainy day by building houses for themselves and banking their savings. Costly chapels were built in some rural areas where no one except workers resided and they were honourably paid for by the generous contributions of the members.

Regrettably, most of the colliers spent the greater part of their hard earned money in the taverns. It is true their families did not go short of food, but once the shop bills had been paid, they were never happy until they had poured the remainder of their earnings into a publican's coffers. They received so much on pay-day that it took Saturday, Sunday, and Monday to spend it, and on Tuesday they would be obliged to return to work until next pay-day.[27]

Like Lot in Sodom, Siân Jones lived among the uncivilized. In her small two-roomed cottage, whitewashed inside and out, the old woman lived happily and contentedly. The mental picture I have of her is one of supreme contentment, always wearing a large bonnet, in and out of the house and her beautiful Indian scarf, and a skirt of homespun material – her stocking and her knitting needles in her hands, her spotted large stool in the centre of the floor – her big Bible with its brass studs on its corners, open on the table – the kettle always on the hob – the cottage door always fully open and the two hens entering with their heads askew, gazing up at her, and Sian humming. How the old woman sustained herself puzzled me. She received her weekly half-crown parish relief, sixpence from Ismael for making his bed and tidying his house, and the two hens' resolution to lay as frequently as they could; that was her total income. But not exactly either, because Mr Pugh sent her half a sovereign on New Year's Day, and a load of coal, together with a sack of potatoes. Sian paid fifteen pence weekly rent to Jeremiah Jenkins, and she unfailingly subscribed one penny every Sunday night to the chapel. She never went begging, but I never saw her in need. Someone must have been giving her a great deal, secretly, and who that was will only be revealed on the day when all good deeds are divulged.[28]

Daniel Owen is humorous in his description of what he sees as major differences between the various religious traditions in his community and points out the distinction between them in a clear and open-minded way. The quotations below are taken from his novel *Rhys Lewis*. The first extract is from a conversation between the eponymous character, Rhys Lewis, and his friends, Will Bryan and John Beck ,who visit him when he is recovering from the thrashing he had received at the hands of the 'Old Soldier'. Rhys's brother Bob is to be brought before the chapel deacons, the *Seiat*, to answer for his retaliatory assault on the sadistic schoolmaster and Will Bryan, a Methodist, explains its meaning to John Beck, an Anglican.

'Do you see, Jack,' said he, 'Society means a lot of good folk who think themselves bad, coming together every Tuesday night, to find fault with themselves, and run each other down.'

'That is where the difference between Church and Chapel comes in,' said Will. 'You Church people think yourselves good when you are bad, while Chapel people think themselves bad when they are good.'

'You don't mean to tell me,' said Beck, 'that all who belong to the Society are good people, and that all who belong to the Church are bad?'

'All,' returned Will, 'who take the Sacrament in Chapel are good people, although they think themselves bad, and all who take the Sacrament in Church think themselves good, while more than half of them are bad. There is the old Soldier – you know very well he takes (the) Sacrament on Sunday morning, just to please Mr Brown, while every Sunday night he goes boozing to the Cross Foxes till he is too blind to see his way home again. Did he belong to the Chapel, look you, he would get the kick out pretty sharp. But when did you see anybody expelled from Church?'

… Will Bryan went on with his exposition of what was meant by 'being brought before the Society.' 'You see,' he said, 'when any one belonging to the Society does wrong – even they, you know, are not perfect – someone else must needs go to the elders and split upon him; and next Society, after that, Abel Hughes will call him to account …'

'… it is more comfortable in the Church, but more safe in the Chapel.'[29]

At the end of the book Will Bryan picks out 'the good points' of the various denominations.

Have you never wondered that a new sect has not risen to take up the good points of all the denominations? Something of this sort, now; let them adopt the style of the Church of England; the smartness of the Congregationalists, the go-aheadedness of the Wesleyans, and doctrine of the old corph. I don't know much about the Dippers (Baptists), but I should think they must have their good points. Each sect excels the other in something. I like the style of the English Church; they are more devotional, don't look about them, or talk to each other during the service; only I think they must be awfully ignorant.[30]

Roman Catholicism

Despite nearly three centuries of persecution, Roman Catholicism survived in parts of England and Wales and the years between the Reformation and Catholic Emancipation in 1829 were known to Catholics as the Penal Times. Holywell in Flintshire was in many ways unusual as it continued to be a place of pilgrimage to the well of St Winefride and the centre for both a Jesuit and secular mission where Mass could be heard in secret. A return of Papists in 1767 revealed that there were 362 Catholics in the diocese of St Asaph, twenty-one of whom were recorded as residing in the parish of Mold. Their occupations included: three farmers, one dealer, three miners, one servant and one mason, with half of this number having been born in the parish. There were another ten Catholics dwelling in the township of Nercwys, whose presence there being the result of the marriage of three gentry Catholic families who had retained their allegiance to the old faith – the Giffards, an old recusant family of Chillington and Blackladies, Staffordshire; the Roberts family[31] of Nerquis and the Hydes of Plas Ucha. 'At a time when the lack of patrons led to the virtual extinction of Welsh Catholicism, the recusant Giffards were able to sustain the failing Catholic communities in Denbigh and Flint.'[32] Chief among these was John Bonaventura Giffard (d. 1797)[33] who had married Elizabeth Hyde, daughter and heiress of Robert Hyde of Nercwys Hall. His mother-in-law had objected to their daughters being brought up in the Catholic faith and insisted that the eldest daughter, Elizabeth, was baptised an Anglican and remained with her mother at Nercwys, whilst the younger child, Eleanor, was taken to Paris by her father, where she was educated by the Blue Nuns. They returned to Nercwys on the death of Madam Hyde in 1786. At the Flintshire Quarter Sessions on 12 January 1792, John Giffard's house at Nercwys was registered as 'a place of meeting for religious worship.' This was therefore the first building in the parish of Mold since the Reformation where Mass was legally sanctioned. By the end of the eighteenth century, Dissenters were beginning to apply for licences to enable them to meet together for worship and the same procedure was now undertaken by Catholics who according to the law fell within a similar category.

In 1829, Prime Minister the Duke of Wellington and Home Secretary Peel were forced, by the actions of Daniel O'Connell in Ireland, to persuade George IV to give his assent to the measure for Catholic emancipation. Although the nation was divided on the issue, the Bill was forced through because of the fear of Irish revolt. In the early decades of the nineteenth century in Mold and elsewhere, Roman Catholics began to increase in number through an alliance between immigrant Irish poor, the devotion of Catholic aristocratic families, middle-class patrons and a multi-national priesthood. There followed a remarkable recovery and growth of Roman Catholicism in Mold and in 1901, the Lenten pastoral letter of Bishop Mostyn outlined the progress made during the long reign of Queen Victoria.

> The British nation is still mourning for our late beloved Queen, whose long and prosperous reign has come to a close in the first month of the new century. We Catholics, however, have many things to be grateful to God for, which have taken place during her illustrious reign. Thanks for the liberty which we have enjoyed, our holy religion has spread far and wide. The Hierarchy has been re-established, Dioceses formed, Churches built, and the members of our faith are now eligible for almost every position of trust in the management of the affairs of the Country.[34]

Bishop Mostyn, a member of the most distinguished Catholic recusant family in Flintshire, had in mind the establishment of the College of Beuno at Tremeirchion by the Jesuits in 1848 and the conversion to Roman Catholicism in August 1850 of Rudolph, viscount Feilding, later earl of Denbigh, and his bride Louisa Pennant of Downing. They transferred the church of St David at Pantasaph, which was in the process of being constructed, to the Roman Catholic diocese of Shrewsbury and invited Capuchin Franciscans to establish a community there. These events were met with strong protest. There was a meeting at the County Hall in Mold on 4 December 1850, summoned by the lord lieutenant 'for the purpose of addressing a memorial to the Queen expressing their astonishment and indignation at the late ecclesiastical arrangements of the Catholic Church in this country.' The motion was carried overwhelmingly and signed by eight peers and nearly a thousand freeholders. In a display of antagonism, Lord Feilding's effigy was burnt in several locations.[35]

By 1895, Catholicism in Wales had grown in sufficient numbers for Pope Leo XIII to appoint Francis Mostyn as vicar apostolic to be elevated three years later to bishop of the newly-created diocese of Menevia. Another sign of progress was Bishop Mostyn's establishment of St Mary's College in Holywell for the training of an indigenous priesthood for his extensive diocese.[36]

The pattern for the establishment of Roman Catholic parishes and deaneries in Wales is a remarkable story of growth when churches had to be built, priests recruited and money found to finance this planting of parishes with their schools and presbyteries begged, borrowed and prayed for. They were totally dependent on the offerings of rich and poor.

The first assistance came from Wrexham when in 1843, Father Tobin rented a room in Mold for

St David's Roman Catholic Church, Mold.

a monthly mass. Because of mass Irish migration as a result of a devastating potato blight, the numbers of Catholics in Mold had increased significantly as may be seen from details of the religious census in 1851 which shows that Catholics were congregating 'at the Chapel Felin Plwm' at Milford House designated 'as not used exclusively as a place of worship.' With space for: 'free 40; standing 60' under the ministrations of Father Michael Scully of Wrexham. On a wet March morning, 133 of the faithful, plus 41 scholars (children), were recorded as present with another 85 plus 26 scholars in attendance. Felin Plwm, Milford House (now known as Holly House), was tenanted by Francis Jones, a retired publican from Holywell, together with Father Scully, who were looked after by a servant. From 1852, the Mold mission was cared for by Italian Capuchin friars, at first from Pantasaph, who quickly established themselves there, and later from Chester where in 1858 they opened St Francis Church.

North Wales was then part of the Roman Catholic diocese of Shrewsbury which, in 1858, acquired a site in Mold upon which to build a chapel and presbytery. The labour for building the chapel was provided by members of the congregation who constructed it between March 1862 and its opening in 1863, when it was dedicated to St David.

> The little stone church with its steep slate roof, was constructed at right angles to Ffordd Fain, so that its gable end at the back of the church faced the road. The altar was at the other end of the church. A small porch with a little pointed bell-tower led inside the back of the church. The small carved wooden altar stood in an angled apse.[37]

In the 1871 census, N[o.] 4 Ffordd Fain is described as the Roman Catholic Chapel.

The first resident priest in Mold was Father Gerard Boen, who served the parish between 1864–84. He was a Belgian-born Capuchin friar who, whilst at Mold, became a secular priest. The twenty years of his ministry were extremely vital and fruitful in the life of the parish. In 1866, Bishop Brown visited and confirmed twenty-one girls and thirty-eight boys and Boen persuaded the earl and countess of Denbigh to act as sponsors on behalf of the candidates. The countess was a generous friend of poor Catholic parishes in north-east Wales and liked to be regarded as their mother.

The first Catholic immigrant population in Mold needed all the help that was available to them. Often treated with hostility and forced to do the most menial of tasks, they naturally turned to the church of their faith to sustain them and sought refuge together in their own living quarters. The census returns show us where they lived, the size and make-up of their households and their occupations. Many were labourers in factories, mines and agriculture; others worked as cotton spinners or weavers; some were costermongers, selling wares from street barrows and market stalls. They lived in an area known as 'Bedlam'[38] long before the Irish arrived, a place where the poor, destitute and unfortunate dwelt. This area included Milford Street, stretching from the top of High Street down to the railway line and ending at the Bridge Inn. Many of the dwellings were two up, two down, with a communal outside lavatory and water tap. Here too were lodging houses. Behind the High Street, near the vicarage, was Princess Yard and off Wrexham Street, Bulleys Yard.

On 21 September 1871, the foundation stone of St David's Catholic School[39] was laid by Edward Thompson of Plas Aney, and the building was opened on 4 March 1871. Thompson was an influential laymen, possibly the only one in Mold to whom the parish priest could turn to for financial support and assistance. The school received the full support of the Thompson family, with the women folk regular visitors and bearers of gifts. He was a coal proprietor, born in Wigan, and was the usual sponsor of candidates for confirmation. Entries in the school log book show not only the academic progress of the pupils but record events in the town.

> 1872   'Poor attendance; most of the children went to a circus which had come into the town, it being the custom every year.'
>
> 1873   August 'A week's holiday was given in consequence of the National Eisteddfod which took place during that time.'
>
> 1876   September 'Visit by the Misses Thompsons who were very pleased with the order of the school and

number of scholars (78), they also gave a nice book ('Shakespeare's dramatic works') to the schoolmistress as a remembrance of the treat.'

1878   September 'Attendance very good. On Thursday the Countess of Denbigh gave a party to the children, she afterwards left calico which was to be presented to the children.'

1895   October 24th – 'In consequence of the funeral of Mr Daniel Owen, Revd Manager thought it better to give the children a half holiday than allow them to take it.'

The new prison had been opened in Mold in 1870 but, when it was taken over eight years later by the Home Office, it was no longer required and the building was eventually sold to members of the Society of Jesus from the Province of Lyon in France who, in the face of persecution, had been forced to flee abroad in 1880. Their search for a suitable building where they could set up a college eventually led them to Mold where they were encouraged to settle and, supported by Bishop Wright of Shrewsbury, built up a close relationship with the neighbouring Jesuit College of Beuno at Tremeirchion.

The purpose of the college was to train members of the society for the priesthood and religious life, the premises becoming a seminary for priests, scholastics and lay brothers. Members of the College of St David's were encouraged to give pastoral support to the clergy and parishioners of Mold where they conducted a parish mission, waged a battle against drink by preaching temperance, prepared candidates for confirmation, converted Protestants and visited Catholics in prison at Ruthin. For respite from these tasks, they acquired a villa at Treuddyn.

Father Lynch appeared to ask the French Jesuits for assistance on several occasions, either because of his failing health, or more likely because of the increasing number of parishioners in both the Mold and Buckley areas.

In the grounds of the college a grotto was built by a stream in honour of Our Lady and close to the house they built stables and pigsties and made hutches for rabbits. The house was improved by the addition of a new library, classroom and wine cellar.

On the 29 September 1897, after nearly twenty years of exile in Mold, the scholastics, priests and other members returned to new premises at Lyon, much to the regret of the Catholics and people of Mold. From this time onwards, the building was used by a variety of occupants: it was a temporary home for the boys of the Catholic Reformatory Ship, *Clarence,* who were rehoused there after a fire had destroyed their berths and the Jesuits used it for confirmation and as a Sunday school. It appears that the next occupants were French Sisters of Charity from Caen, who established a convent school and laundry in the building. During the Great War, it was taken over by the War Office and used as a place of detention for German POWs. From 1919, the premises were untenanted and put up for sale in 1924.[40]

Anglicans

The Parish of Mold continued to be blessed in the nineteenth century, as it had been in the previous one, by the leadership of a number of able and devoted vicars. The Reverend Hope Wynne Eyton and his curate and successor, Charles Butler Clough, were both far sighted incumbents who worked closely and energetically with the leading churchmen of the parish and two reforming bishops of the diocese, William Carey (1830–46) and Thomas Vowler Short (1846–70). This partnership was continued by their successors, amongst whom was Ellis Rowland (1872–84), later bishop of Aberdeen (1906–11). There is evidence of their activity in diocesan and parish records.[41]

Charles Butler Clough may be described as the pioneering figure amongst this group and his outstanding influence could be seen in the number of churches and schools which he built in the townships of Mold, some of which later became parishes in their own right.[42] The Anglican Church was as concerned as the Nonconformist bodies with church extension and many parishes gave generously towards home and foreign missions and auxiliary societies for the promotion of education and church building. Clough served as one of Bishop Short's lieutenants, as archdeacon of St Asaph (1844–54) and dean of the cathedral (1854–9). Many

St John the Evangelist Church, King Street, Mold.
The architectural drawing of John Douglas;
the tower was not built.

critic-ised the bishop for being self-opinionated and arrogant, but Short compensated for this by his energy and gener-osity, and was determined to make up deficiencies such as those revealed by the report of the education inquiry of 1847. His diocese was foremost in Wales for the opening of new schools and the training of teachers. The following new churches were built in the old parish of Mold:

Gwernymynydd School Church opened in 1840[43] as 'Greenhill Church School'. The diocesan strategy was to erect a building, usually in a newly-populated district, which could be used as a school during the week and a place of worship on Sunday. Here at Gwernymynydd near Mold, a lead mining area, a church school was built at a cost of £600, chiefly through the exertions of Dr Hughes.[44] The building remained open until the mid twentieth century.

Gwysaney Mission Room was described as having been built at the expense of '… P.B. Davies-Cooke, Esq, about 1858, it was used as an Infants' Day School until 1894. Sunday School is regularly held in it and services during the winter months … A Church House purchased in 1910 has been adapted and furnished at a cost of £700.'[45]

St John the Evangelist Church, King Street (architect John Douglas), was built in in 1878–9 in the Early English style as a Welsh-language church in the parish of Mold and was used as such until the mid twentieth century. In former centuries, Welsh-language services had been conducted regularly in the Parish Church. The appointment of Joshua Hughes as bishop of St Asaph in 1870, marked a stronger policy in the diocese of providing facilities for worship through the medium of the Welsh language and this may have precipitated the building of this church.

St James' Church New Brighton was opened in 1895. The enthusiasm, dedication and steps taken by faithful parishioners to open this mission church at New Brighton were described in an account in *Mold Parish Church Magazine* as,

The outcome of a labour of love on the part of Miss Thomas, late Head-Mistress of the Mold National Schools, and her friend, Miss Hughes, who formed a Sunday school class in the above village about the year 1885, and from that time until 1893 toiled up there every Sunday afternoon. In the spring of 1893, Mrs Morgan, of Brynhaul, who took an interest in this class, found that the little cottage in which it was held was so incommodious and insanitary, that she determined with the consent of the Vicar to raise a sufficient amount to build a room for a Sunday-School. Mr Frank Bellis drew the plans and when the room had been opened there was a cry for services for which Mr Ellis a lay-reader was engaged. He was succeeded by Mr Ivor Jones, and Mr Field. Two years later it was decided to build a chancel and convert the edifice into a Mission Church and in 1895 New Brighton had a Mission Church, which was licensed by Bishop Edwards in the following year, and dedicated to St James. The site for the Church was presented by Mr Adams of the Park who provided additional land upon which to build a vestry. Other gifts followed of furnishings. In 1897 altar rails were presented by the Vicar of Tremeirchion, altar clothes and stoles by Mrs Philips, of Rhual, and a handsome altar desk by Mr Davies-Cooke. The total cost of the church, chancel and vestry was £350.

It was left to the Reverend Jenkin Davies (1854–72) to oversee the final completion of Mold Parish Church by the addition of a chancel in the years 1853–6. The work, which cost £5,000, was the gift of John Wynne Eyton of Leeswood as a tribute to his father who had been vicar 1792–1825. 'I feel,' he declared, 'the greater satisfaction in now fulfilling the anxious wish of my dear late father who would have erected this chancel years ago had it been in his power to do so.'[48] Architectural historian Edward Hubbard described the chancel as added 'tactfully by Sir Gilbert Scott,' a view shared by the ecclesiologist E.A. Freeman who visited Mold church in 1854 whilst the work was in progress.

> I cannot speak against the carrying out of an original design, which is now taking place at Mold. Whoever looks after such matters there has had the sense to intrust his work to the first architect of the age; and the apse, so long interrupted, is at last rising to perfection under the care of Mr Scott. I hope I am not sinning against my own doctrine of conservative restoration in expressing the wish that he may one day be called upon to complete the clerestory also …[47]

St Mary's Parish Church, Mold, after the building of the chancel.

A local newspaper report summed up the extent of the restoration:

> The alterations, improvements, and additions thereto were commenced about two years ago, and consist principally of the addition of a chancel, the re-modelling of the seats, and the removal of the organ from the west to the easterly end of the church. By Mr Scott's plan 300 additional seats were obtained. The seats are now much lower than the previous unsightly and inconvenient ones in which the sitter was so isolated and cooped up as if totally separated from and disconnected with his fellow worshippers. The chancel is a magnificent piece of building, of an octagonal form, supported by four buttresses, and built of free stone.
> The organ formerly in the West Gallery, now erected at the east end of the north aisle, built by England, had been rebuilt by Jackson of Liverpool and now contains the latest improvements … The organ when finished will be the largest parish church organ in Wales. Mr William Birch was the organist.[48]

However, not everyone was happy with the result, particularly P. B. Davies-Cooke, who remembered that,

> At the so-called restoration in 1856–7, irreparable damage was done inside the Church. The large brass chandelier was taken away, the platforms of the altars in the north and south aisles destroyed, and the vaulting lowered; tombs broken into, and silver to the amount of £50 stolen from the coffins in the Gwysaney vault. The fine wrought-iron gates[49] of about Queen Anne's time, enclosing the platforms, were turned-out. Some of these are now in the garden at Gwysaney, where one has the Davies' crest on it; others at Colomendy; at Gwernafield, and at Cilcain Churchyards. Among other things, a carved wooden-figure from a seat in the Gwysaney Chapel also disappeared. The white marble pavement of the Gwysaney Chapel now forms part of the flooring of the hall in the vicarage. The clerk of the works is said to have plundered the vault …[50]

The opportunity was taken to pay tribute to Charles Butler Clough,

> The central window and the two on the south side were put up at an expense of £400, as a testimonial of respect from the parishioners to their late vicar, and bear this inscription, 'In honour of God and as a record of the eminent services in promoting church extension and religious instruction in the diocese rendered by the very Rev. Charles Butler Clough, M.A., for thirty-eight years curate and vicar of this parish, for a long period a rural dean, afterwards Archdeacon and now Dean and Chancellor of Asaph.' Beneath are three sedilia in stone 'presented and dedicated by the Dean of St Asaph, 1856'[51] and windows by William Wailes (1808–81) showing incidents in the Life of Christ.[52]

Church rates had existed for centuries and were levied on the occupiers of property in the parish, to defray the expenses of running the parish church. They became controversial during the nineteenth century and many Nonconformists began to resist the rate on grounds of conscience and campaigned for its abolition. An example of such opposition occurred in Mold in August 1855, when the legitimacy of the levy was put before the electorate. This received full coverage in an article in the *Chester Chronicle* in September 1855 which gave an insight into the attitudes of opposing sides. Both parties were accused of uncharitableness, ill-feeling and religious jealousy, and the writer took them to task for such a display, observing,

> … that neither side manifested that degree of charity which should characterise men who profess to work for the cause of religion. The indecent conduct of some of the voters – some drunk, and others swearing in the most awful manner in the vestry room – rendered it, altogether, a scene which created in the minds of them who entertained the least respect for religion, feelings of sadness and mortification, that the alterations and repairs of a sacred edifice, should be occasion of so much scandal and contempt of the precepts of that religion which both sides venerated and endeavoured to practice. The contest ended, as might be anticipated, from the conduct of the parties engaged in it. The pro-rate party had marshalled their forces and canvassed the parish, and had cars &c, flying about during the contest to bring their voters to the poll whilst the anti-rate party had neither solicited votes nor made any preparation for mustering their supporters.

The result of the poll was that 301 votes were recorded against and the majority in favour of the rate was 127, 'out of about twelve or thirteen hundred votes eligible to be given at Mold; and so the majority of the ratepayers showed in not coming forward to the poll, that they were not friendly to the rate.' The *Chronicle* correspondent considered that, although the church rate party won at the poll, they knew that they had obtained their victory by not very creditable means, '… the statements that have been made with regard to bribery and coercion are such as cannot be gainsaid. Church rate victories are most damaging to the Church, and bring dishonour on its ministers … and that the Churchwardens would have saved themselves immense trouble by yielding at first to the suggestions made for voluntary contributions.'[53] This suggested policy became law in 1868 with the passing of the Compulsory Church Rate Abolition Act.

In June 1874, the vicar announced in the parish magazine '… that the roof of the Parish Church is giving way. Two of the beams are actually split open and others faulty' and the nave roof, restored less than twenty years before, had to be repaired by Sir Gilbert Scott.

In 1878, the reredos (a decorative screen positioned by the altar of a church), designed by John Douglas and executed in alabaster by Hardman & Company, was installed in the Parish Church.

Further repairs were undertaken in 1911 in accordance with plans drawn up by Messrs Prothero, Phillott & Barnard of Cheltenham who undertook the work at a cost in the region of £8,000. An appeal fund was established, the organisers of which entered into their task with enthusiasm and appealed to their supporters with an imaginative programme of fund raising events. From November 12–15 1912, there was a bazaar held in the Victoria Drill Hall which featured twelve stalls organised by the enthusiastic ladies of the church. Meat, teas and suppers were available from 6 p.m. in the Japanese Smoking Café. 'A high-class' programme of music was performed on three days by the Mold Orchestral Society which, with other entertainments, raised £1,645 11s 9d. One of the patrons was the Earl of Derby. The proceeds met the cost of making the seventeenth century south porch neo-perpendicular in style, renewing some external masonry and replacing the string course of animals and windows of the south side.[54]

The church was again extensively restored from 1951–55 by The Anthony Clark Partnership of Wrexham. Expert opinion had been obtained about the state of the roof-timbers which were found to be severely infected and damaged with death watch and furniture beetles. The seating in the Gwysaney chapel was removed and the Robert Davies memorial (1728) re-sited to the north-west corner of the north side.

In 1856, the vicarage house and land attached comprised the house itself, plus a coach house, stables, shippon, outbuildings and just over four acres of land (along with two private seats in the church). Hugh Lloyd, vicar of Mold, had purchased a house named Trefriew in 1744, not as a vicarage (although he lived there himself), but to secure an endowment of £11 a year for a charity school. He bought it from members of the Barker family, who were agents to the Smelting Company at Gadlys, Bagillt. He considerably enlarged the house and resided there and following his death, Robert Wynne of Garthewin and his wife came to live there. The Trefriew property was finally purchased as a vicarage in 1843[55] by John Wynne Eyton of Leeswood and enlarged in 1868 at a further outlay of £700.

The burial ground, which in 1815 had been described as 'indecorously crowded, there having been 4,000 corpses interred therein,' was deemed to be completely full and all attempts to find a new spot for internments had failed. In 1842, during the purchase of Trefriew, the vestry decided to buy a part of the grounds in order to provide an extension to the churchyard. This was consecrated as a burial ground and added to the old churchyard. In 1849, more room was made available for burials by taking down the old stable and coach house buildings in the new churchyard, the materials salvaged being given to the National School which was then in the course of erection in King Street.

Notes

1. M. Cragoe, *Culture, Politics, and Identity*, Oxford, 2004, p.37f.
2. Henry Richard, *Letters on the Social and Political Condition of Wales 1866*.
3. *The Chester Chronicle*, 23/8/1873.
4. *Journal of John Wesley*.
5. NLW SA/FB/2.
6. F. J. Violet ('Penman'), Mold Gleanings, *The Chester Chronicle* 3/11/1928.
7. ibid, 10/11/1928.
8. The Reverend Roger Edwards, minister of Bethesda, encouraged Daniel Owen.
9. NLW SA/FB/2.
10. *The Chester Chronicle,* 21 March 1834.
11. I.G. Jones, *The Religious Census oif 1851. A Calendar of the Returns relating to Wales, vol.1, North Wales*, Cardiff, 1981, p.119.
12. Ibid, p.119
13. K. Lloyd Gruffydd, 'Baptising in the River Alun during the early Nineteenth Century', *Ystrad Alun*, 9.
14. *The Chester Chronicle,* 28/2 and 20/5/1868.
15. *Y Dreflan*, p.2.
16. Ibid, p.2.
17. 11 December 1907, *Royal Commission on the Church of England and other Religious Bodies in Wales and Monmouthshire*, vol III, pp. 395–8.
18. The statistics for twelve chapels listed in Mold Urban (population 1901 census 4,263) in Royal Commission: total of Chapel sittings 3,898; sittings in school-room attached 1,430; number of communicants 992; number of adherents 2,324; teachers and scholars 1560. Estimated value – buildings and property £24,775 – English Presbyterian £3,087; Bethesda £5,537; English Congregational, Westminster Road £4,400; Pendref £4,050.
19. Andrew Carnegie, Scottish-born philanthropist who made a fortune in America in steel which he used to set up a foundation which provided grants to various public works e.g. public libraries and organs. On a lesser scale was Peter Roberts an entrepreneur, who retired to Bromfield Hall and generously provided the Town Hall in 1911.
20. Cilcain, Rhosesmor, Buckley, Nercwys, Mynydd Isa, the English Presbyterian Church, Mold.
21. Total including renovations and extension £798.
22. Author of *The Life of Daniel Owen – Hanes Daniel Owen*, p.34, published on his centenary in 1936.
23. *Y Dreflan*, p.11.
24. Ibid, p.16.
25. Ibid, p.54.

26. Ibid, pp.37–8.
27. Ibid, p.38.
28. Ibid, p.85.
29. *Rhys Lewis*, pp.65–6.
30. ibid, p.413.
31. Linked to the Parry's of Twysog.
32. P. J. Doyle, 'The Giffards of Nerquis', *Flintshire Historical Society Publications*, vol 24, 1969–70 p.79.
33. His guardian had been Sir Robert Throckmorton of Coughton, Warwickshire.
34. M. Joy, *A History of St David's Parish, Mold*, p.27.
35. The meeting was called in reaction to the Pope's restoration of the Catholic hierarchy. See the *Chester Chronicle.* 7 & 14 December 1850.
36. For example Father Sylvester Baron, parish priest at Mold 1919–30.
37. M. Joy, op cit, p.13.
38. Called after the hospital of St Mary Bethlehem, London, used since 1547 as a hospital for the insane, hence a madhouse.
39. It was a small building – length 35 ft., breadth 18½ft, height 11ft.
40. FRO NT/1825 for extracts from the College Diary and *Mold Gleanings*, op cit, for an account of Mold Gaol.
41. These are deposited at FRO.
42. Gwernaffield, Bistre, Pontblyddyn and part of Rhydymwyn.
43. See *Report of the Commissioners of Inquiry into the State of Education in Wales*, London, 1847, p.106.
44. D.R. Thomas, *History of the Diocese of St Asaph,* vol ii, p.415, 1911.
45. Ibid.
46. *The Chester Chronicle,* 12/8/1854.
47. *Ecclesiologist no CV,* December 1854.
48. *The Chester Chronicle,* May 1856.
49. The iron gates and screenwork were made for the north aisle of the chancel *c.*1726 by Robert Davies, and a matching set in 1732 by Thomas Cheswise. Hubbard, op cit, p.391.
50. P.B. Davies Cooke, *A Short History of Mold Parish Church,* 1905, pp.74–5.
51. D.R. Thomas, *History of Diocese of St Asaph,* 1874 edition, p.601.
52. M. Seaborne, *Victorian and Later Stained Glass Windows in Flintshire Churches,* p.17.
53. 'Church rates at Mold', *Chester Chronicle,* 17/3/1855 and 8 & 15/9/1855.
54. FROP P/40/1/140.
55. FRO/ P40/1/99.

10: Nineteenth-century Mold: education

The debate on the state of education in Wales was polarised between Nonconformists and Anglicans and the passion of their arguments became more vehement as evidenced by the strength of their respective support in Wales. At the beginning of the nineteenth century there was little if any efficient, organised and compulsory system of education anywhere in Britain.[1] The situation was alarming enough in England and Wales to stir the government into action. What existed at the time were vestiges of a previous age. Endowed grammar schools of the Tudor and Stuart Age, most of them by now decayed having lost their classical curriculum, and free schools, dependent on charitable gifts of pious benefactors to educate a limited number of poor children on a shoe string and, if they were fortunate enough, to be clothed. Provision of secondary education for those who had learnt their letters was obtained through indentures, by being apprenticed to a master for a period of up to seven years. The number of places available in schools was becoming more limited as the population grew. The nature of education varied from a basic provision of learning to read, write, and do simple arithmetic alongside the usually compulsory instruction in the Catechism in the Book of Common Prayer, to that of a classical education in endowed grammar schools of the sixteenth and seventeenth centuries. Those in Flintshire were founded at St Asaph, Northop, and Hawarden. There was no official provision in Mold for this standard of 'secondary' education until the end of the nineteenth century.

In the early years of the nineteenth century, attempts to expand educational provision were generated by the activities of Nonconformist bodies and the Church of England. Their schools were called Voluntary Schools.[2] In 1811, the Church of England set up an educational society, the National Society for Promoting the Education of the Poor in the Principles of the Established Church. The teachers were to be practising members of the Church of England and the syllabus included the compulsory study of the Anglican liturgy and catechism. The National Society promoted schools founded on these principles and funded by grant aid. The diocese of St Asaph, under the leadership of Bishop Carey (1830–46) and Bishop Short (1846–70) actively pursued a policy of building churches and schools and training teachers. Bishops and clergy converted local charity schools into National Schools. In Mold, under the guidance of the vicar, Hope Wynne Eyton, and his curate, C.B. Clough (later vicar of Mold, archdeacon and dean of St Asaph) a National School was established in 1819. Their activity in the provision of schools lasted for over sixty years, during the most crucial period of educational change for the old parish of Mold and its division into newly-created parishes. It was the Reverend Clough who promoted the formation of new parishes and the building of churches and schools in the area for the instruction of their pupils in the religious values of the Church of England which became the basis of education in the majority of schools founded before 1850.

The establishment of Nonconformist schools dates from the same decade as the National Society. The movement was initiated by the Quaker, Joseph Lancaster, who between the years 1806–14, strove to establish schools of a non-sectarian nature, where instruction was available to all and the teaching of dogma excluded with the Bible as the only religious textbook in use. In 1814, the British and Foreign School Society was founded in London to promote the education of the labouring and manufacturing classes of every religious persuasion. The society made little headway in north Wales until Hugh Owen took up their cause and advocated the establishment of what became known as British Schools.

With limited financial resources, the Anglican clergy and bishops realised that an adjustment might have

Charles Butler Clough, vicar of Mold.

to be made by diverting existing charitable endowments to the support of schools set up in accordance with the educational ideas introduced by Dr Bell, Joseph Lancaster and the National Society. The government also offered financial support and its blessing to a scheme which it hoped would help to control the lawlessness of the working classes through the discipline and supervision of a system of education. This educational reform was undertaken in a very British manner as a partnership between the state, voluntary societies, and religious bodies.

The Church of England had the support of the National Society and the local diocese. We see this process in operation in the Parish of Mold in 1812 in the correspondence of Bishop Cleaver of St Asaph who wrote to the vicar in May:[3]

The National Society have now established their plan for instituting Schools under every variety of circumstances which are likely to occur that I am incouraged to hope you may find it easy in the Parish of Mold to lay the foundation of a school upon Dr Bell's system.[4]

Six weeks later the Vicar of Mold received further advice from Lord Kenyon who had recently established a similar school in the Maelor district, the 'Madras' School at Penley. He wrote to the cicar of Mold on the subject of setting up one of Dr Bell's schools at Mold commenting that,

… nothing is needful to do so but a room proportioned to the number of children you cd. get to come; the fitting up & books wd. be a very trifling expense; and any steady man, wd. if he is not mad, wd. do to manage the school. If you wd. produce 100 boys and a room to hold them I wd. engage to set you a going very well in 3 days.[5]

The bishop gave his opinion on the legality of diverting existing endowments and advised that a National School could be established 'upon the fund appropriated and the expense of a master from London, or rather a young Teacher under your Master would be temporary only: probably for a few weeks.'[6] For some reason there was a delay in proceeding with the scheme at Mold but, on 8 September 1815, Bishop Cleaver's successor, Bishop John Luxmoore, supported the cautious vicar[7] by repeating previous episcopal assurance of the propriety of 'the application of the Funds to a National School upon the new system by extending its benefits, by complying in the best manner with the intention of the Founders,' in his use of a previous endowment. This action would concur with the bishop's sentiments 'in which the good morals of the lower classes, and the happiness of the higher is so much concerned.'[8]

In 1818, Lord Liverpool's Tory government was seeking to alleviate distress and educate the rebellious masses by providing money for the building of churches and supporting schools and, in order to identify what help was needed, a questionnaire was circulated. The vicar of Mold answered it replying that there was one school in the parish of Mold where eighteen children were taught (originally there had been thirty, but this had been reduced to as few as six) and that salaries and endowments for a master amounted to £17 14s (rent charge for master £9, funds £8 14). To the final query – 'Are the poorer classes in your neighbourhood without sufficient means of educating their children?' He answered simply, 'They are.'[9] His energetic young curate, Charles Butler Clough, was soon made aware of the situation of the number of school places in Mold Parish and the following information was enigmatically inscribed at the top of an undated letter written to the vicar *c.*1819/20.

Ritson's, Thomas Ritson[10] 60, Evans's, [Presbyterian Chapel, New Street] 86, Norbury's 55 [Private Adventure School, Wright's 50,[?] total 251+800 = 1051 Sunday Schools.

Perhaps this calculation is Clough's rough jottings on the number of school places? He lumps together private adventure day schools with Nonconformist Sunday schools. What is more confusing is that the Nonconformists may have held day schools and Sunday schools in chapel buildings! Clough continues to explain the purchase of another site for Hugh Lloyd's charity school which was let to the newly-established Provident Savings Bank. The premises he refers to in the letter below was the Calvinistic Methodist chapel at Ponterwyl, which became the National School.

> Premises have been bought in order to establish a School upon the National Plan – It is expected that it will be opened for Instruction in about Three Weeks. The Building will contain about one hundred & fifty children. The annual Subscriptions promise to be of too small an amount to tender this establishment so useful as the general wants & wishes require.

> Dear Sir,
> The above I should think will be sufficient Answer to Mr Brougham's letter.[11] The Government circular of 1818 sent out by Henry Brougham later Lord Chancellor The Independent School[12] is at Buckley & contains at least to the number I have noted down. Perhaps you had better not notice your answer to the former Questions. I have put the number down from memory & perhaps not correctly; as I believe you have Pierce's return – you can correct them if wrong. They are not however very wide of the truth.[13]

The transfer of the eighteenth-century Mold Charity School (Vicar Hugh Lloyd's school) to the former Calvinistic Methodist Chapel Ponterwyl in 1819 was recorded by the Charity Commissioners in their report of 1837.[14]

> In the year 1819 a subscription was opened for the purpose of purchasing a building theretofore used as a dissenting chapel, in which to open to open a large school, to be conducted on the national system. The amount collected was £267. 8s; to this the National School Society added £100. With £260 of this money the chapel was purchased and with the remainder a stable, attached to the chapel, was converted into a girl's school, and the whole building fitted up for the purpose of education … The number of children educated is about 180; orphans and children of widows are, upon application to the vicar, admitted as entirely free; and the number of these is always larger than the old endowment of the charity-school could possibly educate.[15]

An ever-increasing number of Nonconformist parents were reluctant to send their children to day schools of the Established Church on the grounds of conscience. The Mold novelist, Daniel Owen, born in 1836, received his first schooling at the National School, whilst his older brother, David, was educated at the Cotton Factory School. The Nonconformists had, to some extent, to live in two worlds, the world of the Welsh Sunday school and, in order to make use of the only day school generally available, the Church school.

Evidence of the success of attempts by Nonconformists to fulfil their own educational needs is seen in the action of Hugh Owen, an Anglesey-born civil servant in the Poor Law Commission. He sought to create a balance in school places between the Church of England and Dissenters when, in August1843, he addressed a 'Letter to the Welsh People' on day schools. He advised that British Schools should be established in every district in Wales, run by a committee whose members were to be chosen from among the various religious denominations. In the Mold area, Hugh Jones of Buckley, a Calvinistic Methodist, took up the cause in the townships of Bistre and Ewloe and was instrumental in bringing together Methodists of all branches – Wesleyan, Old and New Connexion, Calvinistic and Primitive, together with Independents – to set up a communal school whereby members were educated together, but worshipped separately on the Sabbath.[16] By 1847, 130 boys (with twelve employed as monitors) and forty-eight girls were being taught. The establishment of a British School in Mold two years later was probably influenced by the opening of the Union School, a British school, at Glanrafon in June 1846. This was an exception in Flintshire at this time in that it did not meet in chapel buildings but was purpose-built.[28] In 1845, the Nonconformists had combined to build a British School in Mold, a display of unity which confirmed their desire to provide an alternative education to the doctrinal teaching of the Anglican Church.

No single publication of the nineteenth century provoked and united the Welsh people in their hostility to the English government than the *Report into the State of Education in Wales* in 1847.[29] They felt themselves victimised as a subject people, insulted and made to feel inferior because of their race and ancient language. It appeared to the Welsh that the English inspectors had scrutinised all parts of their lives in an effort to expose and condemn their morality, pour contempt on their social conditions, mock the language which the inspectors could not speak (judging it to be inadequate for the conduct of commerce) and criticise their intellectual attainments. The inspectors viewed the majority of Welsh people as belonging to a civilization inferior to that of the English and proposed that the solution to all problems was to make the Welsh into English people by not encouraging the use of their language and customs. The chief means of achieving such Anglicisation was through the removal of inadequacies in the educational system, many of which they were not slow to report. The anger of the Welsh nation was roused because the chastity of their women was questioned, their language and customs undervalued and generally speaking what they stood for was treated with contempt.

The quick-witted Welsh soon found an apt phrase to describe the ignominious attack of their old enemy, the Saxons, dubbing the report of 1847 '*Brad y Llyfrau Gleision,*' (the 'Treachery of the Blue Books').[30] Of the three commissioners who inspected schools and wrote the report, Henry Vaughan Johnson[31] was responsible for that of north Wales. With his assistants, he claimed to have inspected 591 schools and examined 19,521 scholars 'in all subjects professed to be taught' amongst which were those in Mold. He wrote an introduction to the report which extended to sixty-eight foolscap pages which highlighted to some extent the situation in Mold as the individual religious groups wrestled against great odds to establish schools.

Dissenting chapels, which are far more frequently employed as schools, are equally inconvenient for the purpose. The promoters of Church schools belong to the wealthy class of inhabitants, and having influence with the proprietors of land, who are all members of the Established Church, are able to procure sites, and by the aid of Government grants, to erect sufficient schools. Whereas Dissenters, and those who establish British and other schools without tests or restrictions in matters of religion, belong to the middle ranks and labouring class, who have neither funds for the erection of a school-room, nor sufficient influence to procure a site for the purpose. It is important to illustrate the inconvenience of these buildings: the British schools which are held in them are among the most efficient schools at present in operation; but the peculiar system of teaching and organisation to which British teachers have been trained are incompatible with the materials they are driven to employ.[32]

The extreme youth of the teachers is a fruitful source of ignorance and disorder in many schools … Still worse results are occasioned by employing aged persons and cripples, who are very more numerous among the class of Welsh teachers.[33]

This was certainly the case in Mold with regards to the age of teachers and in one case, a teacher was recorded as being disabled as a result of losing a leg. Daniel Owen dramatically made use of this in his character of Robin the Soldier in the book *Rhys Lewis*. The Report continued:

Persons are appointed to conduct important schools who are unable to speak or even to understand English …[34]

In schools where English teachers are employed, the confusion and ambiguity is increased …[35]

The teachers in Mold admitted that this was the case.

In many cases the English teachers who are employed appear unconscious of any necessity for interpreting the unknown language which it is their business to teach.[25]

This was not the case in Mold where monoglot English-speaking teachers lamented their inability to teach through the medium of the Welsh language.

However deficient in other apparatus for instruction few schools were found destitute of a cane or birch rod, and the general appearance of the pupils indicated that they were habitually governed by fear, and not by that moral and intelligent influence which by enlisting the affections and awakening the attention and enterprise of children, secures the most perfect discipline and industry, and by accustoming them to the habit of self-government, attains a moral object more valuable than mere outward decorum.[26]

Daniel Owen described in *Rhys Lewis* the sadistic and terrifying use of the cane by 'Robin the Soldier' on his entrance to the classroom,

He walked up to his desk, and drew forth a long stout cane. Each lad shrugged a preparatory shoulder while the old Soldier went the round of the school, caning all, cruelly and indiscriminately. I was the only one who escaped even a taste, and I was the only one who burst out crying, the chastisement having terrified me. The other boys appeared too well-used to the proceeding to mind it. The last of them having received his allowance, the master returned to his desk, put up his hands and said 'Let us pray,' after which he slowly repeated his Paternoster, the boys following. I subsequently learned that some of the wicked ones, in the midst of the general chatter, had uttered words very different from any to be found in the Prayer, thereby eliciting the low laughter of those who were within hearing.[27]

The inspector Henry Vaughan Johnson reported on a variety of schools, all of which he condemned.

Of 578 schools at present in operation, 216 are taught on private adventure, 112 by dames the rest by male teachers. The total number of scholars in such schools amount to 5348. These schools have been carefully examined, and minute notes have been taken respecting their present condition as regards the buildings, furniture, and apparatus; the teachers and their qualifications, and the attainments of the scholars in every branch of instruction. In every one of these respects they are so utterly worthless, that nothing can account for their existence, except the determination on the part of Welsh parents to have their children instructed without interference in matters of conscience … This conclusion is confirmed by the fact that, wherever a British or Foreign or other neutral school is established, private-adventure schools become extinct.[28]

Private Adventure and Dame Schools in Mold[29]
Mrs Alice Jones's school – Dame – established 1845 – Dressmaker
Miss Griffith's school – Dame – established 1822
Miss Norbury's school – Dame – established 1812 – Milliner
Mrs Birch's school – Dame – established – 1846
Mr Henry Smith's school – private – established – Linen Draper

Sunday Schools[30]
Parish Church 1831 – 25 male teachers – 34 female teachers
Pupils under 15 – 210 male, above 15 – 30 usual attends, total 175;
15 – 340 female, above 15 – 30 usual attends, total 255
Wesleyan estab. 1806 – 17 male teachers – 5 female teachers
Pupils under 15 – 37 male, above 15 – 62
Under 15 33 female, above 15 – 43
Calvinistic Methodist established 1795 Newst – 30 male teachers – 20 female teachers
Pupils under 15 – 97 male, above 15 – 99 male

Under 15 – 61 female, above 15 – 47 female
Independents established '1805 Newst – 16 male teachers – 13 female teachers
Pupils under 15 – 46 male above 15 – 31 male
Under 15 – 37 female above 15 – 25 female

Johnson, in his introduction to the report, made a distinction between Sunday schools of the Established Church and those of the Nonconformist denominations of which he said,

The Sunday-schools, as the main instrument of civilization have determined the character of the language, literature and general intelligence of the inhabitants. The language cultivated in the Sunday schools is Welsh.[31]

Their schools, literature, and religious pursuits may have cultivated talents for preaching and poetry, but for every other calling they are incapacitated. For secular subjects they have neither literature nor a language. In Welsh, although they speak correctly they can neither write nor spell. Thus situated, they are compelled to employ two languages, one for domestic intercourse, another for the market, in the courts of justice, at the Board of Guardians, and for the transaction of every other public function: and to increase their difficulties the latter language remains, and must continue an unknown tongue.[32]

The English commissioners incurred the anger of Welsh people by appearing to equate national identity with poverty, drunkenness and sexual immorality. To them it was an unforgiveable slander and gross impertinence to condemn a proud and ancient people in such an arrogant and superior manner. Amongst the comments made by Commissioner Johnson was the condemnation of social evils and behaviour which prevailed in most communities in Britain during the nineteenth century. What was clear is that the English critics misunderstood Welsh traditions and customs and viewed the use of the Welsh language as an impediment to improvement and were not prepared to consider the equality of what they considered was an alien tongue. Evidence given by a Church of England cleric, the Reverend J.P. Foulkes,[33] curate in the neighbouring parish of St Matthew Buckley, was quoted by Johnson.

The state of morals is degraded in respect of drunkenness, profanity, dishonesty, and incontinence; that the latter vice is increasing so rapidly as to render it difficult to find a cottage where some female of the family has not been enceinte before marriage.[34]

Johnson, whatever his prejudices, may have made some attempt to be fair as in his conclusion, he stated that;

Whatever may be the defects of society in North Wales it is free, in the five northern counties, from crimes of a heinous nature, and no signs of disaffection or sedition have appeared within the memory of man.[35]

The reports for seven schools in the parish of Mold parish are given in the report[36] and extracts from the reports of the three schools in the actual town of Mold are given below.[37] The introduction speaks of the generosity of Archdeacon Clough in making up the inevitable short-fall in expenditure because,

Great numbers of the inhabitants are very poor, and the sums raised by the pence of the children are inconsiderable, consequently the standard of education is very low in all the schools above mentioned.
    The British school at Mold is supported with considerable difficulty. The secretary states that the funds are inadequate; that it is impossible to maintain an efficient school in a place like Mold without assistance, in addition to the voluntary contributions of the locality, unless exertions are made which it would be vain to expect; and that it will be necessary to apply for assistance from Government.

Mold Church School
A school for boys and girls, taught respectively by a master and mistress in separate buildings which have been adapted for the purpose … The buildings were originally the chapel and stable belonging to a dissenting

Mold Parish Church and the National School which was located in King Street.

congregation and were purchased and conveyed to the trustees for the purpose of education. It is intended to erect a new building, more suitable for the purpose. The furniture and apparatus from want of means are all ordinary and in a great measure provided by the vicar.

The number of boys 85; girls 85; number of monitors, 10. Subjects taught – the Bible, Church Catechism, reading, writing, and arithmetic. Fees, nominally, 1d per week, but in effect, 40 children are taught free, being unable to pay. Total income of master, £60, of mistress £26. 49 pupils are above 10 years of age, and 43 have attended the school for more than three years.

The master is a young man, aged 21; he has been trained for 18 months at the Battersea training school. He appears capable of improving the school considerably… He expresses a wish to be allowed to introduce more subjects of instruction alleging that the pupils lose their energy and interest when confined to reading, writing, and arithmetic, especially ignorant (as many here are) of the language in which their lessons are conveyed. He is about to commence reading the History of England …

In the girls' school-room I found 50 scholars. They were less perfect in the Catechism and their writing was inferior, 4 of them being better informed in Scripture than any of the boys. The nominal mistress being superannuated, the girls are taught by her daughter, who has never been trained for the purpose.

Mold British School

A school for boys and girls, taught respectively by a master and mistress, in separate rooms of a school built for the purpose. Number of boys, 164; of girls, 149; number employed as monitors, 18. Subjects taught – the Scriptures, reading, writing, arithmetic, English grammar, geography, history, and music. Fees 2d. per week; reduced to 1d, upon subscription of 2s. 6d. per annum. Salary of master £60; of mistress, £40. Both sexes were taught together by the master previously to January, 1847, when the mistress was appointed.

The majority could talk a little English but there were many who did not understand the master. I found that few of them could turn the simplest and shortest sentence of English into any kind of Welsh.

The master is an Englishman, about 25 years of age. He was trained at the Borough Road Normal School. He appeared to be sensible of the disadvantage of not knowing Welsh. His abilities and acquirements are much above the average of Schoolmasters in Wales; and he appears anxious to improve himself. He adheres strictly to the British system.

The mistress, who was formerly an upper nurse in a gentleman's family, has been trained at the Borough Road, Normal School. She has been only two months engaged as a teacher, and is unacquainted with the Welsh language which she considers a disadvantage. Her strictness and care in correcting mistakes, in asking questions on the subjects of instruction, and in general discipline, deserve approbation. The monitors are generally pretty good, with respect to their attainments and mode of discharging their duties.

The proceedings in both departments of the foregoing school were conducted with more noise than is usual even in British Schools. In the boys' departments, the effect was deafening.

Many parents who send their children to school are members of the Established Church, which their children attend on Sunday – JOHN JAMES, Assistant.

Cotton Mill Company's School[38]

A school for boys and girls, taught together by a master in a room in the factory. Number of scholars, 30. Subjects taught – the Bible, Church Catechism, and reading. Master's salary, £20.

I examined this school, March 2. I arrived an hour after the time when the school professed to assemble, and therefore at a time when all should have been engaged with their studies; but I found only 3 children assembled. At length 19 were summoned, among whom I found 2 who could read a verse of the Bible, and answer some Scripture questions. They receive no instruction in writing, arithmetic, or any higher subject. The rest were ignorant of everything secular and Scriptural; they were, for the most part, unable to understand the most familiar phrases in English; their manners were rough and uncouth, their persons were extremely dirty, and their clothes tattered and threadbare.

The master was formerly a carrier. He had no kind of training, and scarcely any education. He appears to have received his present appointment rather out of charity, in consequence of the loss of a leg, than from any other consideration.

The school-room would only accommodate 26 children. It was intensely hot, and filthy in the extreme – ABRAHAM THOMAS, Assistant.

The 1847 report indicated that there was no obligation for parents to send children to the school of the denomination to which they belonged and it was apparent that they were free to choose. Anglicans sent children to the British School and Nonconformists to the National School. It showed that the only language spoken by teachers at the British School was English and that their training had taken place in London. A major criticism in the report was that many Welsh children had difficulty in understanding English whilst the majority of teachers had no knowledge of the Welsh language.

The person who received most praise was Archdeacon Clough, vicar of Mold, who had been instrumental in raising money for building new schools adjacent to the new churches in the newly sub-divided parish. Clough had been generous enough to make good any financial shortfall to ensure that these new schools were viable.

As noted above, the novelist Daniel Owen had received his early schooling in the National School which was under the control of the vicar of Mold, having attended the school at Ponterwyl until the British School was opened in Glanrafon in 1845. His elder brother, Robert, was a pupil at the Cotton Company School at Rhydygoleu. Daniel Owen drew on his own memories and those of his brother for the setting of his novels and it is possible to recognise them as the background to his story-telling.

In his introduction to his first novel, *Y Dreflan*, Owen drew on his experiences at the National School.

It is true we have no Lord-bishop here, but we have a Vicar who regards himself to be the equal of one, which serves the purpose. The Vicar has a large magnificent church of which I have many recollections when things were conducted under the old dispensation, before the opening of the British School, when attendance at church was compulsory for anyone wishing to attend Church School, or he would be obliged to suffer the 'hold out' on a Monday morning. I can well-remember the many hours I spent in the deep pew from which it was practically impossible for me to see, or hear, the parson.[39] I was too preoccupied to be attentive, by the appearance of the 'old flogger', the name by which he was known to us children, passing by, with a stout cane in his hand, on his way up and down the aisle, as stealthily as a cat, during the whole service. We believed that his greatest delight in life was to supply this cane on to our heads and shoulders.[40]

The character of the 'Old Flogger' in *Y Dreflan* was recreated in his later novel *Rhys Lewis* as the sadistic one-legged schoolmaster, Robin the Soldier, about whom he had learned from his brother. Robert Owen reminisced about the one-legged carrier recorded by the inspector, Abraham Thomas, and Daniel Owen turned him into the crippled boozy 6d per day army-pensioner who had been wounded at Waterloo and who was taunted by Will Bryan and his school fellows.

Owen mentions another school in *Rhys Lewis* which appears to be an alternative to the Church School and may have been a Private Adventure School.

When I was a boy there were only two day schools in the town of my birth. One was kept by a gentleman of the name of Smith, whom I remember very well. Mr Smith was the great oracle of the town. He was looked up to by some people with an admiration bordering almost upon worship. He was believed to be proficient in at least seven languages, and he was said to utter words which no one else could understand. I heard my mother declare that Mr Smith and Dic Aberdaron were the two greatest scholars the world had ever seen.[41]

The other school was kept by one Robert Davies or, as he was commonly called, 'Robin the Soldier', who had spent the prime of life in the British Army, where he distinguished himself as a brave, intrepid warrior. He returned to his native village minus his right leg, which he had left behind him in Belgium. Robert supplied this deficiency by means of a wooden leg. The income from the wooden leg being barely sufficient to meet the weekly calls of the Cross Foxes, our old soldier speedily found himself in straightened circumstances.

Owen creates the character of the schoolmaster, who had become a toll-gate keeper, in a couple of vivid sketches. It '… was not Robert who kept the gate, but it was the gate which kept him.' He is said to be 'a devout man who went to church every Sunday, to bed every Sunday afternoon, and to the Cross Foxes, every Sunday night,' who owed his appointment to the indulgent attitude of the vicar and his choice of candidates for the post of schoolmaster. Bobbit was persuaded by Parson Brown, in broken Welsh, to keep school – 'you scholar, you able to read and write and say catechism – you start school in old empty office there – many children without learning hereabouts.'[42]

In his description of the school, Owen may be using the old charity school in Mold.

The 'office' in which the old soldier kept school was a long, narrow structure, round which ran a rough and crooked bench connected with a desk which leaned against the wall … At the other end, close to the fire, stood the master's desk.

Prayer ended, the old soldier in a voice of command, cried, 'Rivets, my boys', a synonym used every Monday morning for 'Pass up with your pence.[43]

The old Soldier's most important business was taking our pence, and the next, in point of diversion, the breaking of a good stout cane on our backs and hands every week or nine days … As far as I can recollect, none of the boys, any more than myself, cared the least bit for learning, while he, to whom our instruction was entrusted, cared less. He seemed to me, at all times, to derive greater pleasure from our failure to say our lessons, than for our success, because it gave him an excuse for our castigation.[44]

I would have written in greater detail my account of Soldier Robin's school, so that the lads of these days might see the increase and improvement that have taken place in schools and school master during less than half a generation.[45]

Rhys Lewis was published in 1885 and was more concerned with painting a picture of life in the community in Mold and of portraying the characters who grew up there, than recording the Welsh nation's reaction to the 1847 commissioners report. It is more than likely that he was present as a nine-year-old school boy when the British School at Glanrafon was inspected on 11 February 1846, but the national debate on education never became his concern.

The people of Wales in general, and Nonconformists in particular, were appalled and angry because of the commissioners' observations on the language, religion and morals of the people. They resented being branded as ill-educated, poor, dirty, unchaste and potentially rebellious. Four years later, they appeared to be vindicated when the religious census revealed without any doubt that Welsh people were more zealous in their attendance at a place of worship than the English. In Wales, 34% of the population attended public worship as compared with 24% of the population in England. In Wales, only 9% of the worshippers attended Church of England services and 87% went to Nonconformist chapels. In England, the Church of England's services attracted 49% of worshippers and Nonconformists 47%. The Welsh were clearly different from the English.

The religious census of 1851 therefore revealed to the Welsh people the strength of Nonconformity, with its language of worship and community conducted chiefly in the ancient British tongue. For the previous fifty years or more, the English had failed to notice, or realise, the impact of the cultural and literary awakening that was occurring in Wales. Why should they, when it was conducted in a language which was foreign to them?

From the time of the circulating schools of the Reverend Griffith Jones (1684–61) and the Sunday schools of the Reverend Thomas Charles (1755–1814), Nonconformists had practised their own curricula of self-improvement in their own institutions, and were able to read their own literature, engage in musical activities, *eisteddfodau* and literary pursuits. The advocacy of temperance reform and religious revival became part of their programme of self-help and came to dominate the various Nonconformist denominations well into the twentieth century. Their religion and community life marked their national identity and brought it into the political arena.

It was a Welshman who had requested an investigation into the state of education in Wales because it was obvious to both him and his fellow countrymen that some changes were necessary. Welsh people did not dispute the need for educational reform and were only too willing to support it. There were gross inadequacies in the existing system and a failure by both the National Society of the Church of England and the Nonconformist British Schools.

Steps to try and remedy the situation had already been taken in Mold before the report of 1847 was published and in 1849, an appeal was launched for the replacement of the National School at Ponterwyl with a new, purpose-built school in King Street.

The Children on the Books of the present National Schools (272) being far more than the rooms will contain (186) – the situation being low, damp, and unhealthy – the building being occasionally surrounded by floods, and the Railway Station having been built within a few yards, not only disturbing the quietness and order of the Schools, but rendering it dangerous for the Children to pass and re-pass the public road adjoining, it becomes absolutely necessary that better provision should be made for their accommodation. An excellent and central site for New Schools has been obtained and Plans and Specification have been approved of by the Committee of Council on Education.

The Schools will contain Four Hundred Children with a Master's House. The Expense is estimated at about Fourteen Hundred pounds.

Subscriptions promised for the new school included:[46]

Committee of Council on Education	£400
The Lord Bishop of St Asaph	£ 50
P. D. Cooke, Esq	£100
J. W. Eyton, Esq	£100
Robert Knight, Esq	£100
Archdeacon Clough, vicar	£100
Honourable E. M. Ll. Mostyn	£ 50

More subscriptions were collected and a small profit resulted. The cost was £1,747, which included the site purchased for £310 from J. Wynne Eyton.

Vicar Clough was one of the bishop's lieutenants in the pursuit of educational reform in the diocese of St Asaph. Bishop Short's immediate reaction to the 1847 report was to remedy some of the defects and with his brother bishop, Connop Thirwall of St David's, they proposed that the government create in Wales a supervised state system of education, with a professional training structure and grants towards salaries and the appointment of two inspectors acquainted with the Welsh tongue.

Bishop Short set up a diocesan board of education composed of representatives of the clergy from the whole diocese. Its secretary, the Reverend H.P. Foulkes, was the clergyman in charge of neighbouring Buckley, who was highly regarded by W.E. Gladstone. Members met in consultation for two days in the spring and later in August and September for three weeks at a meeting of schoolmasters for special training.

The Welsh people generally recognized that a knowledge of the English language was essential for advancement in the commercial world and the broader social sphere, and were prepared to receive secular instruction through its medium. The educational reforms pursued by the state were implemented through the curricula recommended by their inspectorate and the language chosen was limited to English in elementary schools. Other languages – Greek, Latin, French – were taught in higher schools, but not Welsh.

The aims of the government's Department of Education were to increase literacy – the 3 R's, reading, writing, and arithmetic as befitted Britain's commercial interests; a knowledge of the Empire, through the teaching of geography; and patriotic observance of national events and knowledge of English history, poetry and popular songs. The teaching of sewing was compulsory for girls. Emphasis was placed on discipline through orderly movement in the school and playground, and reinforced through a system of punishment and reward for attendance, behaviour and achievement. Strong measures were taken to eliminate the spread of infection and disease through guidance, instruction and intervention by local medical officers of health. Events such as the opening of a new place of worship, the visit of a circus or menagerie were permitted to break the monotony of the school regime.

From 1863 onwards, we are provided with a day-to-day account of school life from entries recorded in log books which it was compulsory for schools to keep. It was the method by which the central Department of Education was able to monitor events in every school under its control. They provided a useful reference source for government inspectors, school managers, members of school boards and head teachers. They also provided a lively commentary on changes in education, attitudes of head teachers, comments of the inspectorate and progress of the behaviour and health of generations of scholars and the concerns of anxious parents. The guidelines published for their use contained advice that 'a teacher who performs this duty simply, regularly, and with discrimination will find it a powerful help in mastering his profession, as well as an honourable monument to his labours.'

The first major event universally described in log books is the introduction of the so-called Revised Code in 1863, the assessment upon which grants to elementary schools were to be paid. It laid down the standards which had to be attained in the government established curricula. Scholars were to be subject to examination by government inspectors in various subjects at six levels and, if successful, schools qualified for a government grant. School attendance was also taken into consideration. This system was heartily disliked and became known as 'payment by results.' The author of the act, Charles Lowe, declared that 'if it [education] is cheap, it shall be efficient; if it is not efficient, it shall be cheap.'

The next significant change in education was W. E. Forster's Education Act of 1870 which, together with electoral reform, was regarded as one of the major achievements of Prime Minister Gladstone's first term in office. For Nonconformists it was a great step forward. The Reform Act of 1867 extended the numbers of those entitled to vote in local and parliamentary elections and in many urban areas in Wales, Nonconformists now made up the majority of the electorate. This came at a time when the new Education Act adopted the principle of an elected authority – a school board – to enforce the new regulations. One of the intentions of the act was to provide an essential minimum of education and eventually to establish compulsory education for all up to the age of fourteen. Free elementary education, however, did not come into being until 1891. The act created school districts, usually larger than parishes, under a board of education that was elected on a triennial basis by ratepayers, and authorized to build schools. The first elected school board for Mold held its first meeting on 19 December 1874, made up of seven elected members consisting of four Nonconformists and three Anglicans under the chairmanship of the Reverend Roger Edwards, the minister of Bethesda Chapel. This marked a major change in the balance of political power in the area.

The school boards were responsible for providing sufficient school accommodation. Existing voluntary agencies, such as those of the Church of England, were given time to provide new schools or increase accommodation in existing schools and for this they would be entitled to government grant aid. Boards were able to make by-laws to compel children to attend school and the act made specific rules concerning religious instruction in all elementary schools which were in receipt of a parliamentary grant. No child was to be compelled to attend any Sunday school or place of religious worship as a condition of admittance to school and parents were given the right to withdraw their children from religious instruction. If no religious provision was desired by a particular school board, the school could be completely secular.[47] The Mold School Board used its new powers to build schools at Leeswood and Bistre and to extend the British School at Mold, which became known as the Mold Board School.

The 1870 Education Act made Nonconformists totally independent of the Anglican Church and they formed their own alternative leadership which was nurtured in British Schools, Chapel worship and the Liberal Party. Ministers, schoolmasters and elected representatives began to unite on a platform which challenged church rates, tithes and eventually called for the Disestablishment of the Anglican church.

The fascinating history of elementary education in Mold is available in school log books which exist for the National, British and Roman Catholic schools from the 1860s.[48] In the elementary schools (before 1944), the main departments were infants, junior and senior boys, and junior and senior girls.

St David's, a purpose-built Roman Catholic school, was erected in 1872[49] in accordance with the terms of the 1870 Education Act, which enabled it to benefit from government grants to allow it to provide for the needs of an increasing Catholic population. This growth is reflected in the number of 'scholars' present at Milford House in 1851 (41 scholars + 133 in the morning and 85 + 25 scholars in the evening) and the increase in numbers recorded in the school log books a generation later. The problems faced by the Catholic population, made up largely of poor Irish migrants, were common to similar communities throughout the country.

William Lloyd Parry, founder of Alun School, Mold.

The Aberdare Report of 1880 recommended that intermediate schools be created to provide education for those eligible between the end of elementary education [+14] and higher education at university or college. The setting up and administration of this new educational tier, through the Welsh Intermediate Education Act of 1889, became the responsibility of the county councils that were set up in 1888.

The Alun School, named after the poet, the Reverend John Blackwell (whose bardic name was *Alun*), was founded as a private school in 1880 at Mold by William Lloyd Parry.[50] It opened in King Street in 1881 and remained there until 1885 when it moved to Broncoed House at the top of Broncoed Lane, and the following year settled at Preswylfa on Hendy Road. At the 1891 school prize-giving held in Mold Town Hall, the chairman was J. Herbert Lewis, JP., and Principal Harry Reichel of the University College of North Wales, Bangor, was announced as visitor, with the dean of St Asaph

Preswylfa, the home of the Alun School, Mold from 1895.

invited to give the address and present the prizes. All three were members of the recently founded Flintshire Education Committee which was engaged in choosing new 'County' schools in accordance with the Welsh Intermediate Education Act of 1889. The school at Mold, along with those at Rhyl, Holywell, Hawarden and St Asaph passed the test and Daniel Owen became a governor of the school before his death in October 1895. The school at Preswylfa re-opened on 7 May 1895 as an intermediate school under the control of Flintshire County Council. It was a matter of pride for Mold to have its first higher educational establishment and a great triumph to William Lloyd Parry to succeed in its establishment.[61]

A further Education Act was passed in 1902 whereby school boards were abolished and local elementary education became the responsibility of Flintshire County Council. The old Glanrafon Board School was re-named Mold Council School.

Notes

1. For information relating to the establishment of schools see *Report … concerning Charities 1819–37 and 1890, Commissioners of Inquiry into the State of Education Wales 1847*, St Asaph Diocesan Records, NLW.
2. A temporary, but effective, effort to teach people to read was made by the Reverend Griffith Jones (1683–1761) of Llanddowror, who is reputed to have set up 3,495 circulating schools in Wales which taught over 158,000 scholars in twenty-five years. There were few of these schools in Flintshire and none in Mold.
3. This paragraph is dependent upon correspondence between Hope Wynne Eyton and C.B. Clough and bishops of St Asaph.
4. FRO D/LE/1187, 13 May 1812.
5. FRO D/LE/118.
6. FRO D/LE/1189.
7. FRO D/LE/1190
8. Ibid.
9. FRO D/LE/1196, 18 July 1818.
10. See *Pigot's Directory*, 1822.
11. The government circular of 1818 sent out by Henry Brougham, later lord chancellor.
12. Founded by Jonathan Catherall II.
13. FRO D/LE/1197.
14. p.209 of the report.
15. The total income of £23 2s went to the master of the National School, with the exception of £1 paid to the vicar of Mold. The income was derived from Hugh Lloyd's rent charge – income from James Hughes (1723) £100 – and Martha Dodd (1780) £100 – and £4 rent from the charity school.
16. See *Making of Buckley and District*, op cit, pp.236–7.
17. M.V. J. Seaborne, 'Education in Flintshire during the early Victorian period', *Flintshire Historical Society Journal*, vol.33, 1992, pp.73–4. This includes a plan of the British School, Mold.

18. See extracts from *Report of the Commissioners of Inquiry into the State of Education in Wales 1847* [abbreviation SEW]

19. This phrase deliberately echoed '*Brad y Cyllyll Hirion*' (the Treachery of the Long Knives) the story of the sixth-century Saxon lord who invited British chieftains to a banquet to celebrate a truce, required them to leave their weapons at the door as a sign of goodwill and had them murdered by his followers who cunningly concealed their own knives about their persons … see G.T. Roberts, *The Language of the Blue Books,* Cardiff, 1998.

20. H.V. Johnson inspected schools in north Wales with assistance from students of St David's College, Lampeter. He was later called to the bar.

21. SEWP 6.

22. ibid, pp.15–6.

23. ibid, p.16.

24. ibid.

25. ibid, p.19.

26. ibid, p.25.

27. Daniel Owen, *Rhys Lewis,* translated James Harries, Wrexham, 1915 ed., p.43.

28. ibid, p.54.

29. SEW, op cit, p.222.

30. ibid, p.298.

31. ibid, p.55.

32. ibid, p.61.

33. Foulkes came from of minor gentry stock in Denbighshire. He was taught Welsh by Ab Ithel.

34. SEW, pp.66–7.

35. ibid, p.67.

36. The schools in the ecclesiastical districts of Bistre, Pontblyddyn, Treuddyn, Gwernaffield, Nercwys and Gwernymynydd are omitted here.

37. ibid, pp.102–3, Mold Church School, Mold British School and Cotton Mill School.

38. The factory was at Rhydygoleu and the school was established following the Factory Act of 1833 which laid down provision for the education on the premises for children of the operatives and compulsory inspection.

39. This is where the mischievous escapade of Will Bryan perpetrated in church on Good Friday occurred when he caused the schoolmaster to fall over by tying cord round his wooden leg. *Rhys Lewis,* ibid, ch IX, p.52.

40. op cit, *Y Dreflan*

41. 'Mr S frequented the "English Church," the Llan.' Dic Aberdaron [Richard Robert Jones (1780–1843) polygot, Methodist who assisted Thomas Charles in producing 1807 edition of the Welsh Bible.

42. *Rhys Lewis,* p.39.

43. ibid, p.43.

44. ibid, p.48.

45. ibid, p.56.

46. FRO P/40/1/172.

47. See Mold School Board by-laws 1893 D/KK/977.

48. See references Norma Platt, 'The Development of Elementary Education at Mold, *c.*1834–1902', *Ystrad Alun,* 4, 2003, pp.31–44.

49. A new Roman Catholic school was opened in St David's Lane in 1961.

50. Tim Erasmus, *A History of the Alun School, Mold: the Lloyd Parry Years (1880–1922),* Mold, 2003.

11: Creating wealth: the nineteenth century

Having examined the importance in people's lives of religion, education and health and the effect each had on the townscape through the building of chapels, churches, schools, a hospital and other civic buildings, it is necessary to explore the creation of wealth in Mold and district. The transformation of the means of production, be it in agriculture, mining, factories or other work places, contributed to the creation of wealth and the building of many public and private buildings. One of the most important factors causing this transformation was the introduction of new ideas into the work place. This had occurred in agriculture during the eighteenth century, through experimentation in animal husbandry, machinery, crop rotation and the reorganisation of land through enclosure. It occurred in industry as a result of the development of the steam engine, the use of coke in the smelting of iron and the factory production of textiles. In the Mold area, innovation was applied to the lead industry by two outstanding engineers, John Wilkinson of Brymbo and John Taylor of Coed Du, and in the cotton and coal industries by a succession of entrepreneurs and speculators. The railway came to Mold in 1849, bringing with it the means for the town to realise its full potential by linking agriculture, trade and industry with extensive markets across the country and abroad. All of this had a significant effect upon the urban area of Mold after 1800.

Agriculture
Mold has always regarded itself as a market town, an agricultural rather than an industrial or manufacturing centre. A farming presence has been maintained throughout the centuries with weekly retail and cattle markets, and annual fairs. Through these activities the town has retained its prosperity and the loyal support of the surrounding population. This is not surprising, with the town located in the centre of a farming region, in a lowland river valley on the edge of a highland zone.

From the end of the eighteenth century, Britain was self-sufficient in food supplies in normal years, although the period 1760–1816 was frequently a time of crisis, with the authorities in Mold having to intervene to supply food to the destitute and hungry when there were a number of unusually poor harvests.

In the decades following the end of the Napoleonic Wars, there was an improvement in British agriculture resulting in higher productivity which involved a close interaction between arable farming and animal husbandry. Animals were increasingly stall-fed with field crops and in return, they were healthier and larger and produced more manure that could then be used to fertilise crops.

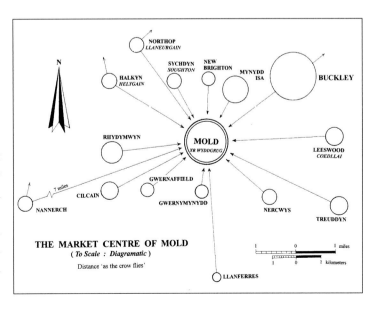

THE MARKET CENTRE OF MOLD
(*To Scale : Diagramatic*)
Distance 'as the crow flies'

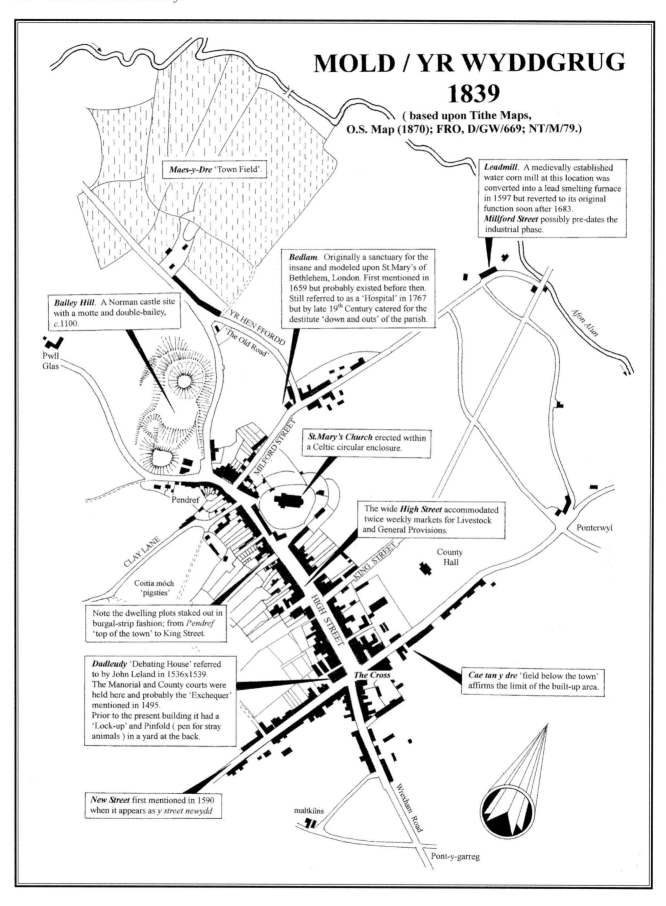

MOLD / YR WYDDGRUG 1839

(based upon Tithe Maps,
O.S. Map (1870); FRO, D/GW/669; NT/M/79.)

Maes-y-Dre 'Town Field'.

Leadmill. A medievally established water corn mill at this location was converted into a lead smelting furnace in 1597 but reverted to its original function soon after 1683.
Millford Street possibly pre-dates the industrial phase.

Bedlam. Originally a sanctuary for the insane and modeled upon St.Mary's of Bethlehem, London. First mentioned in 1659 but probably existed before then. Still referred to as a 'Hospital' in 1767 but by late 19th Century catered for the destitute 'down and outs' of the parish.

Bailey Hill. A Norman castle site with a motte and double-bailey, *c.*1100.

Pwll Glas

YR HEN FFORDD
'The Old Road'

MILFORD STREET

St.Mary's Church erected within a Celtic circular enclosure.

Pendref

The wide *High Street* accommodated twice weekly markets for Livestock and General Provisions.

Ponterwyl

CLAY LANE

KING STREET

County Hall

Coitia môch 'pigsties'

Note the dwelling plots staked out in burgal-strip fashion; from *Pendref* 'top of the town' to King Street.

HIGH STREET

Dadleudy 'Debating House' referred to by John Leland in 1536x1539. The Manorial and County courts were held here and probably the 'Exchequer' mentioned in 1495. Prior to the present building it had a 'Lock-up' and Pinfold (pen for stray animals) in a yard at the back.

The Cross

Cae tan y dre 'field below the town' affirms the limit of the built-up area.

New Street first mentioned in 1590 when it appears as *y street newydd*

maltkilns

Wrexham Road

Afon Alun

Pont-y-garreg

The Mold Enclosure Acts increased the size of agricultural holdings and cultivated land was made more productive by introducing a flexible combination of arable and pastoral farming methods which increased productivity. Fodder crops such as improved grasses, clovers, vetches and turnips were increasingly cultivated and British animals grew fatter and bigger. At a time of rapid population increase, animals were central to the British economy supplying meat, dairy products and raw materials, and before mechanical technology, horses were used as a source of power and a means of transport. In market towns such as Mold, there was a growing sense of self-confidence because of the increasing efficiency of agriculture. Nineteenth-century farming journals and local newspapers were full of advertisements for agricultural equipment – seed drills, threshing and winnowing machines, chaff cutters – the new tools used by improving landowners and tenant farmers. A Flintshire man, James Boydell, exhibited a steam tractor at Blackheath in 1859.[1]

The journals also carried announcements of ploughing competitions and large agricultural shows, organised by local societies and patronised by the gentry, their tenant farmers and large owner-occupiers, with encouragement given to servants and labourers by making them eligible for prizes for long service, good character and exemplary diligence. Local markets such as Mold were vital

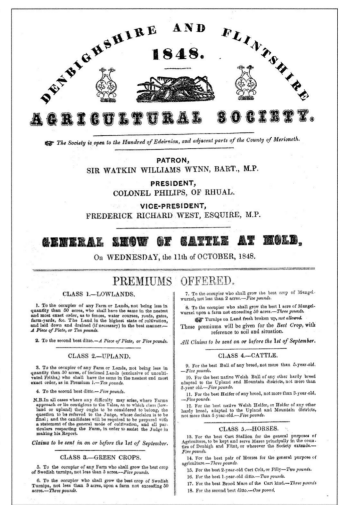

Denbighshire & Flintshire Agricultural Society Cattle Show Programme, 1848.

for the local economy and for the sale and distribution of raw materials such as wool, leather, tallow, barley for brewing, straw and oats.

The Denbighshire & Flintshire Agricultural Society was formed at a meeting held in the Black Lion Hotel, Mold on 24 July 1839, with the intention of 'promoting Agriculture and encouraging Industry' by offering 'premiums for the best cultivated farms and crops, labourers of good character etc.' The annual meetings at which these were awarded developed into an annual show held in turn in Mold, Ruthin and Wrexham. The chairman was appointed annually from amongst the landowners of the two counties of Flintshire and Denbighshire. Amongst the prizes offered were:

1844 – Premiums offered for Farmlands in lowland and uplands for Draining, Fencing etc – Turnips – Livestock (12 classes) – Horses (8 classes) – Sheep (14 Classes) – Pigs (4 classes). Day Labourers being a cottager who has brought up the greatest number of legitimate children without relief … Woman and Man Servant served the longest time in the same family producing the best character. Cottagers – for Cultivation of his land and Garden in the neatest and best style of cultivation.[2]

Amongst the winners were:

1845 – Mr John Catherall of Mold for the best crop of Swedish turnips…Hugh Hughes of Gwernaffield, second best ploughman. A Day Labourer bringing up families – to Mr Edward Roberts of Mold a Day Labourer in husbandry for having brought up 11 children without parochial relief £3. To Mr Jones Carreg-y-llech, Treuddyn for the best Dairy of Cheese not less than 20 nor more than 40 lbs weight … Horned Cattle: Landlord's Bulls to serve the Cows of the Tenantry gratis To John Wynne Eyton Esq. of Leeswood. The medal.

In his description of Dreflan [Mold], a few weeks before Christmas, Daniel Owen gave a vivid insight into the effect of prosperity on the town's trade,

No one suspected that there would be great poverty and distress. There were few beggars about and few were unemployed apart from those too lazy to work. The government of the day was constantly planning improvements and oiling the machinery of industry and; the economy was improving. Everywhere there was work and food. On market days the streets of Dreflan were overcrowded with people and rarely was there a pale face to be seen. The wives of ordinary labourers struggled home under the weight of heavy baskets and many had to procure a conveyance. On Saturday night, the shopkeepers could not close their shops until Sunday morning was upon them, let alone find time to count their money.[3]

Mold has been a market centre since the town was founded in Norman times. It was a meeting place for native Welsh, Saxons and Normans, a natural centre of exchange. Its layout, with a broad main street, wide enough to accommodate market traders, is common to most market towns. In Mold this street (rather than a square) extended from the Cross to the Bailey Hill, with market stalls fronting the shops of merchants and tradesman at the head of their burgage plots. In addition, there was a covered market situated by the Cross, at a point where routes converged and where traders entered the town with their merchandise. This was the business centre of the lordship. Housed in the leet court, with the pinfold for stray animals adjacent, was a covered market which served as the headquarters of the town bailiff, the place where he presided on market day, collecting tolls, directing the visiting traders, and from where, on the four annual fair days, he organised cattle sales in the nearby streets and fields. These three features of the market, the open-street, the covered indoor hall and the cattle auction mart are still retained and have been re-developed as Mold has been adapted to modern planning and traffic arrangements and to meet competition from larger retail concerns.

Civic buildings
Following the Reform Act of 1832, when Mold became a Contributory Parliamentary Borough, 'the authorities thought fit to hold both the Assizes and the Quarter Sessions of the Peace at Mold, and to cause a building called the County Hall to be erected there'.[4] This was built in 1834 to a design by Thomas Jones of Chester

The new Market Hall, 1849.

on what became known as County Hall Fields situated below King Street and westwards behind High Street. This was the beginning of a new civic area for the town which, over the next 130 years became the centre for county administration. Here were built a court house, lock up, militia barracks, police headquarters and education offices.

Sir Thomas Mostyn preferred not to dispose of the building known as *Dadleudy* (debating house) on the corner of New Street and High Street, which from medieval times was used as the manorial and assize court. In 1845, his son was contacted by the chairman of the Mold vestry with regards to the state of the building which was '… considered by the inhabitants to be prejudicial to the health of the town, and that he be respectfully requested

High Street viewed from Wrexham Street with the Market Hall on the left and the fountain and clock that was erected on the Cross.

to cause its removal with the least possible delay.' The Mold Markets Company was formed in the same year and received a licence from the Privy Council to purchase land on which to erect and maintain a building which was to be used as a public market hall.[5] The company agreed to purchase the lease of the old Court Leet building, together with the market tolls for Mold, from the Hon Edward Mostyn Lloyd Mostyn for £315. The old cells at the rear of the building were demolished and a covered market and offices were built on the site in 1849–50. The construction of the Market Hall, with an assembly room above, was built in 1849–50. In 1882, the building was purchased by the Local Board for £2,500 and a third storey was added (part-funded by the proceeds from the 1873 National Eisteddfod) which was used as a meeting place by the local board and and as a library and meeting place for the Cosmopolitan Society. This building was known as the 'Market Hall at the Cross' to distinguish it from a second market building, erected at around the same date, which was known as the Butchers or Tory Market, erected in King Street on land belonging to John Wynne Eyton of Leeswood Hall. The Butchers Market was not a success and was sold, eventually becoming the site of the Drill Hall.

The Militia Barracks was built in 1857–8 to a design by the noted architect Thomas Mainwaring Penson. It

was located on a portion of the ground originally purchased for the county at the rear of King Street and was described as 'A Militia Armoury and Storehouse provided by the County of Flint intended to be enclosed within an acre of ground with accommodation for a Sergeant Major and four Sergeants.' It was demised to the Secretary of State

The Militia Barracks, c.1890.

Mold Gaol, an illustration showing it when it was St Germanus House, occupied by the French Jesuits.

for War for the term of twenty-one-years from 1 April 1879 at the yearly rent of £62.

Under the Local Government Act of 1888 it was provided that 'all County Buildings, Police Stations, works and property should be transferred to County Council of each County.' Eventually, in 1897–8 the Militia Barracks, the Police Station and the County Hall in Mold were converted for use as county offices by Grierson & Bell, on the site known as County Hall Fields.

In accounts passed at the Quarter Sessions of October 1801, it was ordered 'that the Clerk of the Peace settle upon Mr Turner's account respecting the erection of the lock-up House in Mold.' The County also paid the salary of the Master of the Mold House of Correction which in 1835 was £5 5s 6d. In 1865, it was decided to remove the County Gaol from Flint to Mold because of the noisome smells caused by its proximity to the chemical works of Muspratt Bros & Huntley, and a new building was erected for the purpose at Upper Bryn Coch, at a cost of c.£25,000. Designed by Martin and Chamberlain of Birmingham, it was ready to accommodate prisoners by August 1870. A report on the prison appeared in July 1871.

> Mold county prison contains accommodation for 52 male and 20 female prisoners, and the average daily number in custody during the last year has been 29. The average weekly cost of food per prisoner is 2s-7^5/8d and the total ordinary expenditure of the prison, including the salaries of all the officers is £1236 13s. Hard labour of the first class consists of the tread-wheel and weeding and digging in the garden. The wheel accommodates 18 prisoners (twelve on the wheel while six rest), employed there one hour daily; ascent 1,800 feet. Hard labour of the second class consists in picking oakum and cleaning the prison. £453 12s has been received in cash for labour performed by the prisoners. 71 prisoners have had their diet stopped for prison offences, and one has been placed in the dark cells. Prisoners not belonging to the Established Church are offered every facility for being visited by a minister of their own persuasion; and a Roman Catholic priest attends every Sunday. The surgeon is constant in attendance, and the health of the prisoners is said to be good.[6]

The gaol became redundant following the passing of the Prison Act of 1877 and it was closed in 1878 and sold for £3,400. In 1881 the building became St David's French Jesuit Seminary and was used as such until 1918 by French and Spanish religious orders. It was also occupied by boys of the Catholic reformatory training ship, the *Clarence*, and French nuns from Caen. In the 1920s, it was bought for £3,000 by Richard Hughes, a Liverpool merchant.

Mold Police Station and Police Constables' Residence were designed in 1881 and built in County Hall by the architect Lockwood who was instructed to pay attention to 'the defensive capabilities of the proposed building.' In 1883, it was leased to the Secretary of State for War for a term of seventeen years in 1883 at the yearly rent of £25.

Soon after it was established, the Mold Local Board built a fountain and clock at the Cross, the cost of which was raised by public subscription. Two panels contained a profile of Prince Albert and the inscription 'In memory of the late Prince Consort, Albert the Good, A.D., 1865.' The fountain was inaugurated by Mrs Bateson, wife of the chairman, who declared 'that the fountain is now open to the public of Mold, and I hope that they will quench their thirst there, instead of going to the public houses.'[7]

The Mold Markets Company was an example of how the Victorians

Mold Police, 1892.

took the opportunity to use wealth to create further wealth by improving opportunities for trade and retail services. They also disposed of wealth in a philanthropic manner, for the purposes of 'self-improvement' such as the provision of a reading room, or a drinking fountain. Most Victorian high streets were beginning to display their own status symbols which proclaimed the town's wealth and prosperity. The main street became an indicator of the successful creation of wealth. Trade directories, the Yellow Pages of their day, directed customers and attracted commercial travellers. As wealth was accumulated, the number of entries multiplied, listing all manner of service providers: surveyors, surgeons, insurance brokers, mining and colliery agents, hotels, agents, attorneys, etc. By the end of the century, in times of boom when wages were beginning to improve, a consumer culture slowly emerged, stimulated by newspaper adverts.

Industry

In the eighteenth century, the mining of lead and coal was invariably financed either by local landowners themselves who would raise funds out of their own pockets or in partnership with a syndicate of family or friends. In the seventeenth century, the Mostyn family recovered from the debt into which they were disastrously plunged by their support of Charles I in the Civil War, by living frugally in a farmhouse on their estate until they had recouped their losses from the coal mined there. It was common for mineral rights to be leased to London adventurers, city speculators with capital, forerunners of modern venture capitalists. For smaller enterprises, there were country banks which were used by local merchants, businessmen, shopkeepers and artisans. Around 1800, their average size in terms of capitalization was in the order of £10,000. Every country bank maintained an agent or correspondent bank in London, which helped it handle and discount bills of exchange. In Mold for example, in 1835, the bankers Douglas, Smalley & Co. drew on Mastermen, Peters & Co. of London. Douglas, Smalley & Co., with branches in Mold, Denbigh and Holywell, went bust in 1837 and amongst those who lost their deposits were the St Winefride's Well Appeal Fund and the Argoed Mining Disaster Fund. Others suffered in Mold when Samuel & James Knight's bank folded which could have survived, but for a panic and a run on the bank. Through no fault of his own, the vicar of Mold lost money belonging to the Mold Savings Bank for which he was held personally responsible and had to bear the liability himself. Country banks were vulnerable because the law prohibited them from becoming unlimited liability enterprises and so one exposed partner could bring down the entire venture.

The face of Mold Mountain is pock-marked with capped lead workings and deep in the bowels of the earth are two great drainage tunnels, thrust through from Cadole to the River Dee at Bagillt, memorials to generations of miners from Roman times onwards. Looking back to the end of the eighteenth century it might appear that a great price was paid in both labour and investment in an industry which was dying because it was no longer viable. Following the demise of the extraction of lead ore from Mold Mountain efforts were made to revive it by two great entrepreneurs who both worked the lead mines at Llyn-y-Pandy.

The first of these was Bersham iron master, John Wilkinson, who was astute and successful enough to finance his own schemes. He was the ideal man to provide the technical equipment required to rid the deep mines of north Wales of their greatest scourge, underground water. James Watt and Matthew Boulton, the pioneers of the steam-engine cylinder, had recognised him as the only person able to meet their specifications and engaged him to manufacture essential components for their engines. Wilkinson, as well as being an experimenter, adept at improving new technology in both the iron and lead smelting industries, was also an entrepreneur who was willing to supply both the British and French governments with the products of his iron works. He brought this skill, drive and versatility to his industrial concerns which he financed from his profits and, because of the lack of liquidity, issued his own notes and trade tokens for his workers' use when specie was in short supply. When he died in 1808, his most important legacy to the Mold mines was the hope that the new technology he had introduced would revive an ailing industry.

The second entrepreneur was John Taylor, a Cornish man, who was appointed mineral agent to Lord Grosvenor's works at Halkyn in 1813, an association which was to continue with his son, also named John Taylor. The elder Taylor[8] was a man of immense talent and reputation both in Britain and abroad and became involved in all the major metal-mining areas of the British Isles, either as a manager or an owner. He was particularly interested in spreading scientific knowledge and was a fellow of the Royal Society and the Geological Society of London and was one of the founders of London University and later turned his energies to mechanical engineering at Sandycroft Foundry.[9] He attempted to revive the Mold lead mines by using the latest technology in engines and pumping equipment, and by constructing leats and watercourses to sustain the operation of water wheels when the river Alun disappeared into swallow holes. In a report on the Mold mines in 1827[10] Taylor summed up the difficulties he was encountering in making the mines workable and productive,

The mines … were reduced to an extreme state of poverty, and although large deposits of lead were known to have been left by the former proprietors, they could not be got at or worked to advantage unless proper shafts and levels were opened for this purpose.[11]

Considerable quantities of ore were known to have been left in the mine (Pen-y-Fron); there was a prospective of extensive discoveries in the ground which remained unwrought, and no doubt of the ultimate success of the undertaking; but the same difficulties presented itself to the present Adventurers which was found to exist by the late proprietor, – that of a great influx of water; and it was only by employing means more adequate to the purpose of relieving the mines of it than those formerly employed that any success could at all be calculated upon.[12]

The basic equipment Taylor thought necessary included steam engines and four large water wheels for pumping. Taylor relied on attracting

Lead, &c. Mining Companies and their Agents.

Bryn Gwyn Lead Mining Co. Limited, H. Nottingham, agent
Bryngwiog Lead Mining Co. Limited; William Harper, agent
East Westminster Lead Mining Co. Limited; Morris Roberts, agent
Erwfelin Lead Mining Co. Limited; John Lloyd, agent
Frou Hall Lead Mining Co.; John Pryor, agent
Garreg Boeth Lead Mines Co.; Captain J. Lloyd, agent
Glan Alyn Lead Mine Co. Limited; Captain Roberts, agent
Great Fron Fownog Consolidated Lead Mining Co.; Captain Wasley, agent
Hendre Lead Mining Co. Limited; John Lloyd, agent
Llyn-y-Pandy Lead Mining Co. Limited; Captain Francis, agent
Maes-y-Safn Lead Mining Co. Limited
Mold Consolidated Lead Mining Co. Limited; B. Williams, agent
Mount Pleasant Lead Mining Co.; J. Wasley, agent
Nannerch Iron Ore Co.; J. Holden, agent
North Hendre Lead Mining Co. Limited; John Lloyd, agent
Old Westminster Lead Mining Co.; J. Ede, agent
Pant Du Lead Mining Co. Limited; Captain Mansell, agent
Pant-y-Buarth Lead Mining Co.; Edward Jones, agent
Pant-y-Mwyn Lead Mining Co.; Edward Jones, agent
Rhosesmor Lead Mining Co. Limited; Captain Julian, agent

Slater's Trade Directory entry for lead mining companies and their agents in the Mold area in 1874.

substantial investment to finance his ambitious schemes. The London banker, Samuel Hoare, was the largest investor. He must have received a boost to his confidence and satisfaction when in September 1829, a public dinner

> … attended by nearly one hundred of the most respectable miners and smelters in the county with Philip Davies Cooke, Esq presiding, [was given at the White Horse, Holywell for him] by the gentlemen interested in mining and smelting in the County of Flint in general acknowledgement of services rendered by Mr Taylor to the mining interest in the erection of improved machinery on an extended scale and the introduction of a system of economy in the management of mines …[13]

The Flintshire representatives obviously appreciated Taylor's efforts to rationalize working practices and in the amalgamation of the majority of the mines on the mountain as Mold Mines. But overall it must be said that in spite of high investment in technology and expert management such as that introduced by Taylor and his Cornish 'Captains,' production figures never reached expectation throughout the nineteenth century. Despite temporary revivals in the industry from time to time brought about by an increased demand for zinc, or the exposure of veins at lower levels through drainage, there was a slow and general decline both in large and small workings.[14] Taylor estimated that by 1829, he had expended £160,000 for a return of £40,000, a financial disaster which was reflected in the fate of so many local lead mines: Pen-y-Fron closed in 1837; Pant-y-Mwyn closed in 1844 because of the high cost of pumping water; Pant-y-Buarth was worked by Taylor between 1825 and 1833 and then again from 1841–45, producing only an uneconomic 2,296 tons.

The mines leased by the lords of Mold fared no better and their agent reported on twenty-two lead mines in 1863,[15] making such comments as:

> … very little lead being mined, hence small royalties; Gwernymynydd and Cathole unlet; Thorn tree not working; True Blue – 4 men working – very little gotten; Exhibition – 6 men working, very little gotten; Deborah – they have been at work for 2 years and have sold 9 ton; Modlen – at present most productive mine on the mountain last ½ year royalty £74. 3s. 6d; Mount Pleasant – 18 to 20 men last ½ year royalty £56. 9s 1d.[16]

Difficulties encountered throughout Flintshire included sudden flooding through heavy rainfall, poor ventilation and instances of carbon dioxide poisoning.

Great faith was placed in drainage tunnels excavated to reduce levels of water and make lead veins more accessible, and two deep ones were engineered and operated over long periods, the Halkyn Deep Level (1818–1903) and the Milwr Tunnel from Bagillt to Cadole (1897–1958). Their construction was a bold attempt to resuscitate a dying industry, and a great engineering feat conducted at great expense, with no tangible return.

In 1863, commissioners who had been appointed to inquire into the condition of mines in Great Britain, took evidence, under the chairmanship of Lord Kinnaird. Dr Peter Parry, coroner and general practitioner of Mold, when questioned by them about the health of miners, had answered: 'I see colliers who are old, but I cannot find an old miner … they become asthmatical and affected in their breathing and suffer very acute stomach pains.' He told the commission of the seven men who died at the Bryngwyn Mine in September 1854, when an inquest returned a verdict that 'they casually suffocated and smothered in a lead ore mine shaft from the effect of impure air.' The next witness, Mr Robert Parry, a surgeon of Mold, confirmed the injury caused to the health of miners by their working conditions. He believed that working underground for six hours was enough for one shift and that when miners were aged between 25-30, they began to complain of ill health. Their health often improved when they took their customary time off in August to assist in the corn harvest. A Captain Francis Evans of Waun (Gwernaffield) told the commission that when the miners 'get to a certain time of life they contrive to get other occupations,' adding that 'Bread and butter are [their] principal diet' and that they spent their money on drink.

They have a custom, no matter what family they have, of giving their wives 12s a week and no more, and spending the rest … it is no use to give them extra wages, they only stay away from work, and spend their time, and lose their money.

Daniel Owen on the other hand, gives a more sober picture of the way of life of the unemployed or striking miner in adversity.

But to the poor miners who had been accustomed to entirely depend on Pwllgwynt for their sustenance, the stoppage of the mine was a serious and a bitter event indeed. Their wages goodness knows, had for years been pitifully small, scarcely fourteen shillings a week… The fact was that nearly every one of the Pwllgwynt miners kept a pig and planted potatoes in their field. It is a marvel to think on what a small amount of money many Welsh labourers have been able to live and rear a numerous family. . . They were not starving; they were not naked. Indeed they came to chapel as a whole family not only tidy, but were besides able to give something to the 'cause'. How they were able to do this heavens above knows one is driven to the conclusion that their necessities were small, and that we, in these days, spend a lot of money on things that we could do without … Like a bird that lives from day to day without taking any heed for the morrow, so they lived from hand to mouth; and when Pwllgwynt stopped working their poverty and misery was heavy upon them.

The winter and early summer months of 1865/6 saw the Halkyn lead miners come out on strike and a mob, reported to be in the region of 2–3,000 men, caused a disturbance in the town of Mold. The miners were protesting against the Taylor management's attempt to enforce the Cornish system of an eight-hour working shift which meant an increase of two working hours per day. This extended change in time of toil was a long standing grievance between the Taylor family and the workforce. The suggestion had been made by John Taylor, senior, in 1822, when he proposed the extra hours as an 'improved system.' In 1865/6 the miners brought forward the same arguments to make their case against its adoption – the extra time working underground would be injurious to health and the new arrangement would reduce their minimum payment to twenty shillings per month which the miners were obliged to accept if they failed to mine lead for any reason; they were also required to work a month in hand. Accepting these conditions would result in more control over their time by the employer. The new conditions reduced the opportunity for the miners to cultivate their garden or earn extra money elsewhere such as on local farms during harvest time.

Trouble broke out at Taylor's Halkyn colliery where fifty miners came out on strike in December 1865, supported by a large number of miners from other pits. In the middle of January 1866, rumours of black-leg labour turned into a mass demonstration in Halkyn with 2,000 miners from the Holywell district ransacking local cottages. Soldiers of the 85th Regiment arrived in the area from Chester to support the local police. The trouble eventually died down and the troops departed until the beginning of May when the strikers took the law into their own hands and attempted to remove black-leg labour from the county. At the end of May, police armed with cutlasses arrested the ringleaders at 2 a.m. at their homes and brought them to the court house in Mold on 11 June, when fourteen men were committed for trial at Chester. A mob of 2–3,000 colliers gathered outside the old court house to protest at the trial and were held in check by policemen and soldiers from Flintshire and a detachment of the 39th Regiment from Chester. The day passed without any violence and the mob dispersed without incident.[17]

The industrial unrest of 1866 had calmed down and the military had long departed when, at 4.30 a.m. on 16 November, the early risers, the 'knockers up', awakened the sleeping townsfolk of Mold and summoned the Local Board's 'rag taggle' fire brigade to a blaze in the eight-storeyed cotton factory.[18] The company house of Frederick Septimus Bateson, the cotton manufacturer, was fortunately unscathed and the workers had not assembled. Mr Bateson, the patriotic and generous promoter of the water fountain recently inaugurated at Mold Cross, must have wished it was on his doorstop to quench the flames and that the water which his wife had recommended the thirsty to drink, had been available for them on that calamitous dawn. Not only

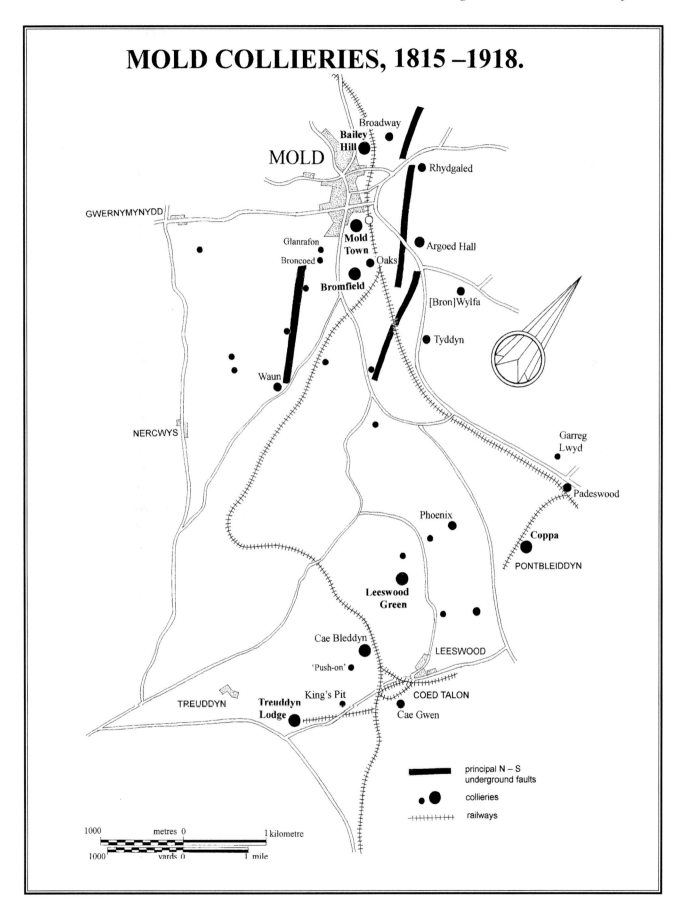

MOLD COLLIERIES, 1815 –1918.

Broadway

Bailey Hill

MOLD

Rhydgaled

GWERNYMYNYDD

Glanrafon

Mold Town

Broncoed

Oaks

Argoed Hall

Bromfield

[Bron]Wylfa

Tyddyn

Waun

NERCWYS

Garreg Lwyd

Padeswood

Phoenix

Coppa

PONTBLEIDDYN

Leeswood Green

Cae Bleddyn

LEESWOOD

'Push-on'

King's Pit

COED TALON

TREUDDYN

Treuddyn Lodge

Cae Gwen

principal N – S
underground faults

● collieries

┼┼┼┼┼┼┼ railways

1000   metres 0   1 kilometre

1000   yards 0   1 mile

was his livelihood in Mold destroyed, but the jobs of two hundred and fifty workers and their dependants also perished as winter approached. The incident was reported in the local press,

> About half-past four o'clock on Thursday morning week, the usual quietude of the Town of Mold was disturbed by the cries of 'Fire'. There stood about half a mile from the town, in Maes-y-dre, a large eight-storied cotton mill, built of brick in the form of a square with outbuildings and offices contiguous. This building which was one of the largest in the district early on Thursday morning was entirely destroyed, and its valuable contents, consisting of a large stock of raw material and a large quantity of new machinery, were consumed. The premises were in the occupation of Mr F. S. Bateson, a gentleman who is well known in Liverpool. There was a strong wind blowing at the time and the efforts used to prevent the spread of the flames were ineffectual. Immediately after the discovery of the fire, which was in the card room, it spread with such alarming rapidity that every part of the building was enveloped in one common sheet of flame. From the first there appeared no hope of saving the premises, and the only piece of machinery that was rescued was a carding machine. Fortunately a large amount of cotton which had only arrived at the station that day had not been despatched to the mill, otherwise the loss would have been more serious. There is no clue to the origin of the fire. The loss is estimated at £20,000 – £25,000, a considerable portion, if not the whole, being covered by insurance. The calamity has cast a gloom over the town, and will throw out of employment upwards of 250 people.[19]

The Mold Cotton Factory had survived seventy years of boom and bust and, whenever prosperity had returned, had always reopened its doors to members of at least two generations of operatives who resided in artisan dwellings in the neighbouring Maes-y-dre, Milford Street, Henffordd and Rhyd-y-Goleu. Unlike the Holywell Woollen Mill, which was burnt down on two or three occasions, the cotton mill did not have the phoenix on its trade-mark and the eight-storey monument to cotton manufacture was never rebuilt and the town lost its textile industry.

The Mold Tinplate Works[20] was located on the banks of the river Alun on a thirty-four acre site, which included a mill-pool of five acres. The site had been in use for centuries, first as a water-mill for lead smelting, and latterly as a textile mill. In the 1830s, steam engines had been installed that were fuelled by coal from the Bedford pits of Bailey Hill and Sychdyn collieries. Convenient road and rail transport added to the desirability of the site for redevelopment and in 1873, it was bought by William Williams (a tinplate manufacturer from Morriston near Swansea), Rowland Morgan (a Llanelli iron-founder) and George Jeremiah. The new enterprise lasted for only three years but was revived in 1878 as the Alyn Tinplate Company in the ownership

Mold Tinplate Works.

Left: Tinplate Workers.

Below: Tinplate Works staff.

of Josiah Richards, David Williams (of the Pontypool Iron and Tinplate Co.), Morgan Morgan (of Pontypool) and Walter M. Spence (of Liverpool). In 1896, following the death of Morgan the company was registered as the Alyn Steel Tinplate Co. Ltd. In 1936, it was taken over by Richard Thomas & Co. and during the Second Word War became an ordnance dump.

The importance of these smaller industries in the creation of wealth in Mold was that they provided a continual presence of manufacturing which sustained the livelihoods of a variable workforce and an inflow of income and local authority rates into the town.

There is little evidence of any major development of coal mining in the lordship of Mold before the nineteenth century. In 1791, the surveyor to the lord of the manor advised 'on the potentiality of coal reserves in the townships of Mold south of the river Alyn.' Although brief reference has already been made to the expansion of the coalfield generally up to the 1840s, against a background of labour unrest across the region, and its effect on the town of Mold, the account of the mining of coal is continued here in more detail in order to describe the main areas of production and the working of the more important collieries.

Throughout the nineteenth century, coal was exploited intermittently from collieries in the districts of the Flintshire coalfield which were once part of the parish of Mold. The owners of mineral rights often leased them for a specified period, subject to the payment of a royalty, with the lessee's company agreeing to observe the conditions of the lease. It was the lessees who obtained the necessary capital to equip the pit and meet the costs of production by issuing shares and selling the coal at a profit. In times of economic depression, when there was little or no demand, the pits usually closed and remained idle until they reopened under new management. A brief gazetteer of collieries is given below to show their grouping and known dates of activity.[21]

Argoed Hall Colliery[22] witnessed what was probably the worst colliery disaster in the district. It occurred on Wednesday 10 May 1837 at the colliery owned by Messrs Hampton and Company, where a flash flood occurred when a pumping engine failed to cope with torrents of water breaking in from old workings, overwhelming the mine and resulting in many fatalities. Those working below never received an order to return to the surface. Some colliers escaped, but many others were trapped by rising flood water to a depth of fifteen feet and were unable to get to safety.

At the inquest held on 15 May, the coroner returned a verdict of loss of life caused by the accumulation of foul air from rising water, which accidentally broke into the colliery. The agents and proprietors were exonerated from any blame. The bodies of twenty-one victims were brought to the surface, amongst them Robert Owen, aged 47, and his two sons, Thomas and Robert, aged 16 and 11. They were the father and two brothers of Daniel Owen who was only seven months old at the time. Unfortunately, the proceeds of the disaster fund established to relieve the sufferings 'of 18 poor families by administering permanently to their wants,' was lost when Douglas, Smalley & Company of the Holywell and the Mold Bank became bankrupt.

Daniel Owen in his fictional autobiography, *Rhys Lewis,* used the occasion of a mining disaster and its effect on the local community to describe the death of the collier's champion Bob Lewis.

When the explosion took place at the Red Fields pit, which caused the death of my brother Bob and divers others, there was, of course, not a moment's warning; and the neighbourhood, which a few minutes before, was all peace and happiness, was plunged into sore and indescribable sorrow … It was not, however, the why and the wherefore of the occurrence, that troubled the bereaved – but the results.[23]

Bailey Hill Colliery – the Bedford Pits were a group of relatively small pits at the north-west part of the town, usefully situated to supply coal to the steam engines of the Cotton Mill during the 1830s. It was known locally as the 'Hard Struggle,' suggesting difficulties in operating it. The pit remained open until the 1890s.[24]

Broadway Colliery, Llwynegryn was called Cae March, no doubt an allusion to the marshy ground near the river. The coalfield was described as 'most faulty.'[25]

Bronwylfa Colliery known to be operating in 1869.[26]

Glan-yr-Afon Colliery ceased working in 1861.

Rhyd Galed Colliery, near Argoed.

Mold Town Colliery.[27]

Bailey Hill Colliery.

Bromfield Hall Colliery[28] was worked throughout the nineteenth century until *c.*1916 and was the most important and productive of the Mold collieries during that period. In 1913 a report[29] was produced on the extent of the coal reserves owned by the company which spoke optimistically of huge coal reserves in the Mold area. These were divided into five locations where there was the prospect of coal extraction. It was reported that the Bromfield company held the property under several leases 'which grant the company the right to mine for coals and other specified minerals under 3,220 acres.' Details were given of royalties payable, the sequence, thickness and depth of the coals found in the Bromfield shafts, colliery sites and buildings, modes of working and pumping operations. It was observed that many of the old underground workings examined had been abandoned years previously. The five areas named in the report were:

1. The Bromfield area where it was estimated that there were workable reserves of over 3 million tons of coal, but geological restrictions and the proximity of the town of Mold meant that a large daily output from this area could not be maintained.

2. The Oaks area to the south of Bromfield Colliery. It was stated that in the past numerous shafts had extensively worked the Hollin and Main coal seams from the Oak's shafts which were flooded at the time of inspection. These were last worked thirty-five years previously (1878) and it was estimated that £4,000 would need to be spent on unwatering to obtain access to reserves of 4.2 million tons of coal.

3. The Pentrehobyn area, situated to the south-east of Bromfield, adjoining the Oaks area, and separated from the Llong area by a geological fault. Main coal had been worked from the pit earlier in the nineteenth century and it was planned to exploit four foot, wall and bench coal. It was estimated that there were reserves of 1.25 million tons of coal.

4. The Llong area adjoining cannel coal was worked from pits now abandoned (thirty years previously *c.*1883) and to the north of the Llong pit's hollin and main coal was worked from the old Argoed Hall shafts. It was calculated that there were reserves of 2.37 million tons of coal.

5. The Nercwys area, to the west of the Bromfield and Oaks area, where earlier the pits worked cannel, hollin and main coals. The report was optimistic and recommended the sinking of two new shafts in a central position near the old Waun sidings and the London & North Western Railway. The surveyors reported, 'we are very favourably impressed as to the future of this area, everything points to there being large areas of coal and, what is more important, large areas of the hollin and main coal seams, the probable quantity available being 16 million tons. The average monthly output had been 10,494 tons at a cost 9/4d per ton. No difficulty appeared to be found in obtaining a market for the output. There was railway freight from the colliery to Birkenhead and Ellesmere Port and owing to the colliery being situated on the immediate outskirts of the town of Mold, a good cart sale and the mixed coal produced could be sold as house and steam coal.'

Johnstone's report failed to mention a colliery worked eighty-six years before, the Tyddyn Colliery.[30]

Mold viewed from Argoed Colliery, watercolour.

Coal Proprietors and Merchants.

Bronwhlfa Colliery Co. Limited,
Bronwhlfa Colliery, near Mold;
Richard Blackburn, manager;
Registered Office in England,
Sunny Bank, Rochdale

Catherall & Co., Buckley

Coed Talon Colliery Co. Limited (and
cannel), Coed Talon ; Jos. Dougan,
agent

Coppa Colliery Co., Limited, Coppa
Colliery, Mold

Ewloe Hall Colliery Co., Buckley ;
Edward Parry, manager

Flintshire Oil & Cannel Co. Limited,
Tryddyn ; Thomas Ollis, manager

Hughes John & Co. (merchants),
Padeswood; office, Pont Blyddyn

Lassey John, Buckley

Leeswood Cannel and Gas Coal Co.
Limited, Leeswood

Leeswood Main Coal, Cannel and Oil
Co. Limited, Leeswood ; Lewis
Howell, manager

Little Mountain Coal, Iron and Clay
Co. Limited, Buckley

Mold Argoed Colliery Co. Limited,
Argoed Colliery ; Andrew Boosie,
manager

Mold Collieries and Mines, Limited,
Pont Blyddyn ; Mr. Holden,
manager

Nerquis Coal & Cannel Co., Nerquis ;
George Parker, manager

Newton Joseph & Co., Cheapside
Colliery, Ewloe Green, near Mold

Oak Pits Colliery Co. Limited, Oak
Pits ; Mr. Jacob Forrest, manager

Parry William, Caergwrle

South Buckley Coal and Fire Brick
Co. Limited, Buckley, near Mold ;
A. J. Barrat, manager; Registered
Office in England, 2 Drake Street,
Rochdale

Spon Colliery Co., Buckley

Sparrow & Poole, Plas Main

Watkinson George & Sons, Limited,
Buckley Collieries

Williams John, Bedford Colliery ;
Edward Wheldon, manager

Ward Samuel P. & Co., Sandycroft
Colliery, adjoining the Railway
Station, Buckley, near Mold

*Slater's Trade Directory entry for
coal proprietors and merchants
in the Mold area, 1874.*

John Taylor's report of 1827 on the Mold mines gives a glimpse of a colliery whose main purpose was to supply coal to an ancillary industry, lead mining, and methods and hazards involved.

Three shafts have been sunk, together 80 fathoms; a steam-engine of 18 inch cylinder, a great extent of trial has been made, a great length of levels driven in different directions in search of coal. The quantity of coal produced is not so great as we had been led to anticipate, being at present 200 tons per week from which the mines are supplied, and the overplus sold to the country. These costs are about meeting the costs of working, but they are not sufficient, to warrant any further expense in opening new ground.

The Broncoed and Oak Pits Colliery operated from the 1820s.[31]
The Nerquis Colliery Company (owned by the Nerquis Hall Estate), operated under lease from the 1850s until closure in 1930 when they were working at a loss of £1,000 a month. It produced cannel coal. Between 1865 and the early 1880s the coal industry was the largest employer, outstripping agriculture, in Nercwys.
Ty'n Twll pit (located near Nercwys School) produced cannel coal.
Hendre Pits near Hendre Isa, where unsuccessful trials lost the operators £30,000.
The Waen and Nerquis Colliery, located a mile south of Mold, only operated from 1890–9. It consisted of two pits, John and Eyton, operated by Thomas Parry & Co. The Waen Colliery winding house later became a cheese factory.

The southern end of the coalfield spread over Treuddyn, Coed Talon, Leeswood and Pontblyddyn, was worked consistently throughout the nineteenth century for its upper seams of good quality hollin, brassey, and main coal. But it was best known for the quality of its smooth and curly cannel coal from which oil was manufactured by distillation. The colliers employed here were often involved in industrial disputes in the district, being on a direct route across the Flintshire and Denbighshire coalfield. Mold was the nearest assize court for the prosecution of colliers and lead miners charged with violent protests in clashes with police and military. In the summer of 1869, a dispute at Leeswood Green Colliery, between the local Welsh workforce and an officious English boss, was the cause of the Mold riots. It was this event that Daniel Owen used as the background to his portrayal of the character of the collier 'Bob' (Robert), based on his own brother and in the novel the brother of the eponymous Rhys Lewis, both of whom were imprisoned for their role in the dispute.

The mining of coal was a highly competitive enterprise and its success or failure depended on a number of factors such as the economic climate, the reserves of coal available, the geology of a particular district and the local transport facilities. The steam locomotive, which had been developed in the coalfields, revolutionised the mining and movement of coal. Britain's economic supremacy in the nineteenth century owed a great deal to this new transport system. The growth of railways and their branch lines in the Mold district was closely bound up with the rise and decline of the coal industry. The creation of wealth in the mining industry was an adventure often entered upon with great optimism, whose progress could be interrupted by flooding, explosion, or industrial action. Finally the cost of getting coal in terms of human lives was sometimes a cause for anger and sorrow expressed by a volatile workforce protesting against conditions they felt to be intolerable. It is this combination of greed, intolerance, frustration and injustice which resulted in the tragedy and unforeseen fatalities of the Mold riots which has entered into the town's psyche and folklore.

Railways[32]

The railway mania of the 1840s and 1860s placed Mold in an advantageous position. The opening of the Mold & Chester Railway in 1847 eventually created a number of branch lines which followed the Alun, Terrig and Wheeler valleys linking the town with the coal-producing areas at the easterly edge of the old parish boundaries, eastwards towards Wrexham and with northerly links to Buckley and Deeside. Many of the new coal and lead mining companies were centred on Mold in order to benefit from the professional services of agents, insurers, and attorneys. As passenger stations grew in number over a larger area so did attendance at Mold's markets and fairs as the wealth of the region began to circulate. The brick manufacturing townships of Bistre and Buckley benefitted from the construction of railway stations, bridges, embankments, etc. Local landowner and politician, William Gladstone, was the chief architect of the Railway Act of 1844 which laid down a standard gauge of track throughout the widening railway network.

Although there were tramways in the old parish of Hawarden, linking the coalfield to the river Dee, proposals in 1825 to open up a tramway from Treuddyn to the port of Flint did not win approval. Mold had to wait for the Chester & Holyhead Railway Company to connect the two places when a station was opened in Mold on 14 August 1849. The versatility of the railways in making direct connections between supplier and market was seen in the establishment of branch lines. The Mold & Chester Railway had branch lines to Nant Mawr colliery and Ffrith to exploit the coal, ironstone and fireclay of the villages of Coed Talon, Leeswood and Pontblyddyn and limestone quarries.

In 1859 the Nerquis Private Railway was constructed to transport the coal of the Nerquis Colliery Company, running eastwards to join the Ffrith branch of the Mold railway at Coed Talon. It was expanded when it was absorbed into the Mold & Treuddyn Railway and opened for mineral traffic on 8 July 1870. The route from Mold Station left the Chester & Mold Railway half-a-mile south-east of Mold station and ran due south to enter the Terrig valley and turn from the Nerquis Private Railway to Coed Talon, where a new junction with the Ffrith branch would be made. This was authorised by an Act of Parliament in 1866, and the Nerquis Railway was finally purchased by the London & North Western Railway Company in May 1868. The line, about four miles in length, cost between £30,000–40,000. It was built to provide sidings for a number of collieries at a time when the district was enjoying an unprecedented demand for cannel coal. In 1849, a patent was taken out 'for obtaining paraffin oil from bituminous coal by slow distillation.' The cannel coal in the region east of Mold was ideal for this process. In 1861, the press announced 'New works in Flintshire, a veritable nursery for oil distillers.' As a result, the Mineral Oil Company was established at Leeswood and Saltney in 1861. By 1865 over 1,000 retorts had been erected locally for the manufacture of oil from the cannel. There was a national demand for cannel coal obtained from mines throughout the district where twenty-three companies were listed in the trade directories as producers, and combined production figures of cannel coal from the Mold/Leeswood area was *c.*120,000 tons.

In 1869, the Mold & Denbigh Railway was established to provide for passenger and goods traffic westward along the Alun valley. Its industrial sidings provided a necessary and invaluable competitive link for a variety of industries along the route including: the Bailey Hill Colliery; the Alyn Tinplate Works; the Mold Colliery Company Ltd (until 1895); the Ruby Brick & Tile Works; the North Hendre Lead Mine (1867–1987); the Hendre limestone quarry and the Glan-yr-Afon Lime Company (1874–*c.*1894).

The railway network built between *c.*1849–70 serviced the main districts where coal was found across the coalfield.

The Mold Riots

The Mold Riots of 1869, perhaps the best-remembered events in the town's nineteenth-century history, link the town, the railways and the mining industry. A colliers' dispute at Leeswood Green Colliery in the summer of 1869 brought tensions into the open which had existed between the workforce and the management since the early years of the century. The community in which the dispute originated had a Welsh-speaking cultural background and the proprietors and managers were predominantly English in speech, religion, and upbringing. These contrasting cultures and use of different languages in the home and the work-place, caused considerable misunderstanding, making communication difficult and relationships strained. An added complication was that these divisions were also experienced in the court room, between officials and defendants giving rise to a sense of injustice and persecution. The resultant frustration and anger perhaps inevitably led to confrontation, riot and for some, imprisonment.

The disturbance appears to have started at Leeswood Green Colliery, initially as a protest by the colliers who were angered by the arrogant and unjust behaviour of the underground manager, John Young, a Durham man who had replaced a local man in 1864.[33] Young had favourites and showed his dislike generally of Welsh colliers. They in turn were alarmed by his inefficiency. On 1 May 1869, a notice was posted at the pit heads announcing a reduction of the cutting price of coal by one shilling. On 19 May violence erupted and Young, confronted by fifty or sixty angry colliers, took refuge in the engine-house. By the time he re-emerged, the crowd had increased tenfold and he was marched to the railway station at Hope Junction where the police intercepted the crowd and took him to Mold. Five days later, the mob stripped Young's house of its furniture which they despatched to the railway station as a result of which two police officers apprehended William Hughes, a collier from Treuddyn. The following day, a police superintendent was attacked by an irate mob whilst escorting Hughes to the Magistrates Court. The crowd managed to release him and carried him shoulder high through King Street and Wrexham Street. Common sense later prevailed and Hughes, along with seven other men upon whom warrants had been served, was persuaded by David Phillips, a miner at Cae Blyddyn, to surrender to the police. Phillips, a former prize-fighter and a Methodist convert, who had the respect and trust of the colliers, wished to avoid violence and wanted to ensure that the defendants received justice and 'fair-play'. The accused appeared before magistrates and were released and bailed to appear at a special session on 2 June.

In order to support their workmates on the day they made their second appearance before the magistrates, colliers from across the coalfield took a day off and gathered in Mold where they spent the day peacefully. All day long the waiting crowd had grown. The court had sat at 11 a.m. but it was not until 5 p.m. that the sentences were passed. The crowd, angered by the severity of the sentences,[34] grew larger and more menacing. It was reported that 500–600 people gathered outside the court house to greet two of the prisoners who were to serve their sentence of a month's imprisonment with hard labour at Flint Gaol. The prisoners emerged after a wait of two hours and were conducted to the railway station to be taken by train to Flint via Chester. Expecting trouble, the whole Flintshire Constabulary of thirty-nine officers, including Chief Constable Peter Browne, were present. Earlier that day, the police had been reinforced by a detachment of fifty men of 2nd Battalion of the King's Own Regiment from Chester.

The police set out to escort the prisoners from the court house to the railway station, via Chester Street, Tyddyn Street and along the railway bridge. The party ran the gauntlet of a large gathering described as 'very demonstrative and hustling', made up of 'groups of sturdy collier youths and men some of them with powder-scarred faces' and including many women. As the escort struggled to the station, the crowd turned nasty and began pelting the police with large stones which the women picked up from the newly-laid surface of Tyddyn Street. The escorting party, clearly distinguishable by their uniforms and overlooked from the high ground of Tyddyn Street, was an easy target. Their progress was halted when they reached the railway station and discovered that the main gate was closed and the only access was by a narrow gate. Chief Constable Browne later testified that at this stage, 'The stones were as thick as hail – the air was black with them – many of the stones were four and five pounds in weight – several of my own men were bleeding copiously, the blood streaming down their uniforms.' The troops who were in the railway station fared no better, with missiles shattering the carriage windows of the waiting train and 'falling with destructive force on the knapsacks and shakos of the soldiers, and helmets of the police.' Two officers, twenty soldiers and twelve policemen were 'severely injured' including Captain Blake and the Chief Constable.

It was essential that the crowd be dispersed and the Chief Constable ordered Captain Blake to fire above the crowd. Blake refused to give the order because the Riot Act had not been read at which point, according to the press, Browne ran up to the front part of the train where he found Mr Clough, a local magistrate. He said to him 'For God's sake give the order to fire or we shall all be murdered.' He then called out 'Fire!' Still Captain Blake was reluctant but, when the crowd stormed the railway platform, he eventually gave the order and between twelve and fifteen shots were fired at which point, the rioters immediately broke up.

No police or military personnel lost their lives, although many were injured. The crowd dispersed taking their injured away with them as they were reluctant to be treated by the doctors present at the scene. Four civilians were killed when the soldiers opened fire. Edward Bellis, 22 years of age, a young blacksmith from Treuddyn, was shot in the abdomen, and taken by his friends to Pontblyddyn where he died next morning. Robert Hannaby, a collier from Moss (near Wrexham), was shot through the face and died in Tyddyn Street. Margaret Husband a woman from Chester, a 19 year old servant of the Reverend Roger Edwards, a spectator who was caught up in the melee, died three days later, as did Elizabeth Jones, aged 50 years, from Coed Talon, who was shot in the back. Charles Keane, manager of the Mold Foundry, an innocent bystander, was shot through the shoulder but later recovered from his wound.

Ten men were eventually brought before the magistrates accused of rioting, six of whom were tried on 6 August before Lord Chief Justice Bovill on charges of riot and assault. They came from Hope, Leeswood,

The riot at Mold Station.

The Illustrated London News *impression of the riot at Mold Station, showing the moment when the troops opened fire.*

Nercwys and Mold. Their defence was paid for by contributions from their fellow miners.

In the meantime, John Young's reappearance at Leeswood Green on 10 June resulted in a strike which held firm until the middle of August. Angered and frustrated the Leeswood colliers and their wives abducted John Young again on 22 July and he was escorted to Queensferry by David Philips, who sought to protect him from harm.

Those arrested for the riot of 2 June and the second abduction of John Young in July, faced separate trials at Mold Assizes beginning on 6 August and lasting for three-and-a-half days. At the trial of the rioters, six of the seven defendants were positively identified, found guilty and sentenced to ten years penal servitude. Three men were tried for the second abduction of Young, found guilty and imprisoned for periods up to eighteen months. David Philips was given the longest sentence, despite Young agreeing that he had protected him from injury and shown him kindness. The jury which reached the verdicts included four coal-owners who were landowners receiving royalties from coal mines. By this time, some of the Leeswood colliers were reported to be begging in the streets of Wrexham. The prisoners were removed in chains, surrounded by cavalry with swords drawn.

After the riots, the Leeswood colliers ironically turned to England for aid and protection and joined the Amalgamated Association of Miners (AAM), a move which eventually helped to reduce tension and misunderstanding between the Welsh and English.

In Mold, the clerk of the local board wrote the day after the trial to thank the police and military for their support and sacrifices during the riot. At a special meeting of the board held on 26 June 1872, it was proposed

That this Board memorialise the Court of Quarter Sessions to intercede with the Lord Chief Justice at the next Assizes on behalf of the Convicts now under sentence of Penal Servitude for participating in the Mold Riot in 1869 and that the Chairman and Clerk be a deputation to present the demand … we have no wish to condone their offences in the least, but rather that the power of the law should always be upheld.

We cannot help thinking, not withstanding, that the men in question were not the leaders of the agitation which led to the riot, but were in fact, entrapped into a violation of the law by others, who have escaped punishment [and] we feel assured that public opinion in the district would justify any steps taken by your worshipful court in acceding to our memorial.'[35]

Daniel Owen was aged thirty-three when the riot took place not far from his workshop in Mold. Two years previously having given up training for the Methodist ministry, he had resumed working as a tailor in Angel Jones's shop where the progress of the strike was closely followed. Customers and passing witnesses provided the staff with continual updates and every snippet of news was devoured, every rumour believed, and eventually justice and injustice measured as assiduously as the fitting of a new suit of clothes. Fourteen years were to pass before Daniel Owen published *Rhys Lewis* in which he fashioned the material he had gathered during those summer months into his own sympathetic story of the events.[36]

The newspaper accounts immediately following the riots gave no time for their authors to reflect on why they had occurred. Obviously they showed no sympathy for the rioters who were generally described by the English correspondents as ignorant, violent, Welsh-speaking colliers, intent on causing destruction to property and trouble to the Tory magistracy. Daniel Owen's veiled account of the Mold riots in *Rhys Lewis* is more than a press report. It is a passionate exercise in the presentation of a Welsh mining community's reaction to an industrial dispute and the divisions it caused. Giving an account of the riots through the vehicle of a novel gave Owen an opportunity to get to the bottom of the motives of all the parties involved. The complexities and complications of the series of events which made up the riots were simplified by him in order to give a clearer understanding of what were the motives and characterisation of the main actors in the drama. For this purpose, he created a group of characters to represent all classes in the district. The social atmosphere in Mold in 1869 appeared to be a prelude to industrial prosperity. The division of the fruits of the earth such as coal and lead and profits were, in the eyes of some social observers, unequally distributed. The story of the riot gave Owen the opportunity to comment on the injustice which existed in society and on a system of production and distribution which many thought was unfairly in the hands of the master and too often left the servant deprived and oppressed. The novel *Rhys Lewis* gave Owen an opportunity to dismiss the officially accepted account of the riot and to present a different view of the rioters themselves the majority of whom he said '… were sober, industrious and moral; but amongst them were a number of worthless characters, given to excessive drinking.'

How some of the colliers set fiercely upon the police who were conveying my brother and his associates to prison; how the assailants were arrested, tried, and found guilty; how the military were called out, were attacked and beaten; and how, under cruellest provocation, they opened fire upon the rioters, killing several, and so on, it does not concern me to narrate. I can say this much, when the disturbance was at its highest, the feeling of the majority, which included some men of reason and intelligence, was in favour of the colliers; but when things had cooled down, and opportunity was given of looking calmly at the circumstances, these same people were obliged to acknowledge the unwisdom and iniquity of the whole proceedings, and to view with apprehension the frightful lengths to which even sensible and religious men may be led when governed by their passions, instead of by reason and by grace.[37]

In order to provide a straightforward narrative, Owen selected, rearranged and combined different events. A good example of this is that the three attacks on the manager John Young (Strangle) are condensed into one. Owen concentrates on the events at 'Red Fields' (Leeswood Green Colliery) and casts Bob Lewis as the colliers' spokesman,

He stood upon a high mound, with a number of the principal colliers at the Red Field Pit about him, and a tremendous crowd below … His subject was the injustice and hardship suffered by the workmen, by reason of the

After the death of Angel Jones, Daniel Owen set up his own business and is seen here(third from the left) with his tailoring staff.

arrogance and incapacity of the official. He proved, to the satisfaction of those who heard him, that the 'Lankies' knew nothing of Welsh mining operations, that they oppressed the men, and ruined the masters by their conduct.[38]

Owen abhorred the treatment of the Welsh workers by their English bosses and was furious at the injustice meted out to Abraham Jones.

At one time 'all things under the earth' were managed by a simple, honest Welshman, named Abraham Jones, a deacon with the Congregationalists. He was a cool, strong-minded man, possessing great influence with those under him. Whatever the dispute arose amongst them, it only wanted Abraham Jones to arbitrate, and everything was settled at once … He proved himself at all times, a sincere friend of the workman, knowing well what it was to have been a workman himself. With him it was a matter of conscience to keep his eyes open to the welfare of the employers who paid him his salary … He was considered one of the most expert practical colliers in the country, and, during his management, everything went on smoothly and without any hitch or disturbance worth the mention.

He laboured under one great disadvantage in his connection with his chiefs; his English was so imperfect that, in consultation with them, it appeared at times as if he were not perfectly straightforward in his story.

The directors asked Abraham Jones to resign, an excuse the workmen thought for the management to replace him with a 'hard-up friend', Mr Strangle, who is described as,[39]

… a middle-aged personage, fat-paunched and blustering, who carried in his own person all the roughness, the slovenliness and ignorance of his tribe at Wigan … His speech, however, was but a trifling drawback compared to his insufferable behaviour towards everybody about him … Abraham Jones's old flannel jacket was much more capable of managing the Red Fields works than Mr Strangle. The antagonism of the man was rivalled only by his own hatred of Wales and the Welsh.[40]

Bob Lewis declares he will fight for justice,

Someone must fight the battle of the Red Fields workmen before they are rid of their tyranny, and if I and my associates fall while sounding the battle-trumpet, let it be so; the call to arms has gone forth, we have justice on our side, and others, even though we do not, will reap the rich fruits of the victory which is bound to follow.[41]

The workmen at Red Fields are paid off and Mr Strangle is seized and abducted,

No sooner did he make his appearance than scores of throats opened out upon him, like a pack of hounds in full cry. A fierce rush was made towards him, and he was carried along the road leading to the railway station like a straw before the whirlwind. The two officers, with incredible pluck, endeavoured to protect him and to rescue him from the infuriated colliers; and so did Bob and others.[42]

Bob Lewis and his companions are arrested for the abduction of Mr Strangle and appear in court.

The magistrates on the bench were Mr Brown, the clergyman, and the gentleman from the Hall. As I have previously observed, Mr Brown was a genial, kindly man; but the owner of the Hall was quite a different personage. The latter was huge, unwieldy, pompous, overbearing, and merciless. One would think that everybody and everything had been created for his service … Nobody ever discovered what other qualifications the gentleman from the Hall possessed for the magisterial bench, except that he was a rank Tory, a zealous Churchman, was very wealthy, and always wore spurs, save when in bed.[43]

Injustice continues in the court room when Bob Lewis and the other prisoners are convicted on the false evidence of Mr Strangle and the two police officers 'although neither overseer nor constables understood a word of Welsh, they declared on oath that Bob had instigated the attack, for they said, they heard him naming Mr Strangle when the rush was made upon that individual by the workmen'.

Bob Lewis and the other prisoners refuse offers to be defended and are sentenced. The prisoners are taken outside and the crowd begin to behave in a riotous manner.[44]

Owen's interpretation of the events surrounding the Mold Riots of 1869 shows his ability to express an informed opinion about the position of the working man in his relationship with those upon whom he was dependent: land-owners, coal and lead work proprietors and their overseers, tradesmen, schoolmasters and all in a position of authority. The foundation of his political judgement and sympathy was primarily the values he had learned from his mother. These were the Biblical values of justice, righteousness and mercy, which were totally opposed to the oppression and exploitation of any member of society. For Owen, the primacy of the gospel message of love in caring for all members of society, through acts of kindness and the exercise of charity, is the basic criterion for the judgement of any word and deed whenever and wherever expressed. Throughout his novels there is fierce condemnation of hypocrisy, cruelty, indifference and intolerance, both to the behaviour of members of the perfect society of the baptised and those in the world at large.

Daniel Owen was an acute observer of people, events, and places happening around him. The apprenticeship he served as a tailor in Angel Jones' workshop had taught him to express himself and argue in defence of those values which he passionately held dear. He had prepared himself to express his views on issues which concerned both the material and spiritual welfare of society. We have two brief glimpses of his potential as a 'people's politician.'

The first is a speech which he made at a Liberal dinner in Mold in 1873. W.H. Gladstone, MP, the eldest son of the Prime Minister was present and he reported to his father that, 'The most striking speech was by a tailor in Mold, Daniel Owen, who I was told went to Bala College to educate himself.'[45] Owen had been nominated to propose the toast on behalf of the working man and, at a time of industrial unrest, spoke up in their defence in an honest and reasonable address which showed common sense, courage and restraint,

Undoubtedly your mind reverts to strikes and trade unions. I am not going to advocate trade-unions here tonight. They are not the best thing for the working man. But on the other hand they are not the incarnation of wickedness that they were represented to be by a gentleman in this room last week. It depends a great deal on your standpoint. The same institution may wear quite a different aspect to the working man, from what it represents to a country gentleman and a magistrate.

He re-echoed Gladstone's passion for social justice and self-improvement as he spoke of the influence of education on their situation,

They are more respected, they are better paid, and best of all they are better educated. A fair majority, I should say of the working men of this country can read their books and their newspapers, and possess the means of what is going on in the world. And what has been the result of this education? You will say uneasiness, discontent – I admit it; with a modification. If you want a man that can never say no – and lick the rod of tyranny, then keep him from his books and papers, bar the way to his intellect…When the education of the working class will be somewhat

TO THE
ELECTORS
OF THE
MOLD URBAN DISTRICT COUNCIL.

LADIES AND GENTLEMEN,

Next Saturday, December 15th, you will be called upon to elect Fifteen Members on the MOLD URBAN DISTRICT COUNCIL. Amongst the host of candidates I find my own name. Strenuous efforts, I know, are being made by many of them to ensure their return, and I find no fault with them on that account. But as I do not myself intend to canvass you personally, nor to enlist anybody else to canvass on my behalf (not that I do not place the highest value on every individual vote, but because I do not approve of canvassing where it can be avoided, particularly in municipal contests), perhaps it will not be out of place for me to state in a few words my views on one or two points around which this election will turn, and upon which the issue will depend.

To many, this will be superfluous, as my record during my five years' service on the LOCAL BOARD is well-known. I trust that the great bulk of the electors will admit that cleanliness, pure air, and pure water, are of paramount importance to every town, and that the furtherance of every measure in that direction is the cheapest and best in the end. On the other hand I honestly think that a great deal of nonsense is spoken about sanitation. I do not believe in a sanitarian who enjoys his bacon for breakfast and smells a pigstye a mile off. In the Local Board I have advocated, almost single-handed, that every cottager ought to have the privilege of keeping a pig, provided he keeps the "*cut*" clean. The pig is not only the working-man's bank, but his delight also.

I feel certain that something in the way of drainage is required in our dear old town of Mold. But at the same time I believe that its low sanitary condition is very much exaggerated in some quarters, and that the town is no worse, if as bad, as many other *old* town in North Wales from a sanitary point of view. To be able to do away with all manner of dirt is Utopian. The Drainage Scheme presented to and approved by the *late* Local Board is, I believe, a good one. The unfortunate part of the matter is that the time is inopportune—trade is bad, and Mold is not what it used to be. Too many of us have a difficulty in making both ends meet. The drainage question is a very big and important question, and ought to be well and carefully handled. Whatever is done in this matter—and something must be done whoever you will elect on your Council—ought, in the face of present circumstances of trade, to be done in the most economical way.

"*Ladies and Gentlemen*," as old Simpson of yore said, "*them is my sentiments.*" If I am elected by you on the Council, I will endeavour to serve you to the best of my poor ability: if I am not elected I shall be satisfied—in good humour, and friendly with you all.

Your Obedient Servant,

DANIEL OWEN.

AT
ETHOLWYR
CYNGOR DINESIG
RHANBARTH YR
WYDDGRUG.

GYD-DRETHDALWYR,

Dydd Sadwrn nesaf, Rhagfyr 15fed, gelwir arnoch i ethol Cyngor sydd i ddisodli y diweddar LOCAL BOARD o dragywyddol, os nad o fendigedig goffadwriaeth. Mae llu o ymgeiswyr am eich ffafr, ac yn eu plith y mae eich anheilwng was. Nid wyf yn bwriadu eich canfasio, ond yr wyf yn anfon atoch y peth tebycaf i mi fy hun a welsoch erioed. Wedi byw yn eich mysg fy holl oes dylech wybod rhywbeth am danaf. Nid oes genyf ddawn i ganmawl fy hun, a phe buasai y ddawn genyf ni buaswn yn ei defnyddio. Os oes gwell dynion ar y maes—os ydynt yn cynnrychioli eich dymuniadau yn well, ar bob cyfrif dewiswch hwynt. Ond cynghorwn bob etholwr sydd yn perthyn i'r Dosbarth Gweithiol, fel fy hunan, ofyn y cwestiwn hwn i bob ymgeisydd :—

'A wyt ti 'n dyfal dal yn dyn
Mai iachus yw cadw mochyn !

Gwyddoch yn burion fy mod wedi dadleu hyn ar y Bwrdd Lleol oreu y gallwn. Peidiwch a gwrando ar ddyeithriaid dibrofiad, ond cofiwch hen air ein cyn-dadau :—

Mae nghorob dda, a ham,
Yn nhop y tŷ 'n gytun ;
A llwyth o datws yn yr hog
Yn hendwr i bob dyn.

Os dewiswch fy ethol fel un o'ch cynnrychiolwyr gwnaf fy ngoreu i'ch gwasanaethu yn ol fy ngallu fei yr ydwyf wedi gwneyd eisoes. Os byddwch yn hytrach yn dewis rhywun arall— pobpeth yn dda—ni fyddwn yn llai cyfeillgar,

Yr eiddoch, mewn natur dda,

DANIEL OWEN.

---

advanced, a better sense will be shown on the part of the employed, and let us hope a little less arrogance on the part of the employer, and disputes will melt away under the congenial influence of arbitration.[46]

The second example of Owen as a 'people's politician' is found in a printed address he made to the electors of the Mold Urban District Council in December 1894. It shows the same qualities of humanity, humour, common-sense and modesty which he demonstrated in *Y Dreflan*. He appealed to the electorate for their support on the record of his five years' service on the local board. He reminded them that the main issue before them was the question of sanitation, which he agreed 'is of paramount importance,' but admitted,

> On the other hand I honestly think that a great deal of nonsense is spoken about sanitation. I do not believe in a sanitarian who enjoys his bacon for breakfast and smells a pigstye [sic] a mile off. In the Local Board I have advocated, almost single-handed, that every cottager ought to have the privilege of keeping a pig … The pig is not only the working-man's bank, but his delight also.

After humouring the electorate he comes to the point,

> The Drainage Scheme is I believe a good one … The unfortunate matter is that the time is inopportune- trade is bad, and Mold is not what it used to be. Too many of us have a difficulty in making both ends meet. The drainage question is a very big and important question, and ought to be well and carefully handled in the face of present circumstance of trade, to be done in the most economical way … If I am elected by you on the Council, I will endeavour to serve you to the best of my poor ability: if I am not elected I shall be satisfied – in good humour and friendly to you all.

The people of Mold did elect him and he became the first chairman of Mold Urban District Council. He died on 22 October 1895, during his term of office.

The town of Mold was shaped and invigorated in the nineteenth century through the prosperity of its industry and trade and the emergence of more repre-

Election campaign posters for Daniel Owen who was seeking election onto the Mold UDC (top) and Mold Town Council (bottom).

TOWN HALL, MOLD, FLINTSHIRE.

For Theatrical and Dramatic Performances, Magic Lantern and Ghost Entertainments, Concerts, Balls, Lectures, Meetings, &c.

Dimensions :— 52 by 44 clear of the Platform.   Platform 12ft. deep, 26ft. wide.
Two Ante-rooms 18 by 16 feet each.   Lavatories, &c.

SCALE OF CHARGES :—

Concerts, Lectures, Meetings, &c.	£	s.	d.	Theatrical, Dramatic, and other Entertainments.	£	s.	d.
One Night	1	15	0	One Night	2	2	0
Two Nights...	3	3	0	Two Nights...	3	15	0
Three Nights	4	4	0	Three Nights	5	0	0
Each succeeding Night...	1	1	0	Each succeeding Night...	1	5	0

The above Charges include Gas.

	£	s.	d.	SMALL ROOMS ONLY.			
Per Day (till 5 p.m.) without Gas ...	1	5	0	Without Gas (till 5 p.m.) One room 4/-, Both 6/6			
Ball (Day and Night)	5	5	0	With Gas ... ... ,, 5/-, ,, 7/6			

For all other particulars as to Payments and Regulations, apply to **Mr. Isaac Jones,**

Advert for theatrical and dramatic performances at the Town Hall, c.1900.

sentative institutions of government which were centred there. The townscape on the eve of the Great War reflected both the solidity of Victorian values and the confidence and flamboyance of the Edwardian summer which briefly blossomed before the horror of war erupted.

Notes

1. See T. W. Pritchard, *History of the Old Parish of Hawarden,* op cit, p.179.
2. FRO D/GW/1959.
3. Daniel Owen, *Y Dreflan,* ms translated by T. Ceiriog Williams, p.38.
4. Henry Taylor, *Historic Notices of Flint,* p.109.
5. See discussion in Mold Gleanings by *Penman,* F.J. Violet, Feb/March, FRO and County Library.
6. *Chester Chronicle,* 8 July 1871.
7. *Wrexham Weekly Advertiser,* 23 September 1865.
8. See entry in the *Oxford Dictionary of National Biography.*
9. T.W. Pritchard, *Old Parish of Hawarden,* op cit, p.208.
10. FRO D/DM/219/2.
11. ibid, p.11.
12. ibid, p.4.
13. *The Chester Chronicle,* 11/9/1829.
14. Figures for Flintshire production: 1865 – 6,000 tons; 1885 – 2,000 tons. Employment: 1901 – 1,004; 1911 – 448; 1914 – 400.
15. FRO D/DM/5218. 2/11/1863 J. Tolson White's report 'the Mines and Minerals on the Mostyn Estate.'
16. ibid.
17. Tim Jones, op cit, *Rioting in North East Wales, 1536–1918,* Wrexham, 1997, pp.49–50.
18. See chapter 7 for its beginning in 1792 and also Diane J.P. Johnson, *Ystrad Alun,* 4, 2003.
19. *The Flintshire Observer,* 16/11/1866.
20. FRO NT/2 and NT/1326.
21. This list does not claim to be complete. For example the Bistre, Buckley and Ewloe area is omitted from the discussion, but see T.W. Pritchard, *The Making of Buckley and District,* op cit.
22. See L. Lloyd Gruffydd, *Ystrad Alun* 2 and the *Chester Chronicle,* 12 May 1837.
23. *Rhys Lewis,* trans, p.194.
24. Finally under the management of G.H. Hollingsworth 1889. In liquidation 1896 FRO D/CL/118.
25. FRO D/DM/90/1, Plans and sections 1861–1910.
26. Worked in 1869, ibid.
27. *Chester Chronicle* 4 October 1844, and leases of mines in Mold DM/KK/991, 993–5.
28. FRO D/DM/344/1–3.
29. Report by Ronald Johnstone & Sons, mining engineers, Glasgow. Transcript by K. Lloyd Gruffydd.
30. Op cit, Taylor Report Mold Mines 1827 D/DM 219/92, p.7.
31. See Johnstone Report 1913 for Nercwys area; and J.R. Thomas and M. Thomas, op cit.
32. The railways in the Mold district are thoroughly discussed by M. Griffiths and J.R. Thomas in 'Industrial Railways and Tramways of Flintshire [7 parts], *Archive,* nos. 14–22, 1998–9.
33. Widely reported in National newspapers. For local reports see the *Chester Chronicle, Flintshire Observer* and *Baner ac Amserau Cymru,* etc., May and June 1869.
34. Ishmael and John Jones received sentences of one month's hard labour. William Hughes and Edwin Jones were fined 10s each with costs.

Robert Davies, Richard Taylor, John Hughes and Thomas Jones were fined £1 each with costs.

35. FRO Mold Local Board minutes, p.372 for 26 June 1872.
36. This was discussed by Bedwyr Lewis Jones in 1982 in the seventh Daniel Owen Memorial Lecture *The Two Phases of Daniel Owen's Career as a Writer*. The events surrounding the Mold Riots in 1869 are used in *Rhys Lewis,* particularly in chapters xvi–xvii. This section depends on these sources.
37. *Rhys Lewis,* trans pp.127–8.
38. ibid, pp.108–9.
39. ibid, p.110f.
40. ibid, p.112.
41. ibid, p.115.
42. ibid, p.118.
43. ibid, p.124.
44. ibid, pp.124–5
45. FRO D/DM/521/31/3.
46. *Wrexham Advertiser*, 25 January 1873.

12: The twentieth century

The twentieth century was a period when the main influences in society were local government and national events. Developments in Mold were in the main shaped by the policies of central government, which controlled expenditure and promulgated legislation, and by local agencies who implemented them. As far as Mold was concerned, the local agencies were Mold Urban District Council (1895–1974) and Flintshire County Council (1888–1974). The dominance of the Liberal party in Wales stemmed from the time of the leadership of William Gladstone in 1869 to the charismatic years of Lloyd George, who was in decline by 1922. During this time, Welsh society had found a new confidence through the partnership of the Liberals and the Nonconformists. Governments, both national and local,were chosen by an increased electorate composed mainly of Nonconformists, and the role of the gentry was significantly reduced.

Overshadowing all the changes in government were the two world wars and the major economic depressions of the 1920s and 1930s, which resulted in poverty, unemployment and social deprivation, issues which were not resolved until the introduction of major welfare reforms in health, housing and education in the years after the Second World War.

The landscape of both town and countryside was transformed to a greater extent during the twentieth century than in the previous two thousand years. The petrol engine and road transport made local railways uneconomic and horse transport archaic, and created an insatiable demand for parking spaces in town centres making the construction of roads to by-pass them a necessity.

Throughout the twentieth century, life for the entire population was transformed by electricity, radio and television, enhanced by new technology, and lengthened by improvements in medicine and care. All these raised the general standard of living and changed the environment. On the employment front, mining almost ceased in the region and agriculture became mechanised, thereby providing work for fewer people.

The map on page 234 distinguishes periods of growth between c.1100 and 2010 which have been the subject of successive chapters of this study. At its core is the extent of the first phase of development between 1100 and 1536. This is the medieval borough, the 'decayed' town seen by John Leland in 1539, with its limits as far south as Chester Street. The next major period of growth lasted from 1536 to 1839 and the map shows the extension of Mold towards the south east, along Wrexham Street, Ruthin Road, Chester Street and the rear of High Street. The expansion in the shorter period between 1839 and 1910 included important additions to commercial life, including the development of professional services, retail trades, the establishment of civic buildings in response to local government reform, and Victorian and Edwardian urban housing. The final phase of growth, from 1910 to 2010, is that which experienced the greatest geographical expansion of the town. This is best analysed on the second map, 'Mold: Yr Wyddgrug, 2012' which shows details of the following aspects of the urban townscape.

1. Habitation – the growth of housing estates throughout the urban area, although the major central medieval artery remains at the centre of the town.

2. The commercial centre – throughout the centuries this has been in the area of High Street, Chester Street, Wrexham Street and New Street. It was joined at the beginning of the twentieth century by Earl Road and in the 1980s by an open shopping precinct which leads to nearby retail markets. All of these developments have

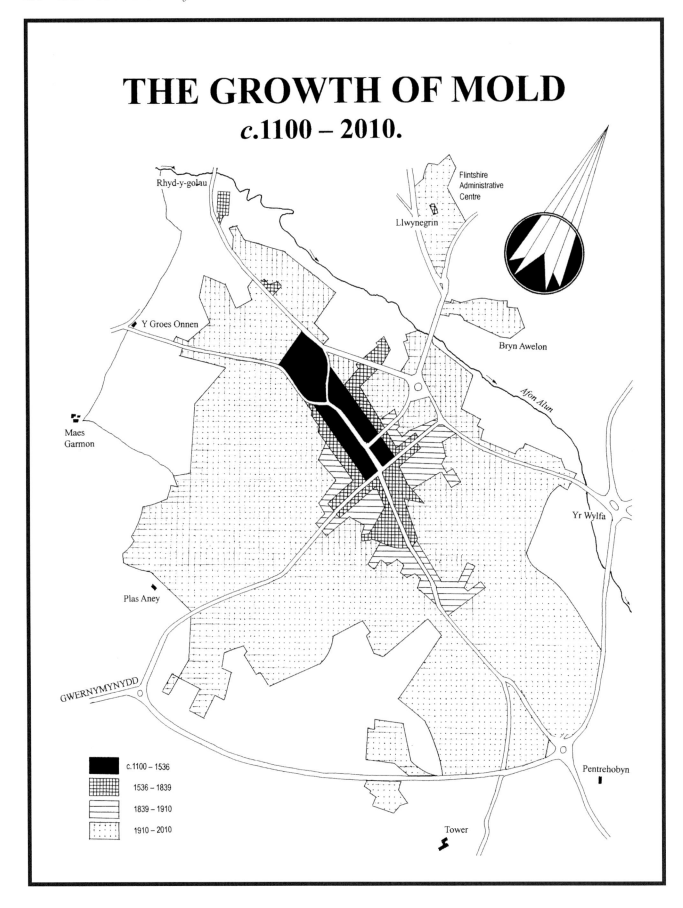

THE GROWTH OF MOLD
*c.*1100 – 2010.

Rhyd-y-golau

Flintshire
Administrative
Centre

Llwynegrin

Y Groes Onnen

Bryn Awelon

Afon Alun

Maes
Garmon

Yr Wylfa

Plas Aney

GWERNYMYNYDD

Pentrehobyn

	c.1100 – 1536
	1536 – 1839
	1839 – 1910
	1910 – 2010

Tower

necessitated the provision of car parking spaces a major factor to be considered by any planning committee. Community facilities have been introduced on the periphery of the urban area in the form of schools, community centres and recreation areas. With the decline and closure of coal mining after the First World War land became available for redevelopment close to the boundaries of the urban area. The largest of these sites, at Bromfield and Broncoed, were developed into industrial estates, providing employment in light industries.

Members of the Bromfield Mine Rescue Team, pre 1914.

The major impression conveyed by the two maps is the compactness of the town of Mold and the achievement of the local authorities and planners in containing the town and maintaining a balance of essential community services. This arrangement has generally succeeded in integrating a number of separate developments which include the conservation and promotion of historic buildings, the introduction of community and leisure facilities, the replacement of school buildings and the formation of major industrial parks.

The viability of the town depended on the establishment, maintenance and adaptation of the free movement of traffic into and out of the town. Those who do not wish to use the town centre have been provided with an alternative route as well as those who seek a quick exit. The authorities have successfully ensured that alternative traffic systems are in place to facilitate a pedestrianised area for the twice weekly street markets. Mold also has a livestock mart on Monday and Friday where dealers, farmers and auctioneers gather to do business on the same site they have occupied for over a century. The survival of the old traditional commercial activity in the town centre has been achieved through the creation of a new out of town administrative centre, County Hall, on the former Llwynegryn estate which brings together county offices, law courts, library headquarters, Theatre Clwyd (which incorporates a cinema and is now called Clwyd Theatre Cymru). The site is easily accessible by road and does not impede other traffic. The transfer of civic functions to this site during the 1970s removed the pressure from overcrowding of civic buildings and an increasingly congested town centre and enabled the re-use of the former County Hall Fields site. It has provided a choice of other options to town planners, the most beneficial of which was the siting of the bus station there.

The character of the town of Mold was not destroyed in the twentieth century and it continues to have a viable community and its development has followed the same historic pattern identified in previous centuries, that of an historic market town which serves as a civic centre, providing a limited variety of opportunities for employment and retaining its Anglo-Welsh cultural traditions.

Politics

Mold became a Contributory Borough in 1832 and, for electoral purposes, was part of the Flint Boroughs' constituency until 1918. The electorate then voted in the Flintshire County constituency until 1950 when the county was divided electorally into East and West Flintshire. Further reorganisation of the electoral boundaries were made in 1983. Before electoral reform was instigated in 1832, parliamentary representation of both the county and borough seats in Flintshire was shared between the leading county families of Mostyn, Glynne, Hanmer and others, either by contest or arrangement. The extension of the franchise in 1867, 1884

Sir John Herbert Lewis, MP.

and 1918 led to a substantial increase in the electorate and the end of domination of local politics by the gentry.

The period of Liberal domination (under Gladstone, Asquith and Lloyd George), which lasted from the 1880s to 1920s, was marked by a combination of a strong Welsh economy and a large Welsh Nonconformist pressure group which pushed local government and educational reform and an Act for the Disestablishment and Disendowment of the Anglican Church in Wales through Parliament. This political ascendancy however ended in 1922, when the party was exhausted and disillusioned by a war that had been unparalleled in its cost, carnage and consequences. The Liberal party gradually surrendered its power to its old adversaries, the Conservatives and the rising Labour party.

Local personalities who were involved in politics during these years were:[1]

Members of Parliament for Flint Boroughs

1874–8 — Peter Ellis Eyton (born Rhyl 1827, died 1878), Liberal party. He was registrar of the County Court for Mold and Flint. He gave £210 to the Mold Local Board towards library facilities.

1878–92 — John Roberts of Abergele (born Liverpool 1835, died 1894) was a Liberal and a Gladstonian, who successfully retained the seat on three occasions before his retirement.

1892–1906 — Sir John Herbert Lewis (born Mostyn 1858, died 1933) the son of a Liverpool merchant and great-nephew of Thomas Jones of Denbigh, a Calvinistic Methodist minister. A lawyer by profession, in 1889 he became first chairman of the new Flintshire County Council. He entered Parliament in 1892 as a Liberal, representing the Flint Boroughs until 1906, the County until 1918, and the University of Wales until his retirement in 1922. He has been described as 'an honourable, peaceful man of Flintshire, who fought the good fight for educational and other reform, and who stuck to Lloyd George through thick and thin.'[2] He held an influential position in the Liberal administration as a whip and Secretary of the Local Government Board in 1909 and Parliamentary Secretary of the Board of Education in 1915. Lewis was a successful advocate for public grants to the National Museum of Wales and the National Library of Wales and was the latter organisation's president from 1926–33. It was said in his obituary 'that during his time in parliament Lewis did more constructive work for Welsh institutions than anybody else.'[3]

1913–8 — Thomas Henry Parry, DSO (1878–1939), the last member to hold the Flint Boroughs seat before it was abolished in 1918, when he was returned unopposed as the Liberal member for Flintshire. He was re-elected in November 1922 and sat until he was defeated in 1924. He was the son of Thomas Parry of Mold, a distinguished Calvinistic Methodist. Educated at the Alun School, the University College, Aberystwyth and Christ's College, Cambridge, he practised as a barrister on the Chester circuit. During the First World War he had a distinguished record commanding the 5th and 6th Battalions, Royal Welsh Fusiliers and was wounded at Suvla Bay and later at Gaza. Serious illness prevented his presence at the electoral contest of 1924 when he was defeated by E.H.G. Roberts the Conservative candidate.

Colonel Thomas Henry Parry, DSO, MP (right).

Town Hall, Mold.

The ascendancy of the Liberal party and their partnership with the Nonconformists was at an end. Lloyd George failed to receive sufficient support from a splintered and confused party whose members could not decide how to vote. Lloyd George had abandoned free trade, the Nonconformists had lost interest in politics and increasing unemployment was turning other members of the party in Wales to the left.

During the first part of the twentieth century, the daily life of the people of Mold was dramatically improved by the interaction of two new local authorities both of which had a presence in Mold. The first and largest of these was Flintshire County Council which was established in 1888 with particular responsiblity for education, health and roads. With the existing Quarter Sessions, the newly-formed County Council also became the statutory police authority. It influenced improvements in agriculture and horticulture through its educational services and as the landlord of a number of newly-acquired smallholdings. The second body was Mold Urban District Council, a newly-established local government authority which replaced the local board in 1894. It had fifteen elected representatives and its actions and decisions created and improved the infrastructure of the town with the continuing aid of government grants for sewerage, drainage, sanitation, water supply, street lighting, slum clearance, the building of corporation housing and the provision of community services and leisure facilities.

Due to central government legislation being required to enable local authorities to introduce measures to improve education, health and welfare, many such reforms were costly and were not implemented until the passing of the Parliament Act of 1911 enabled the Liberal government to carry through its radical budget of welfare reform on a national scale. Chancellor of the Exchequer, David Lloyd George, introduced a programme of legislation which changed the lives of the people of Britain by introducing state pensions, unemployment insurance, school medical inspections and the first tentative provision of school meals (for large families only). The core of welfare legislation laid down by the Liberal government before 1914 was the only safety-net available for the poor, the sick and the unemployed.

As a result of the local political reforms and changes, Mold gradually became an important administrative centre for Flintshire. This demonstration of the increasing functions of local government was marked by the construction of new civic buildings. The outstanding Mold architect of the twentieth century was Frederick A. Roberts, who created a group of distinctive buildings in the town centre. He was born in 1885 and educated at the Alun County School and Grosvenor Art School Chester. He was articled to James Strong of Liverpool and commenced practice in Mold 1906. He was responsible for a number of buildings grouped together in Earl Road which were described by the architectural historian, Hubbard, as 'an Edwardian

Bromfield Hall, Mold, home of Peter E. Roberts, JP.

Post Office, Chester Street.

Baroque group of limestone and bright red brick, with "Queen Anne" detail'. These buildings included the Town Hall (1911–12), 'only five bays but effectively proud and confident' which was the gift of Peter E. Roberts, JP of Bromfield Hall. A native of Mold, Roberts began his business life in the town in the early 1850s when he was apprenticed to a draper. He later went to Chester, Bury in Lancashire and London before settling in Burnley where he built up a large drapery business. He made his fortune through developing the idea of and manufacturing the Wood-Milne rubber heel that could be fitted to a boot which was sold world-wide. Peter Roberts eventually returned to Mold, entered public life and was a member and chairman of Mold Urban District Council. As a mark of loyalty to King George V, and of affection for his native town, he made a gift of the Town Hall. The foundation stone was laid at the time of the Coronation in 1911 and the building was opened in October the following year. It consisted of a council chamber, a lecture hall, public library and reading room. The library was presented by the Mold Cosmopolitan Society and a donation for the purchase of more books was made by J.W. Summers, MP. Peter Roberts left Mold in 1915 for health reasons to reside in Bournemouth and died there the following year.

Other buildings in the Earl Road group are Cambrian House (the former County Court offices), Earl Chambers and the Territorial Association Building next to the Town Hall, the administrative centre for the county's volunteer battalions.

Also designed by F.A. Roberts was the Post Office, opened in Chester Street in 1906, which was later demolished to build a telephone exchange.

County Offices and the old Militia Barracks, collectively known as County Hall Fields.

The First World War

Mold was not unfamiliar with the presence of soldiers as a militia had been raised in Flintshire for centuries and used at the beginning of the nineteenth century to control striking miners. In the absence of militia, regular troops were called upon when the situation was serious enough to assist the county constabulary to restore order, notably on the occasion of the Mold riots. By the time of the declaration of war in August 1914, the town possessed two buildings that were associated with the military, the Drill Hall in King Street and the recently built Territorial Force Association building in Earl Road. The experience of conflicts in far-flung corners of the Empire and from threats from other world powers such as France and Russia, as well as from Fenians in Ireland, resulted in a complete reorganisation of the British Army by the Secretary of State for War, Richard Haldane. The Territorial and Reserve Forces Act of 1907 led to the formation of the Territorial Force which merged the old Volunteer units of each county into a new Territorial Force battalion of existing line regiments. In Mold, the 5th (Flintshire) Battalion, Royal Welsh Fusiliers was formed on 1 April 1908 and received its colours from King Edward VII at Windsor.

The Great War which broke out on 4 August 1914, claimed the lives of approximately 370 Mold men and women, whose names are recorded on the War Memorial erected in 1925 beside the entrance to Bailey Hill, erected by Mold UDC (F.A Roberts, architect). Chapels, churches and schools remembered their own dead on their own memorials. Within a fortnight of the signing the Armistice on 11 November 1918, members of the congregation of Mold Parish Church decided to set aside the north chapel as a memorial to over 130 members who had 'laid down their lives for King and country.' The large plaque was a design of Sir Thomas Jackson. The church also decided to install a new organ as a tribute to their sacrifice. Mold men and women served in every theatre of the war – France, Gallipoli, Mesopotamia, Salonika, Palestine, Africa and India. They served in all ranks in many regiments, but particularly in the Royal Welsh Fusiliers (most notably in the 5th Battalion). Others died at sea and a few in prison camps. Every street lost someone and the old gentry families from Pentrehobyn, Rhual, Plas Teg, Fron and Tyddyn also suffered losses. On the home front Leeswood Hall became a military hospital.

One of the local war heroes was the Member of Parliament for Flintshire Boroughs, Lieutenant-Colonel Thomas Henry Parry, who commanded the 5th Battalion, Royal Welsh Fusiliers at Suvla Bay in Gallipoli and

Members of 5th Battalion, Royal Welsh Fusiliers (TF) on Mold Station, c.1914.

Mold Church Organ Fund appeal, offering a new Ford motor car as the first prize in a raffle. Seated in the car are women munitions workers from the Queensferry works.

later at Gaza in Palestine where he was awarded a DSO. He was a member of Bethesda Chapel and his father, Thomas Parry, JP, was a much-respected Nonconformist local politician, who described himself as a merchant and was therefore ideal for his appointment in 1917 as chairman of the Mold Food Control Committee.[5] They received their orders from Lord Rhondda, Lloyd George's minister of food, who was prodigal with his directives, sending out over 500, at the rate of one a day. By 1917, with no sign of an end to the war, and food being in short supply, people of the calibre of Thomas Parry senior were needed to raise public morale. The work of the Mold committee was to prevent shortages which they only succeeded in doing when food rationing was introduced. They worked hard to control prices and increase the supplies of flour, sugar and meat. Other difficulties that the committee had to deal with included overcharging, price fixing and general complaints from the population. In July 1918, J. Bradbourne Price, the auctioneer at the Mold livestock mart, informed the committee that, over the previous three years, an average of '40 cattle, 500 sheep, 200 pigs and 50 calves per week' were sold in Mold. Through the Cosmopolitan Society, they arranged a series of demonstrations on economical cookery. They advised 'that an application be made to secure for the Town a supply of cheese from the Nercwys factory.' Frustrated by the rise in the price of milk they threatened to resign on grounds that it would 'cause hardship and suffering to children and the poorer classes.' The committee was dissolved in June 1918.

Agriculture, 1919–39

In the years following the First World War, when the coal industry declined and unemployment increased, the traditional farming community in the surrounding rural townships of Mold sustained the trade of the

Group of officers from the 5th Bn, RWF. Back row: 1st left A. T. Keene; 2nd left T. H. Parry, Front row, centre, Lt. Col Basil Edwin Philips of Rhual (killed at Gallipoli 1915).

market town of Mold through its livestock, produce and custom. A 1930 report on Welsh markets placed the market at Mold as

… the second in Wales in turnover of stock. The mart is somewhat small for the number of stock entering it, but congestion is eased by holding of special stock sales in season on a different day from the usual Wednesday market. Special sales of store cattle and dairy cows are held on alternate Fridays from the end of March to June, and special store sheep and cattle sales on alternate Fridays from the end of July to October.

Mold was the largest market in Flintshire, handling over 80,000 head of stock and the report concluded that

Mold is primarily a store stock market. It is the principal market in Wales for dairy cows, which are bought locally and by farmers and dealers from Cheshire, Shropshire and, at times, Staffordshire. The entry of store sheep is also larger than in any other Welsh market with the exception of Brecon and possibly Welshpool and Knighton. The store pig trade is an important feature and a few live poultry are sold by auction.

The retail market-hall in the centre of the town, open twice a week, is used almost entirely for retailing miscellaneous goods; some of the stall-holders, however, receive deliveries of farm produce, such as eggs, on market days from farmers. There is a direct trade in eggs and poultry between farmers and shopkeepers in the town and between farmers and dealers in inn-yards, etc.[6]

Mold auction mart benefited from an increase in the number of beasts sold because of a fall in the amount of arable farming and an increase in permanent grass. Demand for agricultural produce increased in line with the effective purchasing power of the population which led to a greater demand for meat, butter and liquid milk. Marketing conditions improved and a vital cash flow was provided to the local farming community when the Milk Marketing Board came into operation in October 1933 and the provision of free school milk was a valuable economic

Farmers at Mold Mart, c.1930.

lifeline for dairy farmers – between November 1937 and April 1938 it was estimated that nearly 38,000 gallons of milk were supplied to the schools of Flintshire alone. There were also schemes in place for marketing pigs and potatoes.

The typical farm in Flintshire was run by a family and there had been a decline of 60% in the number of agricultural labourers between 1831 and 1931. There were increased educational opportunities available to prospective farmers through the University College of North Wales, Bangor, with training available at its dairy college at Llewenni Hall and Padeswood Hall Demonstration Centre, which provided instruction in horticulture, poultry farming and bee keeping. Cheese making had been taking place in small factories established in the neighbouring townships of Nercwys and Treuddyn.

The pre First World War Liberal government had given power to county councils to become landowners through the Smallholdings and Allotments Act of 1908 and the Land Facilities Act of 1919 enabled them to purchase and develop acquisitions. By 1937, Flintshire County Council had purchased over 4,600 acres and

Long Row (birthplace of Daniel Owen), demolished by Mold UDC.

leased another 162 acres which provided a rent roll of about £11,000. Argoed Hall Farm, together with 198 acres, was purchased in 1934 and sub-divided into ten separate units. Other farms (Bryn-y-Baal, Prenbrigog) in what was once the Stanley lordship of Mold were divided up and made into smallholdings.

The above initiatives to make land available for those unable to purchase it and to instruct the farming community in advantageous and profitable techniques were the means by which farming was sustained between the wars. It showed the traditional advantages which agri-culture had which enabled it to adapt and survive economically because of its sustainable resources, adaptable manpower and changing markets of which Mold and district was a good example.

Industry, 1918–39

A report of 1923 optimistically described the economic prospects for Flintshire as an area with '… great reserves of mineral resources awaiting exploration, [and] a valuable and apparently inexhaustible supply of water and was well situated for an early supply of electricity.' Unfortunately the large reserves of coal and lead could not be mined profitably because of the ingress of water into the underground workings. In addition, foreign markets and competition made investment unprofitable and only one of the eight coal mines in the Mold area was working in 1921. The coal owners claimed that they were unable to give their employees a decent wage and as a result, the General Strike was called in 1926. After a brief post-war boom in house-building, the number of men from Mold employed in the area's brickworks declined to thirty-eight. Work to drain water from the lead mines ceased at the Milwr tunnel in 1921 when the Government withdrew its financial support and it was not until 1934 that the Halkyn mines were again working at full strength. In Mold, the Alyn Steel Tinplate Works were the most reliable employers, with a workforce of 200 but they closed in 1938. The trade directories for 1929 and 1936 make no reference to the mining industries, with only house building showing signs of economic recovery during the 1930s.

When the textile industry at Flint and Greenfield and steel at Shotton began to show signs of recovery, the high unemployment rate in Mold was not affected because of the distance people would have had to travel to find work. The Mold Unemployed Welfare Association could offer no practical help and as elsewhere in the county, in the absence of real jobs, all that was offered were food tokens in payment for labour, and social centres for recreation. So strict were the qualifying terms for claiming money that it was even questioned whether working in their own allotments without forfeiting their benefits was allowed.

Local government

The fifteen elected members of Mold Urban District Council (UDC) decided what was needed for the benefit of the community. Their duty was to enforce government and local regulations (the town's by-laws) in the interests of the local population. Their authority, supported by that of the County Council and aided by government inspectors, reached into all corners of the borough – streets, lighting, rubbish removal, shops, houses, the market place, workplace, schools, public health, sanitation and even burial. What they could provide was determined by the money available from local rates and government grants. Much of the work was carried out by local government officers supported by their own workforce.

The UDC met in session at least once a month, with a number of other more frequent committee meetings. A report of their meetings was printed and gave a full coverage of how they provided for the needs of the people of Mold,[7] the numbers of which, in spite of the economic depression, increased from 4,767 in 1921 to 5,791 in 1939.

The UDC had its own medical officer of health who reported to both central and local government on the state of the population's health, with an analysis which provided birth and death statistics, with details of the age and cause of death. In observance

Mold County Offices, later used as the County Education Offices.

of the regulations laid down in various Public Health Acts, statistics were reported for infectious diseases, housing conditions, sanitary conditions, nuisances, water supply and the remedies enforced.

In their implementation of the Housing Act of 1930, the UDC drew up a modest five-year programme of house clearance and erection of new dwellings. The plan was to clear fifty unsuitable dwellings scattered throughout the town and new houses were erected by the council in the 1920s and 1930s in Broncoed Park, Alexandra Road, Dreflan, Bryn and Nant Garmon. Associated with the building of new houses was the provision of sewage disposal which became the responsibility of the Welsh Water Authority.

An elementary provision was made for leisure facilities including a library committee and during the 1930s it was observed that an increase in the number of books borrowed coincided with the rise in unemployment.

The County Council provided ante-natal, school (including dental treatment), orthopaedic and tuberculosis clinics and vaccination programmes.

Culture and leisure

The Mold Cosmopolitan Society was founded in November 1892 in the King Street office of George H. Bradley, a solicitor who lived at Trebeirdd. He served as clerk to the local board and was a man of broad intellectual interests which he wished to share with others. He saw the opportunity of the new Cosmopolitan Society using the extra storey in the Town Hall as a place to meet. It had been adapted for use as an assembly room from the 'Mold Reading Room and Institute Fund' and he suggested that its use might be extended to allow the society to provide various social and cultural facilities. In 1895, following the creation of the Mold UDC, it was agreed that the society could take over the top floor of the Town Hall at a rent of £10 a year, where it ran a library until the end of 1912. At their annual meeting in 1900, the librarian announced that 1,300 volumes had been borrowed the previous year and amongst the lecturers had been J. Herbert Lewis, MP, who had spoken on the subject 'Life in the House of Commons.' The Cosmopolitan Society provided intellectual stimulus for seventy to eighty male members with women eventually being allowed to join. One of the cultural highlights arranged by the society was the staging of an exhibition of the paintings of Mold aritist, Richard Wilson.[8]

In 1873, the National Eisteddfod was held in Mold for the first time, the occasion when William Gladstone, as Eisteddfod President of the Day, made his memorable speech on Welsh identity. When it returned to the

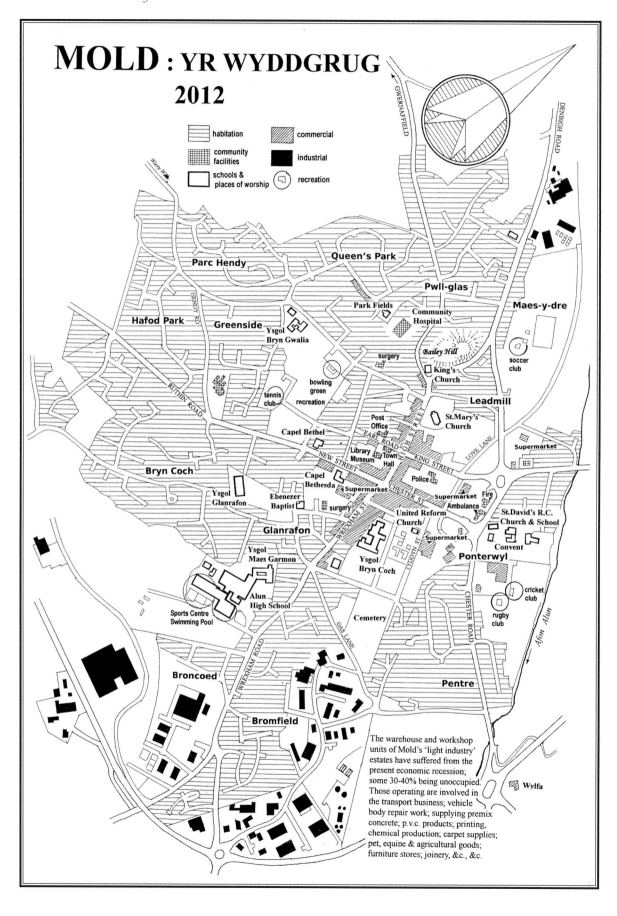

MOLD : YR WYDDGRUG 2012

habitation

community facilities

schools & places of worship

commercial

industrial

recreation

Gwernaffield

Denbigh Road

Wern Hall

Parc Hendy

Queen's Park

Pwll-glas

Maes-y-dre

Hafod Park

Hendy Rd

Greenside

Ysgol Bryn Gwalia

Park Fields

Community Hospital

soccer club

Bailey Hill

surgery

King's Church

Leadmill

Ruthin Road

bowling green recreation

tennis club

Capel Bethel

Post Office

St.Mary's Church

Earl Road

High Street

King St

Love Lane

Supermarket

New Street

Library Museum

Town Hall

Police

Bryn Coch

Capel Bethesda

Supermarket

Supermarket

Fire

Ambulance

St.David's R.C. Church & School

Ysgol Glanrafon

Ebenezer Baptist

surgery

Chester St

United Reform Church

Supermarket

Convent

Ponterwyl

Glanrafon

Ysgol Maes Garmon

Ysgol Bryn Coch

Nigel St

cricket club

Alun High School

Chester Road

rugby club

Sports Centre Swimming Pool

Cemetery

Gas Lane

Afon Alun

Broncoed

Wrexham Road

Pentre

Bromfield

The warehouse and workshop units of Mold's 'light industry' estates have suffered from the present economic recession; some 30-40% being unoccupied. Those operating are involved in the transport business; vehicle body repair work; supplying premix concrete; p.v.c. products; printing, chemical production; carpet supplies; pet, equine & agricultural goods; furniture stores; joinery, &c., &c.

Wylfa

*Dame Margaret Lloyd George and the Gorsedd
of the 1923 National Eisteddfod.*

town in 1923,[9] Mr Lloyd George addressed the eisteddfod before the chairing ceremony of the bard, when he informed them that, 'I like patriotism in the eisteddfodic garb full of instruction and enjoyment, doing good to Wales, and harm to no one else.' Accompanied by Dame Margaret Lloyd George and their daughter, Megan, and their host, Sir J. Herbert Lewis, he returned unexpectedly to attend the *Cymanfa Ganu* which was held in the Pavilion. In preparation for this festival of song, a special collection of hymns and anthems (with music) had been published, amongst which were compositions by John Ambrose Lloyd (1815–74).[10]

In addition to the traditional forms of entertainment, the twentieth century saw the advent of the cinema as a major feature in very town. The Cinematograph Act of 1909 laid down rigorous safety standards, which were administered by the local authority who also issued a licence to cinemas annually. In Mold, films were first shown to the public who were seated on benches in the Assembly Hall. In 1926, the Savoy Cinema opened in Chester Street where it operated until its closure in 1972. The Savoy building was demolished to enable the extension of the adjacent Telephone Exchange. For a period of half a century its dark, smoke-ridden interior enraptured its patrons with romance, thrilled them with horror, moved many to tears and above all, provided an escape from reality.

Second World War, 1939–45

During the 1930s, the newsreels conveyed startling pictures of the clouds of war drifting across Europe and the Far East: the Japanese invasion of China; the Italian invasion of Abyssinia; the slaughter of large numbers of civilians in the bombing of Guernica in Spain; the military re-occupation of the Rhineland and Czechoslovakia. While the arrogant strutting and salutes of the fascist dictators, Hitler and Mussolini, to their goose-stepping troopers caused amusement to the British, people became alarmed at the prospect of air-raids and gas attacks on Britain. In June 1938, there were public meetings in Flintshire asking for volunteers to act as air-raid wardens and to serve in casualty stations. On 5 June 1939, all men aged twenty had to register at the Labour Exchange under the

Madame Douglas-Adams had sung at Covent Garden in the 1870s (under her maiden name of Miss Maude Manley) before retiring to Mold by 1880 where she married Walter Douglas. When he died, leaving her with two young daughters, she married Thomas Smith Adams, the founder of the firm of estate agents. In 1882 began presenting musical performances which were to continue for twenty-two seasons until her death in 1904. These operatic performances took place in both Mold and Chester.[11]

The Savoy Cinema, Chester Street, photographed just before its closure in 1972. The film showing is Skyjacked, *starring Charlton Heston.*

Military Training Act and on 3 September, war was declared on Germany.

Flintshire was heavily involved in the war effort which provided employment for many from Mold who had lived for years on public assistance. Many travelled to the Vickers aircraft factory at Broughton which produced 5,540 Wellington and 235 Lancaster bombers between 1939 and 1945. There was also ample work at Shotton Steel works where, on 276 acres of marsh land, new mills had been built and the first slab was rolled out on 9 November 1939. Soon, the works was making 400,000 Anderson air raid shelters. RAF Sealand was the home to No. 32 Maintenance Unit and RAF Hawarden trained pilots. Like every town in the country, Mold had its own Home Guard detachment, a Women's Voluntary Service unit and an Air Raid Precautions unit (ARP) based in Wrexham Street. The Mold UDC was involved from the outset, purchasing sandbags to protect electricity substations, making 'arrangements for the Tinplate Works hooter to be available for sounding air raid warnings,' borrowing £2,100 to establish and equip a fire station and urging upon the Home Office '… the importance of delivering at an early date, helmets for the protection of babies in the event of an air raid.' Perhaps the most significant change to the town was the arrival of child evacuees from Liverpool in the autumn of 1939. This placed a great strain on inadequate housing stocks and places in local schools. By November, there were 1,273 extra children in the Mold district, about 500 of whom were in the town itself. More arrived in May 1941 (although many of the first arrivals had gone home by then) and a third wave arrived from London in July 1944, at the time of the flying bomb Blitz. Young women doing their National Service in the Women's Land Army had hostels at Windover House on Leeswood Hill and in Mold.

A brief list of some of the many wartime events in Mold will give an idea of the effect of the war on the town.

1939 — The first of many young men were conscripted into the armed forces. The Territorial Army was mobilised and joined the British Expeditionary Force in France.

1940 — In April it was reported to the UDC that Stoker William Davies of Bromfield Park had arrived back in Mold 'after his escape when HMS *Gurkha* was sunk after being bombed by a Nazi plane in the north Sea.'

In June the UDC began to search for cellars to use as emergency air raid shelters until September. They decided to erect twelve public shelters in the town which could accommodate 600 people.

1941 — Bomb damage in the Mold district.

'Wings for Victory' parade, 1943.
One of the many fund-raising parades marching through the streets of Mold.

1942 — In August it was reported in the UDC's minutes that two pigeon lofts in Mold had been accepted
        as being suitable for training pigeons for use with the Home Guard Pigeon Service.
1943 — 'Wings for Victory' week was held, one of several fund-raising events staged in the town.
1944 — Salute the Soldier Week.

The secret government establishment at the Valley Works, Rhydymwyn was probably the area's main
contribution to the war effort, Rhydymwyn being one of the main storage and production facilities for
chemical weapons. It had been used during the Great War as an underground munitions store and was ideal
because of its remoteness and it was near enough to the ICI factory in Runcorn. The use of the facility was
authorised in August. During the war *c.*£3 million was spent on the Valley Works site. It was used as a storage
site for mustard and tear gas bombs and shells. As well as having good underground storage facilities (which
were accessed by four tunnels), Rhydymwyn also had good road and rail links for transporting raw materials
and finished products. By 1941 there was a workforce of 262 on on the site. By 1943 work on the production

Storage Chamber A at Rhydymwyn.

of chemical weapons began to wind down and was replaced in April 1943 by Project 'X'. No one in residence was informed of the intention and purpose of the new arrivals who now occupied a building mysteriously known as P6. They were a group of scientists from the University of Birmingham, Metro-Vickers, ICI Billingham, the Clarendon Laboratory, Oxford, and other places who were tasked to create an isotope separation plant as part of the ultra-secret development of the atomic bomb. Many of these scientists were housed at Maes Alyn, opposite Gwysaney Hall. At the end of the war, 928 bombs containing the nerve gas tabun were brought to Rhydymwyn from Germany for storage in the underground chambers. Project X, the Rhydymwyn effort, had made a valuable contribution to the overall Atomic weapons programme and given it its vital initial impetus, it also 'made fundamental (ones) … to British nuclear technology' in the post war period.[11]

In a very tenuous way, the town of Mold unknowingly played a small part in a drama of deception, known as Operation 'Mincemeat', which saved thousands of lives by tricking the German High Command. False information was planted on a dead body which the Nazis found washed up on the coast of Spain. This appeared to be the corpse of a Major Martin, who had drowned after a plane crash. In his pockets, German agents found forged papers containing secret information on preparations for the Allied forces to land in Greece and Sardinia rather than Sicily. It later transpired that the body was that of a man named Glyndŵr Michael, a Welsh vagrant, who had died through eating rat poison whilst sleeping rough in a London warehouse. Amongst the papers were two letters allegedly written on headed notepaper from the Black Lion Hotel, Mold, in April 1943.[12]

Following the end of the war in 1945, forty-eight names were added to the town's war memorial at Bailey Hill.

Education[13]

In the closing years of the nineteenth century, the Alun County School was opened initially as a private school in King Street but it was later moved to Broncoed House and then in 1886 to Preswylfa in Hendy Road. The school then relocated in 1899 to newly-built premises in Victoria Road which were opened by the Duchess of Westminster. It became the County School following the Welsh Secondary Education Act of 1902. To gain admission to the school, pupils had to pass a scholarship at the age of eleven and even then, because fees had to be paid by parents for books and uniforms, the prospect of taking up a place at the County School was out of reach for many pupils from poor families. For those pupils who failed the scholarship, or whose parents could not afford the fees, there was no alternative but to stay on in the elementary school until they reached the school leaving age of fourteen. Following the recommendations of the Hadow Report, a new Central School was built in the Broncoed Park area in the late 1930s which could accommodate these older pupils unable to enter the County School. It opened as war broke out in September 1939 and its first and only headteacher was Mr T. Ceiriog Williams.

After the passage of the 1944 Education Act, the County School became the Grammar School, and all fees were abolished so enabling children who passed the 11-plus examination to take their place in the school. Mr Joseph Jones was the headmaster until his retirement in 1958, when he was succeeded by Mr Gareth Lloyd Jones.

Grammar School pupils followed more academic courses in English, mathematics, Welsh, classics, modern languages and sciences. While the majority of pupils left school at fourteen for employment (until 1944 when the leaving age was raised to fifteen and sixteen in 1972), a few went on to the sixth form to study for Advanced Level examinations which would enable the successful candidates to apply for university or college places.

Those who failed the 11-plus examination went to the Secondary Modern School, the former Central School, where they followed more practical courses such as woodwork, metalwork, gardening (for boys) and commercial courses and home economics (for girls). These courses were aimed at equipping boys and girls for industrial, agricultural, domestic and clerical occupations when they left school, usually aged 15, without any nationally recognised qualifications, although the brighter pupils took the Union of Lancashire and Cheshire

Mold War Memorial.

Institutes examinations in mathematics and English and some other subjects. These were replaced by the Flintshire School Leaver's Certificate in 1959. The secondary modern school was named Ysgol Daniel Owen, after the famous nineteenth-century Welsh novelist.

Following the adoption of comprehensive education in Flintshire in 1967, Ysgol Daniel Owen merged with the Alun Grammar School to form the Alun High School, under the headship of Mr D. V. Leadbetter, the former head of English at the Alun Grammar School. For the first few years, the school operated on the split sites of the former schools until the Daniel Owen building was remodelled and extended so as to accommodate all the pupils in 1974.

The vacated former grammar school building in Victoria Road was then refurbished and occupied by Bryn Coch Primary School, under its headteacher Mr Robert Taylor. Its former building in Bryn Coch Lane, which had opened in 1961, was then available for occupation by Ysgol Glanrafon Welsh primary school, which moved into the building in 1975. This school, under the headship of Mr Ron Parry, had formerly operated from the school room of Bethesda CM Chapel in New Street and in a wooden classroom in the school field of the old county primary school in Glanrafon.

In 1961, a newly-built Welsh Medium Secondary School, Ysgol Maes Garmon, was opened on land between Conway Street and Highfield Villas, which provided a continuation of Welsh-medium education for those pupils who had already received their primary education at Ysgol Glanrafon. The first headteacher was Mr Elwyn Evans.

The former Church in Wales Voluntary Controlled School in King Street, had been closed and replaced by a new county primary school, Ysgol Bryn Gwalia, in Clayton Road in 1968 under its headteacher, Mr Cyril Hewitt.

The St David's Roman Catholic School had been established in 1863 alongside St David's Catholic Church in Ffordd Fain (now St David's Lane). A new St David's Primary School was built in two phases in 1961 and 1965. In 1954 a new Roman Catholic secondary school, the Blessed Richard Gwyn School, was opened in Flint.

Employment[14]

In 1926, Jones Brothers had begun to produce hay balers at the Esmor Works in Rhosesmor. The business proved to be successful and soon their balers were to be seen at work on farms throughout the country. In 1958, they opened a much larger factory in Wrexham Road, retaining the Rhosesmor works for spares and experimental work. They were soon employing 400 workers and producing and exporting large numbers of balers. In 1961, the company sold out to the American agricultural engineering company, Allis Chalmers, which continued production until 1980. After that, the plant was sold to Bamfords who produced tractors and diggers for several years until they closed.

In 1950, the Synthite Company opened a chemical factory which produced formaldehyde on the site of the former Tinplate Works. In 1969 it employed eighty people. Their products were used in the plastic industry, for the tanning of leather, the manufacture of emulsion paint, and in crease- and water-resistant fabrics.

As the town and its surrounding villages grew in population, particularly after the baby boom following the war, it was very apparent that more jobs would be needed and it was also appreciated that, after the experiences of the 1930s, the area needed to have a greater diversity of employment opportunities as the old industries of coal mining, iron and steel making and textiles declined. Local authorities took a leading role in this development. Mold Urban District Council for example planned the new Bromfield Industrial Estate

Jones balers being shipped out of Mold railway station, 1960s.

for light industry and businesses on the site of the old Bromfield Colliery. Government grants were obtained for clearance of the old colliery slag heaps which had blighted the area for years, and the new estate was planned and constructed. After 1974, this work was completed by the UDC's successor, Delyn Borough Council. Units were built and incentives such as rent or rate free periods were offered to attract companies to come into town and open up new small-scale factories and businesses to provide a range of new jobs for local people. Later on, other industrial estates were built in the town such as at Maes-y-Gwern, on the site of the old Broncoed Colliery, and the Whitely's private estate, on the old Bamford's site, which again attracted new industries and businesses and provided employment opportunities for local people. In this way new employment was created on the brown field sites previously occupied by the old defunct industries which had once served the town and provided work for previous generations.

While other town markets have declined, thankfully Mold has not and it still hosts thriving markets on Wednesdays and Saturdays throughout the year. In the late 1970s, the market was extended with stalls being positioned in the Daniel Owen Square as well as on the High Street. The draw of the bustling market helped to sustain the many small, independent shops in the town centre and also generated interest from supermarket chains and national shopping outlets which wanted some of the trade for themselves. In addition to such shops as Tesco, Aldi, the Co-operative, Iceland, Lidl and in the near future Sainsbury's, the town has a large number of independent shops which add to the range of goods which can be bought and enhance the town's attraction as a shopping centre.

In the early 1970s, the former Mold UDC planned to demolish some of the old dilapidated properties in the town centre and in 1974 signed a deal with a property developer to redevelop the area between Earl Road, New Street and the Lower High Street to create the new Daniel Owen Shopping Precinct and new indoor Market Hall. This development provided over twenty-five new shops in the town centre, which increased the range of retail outlets and purchasing opportunities available as well as providing a much improved indoor market to replace the run down former market hall that had been located on the ground floor of the old Assembly Hall on the Cross. The development also provided good new pedestrian links between the High Street, New Street and Earl Road opening up the shopping frontages through the precinct.

This development certainly helped to enhance the attraction of Mold as a shopping centre, not only for residents of the town but also for those living in the surrounding villages. The town is particularly fortunate in having a wide catchment area, with a growing population which looks to Mold for its shopping facilities and services. This significantly helps to sustain the town as a thriving retail centre.

Of course, the supermarkets, shops, banks, estate agents, offices and other businesses which are also located in the town, all combine to provide a wide range of jobs for local people.

Local government[15]

In the late nineteenth century, Mold as the county town of Flintshire, became the centre and headquarters of the new Flintshire County Council, located in the old County Buildings in County Hall Fields, where their offices remained until 1969 when the new Shire Hall was opened on the site of the old Llwynegryn Hall,[17] which the County Council had bought in 1947. When local government re-organisation occurred in 1974, merging Flintshire and Denbighshire into the new county of Clwyd, Shire Hall was a more modern and superior building to any other owned by the other merging authorities and had sufficient land on which to expand, so it was inevitable that it became the headquarters of the new County Council. Mold therefore became its county town. A County Library headquarters and new Law Courts had also been built on the Llwynegryn site and were opened in 1969. Shire Hall was extended in 1974. Most of this development was the result of the vision and drive of T.M. Hayden Rees, the former Chief Executive of Flintshire County Council and the first Chief Executive of Clwyd County Council. Naturally, these executive developments on the Shire Hall campus gave rise to a wider range of employment opportunities in various council departments, the courts, the library service and Theatre Clwyd (Clwyd Theatr Cymru).

The local government re-organisation of 1974 also merged Mold UDC with Flint Borough Council, Holywell UDC and Holywell RDC to form the new Delyn Borough Council. Initially the new council operated from a number of offices based in Mold Town Hall, Flint Guild Hall, Holywell Town Hall and Holywell RDC offices until new temporary offices were built in Holywell and later, new purpose-built offices were built at Delyn House in Flint. Delyn formed the second tier of local government. Although the town and community councils have limited powers, they have continued to represent local viewsand have taken up local causes and concerns through representation to the higher tiers, for example on matters of controversial planning applications, highways issues, as well as providing litter bins, public seating, additional street lighting, CCTV coverage, Christmas lights, local groups with financial support and maintaining flower beds and hanging baskets to enhance the area.

By 1996, it was felt that the large county councils such as Clwyd, covering as it did the whole of north-east Wales, were too large and remote from most people and that there were too many tiers of local government. New, smaller county councils were therefore created which were to be all-purpose, unitary authorities, combining the power

Llwynegryn Hall, the heart of the Shire Hall civic complex developed during the 1960s and 1970s.

and responsibilities of the former county and borough and district councils like Delyn. The services that came under their control included finance, education, libraries, culture, social services, leisure services, highways, transportation, strategic planning, development and control, public protection, economic development and licensing. The newly-formed Flintshire County Council area was smaller than the old pre-1974 county and extended from Gronant in the north-west to Llanfynydd in the south-east and was formed through the merger of the former Delyn Borough and Alyn and Deeside District Council areas.

Leisure

The local schools all had their own football, cricket, netball, hockey and athletic teams which provided after school opportunities for games, but also competitive sport between the schools in the county. Most adult leisure activities were provided by local clubs such as Mold Alexandra Football Club, Mold Cricket Club and Mold Rugby Club (which had operated in the 1930s, fallen into abeyance and was then revived in the 1960s). Most of these clubs also had junior teams to encourage interest and skill in the sport and provide new blood for the main teams. There was also a very active tennis club and several crown green bowling clubs such as Bailey Hill, Mold Recreation Ground and the Mold Subscription Bowling Club which had a green behind the Dolphin Hotel. In addition to these sporting clubs, there were also two pigeon clubs active in the town and most of the pubs and clubs also had their darts and domino teams which engaged in inter-pub competitions as well as Sunday league football teams which were very popular in the 60s, 70s and 80s.

The Assembly Hall was renovated in the 1980s at a cost of £285,000. It may now be regarded as an ancient building which has received famous visitors, ranging from General Booth (founder of the Salvation Army) in 1906, to the Beatles in 1962. On both occasions, there was a full house. The hall continues to attract dancers of all ages and all styles including civic and police balls and has provided old-time, rock and roll, and other musical genres.

There are two social clubs in the town – the Bryn Griffith Workingmen's Club and the Ex-Servicemen's Club, known locally as the Top Club and the Bottom Club, perhaps not surprisingly since one is at the top of the town and the other at the bottom!

In the 1970s and 1980s, pub quizzes became very popular and most pubs established a quiz team. The original quiz league was organized by Ken Corbett and was sponsored initially by the *Chester Chronicle* newspaper. Today, it is sponsored by the *Leader* newspaper.

The new dual-use leisure centre on the Mold Alun Campus site was opened in 1974 and it spawned a number of new clubs and activities such as the swimming club, canoeing, jogging and badminton. There are also several walking groups within the town, such as the local Ramblers, who organise regular weekly walks in the very beautiful countryside which surrounds Mold.

In 1974, the new Library, Youth and Community Centre, was opened in the Daniel Owen Centre. This facility enabled a number of new groups to be formed using rooms in the centre for their meetings, as well as providing a drop-in facility for people just to call in for a coffee or lunch in the café. The centre also provides opportunities for groups to hold coffee mornings and fund-raising sales in support of various play groups, local sporting and social clubs, as well as local charities. When Clwyd County Council threatened to close the centre to enable savings to be made, a local charitable trust, the Daniel Owen Community Association, was formed to rescue the centre and maintain the facilities for the benefit of the whole community which it has done since 1991.

In the early 1990s, a town museum was created on the upper floor of the library which highlights and exhibits objects from the town's rich history and houses a Daniel Owen museum which celebrates the life and work of the Mold-born Welsh novelist. The museum provision was a joint venture by Clwyd County Council, Delyn Borough Council and Mold Town Council. Originally accommodated on the ground floor of the library, it has now been moved upstairs and the space which was released on the ground floor was then occupied by the Tourist Information Office which seeks to encourage visitors and local tourism by advertising local attractions as well as places to stay in the area.

The town has a very successful civic society, established in 1997, which strives to maintain interest and knowledge of the area's history and heritage. It holds monthly meetings where talks are given by various speakers on matters of local interest such as the history, flora, fauna and geology of the area. Art classes, yoga, Darby and Joan club, a camera club, the Mold Choral Society, the Llwynegryn Singers, Cymdeithas Wil Bryan, the University of the Third Age, the Contact Club, the Mold Town Concert Band are among the many other groups and societies to be found in the town.

Notes

1. This is not a complete list. The selection of names is of those with association with Mold.
2. Kenneth O. Morgan, *Rebirth of a Nation; Wales 1880-1980,* Cardiff, 1981, p.34.
3. Entry in Oxford Dictionary of National Biography quoting the *North Wales Times*, 18 November 1933.
4. D.J. Dutton, 'Liberalism in crisis: Liberal Nationals and the Politics of North East Wales, 1931–1935', *The Welsh History Review,* vol 23, No. 1, Cardiff, June 2006.
5. FRO D/DM/526/1.
6. *Ministry of Agriculture and Fisheries Economic Series*, No. 26, 'Markets and Fairs in England and Wales', part v, 'Welsh Markets', pp.51, 70–2.
7. FRO UD/Mold.
8. M. Roberts, *Mold Heritage Walks,* 1982, p.153f.
9. Newspaper accounts 6–10 August 1923, selection from the *Flintshire Observer, Western Mail* and *Oswestry Advertiser.*
10. John Ambrose Lloyd (1815–74) was the son of Enoch and Catherine Lloyd his father was a cabinet maker who preached with the Baptists and in 1830 was ordained minister. His birth place in High Street, Mold is now the site of Barclay's Bank and is commemorated by a plaque which reads, 'In this house was born John Ambrose Lloyd (1815–1874), musician and composer.' The composer later became a member of

County Hall (formerly Shire Hall).

The Daniel Owen Centre.

the Congregational Church. Although he was a teacher by profession he earned his living as the representative of a Liverpool tea company and travelled throughout north Wales. His life was devoted to music and in the 1840s he founded and conducted the Liverpool Welsh Choral Society. He wrote his first hymn tune Wyddgrug at the age of sixteen. Lloyd achieved a great reputation and respect as a composer particularly in religious and choral music. He published two collections of hymn tunes and anthems, *Casgliad o Donau* and *Aberth Moliant* which included *Teyrnasoedd y Ddaear*.

11. *The X Site: Britain's most Mysterious Government Facility*, Tim Jones, Rhyl, 2000, p.39. Colin Barber, 'The Valley Works at Rhydymwyn', *Flintshire Historical Society Journal*, vol.38, 2010, pp.207–17.

12. *Operation Mincemeat. The True Spy Story that changed the Course of World War II*, Ben McIntyre, London, 2010.

13. I was anxious to provide accurate information about certain changes in Mold and Mr Chris Bithell generously gave me this information.

14. The bulk of this account was provided by Mr Chris Bithell.

15. Courtesy of Mr Chris Bithell.

16. Llwynegryn, an ancient estate in Mold and the name of a township. In the nineteenth century it was owned by the Raikes family (hence Raikes Lane). Henry Cecil Raikes (1838–91), MP, Deputy Speaker of the House of Commons and later Postmaster General. The County Council bought the estate *c.*1947 and developed it in the 1960s into the Shire Hall complex, a stroke of genius which enhanced the status of the town of Mold and preserved the town centre from overcrowding.

Sources

Manuscript collections

Flintshire Record Office

     Glynde

     Grosvenor

     Gwysaney

     Keene and Kelly – Mold Parish Church, lords of Mold, manor of Mold

     Leeswood

     Mostyn of Mostyn

     Nerquis Hall

     Pentrehobyn

     Plas Teg

     Rhual

     Quarter Sessions

     Enclosures

     Mold Local Board

     Mold Urban District Council

     Flintshire County Council

     Clwyd County Council

     Delyn District Council

The Law Courts (Crown Courts and Magistrates' Courts)

Parish Records
Registers, churchwardens, vestry, overseers, charities, schools, tithes
Mold, Nercwys, Treuddyn, Bistre, Gwernaffield and Pontblyddyn

National Library of Wales
St Asaph diocesan records
The account book of the Reverend Hugh Lloyd

Principal journals
Archaeologia Cambrensis
Clwyd Historian
Denbighshire Historical Society Transactions
Flintshire Historical Society Publications and *Journals*
Ystrad Alun – Journal of the Mold and District Civic Society

Newspapers
Chester Chronicle
County Heralds
Mold, Deeside and Buckley Leader

Photographic collections
Flintshire Record Office, Hawarden
Flintshire County Library, Mold
Mold and District Civic Society Archive
David Rowe Collection
National Library of Wales, Aberystwyth

Books and articles
These are given in the text notes at the end of each chapter.

Clwyd Theatr Cymru (formerly Theatre Clwyd)

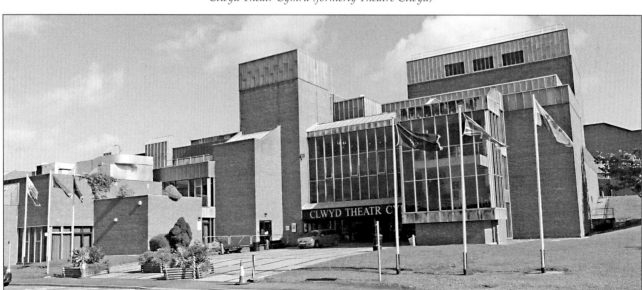

Index